THE LIFE OF GEORGE ROGERS CLARK

STATUE OF GEORGE ROGERS CLARK, QUINCY, ILLINOIS
Erected by the State of Illinois, Charles J. Mulligan, sculptor

THE LIFE OF
GEORGE ROGERS CLARK

By

JAMES ALTON JAMES

William Smith Mason Professor of American History
Northwestern University

GREENWOOD PRESS, PUBLISHERS
NEW YORK

TO MY WIFE

Preface

SOME twenty years ago, upon the recommendation of the Advisory Commission of the Illinois State Historical Library, I began the collection of letters which pertain to the career of George Rogers Clark. While the well-known Draper Manuscripts of the Wisconsin State Historical Society contain a great wealth of material on Clark and his contemporaries, the quest took me to numerous other centers. Notable among the collections drawn upon were those of the Library of Congress and the Department of State, the Virginia State Archives, the Durrett Collection, the Missouri Historical Society (St. Louis), the Bancroft Collection, the British Museum, Public Record Office, and French Archives, especially foreign relations. Transcripts from the Spanish archives were made accessible in the Ayer Collection of the Newberry Library.

During the year 1912 the first volume of the *George Rogers Clark Papers* was published (*Collections of the Illinois State Historical Library*, Vol. VII, *Virginia Series*, Vol. III). It contains the Clark material, then available, for the years 1771 to October 1, 1781. A second volume pertaining to the activities of Clark from 1781 to April 3, 1784, was published in 1926 (*Illinois Historical Collections*, Vol. XIX). The primary aim in these volumes was to make accessible the documentary evidence by which the chief phases of the Revolution in the West might be interpreted.

The material presented in these volumes supplemented by that which is to constitute three other volumes, already transcribed, has furnished the foundation for a number of papers which I have at various times presented. At no time have I approached the study in an attitude of defense or of eulogy. It has been my desire to present a sympathetic interpretation of the personality of Clark and of his influence. As explorer, surveyor, captain of militia, and general in command of western troops, he was dealing with the problems incident to the frontier. His undoing through the machinations of James Wilkinson, his relation to Spanish officials, and the opening of the Mississippi River to free navigation, and even his imprudent conduct in accepting a commission from the French government may be fully understood only when they are interpreted as phases of the expansion of the frontier.

The letters of Oliver Pollock, financier of the Revolution in the West and agent indispensable to Clark's success, will be published at an early date.

Three-quarters of a century ago Lyman C. Draper, in a letter to a nephew of General Clark, writes of having devoted fifteen years of close study to Clark's character and services. Dr. Draper's desire to write the biography of Clark, for whose memory he cherished, as he says, "feelings akin to filial love—nay almost adoration itself," was never fulfilled. While carrying on the collection of documents for this purpose he exhausted all of his own means and additional funds, amounting to four thousand dollars, which were loaned him by a relative. No adequate portrayal of the life of Clark would have been possible had it not been for the indefatigable labor of this man who has been well characterized as "the knight errant of historic adventure." The Draper Manuscripts, constantly referred to, must always be regarded as the real monument to his memory.

Nor could this volume have been brought to completion had I not profited through the researches of a number of persons, especially of Dr. Reuben G. Thwaites, Dr. Louise Phelps Kellogg, and Dr. Frederick J. Turner. All were generous in their suggestions and criticisms. Much space would be required were I to give even a partial list of the names of those to whom I am indebted. The courtesies extended to me by the authorities of the institutions referred to will always be recalled with gratitude. Dr. William Smith Mason not only gave me free access to the unpublished documents in his library but manifested, at all times, interest in the progress of the study.

Among others from whom I have received advice on special points have been: Dr. J. Franklin Jameson, Dr. Clarence W. Alvord, Dr. Theodore C. Pease, and Dr. James A. Robertson. I wish to express my gratitude also to my colleagues, Dr. I. J. Cox, Dr. A. G. Terry, and Dr. Clyde L. Grose for reading portions of the manuscript.

JAMES ALTON JAMES

EVANSTON, ILLINOIS
April 5, 1928

Contents

CHAPTER   PAGE

I. YEARS OF PREPARATION 1

II. EVENTS PRELIMINARY TO THE OUTBREAK OF THE REVO-
LUTION IN THE WEST 28

III. ORGANIZED DEFENSE OF THE FRONTIER 51

IV. THE ILLINOIS COUNTRY 69

V. SPANISH INFLUENCE IN THE WEST DURING THE FIRST
YEARS OF THE REVOLUTION 89

VI. CAPTURE OF THE ILLINOIS COUNTRY—KASKASKIA . . 109

VII. CAPTURE OF VINCENNES 131

VIII. RESULTS OF AMERICAN SUCCESSES AND THE ORGANIZA-
TION OF GOVERNMENT IN THE CONQUERED TERRITORY . 147

IX. CLARK'S PROBLEMS IN EXTENDING HIS CONQUESTS . . 169

X. NEED FOR MEASURES OF DEFENSE, 1780 195

XI. RENEWAL OF PLANS TO CAPTURE DETROIT 229

XII. THE LAST YEAR OF THE REVOLUTION IN THE WEST . . 254

XIII. WESTERN PROBLEMS AT THE CLOSE OF THE WAR . . . 288

XIV. THE BRITISH CONTINUE IN CONTROL OF THE NORTHWEST 310

XV. EFFORTS OF AMERICANS TO GAIN POSSESSION OF THE
NORTHWEST 322

XVI. RETALIATION ON INDIANS AND SPANIARDS 347

XVII. FRONTIER EXPANSION AND SPANISH CONSPIRACY . . 363

XVIII. CLARK AND THE GROWTH OF FRENCH EMPIRE . . . 408

XIX. LOUISIANA CONTINUES TO BE THE CHIEF FACTOR IN
INTERNATIONAL AFFAIRS 438

XX. LAST YEARS 457

APPENDIXES   PAGE

    I. Clark's Memoir 474

    II. Clark on the Mound Builders 495

    III. Improvement in River Navigation 500

    IV. Speech of Chief Logan 502

    V. Letters of Clark Pertaining to His Relations with
       the French Government, 1798, 1799 511

Bibliography 516

Index 527

Illustrations and Maps

ILLUSTRATIONS

GEORGE ROGERS CLARK STATUE, QUINCY, ILLINOIS . *Frontispiece*

FACING PAGE

A KENTUCKY FORT 21

FORT CHARTRES AS IT IS TODAY 70

POWDER MAGAZINE, FORT CHARTRES 76

FROM A PORTRAIT PAINTED BY JOHN WESLEY JARVIS . . . 415

MAPS

I. THE ILLINOIS COUNTRY 69

II. CLARK'S ROUTE 117

CHAPTER I

Years of Preparation

DURING the years between 1730 and 1750 groups of Scotch-Irish and Germans from Pennsylvania, together with a few English, had been pushing their way along the valleys between the Blue Ridge and the Alleghany Mountains. By the middle of the century their settlements had reached the Upper Yadkin River in the northwestern part of North Carolina. These pioneers sought lands which were granted by Virginia and the Carolinas on more liberal terms than those offered by Pennsylvania. Among the settlers who staked a claim in the valley of the Yadkin early in 1752 was Squire Boone, the father of Daniel Boone, who came with his family from the valley of the Schuylkill River when Daniel was eighteen years of age.

Meantime, grants of land were being made by Virginia in the valley of the Shenandoah River. The Virginians who came to this region found the log cabins of the Scotch-Irish and the Germans scattered here and there. Other wanderers passed beyond the headwaters of the James to the headwaters of the river later named the Greenbrier.

Among those who migrated from King and Queen County during the year 1749 to this land of opportunity in the back country were John Clark and his wife, Ann Rogers Clark. Some of their relatives and friends were among the farmers and small planters who had already built their cabins in the newly created frontier county of Albemarle. Moreover, John Clark was the owner of a 400-acre farm, located on the Rivanna River, two miles east of Charlottesville, which had been patented and willed to him by Jonathan Clark, his father. Here the second son of John and Ann Rogers Clark, George Rogers Clark, was born on the nineteenth of November, 1752.

Little is known of Clark's paternal ancestors, but it is said the first representative of the family in America came from England early in the seventeenth century and became a tobacco planter on the James River. The grandfather of Ann Rogers also migrated from England about the same time and located in King and Queen County. Her mother, Mary Byrd, was of a well-known Virginia family.

Two miles and a half to the southeast from Clark's home lay Shadwell, the birthplace of Thomas Jefferson. The friendship between these two in mature manhood was due in part, no doubt, to the recollection that they were born in the same locality.

While English settlements were advancing toward the mountains, English and French traders were competing for the control of the fur trade northwest of the Ohio River.[1] Throughout the West the cry was heard: "The English are coming; they are on the Ohio; among the Chickasaw; everywhere they are robbing us of our trade." In 1749 the Ohio Company of Virginia, organized the year before by certain of the tidewater gentry, received from the Crown a 200,000-acre tract of land between the Monongahela and the Kanawha rivers.

The French were not unmindful of the effect of the

---

[1] For a half century and more Carolinians had been carrying on trade with the Cherokee on the upper waters of the Tennessee River and frequenting the Creek and Chickasaw villages in the southern Appalachian region, and early in 1700 a group of British traders reached the post established by Tonti on the Arkansas River.

English policy on their claim to the Ohio and the Mississippi valleys based on the discoveries of Marquette and La Salle, and were determined to assert their rights. The year in which George Rogers Clark was born, the Marquis Duquesne, who had shortly before come to Canada, sent a detachment of men to construct forts in the Ohio Valley. The same year Governor Robert Dinwiddie of Virginia, who aspired to secure the forks of the Ohio for the English, sought aid from the board of trade in building forts on that river, and asked for small cannon for their defense. During the period of the French and Indian War, which shortly followed, the advance of settlements was, in large measure, retarded.

When Clark was five years of age his parents sold their farm and returned to Caroline County. For the next quarter of a century they made their home in the southwestern corner of this county on an estate which had been bequeathed to them by their uncle, John Clark.[1] The early years of George Rogers Clark, spent on a small plantation, under the influence of parents who were always spoken of as persons of force and strength of character, were years of preparation which gave promise for a successful future.

As was the custom among good Virginia families, the sons were given an opportunity to secure a classical education. George Rogers, at eleven years of age, was sent with his brother Jonathan, two years his senior, to live with their grandfather, John Rogers, in order that they might enter the well-known private school, conducted by Donald Robertson, which was located a short distance from Dunkirk on the Mattapony River.[2] James Madison and John Tyler were among the boys who were then attending this

[1] Draper Manuscript Collection (Wisconsin State Historical Library), 10 J 115. Near the line between Caroline and Spotsylvania.

[2] Draper MSS, 7 J 148.

school. Tradition states that George Rogers was unable to acquire the elements of Greek, Latin, and French as taught by his Scotch schoolmaster, and so at the end of six or eight months he was sent home. The events in the life of this tall, strong-framed, red-haired youth with black, penetrating, sparkling eyes during the years immediately following can only be conjectured. The horse-racing, fox-chases, shooting-matches, and other free fun of Virginia holidays doubtless appealed to him, for he was later regarded as an authority on fine horses. His robust nature also fitted him to take part in the "whimsical and comical diversions" on these social occasions, such as: "that twelve boys of twelve years of age, do run one hundred twelve yards, for a Hat of the cost of twelve shillings." Another item provided "that a pair of silver Buckles be wrestled for by a number of brisk young men."

As the oldest, but one, in a family of six sons and four daughters, he was called upon to assume certain responsibilities on the plantation, for his father owned only a few slaves. Connected with these duties, probably, was the opportunity of going to Richmond, some forty miles to the south, or Fredericksburg, about the same distance to the north, during "fair" days. At both these frontier towns, as authorized by the legislature, fairs were held during the months of May and September for the purpose of "selling cattle, victuals, provisions, goods, wares, and merchandizes." A feature of these fairs was the horse-racing. Large sums of money were offered in prizes, and betting was common. Fredericksburg was slowly developing the external features of the more easterly towns, for an act of the legislature forbade the construction of wooden chimneys in that town after 1763; swine and goats were no longer permitted to run at large within its limits; and by special tax on the owners and proprietors of lots a fund was provided for the repair of the streets, "using stone and timber."[1]

Conditions in Richmond were more primitive, and ten years were to elapse before the legislature forbade the construction of wooden chimneys in this village and prohibited stock from running at large in the streets.[2] The dwellings were described as poor, mean, little wooden houses. The streets were unpaved, "deep with dust when dry and so muddy during a rainy season that wagons sank up to the axles. The principal amusement was card-playing, in which everybody indulged, and drinking intoxicating liquors was the common practice."[3]

These were years when Clark began to acquire a knowledge of history and geography and an interest in natural phenomena to which there is frequent reference in his letters, for he was an apt pupil in the rough school of nature. The wilderness held him in subjection and he was quoted through life as one who knew all the characteristics of Indians and of wild animals. It was his good fortune, as a boy, to have come into contact with his father's friend, George Mason, one of Virginia's ablest lawyers and one of the finest types of gentleman. How intimate this relationship was is shown in the correspondence of Clark at the height of his career.

At nineteen he began the study of surveying under the direction of his grandfather, Rogers, and this step proved to be the opening of his career. For two decades the Upper Ohio had attracted unusual attention from Virginians, and George Washington and other surveyors, while running the boundaries for land companies, had themselves acquired

---

[1] W. W. Hening, *Statutes at Large* (Richmond, 1819–23), VII, 652.

[2] *Ibid.*, VIII, 656, 657.

[3] Beveridge, Albert J., *The Life of John Marshall* (Cambridge, 1916), I, 171.

titles to choice lands in that region. During the five years
since the retaliatory expedition of Colonel Henry Bouquet,
which followed the conspiracy of Pontiac, Virginia and
Pennsylvania backwoodsmen had been crossing the divide
over Braddock's Road and Forbes's Route and pushing
into the Monongahela Valley and beyond to the Ohio country. By blazing a tree near a spring and marking the date
and number of acres they set up what was known as the
"tomahawk claim." After clearing and planting a certain
portion of this land they established what was designated
as a "corn title" to the land. By the royal proclamation of
1763, purchase of land and settlements were prohibited,
without special license, in the region beyond the headwaters of the rivers flowing into the Atlantic.[1] Enforcement of this decree would mean not alone the development
of the fur trade, which was enriching many London merchants, but it would likewise keep the frontiersmen under
English political control. But the pioneers ignored completely this expression of "royal will and pleasure," and
Lord Dunmore characterized their disregard for measures of
restraint in the following letter to the Colonial Secretary.

I have learnt from experience that the established authority
of any Government in America, and the policy of Government
at home are both insufficient to restrain the Americans; and that
they do and will remove as their avidity and restlessness incite them.
They acquire no attachment to Place; but wandering about seems en-
grafted in their nature; they do not conceive that Government has any
right to forbid their taking possession of a vast tract of country either
uninhabited or which serves only as a shelter to a few scattered tribes
of Indians. Nor can they be easily brought to entertain any belief of
the permanent obligation of Treaties made with those People whom
they consider as but little removed from the brute creation.[2]

[1] Proclamation, October 7, 1763. *Wisconsin Historical Collections*, XI,
46–52.

[2] *Dunmore's War*, ed. Reuben G. Thwaites and Louise P. Kellogg (Madison,
1905), p. 371.

If British crown officers in America ever regarded the proclamation of 1763 as other than a temporary expedient to control westward expansion they soon saw the futility of efforts to enforce its provisions, for some thirty thousand whites, it has been estimated, settled beyond the mountains between 1765 and 1768.

Discontent increased among the Indians at the encroachment on their hunting-grounds. In a conference with the Iroquois at Fort Stanwix in 1768 Sir William Johnson purchased such title as these Indians possessed to lands south of the Ohio River. Two years later, at the treaty of Lochabar, the Cherokee claims north of the Kentucky River were acquired by Virginia.[1] While the Shawnee, Miami, Delaware, and other tribes were, for the time, made secure in their hunting-grounds north and west of the Ohio, they denied the validity of the Iroquois cession. Meantime, numerous plans were proposed for locating colonies on the Ohio, the Wabash, and the Illinois rivers. Some of these projects were promoted in England, where half the people were said to have been "New Land mad."

Benjamin Franklin, who seemed to catch a vision of the West to be, was one of the chief promoters of plans for establishing colonial governments beyond the mountains. Shortly after the Albany Congress, which made provision for the purchase of Indian lands and making settlements thereon, he advocated the establishment of two colonies which were to be located between the Ohio River and Lake Erie.[2] In a letter of 1756 to George Whitfield he said:

[1] Dunmore, himself, was not unmindful of the opportunities for financial advancement through speculation in western lands, and desired to become a great landholder. C. W. Alvord, "Virginia and the West," *Mississippi Valley Historical Review*, III, 26.

[2] Even Franklin supposed it might require "some centuries" for this to be realized, Benjamin Franklin, *Life and Writings*, ed. A. H. Smyth (New York, 1905-7), IV, 55.

I sometimes wish that you and I were jointly employed by the Crown to settle a colony on the Ohio. I imagine that we could do it effectually, and without putting the nation to much expense; but I fear we shall never be called upon for such a service. What a glorious thing it would be to settle in that fine country a large, strong, body of religious and industrious people! What a security to other colonies, and advantage to Britain, by increasing her people, territory, strength, and commerce. Might it not greatly facilitate the introduction of pure religion among the heathen, if we could, by such a colony, show them a better sample of Christians than they commonly see in our Indian traders—the most vicious and abandoned wretches of our nation.[1]

Franklin and other prominent men continued, until the outbreak of the Revolutionary War, to present to the British government the necessity for carrying out these projects.[2]

On the Watauga River, tributary of the Holston, the first permanent settlement was begun (1769) in what is now the state of Tennessee. This was made on a tract of land which was leased from the Cherokee Indians for eight years, in consideration of goods received by them amounting to six thousand dollars. During the spring of 1772 what was known as the Watauga Association was established, by which the Watauga settlement and two other stockaded hamlets combined for the purposes of government and protection under the first written constitution drawn up in the Mississippi Valley. The leading spirit in this movement was James Robertson, a Scotch-Irish trader and well-known Indian fighter. He was ably assisted by John Sevier, a young trader of Huguenot ancestry who was

[1] Benjamin Franklin, *Complete Works*, ed. John Bigelow, II, 467.

[2] For maps of the proposed colonies between the years 1748 and 1775, consult C. W. Alvord, *Mississippi Valley in British Politics*, I (frontispiece), 97, 317; II (frontispiece). These volumes are likewise invaluable for a study of the influence of this phase of western history. See also, G. W. Alden, "New Governments West of the Alleghanies before 1780," *Bulletin of the University of Wisconsin*, Vol. II, No. 1.

well educated, and by Evan Shelby, a Welsh trader and cattleman who had seen service in the armies of Braddock and of Forbes. The simple form of government adopted provided for an elective legislature which met at Robertson's cabin on an island in the Watauga River. The legislature was to choose a committee of five men, two of them being Robertson and Sevier, which was to exercise certain executive and judicial functions. Provision was made for a chairman, a clerk to keep the records, and a sheriff to serve warrants and make arrests. This constitution continued in force for a period of six years, when the state of North Carolina established its claim over the country west of the mountains and the Watauga Association was superseded by Washington County. The five committeemen remained in power for some years, however, and there was little to mark the change except the name.

On June 9, 1772, Clark, together with a few other adventurers, set out in canoes from Pittsburgh on an exploring expedition down the river. Reaching the mouth of the Kanawha River, they spent a month in the exploration of lands on the Ohio and its upper tributaries.[1] That the journey was well suited to inure these young men to lives of adventure and hardship may be gathered from statements of one member of the party. They crept past Indian villages, fearing discovery, and the narrator exclaims relative to a typical experience: "Instead of feathers my bed was gravel stones by the river side."

In the autumn Clark returned for a short time to his home, an event of importance in the community, for he was among the first from that section who had visited the Ohio country, the new world, as it was called. His glowing descriptions of the fertile soil, of the exquisite beauty and

[1] *George Rogers Clark Papers*, 1771–81, ed. James A. James, *Illinois Historical Collections*, Virginia Series, III (Springfield, 1912), VIII, 2.

stateliness of the trees, walnut, hickory, ash, elm, and oak; and his stories of the buffalo, deer, and turkeys so plentiful in the region induced his father, among others, to accompany him on his return, for he had determined to locate permanently in the West. Leaving the company at the mouth of Fish Creek, 130 miles below Pittsburgh, where he had already selected a body of land, Clark and a single companion descended the river another 170 miles. By the middle of November they were again at Fish Creek, where they spent the winter, the others going back to their homes. The two devoted their time to hunting, cutting rails, girdling trees, and burning brushwood in preparation for the cultivation of the land. Settlers were then coming in numbers to this region, and Clark gave considerable attention also to surveying their farms. Settlement had reached the mouth of the Scioto River, and the cost of improved land on the Upper Ohio was almost as great as east of the mountains.

During April, 1773, Clark joined a company of adventurers from Virginia with the aim of surveying the interior of Kentucky. After accompanying them a short distance he returned for a brief visit at his old home in Caroline County. By September he was again at the Fish Creek settlement in time to harvest his crop of corn. Early the next spring Clark, with some ninety men, gathered at the mouth of the Little Kanawha in order to descend the Ohio and form a settlement in Kentucky. There were other parties of surveyors, hunters, and adventurers who descended the Ohio to explore and locate tracts of land south of that river. At the time the alarm was general in the frontier communities over the report that the Shawnee were determined to kill all the Virginians and rob all the Pennsylvanians they could find on the Ohio.

During the preceding five years, also, Daniel Boone and other hunters and explorers had pushed out through Cumberland Gap into Kentucky. Their reports on the natural beauty of the land, the indescribable fertility of the soil, and abundance of game quickened the interest among the settlers of the upper North Carolina and Virginia valleys in migrating to this land of promise. To no one was the prospect more alluring than to Boone himself, who, during September, 1773, sold his home on the upper Yadkin and formed a company for the settlement of Kentucky, made up of his own and other families of the neighborhood, a few pioneers from the Clinch River, and a band of hunters, numbering in all eighty persons. They reached Powell's Valley early in October, where they went into camp and waited for the return of seven of their number who had been sent to secure some supplies.[1] When but a short distance from the main body of their companions they were surprised by a band of Shawnee warriors and five were killed. Despite this tragedy, in which he lost his eldest son, Boone advised going forward. He was not able, however, to overcome the consternation of his companions, and was forced to yield to their entreaties to return to the settlements. It was apparent that a conflict was inevitable. During the winter traders reported that the savages were sullen and were exchanging their peltries at Detroit for powder, shot, and tomahawks. Savage depredations became more frequent.

These hostilities were, in the main, committed by the Shawnee, richest and bravest of the tribes. The terms of the treaty made with them ten years earlier by Colonel Bouquet had never been complied with. Messengers who were sent to invite them to a conference for "brightening

[1] Reuben G. Thwaites, *Daniel Boone*, pp. 102 ff.

the chain of friendship" were fired on and with difficulty they escaped with their lives.[1] During May, 1774, a series of such conferences were held at which there were present Dr. John Connolly and Arthur St. Clair, representing respectively Virginia and Pennsylvania, and George Croghan and Alexander McKee, Indian agents, and the representatives of the Iroquois, Delaware, Shawnee, Munsee, and other tribes. The white men, in their speeches, expressed regret for the outrages which had been committed against the Indians, declared that they were the acts of ill-disposed men and were in no way countenanced by their governments. All of the Indians, save the Shawnee, counseled a continuance of friendly relations and disavowed the deeds of their young braves who had gone on the warpath. The Shawnee were openly defiant, called the messages heretofore sent them mere lies, and acknowledged that it was within their power to prevent the depredations of their warriors when they chose so to do.[2]

Their criticisms were aimed chiefly at the Virginians who were founding settlements and building forts along the Ohio Valley. The influence of Dr. Connolly was especially objectionable to them. To Connolly, a bold, enterprising, restless, and withal unprincipled character, who was a lieutenant of Governor Dunmore, had been granted the exclusive privilege of trading on the Virginia frontier.[3] Pennsylvania traders had already established relations with the Ohio tribes, and these Connolly attempted to checkmate. The militia under his direction at Fort Pitt were directed to fire on the Indians who returned with the Pennsylvania traders as protectors.[4]

A clash between the borderers of the two colonies was

---

[1] *American Archives*, 4th series, I, 1015.

[2] *Ibid.*, p. 479.

[3] *Ibid.*, p. 549.   [4] *Ibid.*, p. 484.

inevitable, for the Pennsylvanians, engaged primarily in
trade, desired to have the natives remain in undisturbed
possession of their forests, whereas the Virginians sought
to gain actual possession of the soil. Pennsylvania traders
were accused by the settlers of inciting the Indians to commit hostilities and of supplying them with the necessary
means therefor. Moreover, Virginia, under her charter,
claimed jurisdiction over that portion of western Pennsylvania which included Fort Pitt and the valley of the
Monongahela. The controversy between the two colonies
which was thus aroused continued for a number of years in
spite of the efforts of commissioners to adjust it, and, as
will be seen, Clark found this a leading obstacle in carrying
out his plans for the revolution west of the mountains.

It was not strange, then, that a character such as Connolly, looking to his own interests, should seize the occasion
for fomenting this quarrel. Prospect of war with Pennsylvania or with the Indians was to him a matter of indifference. By his orders magistrates who obstructed his
wishes were arrested and sent to a Virginia jail, and the
property of Pennsylvania private citizens was confiscated
and their cattle, sheep, and hogs were shot. While St. Clair
maintained that reparation should be made the Indians
for injuries they had sustained, and that an honest, open,
intercourse should be established with them, Connolly
avowed that he was no longer to be a dupe to their amica-
ble professions and would pursue every measure to offend
them.[1] Early in the spring of 1774 a party of hunters was
fired upon by a band of Indians, but they made their
escape.

Clark and his companions, delayed at the mouth of the
Little Kanawha, organized for a retaliatory attack on an
Indian town at the mouth of the Scioto, but were dissuaded

[1] *Ibid.*, p. 679.

from doing so by their newly chosen leader, Michael Cresap, who, noted Indian fighter that he was, now pled for peace.[1] They ascended the Ohio to Wheeling as a convenient post to learn what was taking place. Here they received a communication from Connolly, who was at Fort Pitt, which in effect marks the opening of hostilities in Dunmore's War.

They were informed that war was really begun and were urged to participate in the defense of the frontier. The response was ready from this company now augmented considerably in numbers through the addition of hunters and other men who had flocked in from all quarters for protection. In formal fashion, a council was called; war was declared; the war-post was planted and the war-dance and such other ceremonials as were common among the savages on such occasions were performed.[2] The following day, thoroughly aroused over finding two white men who had been scalped, Cresap led a company, of which Clark was a member, in pursuit of a party of Shawnee. Overtaking them, one of the Indians was killed and another was taken prisoner. One of the whites was seriously wounded.[3] On their return it was planned to make an attack on a party of Indians, "Logan's Camp," at Yellow Creek, some 50 miles below Pittsburgh. Logan was the son of a former noted Oneida chieftain and was himself a Mingo chief well known for his sobriety, honesty, and friendship for the whites.[4] He was described as a man of fine physique, over six feet tall and straight as an arrow, a skilful marksman, a great hunter, and in the words of a pioneer "he was the

[1] *Clark Papers*, p. 5.   [2] *Ibid.*, p. 7.

[3] This affair took place April 27, at the mouth of Pipe Creek, about 15 miles below Wheeling (*Dunmore's War*, p. 11).

[4] *Clark Papers*, p. 4. Logan's father was French. As a boy he was made a prisoner by the Indians. Logan's mother was of the Oneida tribe.

best specimen of humanity he ever met with, either white or red." In later life he drank to excess and is said to have become ferocious toward everyone, meeting death at the hands of one of his Indian relatives.

After marching a few miles toward Logan's Camp a halt was called and Cresap argued against the undertaking by reminding his followers that they were about to attack a party of friendly Indians out on a hunting trip and accompanied by their women and children.[1] These facts were well known and the expedition was forthwith abandoned.

Two days later, on April 30, six of these Indians were the victims of an assault, one of the most inhumanly brutal among those related in frontier annals. Five men, one of them a brother of Logan, and his sister with her babe, crossed the Ohio, as had been their custom, to visit with a family named Greathouse, and to secure a supply of rum. After three of the Indians had been made helplessly drunk and the two others, accepting a challenge to shoot at a mark, had discharged their guns, they were set upon by Greathouse and his criminal associates and all were killed.[2]

The Mingo called on the other tribes to aid them in avenging this wrong done their chief, and Logan raised his hatchet with the declaration that he would not ground it until he had taken ten for one. Returning from an expedition, toward the end of June, with thirteen scalps and one prisoner, he declared that he was now satisfied for the loss of his relatives and was prepared to hear what the white chiefs had to say.[3]

By this time the panic had become general along the whole Virginia frontier and a thousand settlers abandoned

---

[1] *Ibid.*, p. 8.

[2] *Dunmore's War*, pp. 10–12. The life of the baby was spared.

[3] *American Archives*, 4th series, I, 471, 475, 546.

their farms and retreated across the Monongahela River in a single day. The blows were aimed especially at the Virginians, for the Indians had sworn not to molest a Pennsylvanian, Pennsylvania traders having been protected by the Shawnee from Logan.[1] While no red men appeared against the Pennsylvania frontier, some of the people were killed by mistake. Large numbers left the country, a hundred families and two thousand cattle passing along a single twenty miles on Braddock's Road in one day.[2] Those borderers daring to remain gathered for defense in numerous small stockaded forts, and scouts were constantly on the alert along the trails seeking for any signs of Indians. Governor Dunmore, alarmed by the reports, took the initiative early in June by calling out the militia of the western counties. Daniel Boone, with a single companion, Michael Stoner, was sent from the Clinch River settlement with warnings to the surveyors and any outlying settlers of Kentucky. Near the site of the present Harrodsburg they found James Harrod with a company of pioneers beginning a settlement. After an absence of sixty-two days, in which he went as far north as the falls of the Ohio, Boone returned to his home, having traversed 800 miles of wilderness.[3]

During July and August bands of Shawnee, Cherokee, and Miami continued to cut off the detached settlers and surprise the little stockades along the entire frontier from Lake Erie to Cumberland Gap. Their barbarities stirred the frontiersmen to a frenzy of rage, and early in August an expedition of which Clark was a member was sent from Wheeling against the upper Shawnee towns on the Muskingum. Cabins were burned and the crops of corn were

[1] *Ibid.*, p. 468.
[2] *Ibid.*, p. 466.
[3] Thwaites, *Daniel Boone*, p. 107.

destroyed, but the savages escaped and were aroused to still greater acts of ferocity. The decisive stroke in what is known as Lord Dunmore's War soon followed.

An army of nearly three thousand Virginia militia, in two sections, advanced toward the Shawnee strongholds in the Scioto Valley. Governor Dunmore was in command of the right wing, which moved down the Ohio from Fort Pitt to Fort Fincastle, recently built at Wheeling. Among those accompanying him were Captain Cresap, George Rogers Clark, recently made a captain of militia, and Joseph Bowman, who was to become Clark's chief aide in the Illinois campaign. Colonel Andrew Lewis, companion of George Washington during the French and Indian War, commanded the left wing, composed of eleven hundred militia gathered from the frontier hamlets, little clearings, and hunters' camps of western Virginia and from Watauga and the valley of the Great Kanawha.[1] With Colonel Lewis were Colonel William Fleming, Captain Evan Shelby, Lieutenant James Robertson, John Floyd, and other leaders whose names were to become famous in the annals of the frontier. Greatly fatigued, the troops reached Point Pleasant at the junction of the Kanawha and the Ohio on the sixth of October.

Cornstalk, the Shawnee chieftain, with military sagacity unusual among the savages, learning of the approach of these armies, determined to attack them before they united. With his confederated army composed of about a thousand Shawnee, Miami, Wyandot, and Ottawa braves, he crossed the Ohio, and at break of day on the tenth of October came up with and attacked the force under Colonel Lewis.[2] For many hours the uncertain contest went on, waged by both sides, when possible, from behind tree trunks, logs, and stones. In the early afternoon Lewis

[1] *Dunmore's War*, p. 301.   [2] *Ibid.*, pp. 257 ff.

determined to try a flank movement. This proved successful, for the Indians interpreted the attack from an unex-
pected quarter as the arrival of reinforcements. An hour
before sunset they began to retreat, and during the night,
with their dead and wounded, recrossed the Ohio. Lord
Dunmore's force, on the march toward the Scioto towns,
learned with great joy of the victory at Point Pleasant.
When they were within a few miles of Chillicothe, the
Indian capital, they were met by a deputation with a request for peace. Cornstalk, who had been unable to prevail upon the disheartened Indians to attack this new
enemy, reluctantly joined the other chiefs in the negotiations at Camp Charlotte. In this treaty the Indians agreed
to accept the Ohio as the boundary between them and the
whites. They were to return all prisoners, make good the
horses stolen, and permit the navigation of the Ohio without molestation.[1]

Chief Logan returned to the Indian towns after the
negotiations were begun, but did not appear at the conference. The reason, as stated by Clark, was "that he was
like a mad dog, his bristles were up and were not quite
fallen, but the good talk now going forward might allay
them." Noting his absence, Governor Dunmore sent John
Gibson, a veteran trader who was well known to Logan,
to bring him to the council. This he failed to do, but on
his return brought a message from Logan which he had
written down as it was given, and, after translating it, presented it to Lord Dunmore. It was read before the army,
and making a profound impression at the time, it soon
came to be quoted as an outstanding example of Indian
eloquence. The speech is as follows:

I appeal to any white man to say if ever he entered Logan's cabin
hungry, and he gave him not meat; if ever he came cold and naked

[1] *American Archives*, 4th series, I, 1014; *Dunmore's War*, p. 304.

and he clothed him not. During the last long and bloody war, Logan remained quiet in his cabin, an advocate for peace. Such was my love for the whites, that my countrymen as they passed, said, "Logan is the friend of white men." I had even thought to live with you, but for the injuries of one man, Colonel Cresap, who the last spring, in cold blood and unprovoked, murdered all the relations of Logan, not sparing even my women and children. There runs not a drop of my blood in the veins of any living creature. This called on me for revenge. I have sought it; I have killed many; I have fully glutted my vengeance. For my country, I rejoice at the beams of peace. But do not harbor a thought that mine is the joy of fear. Logan never felt fear. He will not turn on his heel to save his life. Who is there to mourn for Logan. Not one.

The men of the army knew that Cresap was innocent of the crime thus attributed to him, and joked about it, Clark saying to him "that he must be a very great man, that the Indians palmed everything that happened on his shoulders."[1] Clark was well acquainted with all the parties named, and his statement that the substance of the speech was actually delivered by Logan is now cited as the best proof of its authenticity.[2]

Victory for the Long Knives, as the Indians called the Virginians, was dearly bought, for the sacrifice of forty-six men killed and eighty wounded was greater than that of their foes. There resulted incalculable suffering and privation throughout the frontier communities. The war cost Virginia ten thousand pounds sterling, but the blow humbled the Indians and peace for the time seemed assured.

In after years Lord Dunmore was accused of the design to sacrifice Colonel Lewis and his followers to their fate at Point Pleasant, but there is slight foundation for

[1] *Clark Papers*, p. 8.

[2] For the controversy over Cresap, consult Thomas Jefferson, *Notes on Virginia*, Appendix IV; *Clark Papers*, pp. 4, 5; Theodore Roosevelt, *The Winning of the West* (New York, 1889 and 1896), I, Appendix F, 3. See also, Appendix IV, of this volume.

the criticism, the officers of the army, while halting at
Fort Gower on their homeward march, uniting in resolutions of respect for their commander.[1] They exulted over
the outcome of the three months' campaign in the woods,
during which they had lived for weeks without bread or
salt, or shelter, and proudly asserted that their followers
were on the march and as marksmen, the equal of any in
the world.

The colonists cited the victory as evidence that there
was no need or desire for the protection of a standing army,
since Americans had there shown that they were able and
willing to protect themselves.[2] While proclaiming their allegiance to King George III, they declared that beyond
every other consideration was their attachment to the
interests and just rights of America, and they united in
pledging all of their powers for the defense of American
liberty. Most of the officers and men who served in this
campaign early enlisted in the army of the Revolution.
It was General Lewis who drove Lord Dunmore from
Virginia, and in August of 1775 Captain Cresap, at the
head of a company of 130 backwoods riflemen, some of
them coming from the Ohio country, marched 550 miles
to join General Washington's army at Cambridge.[3]

Soldiers in the armies of Lewis and Dunmore had heard
from their companions, the hunters and surveyors, wonder-
ful stories of Kentucky, and the movement for western
migration began with greater vigor than at any previous
time. Early in the spring of 1775 Clark set out for the Kentucky River, where he engaged in surveying lands for the

---

[1] *American Archives*, 4th series, II, 962, 963. Fort Gower was located at the
junction of the Ohio and the Hocking rivers.

[2] *Ibid.*, p. 1018.

[3] *Ohio Archeological and Historical Publications* (Columbus, 1887), I, 162.

A KENTUCKY FORT

Ideal sketch, from contemporary descriptions and plans, by James R. Stuart. From Reuben G. Thwaites *How George Rogers Clark Won the Northwest.* By permission of A. C. McClurg & Company.

Ohio Company and located land in his own name in what he declared to be one of the richest and most beautiful countries to be found in America.[1] He found Captain James Harrod and fifty companions who, since March 15, 1775, had been engaged in reoccupying the site which they abandoned the year before but which was now, as Harrodsburg, to become the first permanent settlement in Kentucky. He visited Boiling Spring, 7 miles from Harrodsburg, and St. Asaph, or Logan's Fort, where settlements were begun about the same time. Some twenty persons were building log houses at Hinkson's, later called Ruddell's Station, and during the summer Clark assisted in laying out a town on the Kentucky River about a mile from the present Frankfort. So pleased was he with the advantages of the region that he determined to make it his home.[2]

In the meantime, impressed with the reports which Daniel Boone, serving as his confidential agent, gave of the richness of the soil, good climate, and beauty of scenery in Kentucky, Richard Henderson, formerly judge in the highest court of North Carolina and a man distinguished for his ability and influence, determined to establish a colony there. With eight associates he organized the Transylvania Company. On March 17, 1775, a treaty between the Company and the Cherokee chiefs was concluded at Sycamore Shoals, on the Watauga River, in which Henderson and his partners secured in exchange for ten thousand pounds sterling, chiefly in clothing, ornaments, and firearms, title to some 20,000,000 acres of land between the Kentucky and the Cumberland rivers. This constituted

[1] *Clark Papers*, p. 10.

[2] The place was called Leestown. This attempt to found a town ended in failure.

one-half of the present state of Kentucky and adjacent portions of Tennessee and Virginia.[1]

When the treaty was concluded, Boone, as directed by Henderson, was well on his way from Cumberland Gap with a company of about thirty backwoodsmen clearing a trail to the Kentucky River, Boone's trace, later known as the Wilderness Road. On April 5 he began the construction of a fort on this river some 50 miles east of Harrodsburg. Two weeks later Henderson, with a company of some forty men and boys and forty pack horses, the day following the battle of Lexington, reached the post, and here Clark found them beginning a settlement, Boonesborough, which was planned as the capital of Transylvania.[2]

From the outset it was the design of Henderson and his associates to establish an independent government. A land office was at once opened and a store established. A meeting of delegates from Harrodsburg, Boiling Spring, St. Asaph, and Boonesborough, the four settlements within the bounds of the colony, was called for the purpose of drawing up a plan of legislation. These eighteen delegates, in response to the summons, assembled at Boonesborough May 23, 1775. This first representative body of American freemen west of the mountains met in the open air under a gigantic elm. Their foresight was manifest in the laws which provided for the preservation of game and of the cattle-range and for improving the breed of horses. The compact agreed upon provided for religious liberty and a militia and a judicial system.

[1] Archibald Henderson, "Richard Henderson and the Occupation of Kentucky, 1775," *Miss. Valley Hist. Rev.*, I, 353; Henderson, *The Conquest of the Old Southwest*, pp. 216–25.

[2] Henderson, *Miss. Valley Hist. Rev.*, I, 355.

But the promise for a successful development of the colony was transitory. Governor Martin of North Carolina denounced the "lawless undertaking" and called the projectors "an infamous Company of land Pyrates." Governor Dunmore, who was greatly interested in western land companies, proclaimed them disorderly persons who, contrary to law, were seeking to acquire lands within the bounds of Virginia.[1] Discontent grew apace among the settlers, whom Henderson characterized as a set of scoundrels who scarcely believed in God or feared the devil and who regarded the wilderness as free public domain. Many of these pioneers were adventurers; some of them were restless over the conditions upon which lands were granted; and others were disturbed because of Indian outrages. Food became so scarce that they were forced to subsist on a diet of meat without bread, and at times the meat was limited to "fat bear and a little spoiled buffalo and elk." The supply of salt was exhausted. So general were the desertions that by the middle of July the number of settlers was reduced from three hundred to fifty. Boonesborough could muster not more than ten or twelve men, and Harrodsburg and the other settlements together, only about twenty. Henderson continued to be the soul of the undertaking and during these dark days wrote cheerful letters to his partners describing the country as a paradise. "A description of our country," he says, "is a vain attempt, there being nothing elsewhere to compare it with and therefore can be only known to those who visit it." During the fall, migration along the Wilderness Road again set in and by the close of the year the population of Kentucky numbered two hundred. The return of Daniel Boone with his

[1] John Mason Brown, "The Political Beginnings of Kentucky," *Filson Club Publications* (Louisville, 1889), VI, 30 ff.

wife and daughters, and three other families, the first who came to Kentucky, together with twenty-seven men, served to establish the settlements more firmly.

Meantime, efforts were made by the Company to secure recognition from the Continental Congress for Transylvania as the fourteenth member of the United Colonies. With a memorial setting forth this appeal, James Hogg, who was elected by the proprietors a delegate to the Continental Congress, reached Philadelphia in October, 1775.[1] In his interviews with certain of the members, among others John and Samuel Adams, criticisms were freely expressed on some features of the colony, especially the provision for quit-rents, which was characterized as a mark of vassalage. Since Transylvania lay within the original Virginia grant, action was refused until the consent of the delegates from that colony should be secured. But Thomas Jefferson and his colleagues, although they sympathized with the movement, were unwilling to assume this responsibility without the approval of their constituents in convention.[2] It was at Williamsburg, before this body, that the hopes of the Company were finally shattered, and mainly through the efforts of George Rogers Clark.

Fully aware of the discontent among the Kentuckians because of the claims of the Transylvania Company, Clark, while spending the winter in Virginia, came to the determination to contest these claims. Returning to Kentucky in the spring of 1776, he again visited the settlements and camps and by his engaging personality and enterprising spirit gained the confidence of the settlers. He proposed a general meeting at Harrodsburg on the eighth of June for the purpose of electing deputies who should attempt to bring about a more definite connection with Virginia. In

[1] Brown, *Political Beginnings*, p. 33.
[2] Henderson, *Miss. Valley Hist. Rev.*, I, 361.

case they failed to secure concessions he advocated the establishment of an independent state. Upon arriving at Harrodsburg he was surprised to find that the assemblage had elected John Gabriel Jones and himself delegates, instead of deputies, to represent the western part of Fincastle County in the Virginia Assembly. They were to present a petition setting forth their distressed and defenseless situation, urging that efforts should be made to send them relief and protection, and praying for recognition as a separate county.[1] Within a few days they set out for Virginia. Their journey over the Wilderness Road was full of hardships owing to the heavy rains and their suffering from cold and hunger. They were in constant fear of being ambushed by Indians.[2] Learning that the Assembly had adjourned, Jones returned to the Holston settlements to aid in repelling an attack of the Cherokee, while Clark pushed on to Hanover County, where he secured an interview with Patrick Henry, then governor of Virginia.[3]

A more willing auditor than Governor Henry could not have been found, for as a man of the Virginia up-country and owner of Kentucky land, he well understood the spirit of the people now appealing to him for assistance. With a favorable letter of introduction from the Governor to the Executive Council, Clark appeared before them and at once requested five hundred pounds of powder then sorely needed for the defense of Kentucky. He knew that if this appeal were met the assertion of control by Virginia over the territory would follow. But the Council was wary and declared that, while they were not given power to grant the request of a people not legally united to Virginia, they stood ready to make a loan of the ammunition. Clark was himself to become responsible for its full value providing

---

[1] *Journal of the Virginia House of Burgesses* (1776), p. 19.
[2] *Clark Papers*, p. 210.   [3] *Ibid.*, p. 212.

the Assembly refused to regard them as citizens of the state. This offer he rejected in no uncertain fashion, saying that "if a country was not worth protecting, it was not worth claiming." Fearful lest the Kentuckians should seek protection elsewhere, as threatened by Clark, the Council finally acquiesced and issued an order for the delivery of the powder at Pittsburgh subject to his demand.

Successful in this step, Clark waited for the fall meeting of the Assembly, where he was called upon to defend the petition for their recognition as an independent county of Virginia. Judge Henderson, noted for his persuasive eloquence, assisted by the best legal talent in North Carolina, opposed the motion. Their efforts proved unavailing against the arguments presented in the petition itself backed by the personal force of Clark, who was assisted by the advice of Patrick Henry. Should they be taken under the protection of Virginia, then their population would increase, trade would develop, and a respectable body of fine riflemen would furnish an effective guaranty for the safety of the interior counties against Indian attacks.[1] The validity of the purchase was questioned. The policy adopted in the "New Independent Province," as Transylvania was called, was not in harmony, it was argued, with that adopted by the United Colonies, and if carried out might constitute Kentucky an asylum to those "whose principles are inimical to American freedom." The victory was complete. Out of the ill-defined territory constituting Fincastle County the Assembly formed three counties known as Washington, Montgomery, and Kentucky.[2] Kentucky County, with an area about the same as that in the present state of Kentucky, became a political unit of Virginia. Thus ended the last attempt to establish a proprietary

[1] *Ibid.*, p. 13.

[2] Hening, *Statutes at Large*, IX, 257.

colony on American soil. Two years later Colonel Henderson and his associates received as compensation a grant of 200,000 acres of land from the Virginia Assembly between the Green River and the Ohio. A like amount was later granted them between the Powell and the Clinch rivers, in Tennessee, by North Carolina.

CHAPTER II

Events Preliminary to the Outbreak of the Revolution in the West

EARLY in December, 1776, Clark set out for Kentucky, going by the way of Pittsburgh, for his orders to take down the river the consignment of powder and other supplies granted by the Virginia Assembly had not been fulfilled. He determined to carry out the project himself, in spite of the fact that he was aware that the Indians of the upper Ohio had learned of his proposal and were preparing to intercept him. Embarking secretly with John Gabriel Jones as his companion in a small boat propelled by seven boatmen, they landed at the mouth of Limestone Creek, where the powder was secreted at various points. As a ruse they dropped down the river a few miles, abandoned the boat, and struck out for Harrodsburg in order to secure a guard sufficiently large to bring on the cargo. The third day they reached some abandoned cabins of the Hinkson settlement on the west fork of Licking Creek. Here they met four surveyors who informed them that John Todd was in the neighborhood with a party of men which, together with Clark's, would be adequate to convey the hidden supplies to Harrodsburg in safety. Clark, with two companions, hurried forward, leaving orders to await his return. Shortly afterward Todd arrived, and it was determined that he should go with nine men to bring on the powder. While returning on the trail they were attacked by a band of Indians

which was coming in pursuit of Clark. Jones and another
white man were killed; two were made prisoners; and the
others escaped.[1] Early in January the powder was taken
to Harrodsburg by a force of thirty men. It came at the
right moment, for the Kentuckians, cooped up in their
three small stockaded forts at Harrodsburg, Boonesborough, and Logan's Station, were forced to defend themselves against a succession of Indian attacks, organized
by British officials at Detroit, through which they hoped
to gain control of the whole West.

From the opening of the Revolution American leaders
desired the conquest of Detroit, the key to the fur trade
and control of the Indian tribes northwest of the Ohio.[2]
Throughout the war this post, in the possession of the
British, continued, as Washington wrote, "to be a constant
source of trouble to the whole Western country." From
this post a trail led by way of the Maumee River across
the upper Wabash to Post St. Vincent; another extended
to Kaskaskia and other posts on the upper Mississippi.
Not only was it the chief fur-trading center, but in years
of good harvests flour and grain were carried to the other
posts from Detroit.[3] In spite of the careless methods employed in farming, the soil was so fruitful that there was
a good yield of wheat, Indian corn, barley, oats, buck-
wheat, and peas. Very few cattle and no sheep were raised
before the British took possession. The log and frame
houses—for the French neglected to use the stones near
at hand for building—were located for a distance of 13
miles on the north side of the strait or 8 miles on the opposite side. Fruits were plentiful in the woods. Orchards
were common in which were to be found peaches, plums,

[1] *Clark Papers*, p. 20.

[2] *American Archives*, 4th series, III, 1368.

[3] Draper MSS, 46 J 9.

pears, and apples. Melons and grapes were also grown. During the French régime this post had been of prime importance, contributing French militia and Indians to swell the numbers in the army of Montcalm on the Heights of Abraham.

The garrison at Detroit, at the beginning of the year 1776, consisted of 120 soldiers under the command of Captain Richard B. Lernoult. The fort was surrounded by a "Stocade of Picquets about 9 feet out of the earth, without Frize or ditch." Three hundred fifty French and English constituted the whole number of men capable of bearing arms out of a population of some eighteen hundred in the town and nearby country. The majority of them were French militiamen assembled under their own officers. Commanding the fort were two British armed schooners and three sloops manned by thirty seamen and servants. Among the crews, who were dissatisfied with the service and incapable of making much resistance, there was not a single gunner.

Three hundred miles away was Fort Pitt, the chief American post, in 1775, guarding the long frontier stretching from the Greenbrier River in southwestern Virginia to Kitanning on the upper Allegheny. This fort was without a garrison, and the inhabitants of the town, about one hundred in number, were dependent on the militia of the neighboring counties for protection. It was reported that there was scarcely powder enough west of the mountains to prime the gun of each man, and that there were only 200 pounds in the fort.[1]

At Detroit and Pittsburgh, in council after council during the years 1776 and 1777, was exercised all the diplomatic finesse of British and American agents in their attempts

[1] Letter of George Morgan to Lewis Morris, May 16, 1776. *Papers of the Continental Congress*, CLXIII, 237.

to gain control over the Indians of the Northwest. Assembled at some of these conferences were the chiefs and other representatives of the Delawares of the Muskingum and the Ohio, the Shawnee and Mingo of the Scioto, the Wyandot, Ottawa, and Potawatomi of Lake Michigan, the Chippewa of all the Lakes, and besides these, the Miami, Seneca, Fox, Sauk, and numerous other tribes. All told, the Northwestern tribes numbered some eight thousand warriors.[1]

Even before the actual outbreak of hostilities, leaders on both sides were considering the Indian as a factor in the contest. In March, 1775, the provincial government of Massachusetts accepted the proffered services of a number of Stockbridge Indians and enlisted them as minutemen.[2] Colonel Guy Johnson, obedient to orders, removed dissenting missionaries from among the Iroquois. One of these men, Samuel Kirkland, who had been forbidden to return to his post among the Oneida, declared that in attempting to keep the Indians neutral his interpretation of the acts of Congress to the sachems "had done more real good to the cause of the country or cause of truth and justice than five hundred pounds of presents would have effected."[3] Through him the Massachusetts Provincial Congress, April 4, 1775, appealed to the Iroquois "to whet their hatchets and be prepared, together with the colonists,

[1] George Morgan, *Manuscript Letter Book*, March 27, 1778 (Carnegie Library, Pittsburgh), Vol. III. According to Morgan's estimate, the Delawares and Munsee together numbered 600; the Shawnee, 600; the Wyandot, 300; the Ottawa, 600; the Chippewa, 5,000; the Potawatomi, 400; the Kickapoo, Vermilion, and other small tribes of the Wabash, 800; the Miami or Pickawillanee, 300; and the Mingo of Pluggys Town (Scioto River), 60. The Sauk, Foxes, and Iowa numbered some 1,400 warriors in the year 1806. H. R. Schoolcraft, *Archives of Aboriginal Knowledge* (Philadelphia 1860–65), III, 560.

[2] *American Archives*, 4th series, I, 1347.

[3] *New York Colonial Documents*, VIII, 656.

to defend their liberties and lives."[1] It was declared that since the colonists were to be deprived of guns and powder by order of the British government, the Indians would, in consequence, be unable to secure the necessary means of procuring food and clothing.

It is not certain which of the urgent invitations to take up arms issued to the Indians in May, 1775, by Colonel Guy Johnson and by Ethan Allen met with the earliest response. The latter wrote to some of the Canadian tribes:

I want your warriors to come and see me, and help me fight the King's Regular Troops. You know they stand all along close together, rank and file, and my men fight so as Indians do, and I want your warriors to join with me and my warriors, like brothers, and ambush the Regulars; if you will, I will give you money, blankets, tomahawks, knives, paint, and anything that there is in the army, just like brothers; and I will go with you into the woods to scout; and my men and your men will sleep together and eat and drink together, and fight Regulars, because they first killed our brothers.

Ye know my warriors must fight, but if you our brother Indians do not fight on either side, we will still be friends and brothers; and you may come and hunt in our woods, and come with your canoes in the lake, and let us have venison at our forts on the lake, and have rum, bread, and what you want and be like brothers.[2]

At first the American policy tended toward securing Indian neutrality, which was clearly stated by the Continental Congress in a speech prepared for the Six Nations early in July, 1775. The war was declared to be a family quarrel between the colonists and Old England, in which the Indians were in no way concerned. It was urged that they should remain at home and not join on either side, but "keep the hatchet buried deep." Since they were apprehensive of the policy to be pursued by the British, three departments of Indian affairs, the northern, middle, and

[1] *American Archives*, 4th series, I, 1349.
[2] *Ibid.*, II, 665.

southern, were created.[1] In the northern department were included the Six Nations and all other Indians to the north of these tribes. In the southern were the Cherokee and other tribes of the Southwest. All tribes between these two constituted the middle department. Five commissioners were assigned the southern tribes and three each to the two other divisions. They were to treat with the Indians in order to preserve their peace and friendship and prevent their taking part in the war. They were to superintend the distribution of such arms, ammunition, and clothing as were essential to the existence of the Indians.

Within a year, however, a resolution was passed that it was highly expedient to engage the Indians in the service of the United Colonies, and especially to secure their co-operation in bringing about the reduction of Detroit. Notwithstanding the arraignment of the British government in the Declaration of Independence for the enlistment of savages, Congress granted Washington full power to use Indians as auxiliaries and to offer them bounties for all their prisoners.[2]

In a dispatch to Congress Colonel George Morgan outlined the plan which, in general, was pursued by Indian agents of the best type on the frontier. "We shall ever hold it our duty," he wrote, "to exert our utmost influence to prevent hostilities and to promote peace and Harmony with the Indian Tribes. . . . . The cheapest and most humane mode of obtaining an alliance with the savages is by buying of their Friendship; they have been long taught by contending Nations to be bought and sold. . . . . We are well satisfied we can bestow our Country no service more essential to her Interest, than by restraining the hostilities of the Indians, and giving ease to the minds of our

[1] *Ibid.*, p. 1879.

[2] *Journals of the Continental Congress* (new ed.), IV, 395, 452.

Frontier Inhabitants."[1] Indeed, this was the safest course
to pursue, for on the frontiers constant danger from retaliatory attacks outweighed any advantage which might
be secured through the enlistment of savages.

The British early employed the Indians to cut off outlying settlements. Under plea that the "rebels" had used
Indians in their hostilities on the frontier of Quebec, after
the capture of Ticonderoga, and that they had brought
savages for the attack on Boston, General Gage urged that
General Carleton might be privileged to use Canadians
and Indians for a counter-stroke.[2] The letter which followed, containing "His Majesty's commands for engaging
a body of Indians," and promising a large assortment of
goods for presents, was a form merely, for on the day it
was written five hundred Indians were brought to Montreal to join the English army.[3] Thereafter the British
were to enlist Indians for service with the regular army
as well as to employ them with more terrible results in
cutting off outlying settlements and raiding the frontiers.

There was necessity for prompt action on the part of
the Americans in order that they might gain the friendship of the tribes beyond the Ohio. In the provisional treaty at Camp Charlotte, Governor Dunmore promised the
Indians that he would return in the spring and bring it
to completion. By that time the revolutionary movement
had assumed such proportions that he deemed it inadvis-
able to risk a journey to the frontier. Once more he found
a ready agent in Dr. John Connolly, who had been left
in command of the garrison of seventy-five men at Fort

[1] Morgan, *Letter Book*, July 30, 1776, Vol. II.

[2] General Gage to Lord Dartmouth, June 12, 1775, *American Archives*, 4th
series, II, 968.

[3] July 24, 1775. *New York Colonial Documents*, VIII, 596.

Dunmore.[1] In a conference at Williamsburg in February Connolly was instructed by Lord Dunmore to use his efforts to induce the Indians to espouse the cause of Great Britain. In this he succeeded, in so far as he was able to bring together at Pittsburgh the chiefs of the Delawares and a few Mingo, whom he assured that a general treaty was soon to be held with all the Ohio Indians.[2] Disbanding the garrison in July, he returned to find Lord Dunmore a fugitive on board a man-of-war off York. Together they concocted a plan fraught with grave consequences for the back country and for the American cause in general. In a personal interview Connolly won the assent of General Gage to the plan and received instructions for its development.[3] It was designed that Connolly should go to Detroit, where he was to take command of the garrison from Fort Gage, led by Captain Hugh Lord. This nucleus of an army, together with the French and Indians of Detroit, was to proceed to Fort Pitt. It was hoped that this force would be strengthened by the Ohio Indians, for whom liberal presents were provided, and by numbers of the militia from Augusta County, who for their loyalty were to be destroyed, should they offer resistance. They were then to take and fortify Fort Cumberland and capture Alexandria, assisted by troops led by Dunmore which were to be landed under protection of the ships of war. In this way the southern colonies were to be cut off from the northern.

Conditions promised well for the success of the enterprise. Connolly had won the favor of the Indians; Fort Pitt, as already noted, was in condition to offer but little

---

[1] *Pennsylvania Archives* (Philadelphia, 1852–60), IV, 477, 484, 485, 637, 682.

[2] *The Revolution on the Upper Ohio*, 1775–77, ed. R. G. Thwaites and Louise P. Kellogg (Madison, 1908), p. 35.

[3] For details of plan see, *ibid.*, pp. 140 ff.

defense; and the backwoodsmen were without the necessary equipment in arms and ammunition to obstruct such an expedition. They were disunited also because of the Pennsylvania and Virginia boundary dispute. A letter from Connolly to a supposed friend at Pittsburgh led to his betrayal. Virginia authorities were informed of the intrigue and runners bearing orders for his arrest were sent out from all the southern provinces among the Indian tribes through which he proposed to pass.[1] Together with three associates he was captured near Hagerstown, Maryland, while on their way to Fort Pitt.[2]

For upward of two years the frontier was free from any general participation in the war. Meantime, immigration to the West continued, and the contest went on between British and American agents for ascendancy over the Indians of that region.

Connolly had conducted his treaty with the Indians at Pittsburgh in the presence of the Committee of Correspondence of West Augusta County. The provisions and goods furnished by the committee on that occasion assisted materially in gaining the good will of the Indians for later negotiations. A petition to Congress from the committee followed at an early date, setting forth their fears of a rupture with the Indians on account of the late conduct of Lord Dunmore and asking that commissioners from Pennsylvania and Virginia be appointed to confer with the Indians at Pittsburgh.[3]

On June 24, therefore, six commissioners were appointed by Virginia for the purpose of making a treaty with the Ohio Indians, and a sum of two thousand pounds sterling was appropriated for that purpose. Captain James Wood, one of the commissioners, well versed in frontier affairs,

---

[1] *American Archives*, 4th series, III, 1543.

[2] *Ibid.*, p. 616.   [3] *Jour. of Cont. Cong.*, II, 76.

was delegated to visit the tribes and extend to them an invitation to attend the conference at Pittsburgh. He was likewise to explain the dispute to the Indians, make them sensible of the great unanimity of the colonists, and "Assure them of our peaceable Intentions towards them and that we do not stand in need of or desire any Assistance from them."[1]

The day following, Captain Wood set out from Williamsburg on his hazardous journey of two months, accompanied by Simon Girty, his sole companion, who acted as interpreter. Girty, when a boy, was captured by the Indians and lived with them for three years. The report Wood made on his return was not promising for the cause he represented. His reception by the Delaware, Shawnee, and other tribes was friendly, for the fear excited by the battle of Point Pleasant was still upon them.[2] He learned, however, that two British emissaries had already presented belts and strings of wampum to seventeen nations, inviting them to unite with the French and English against the Virginians.[3] They were warned that an attack by the Long Knives, as they called the Virginians, was imminent from two directions, by the Ohio and by the Great Lakes. The Virginians were a distinct people, they were assured, and an attack upon them would in no case be resented by the other colonies. Besides, the invitation to treat, which would be extended to them, should under no condition be accepted, as the representatives who were to meet at Pittsburgh could not be depended upon. Similar advice was given the tribes of the upper Allegheny brought together at Niagara. Many of these Indians, at the instigation of

---

[1] *Rev. on Upper Ohio*, p. 35.

[2] These two tribes had invited others to unite with them against the British in 1764. *Wis. Hist. Coll.*, XVIII, 262.

[3] *American Archives*, 4th series, III, 76 ff.

Governor Carleton and Guy Johnson, were induced to go to Albany, and many more to Montreal, to join the British armies.

The Virginia commissioners, together with those appointed by Congress, assembled at Pittsburgh September 10. Thus, notwithstanding British opposition, which in a measure had been overcome by traders, chiefs and representatives from the Seneca, Delaware, Wyandot, Mingo, and Shawnee tribes gathered slowly for the conference. Each tribe, on arrival, was received with "Drum and Colours and a Salute of small Arms from the Garrison."[1]

During a period of three weeks the commissioners strove, by speeches and through presents of clothing and strings of wampum, to convince the Indians that they should keep the hatchet buried and use all endeavor to induce the Six Nations and other tribes to remain absolutely neutral. They were assured that the cause of Virginia was the cause of all America. "In this dispute," they said, "your Interest is involved with ours so far as this, that in Case those People with whom we are contending should Subdue us, your *Lands*, your *Trade*, your *Liberty* and all that is dear to you must fall with us, for if they would Distroy our flesh and spill our Blood which is the same with theirs; what can you who are no way related to or connected with them [to] Expect? . . . . We are not Affraid these People will Conquer us, they Can't fight in our Country, and you Know we Can; we fear not them, nor any Power on Earth."

In the event of American success, they declared, with true American assurance, they would be so incensed against those Indians who fought against them "that they would march an army into their country, destroy them, and take their lands from them."[2] To convince the Indians still fur-

<hr/>

[1] *Rev. on Upper Ohio*, p. 74.   [2] *American Archives*, 5th series, II, 518.

ther of their invincibility, they asserted that the Indian tribes at the north were ready to become their allies, and that the people of Canada, with the exception of a few of Governor Carleton's fools, were friendly to the American cause.[1] The natives were invited to send their children to be educated among the white people without expense to themselves. No little trouble was experienced in inducing the Indians to agree to surrender all prisoners and Negroes and deliver up stolen horses. With these steps accomplished, peace, "to endure forever," was established.

That these children of the woods were greatly divided and at a loss how to act is in no way surprising. Promises of the British emissaries for a successful issue of their arms were presented in a fashion quite as alluring. Shortly after it was concluded, Lieutenant-Governor Henry Hamilton, who had been in charge at Detroit since 1775, learned of the treaty through an Indian who was present and a Frenchman who had been stationed near Pittsburgh. The special mission of this Frenchman was to discover the effect of the treaty upon the savages and to neutralize the results wherever possible.[2] Hamilton felt convinced that any treaty which might have been made would endure for a brief period only, on account of the "haughty, violent dispositions" of the Virginians. Arms, ammunition, rum, and other presents in ever increasing quantities were the ready means of winning savage favor. "But the Indians must have presents," an official exclaimed; "whenever we fall off from that article they are no more to be depended upon."[3] That the colonists might make a show of presents at first, but that they would be unable to furnish the dif-

---

[1] *Rev. on Upper Ohio*, p. 95.

[2] *Ibid.*, p. 127.

[3] DePeyster to Haldimand, *Michigan Pioneer and Historical Collections* (Lansing, 1877), IX, 375.

ferent nations with their necessary wants, was an argument shrewdly used by British officials, for the savages had already become aware of American poverty. Threats to send canoe-loads of goods back to Montreal were effective whips upon such tribes as might show any disposition to waver.

The jealousy of the Indians was most quickly aroused, however, by accounts of encroachments upon their lands. The contest for their alliance brought out what seemed to the Indians to be two distinct policies. Congress decreed that no encroachments should be made upon the line agreed upon at Fort Stanwix. The commissioners at Pittsburgh declared it to be their purpose not to encroach on Indian lands and to retain only the areas acquired by treaty.[1] It became increasingly difficult for the authorities to keep faith with the Indians, since the acquisition of extensive tracts of their lands beyond the fixed boundary was continuous. Frontiersmen continued to push the line of settlement forward in total disregard of proclamations and boundaries. There were many who even hoped for a general Indian war in order that the seizure of lands might be continued. To this end parties were formed for the purpose of killing Indians on their way for a friendly visit and for waylaying hunters on their own lands. Scouting parties employed by the county-lieutenants on the Monongahela and the Ohio were guilty of acts of lawlessness which pointed to a premeditated design to bring about general hostilities.

According to an English proclamation, no deeds to lands were considered valid until they were passed by the authority of the chief governor, registered at Quebec, and entered at the office in Detroit. Lieutenant-Governor

[1] *Rev. on Upper Ohio*, pp. 98, 118.

Hamilton declared at the close of the year 1778 that he had never granted lands even at Detroit. He said: "As there has been a restraint laid upon the granting land to the settlers at this place, whose farms are small and families numerous, the consequence has been, young men growing to age engage as canoe men, go off to distant settlements and in general become vagabonds, so that the settlement does not increase in numbers as may be seen by comparing the recensement of 1776 with that of 1766."[1]

The attention of the Indians was called to the fact, of which they were already well aware, that the Big Knives had been pushing them back for many years and would not rest until they were possessed of all this country. The origin of the following message, therefore, from the Six Nations and Chippewa to the Virginians and Pennsylvanians early in the year 1777 may be easily discerned.[2] "You have feloniously taken Possession of part of our Country on the branches of the Ohio, as well as the Susquehanna, to the latter we have some time since sent you word to quit our Lands as we now do to you, as we don't know we ever give you liberty, nor can we be easy in our minds while there is an arm'd Force at our very doors, nor do we think you, or anybody else would. Therefore to use you with more lenity than you have a right to expect, we now tell you in a peaceful manner to quit our Lands wherever you have possessed yourselves of them immediately, or blame yourselves for whatever may happen."

Another significant problem considered by the commissioners was the means of capturing Detroit. A plan outlined by Arthur St. Clair, their secretary, proposed a volunteer expedition for the surprise of Detroit, providing

<hr/>

[1] *Mich. Pioneer and Hist. Colls.*, IX, 474.

[2] Morgan, *Letter Book*, February 2, 1777, Vol. I.

it should not be opposed by the Indians.[1] Because of the approval of the project by his associates, St. Clair proceeded to raise five hundred men for the expedition. They were to furnish their own horses and provisions. Ammunition, which could not be procured in the West, was to be provided at the expense of the government. The proposal was discussed in Congress, but the season was thought too far advanced for undertaking such an expedition.[2] Besides, there was a feeling generally prevalent that Benedict Arnold was about to capture Quebec, and as a result that Canada and the West would come into possession of the Americans. Washington shared this view, and it is probable his attitude led to the disapproval of St. Clair's plan by Congress. "The acquisition of Canada," he wrote to General Schuyler, "is of immeasurable importance to the cause we are engaged in. If you carry your arms to Montreal, should not the garrisons of Niagara, and Detroit, also, be called upon to surrender or threatened with the consequences of a refusal? They may, indeed, destroy their stores, and, if the Indians are aiding, escape to Fort Chartres; but it is not very probable."[3]

That expedition failing, a committee of Congress was instructed to prepare plans for an expedition against Detroit, with an estimate of the expense. General Charles Lee urged the absolute necessity of straining every nerve to possess Niagara, headquarters of New York Loyalists, if not Detroit.[4] The committee recommended that an expedition should be sent immediately against Detroit, for

[1] W. H. Smith, *The Life and Public Services of Arthur St. Clair* (Cincinnati, 1882), I, 15.

[2] *American Archives*, 4th series, III, 717.

[3] November 5, 1775; *ibid.*, p. 1368.

[4] Twenty-three hundred Indians were assembled at Niagara during December, 1777, to receive presents.

it was understood that the 120 soldiers in that garrison were indifferent, the French neutral, and the Indians wavering.[1] Final action was postponed, however, until the arrival of Washington. While he sanctioned the project, it was found that it could not be carried out because of insufficient funds. Moreover, the Iroquois were averse to having an army march through territory to which they laid claim.[2]

While the treaty at Pittsburgh had been made, in the language of its text, to last "until the sun shall shine no more, or the waters fail to run in the Ohio," both of these conditions had taken place, to the Indian imagination, by the following spring. In the meantime they had been visited by British agents to secure their adherence. The trails to Detroit were well worn by the tribes assembled there to meet Hamilton, who strove in every possible way to excite the Indians to take up the hatchet.[3] To this end British officers were generous with their presents and lavish in their hospitality, partaking with the Indians in the feast of roast ox, and, as the Indians said, "recovering their dead anew with rum." Even Hamilton himself, cultured Englishman that he was, painted and dressed as an Indian, joined the savage hordes in the wild songs and dances incident to these councils.

Various desultory expeditions by the Indians kept the frontiers in continuous alarm. During the conference at Pittsburgh wandering bands of Wyandot and Mingo went to the mouth of the Kentucky "to look at the White people." On their return they shot two white boys at Boonesborough. Three warriors, of the Six Nations, returned in

[1] *American Archives*, 5th series, I, 35 ff.

[2] *Letters of Richard Henry Lee*, ed. J. C. Ballagh (New York, 1911), I, 185, 193.

[3] Morgan, *Letter Book*, August 31, 1776, Vol. II.

June with two prisoners. A party of four Shawnee, returning in August from the Cherokee country, killed two white men at Big Bone Lick. The frontiersmen retaliated by shooting two Indians.

Congress, early in April, appointed Colonel George Morgan Indian agent for the middle department. The choice was a wise one. For a number of years he had been a trader in the Illinois country, where he had become noted among the Indians for his generosity and strict honesty. No man of the time better understood the methods necessary in winning the friendship of the western tribes. He was instructed to forward at once the great belt presented to the Indians at Pittsburgh.[1] The commissioners for the middle department were directed to conclude a treaty with the western tribes at the earliest convenient time. Morgan was, so far as possible, to adjust all differences through arbitration and "inspire them with sentiments of justice and humanity, and dispose them to introduce the arts of civil and social life, and encourage the residence of handicrafts-men among them."

In pursuance of this general policy assurance had already been given to the Delawares by Congress, upon the request of their chief, that in addition to the establishment of satisfactory trade relations and the protection of their rights to the lands, there should be sent to them a schoolmaster, a Christian minister, and a man competent to give them instruction in agriculture.[2] The November preceding, two blacksmiths had been employed to reside with the Iroquois.

Arriving at Pittsburgh May 16, 1776, Morgan, in his endeavor to prevent the attendance of the Indians at a council called by Hamilton at Detroit, proceeded at once to the Shawnee towns. William Wilson, a trader who ac-

[1] *Jour. Cont. Cong.*, IV, 268.   [2] *Ibid.*, III, 366.

companied Morgan, extended the invitation to other tribes to assemble at Pittsburgh, September 10, for the purpose of making a treaty.

No incident better illustrates the situation which Americans were forced to meet in these critical preliminary years than Wilson's reception by Hamilton. With three companions, Wilson, on invitation of the Wyandot, visited their village opposite Detroit and delivered to the chiefs the speech and belt sent by Morgan. Hamilton having expressed the desire to speak with him in a friendly manner, Wilson accompanied the chiefs to Detroit. In explaining the message to the Indians, Hamilton declared that the people who sent it were enemies and traitors to his King, and that he would prefer to lose his right hand rather than take one of them by the hand. Tearing the speech asunder and cutting the belt to pieces, he then spoke to the assembled Indians on a tomahawk belt. White Eyes, chief of the Delawares, who accompanied Wilson, was ordered to leave Detroit before sunset, "as he regarded his head." Wilson likewise was directed to leave at once, receiving a parting word from the governor which was well calculated to excite fear among the frontier folk and enthusiasm for the British cause among the savages. In reporting the affair Wilson thus quoted Hamilton's remarks: "He would be glad if I would inform the people on my return of what I had seen; and that all the Indians I saw there at the treaty were of the same way of thinking; and that he would be glad if the people would consider the dreadful consequences of going to war with so terrible an enemy, and accept the King's pardon while it could be obtained."

Hamilton then informed Wilson that an army of twenty thousand men were landed in Canada; that they had driven the rebels entirely out of that government and were pursuing them to the southward; that twenty thousand more were landed in New York and the same number to the southward, with the completest train of artillery that ever came out of Europe on any occasion; and that the King's triumph was assured. At the same period a dispatch from Lord Germain declared, "Upon the present appearance of things, I look upon the further progress of this army for the campaign to be rather precarious, an attack upon Rhode Island excepted."[1]

A general confederation of all the western tribes was reported for the purpose of destroying all frontier settlements as soon as their scattered young men could be called in and the corn necessary for subsistence should ripen. In a speech to the Mingo, most desperate of savage tribes, Hamilton is said to have stirred up their most brutal instincts. As he delivered to them the tomahawk, bullets, and powder, having previously taken part with his officers in the war song, he declared: "That he wondered to see them so foolish as not to observe that the Big Knife was come up very near to them, and claimed one-half the water in the Ohio, and that if any of the Indians cross'd over to their side of the river they immediately took him, laid his head on a Big Log and chopp'd it off—that he had now put them in a way to prevent such Usage, and that if they met any of them they should strike their Tomahawks into their heads, cut off some of the hair and bring it to him."[2]

John Stuart, Allen Cameron, and other British agents were, during the early summer, engaged in uniting the southern Indians, numbering some ten thousand warriors, and the Loyalists for an attack on the Tennessee settlements and the frontiers of the Carolinas and Georgia. The Cherokee, most powerful of southern tribes, although they had sold land to the Watauga settlers, were jealous of their progress.

---

[1] *American Archives*, 5th series, II, 518.

[2] Morgan, *Letter Book*, August 18 and 31, 1776, Vol. II.

Lawless elements among the Georgia backwoodsmen, in spite of regulations, were trespassing on Creek property. Signs of preparation for war, such as mending guns and beating grain into flour, were first observed in the Cherokee villages, numbering some two thousand warriors, located in the mountains to the south of the Watauga settlements.[1] A pack train of fifty horses, sent by British agents, supplied them with ammunition. Six hundred Cherokee were reported as ready to strike the Virginia frontier with the determination to kill or make prisoners of all the people. This tribe had also accepted the war belt from the Shawnee and Mingo and agreed to fall on the Kentucky settlements.

The first blow was aimed at the settlers on the Holston River, but, warned by a friendly squaw, they took refuge within their stockaded forts and prepared for defense. Those failing to heed the warning were cut off in the usual fashion and general destruction of property marked the coming of the invaders.

On July 20 some seven hundred warriors advanced in two bands, one against the Watauga fort, the other, led by "The Dragging Canoe," to attack Eaton's Station, 6 miles distant. Defenders of the latter post, numbering 170, deciding to meet the enemy in the open, marched out in two parallel lines toward Long (Big) Island Flats, where the battle took place. A sudden attack by the scouts on an advance party of Indians was so furious that they fled precipitately. On withdrawing to the fort at the close of the day the Indians attacked them from the rear. Quickly extending their line in both directions, to protect their flanks, a movement which was mistaken for retreat by the enemy, the frontiersmen met the onset of the savages at close quarter and completely routed them. Thirteen of the Indians were killed and their chief was badly wound-

[1] *American Archives*, 5th series, I, 111.

ed. The whites took a great quantity of plunder, including guns and ammunition, while only four of their number were seriously injured.

On the same day the Watauga fort, crowded with women and children and defended by forty men, was attacked. So well organized was the defense under Robertson and Sevier that the attempt failed. During the following three weeks an irregular siege of the fort was kept up, three or four of the settlers losing their lives by venturing beyond the gates. Frustrated in their object, the Indians withdrew just as rescue parties appeared from the neighboring forts. These attacks had been projected as a diversion to assist the movement of General Clinton against Charleston, but that officer had abandoned his plan three weeks earlier and sailed for New York.

Other bands of Cherokee, together with Creek and Tories, carried on depredations against the outlying settlements of the Carolinas and Georgia, thirty-seven persons losing their lives within two days along the Catawba River. Stirred by these inroads, the southern colonies united to avenge themselves on the Cherokee. As planned, Virginia troops were to march against the Overhill Cherokee, while the militia of the Carolinas and Georgia were invading the valley and lower towns.

Early in September General Griffith Rutherford led a force of twenty-five hundred North Carolinians over the mountains and fell on the Middle Cherokee towns, which were totally destroyed. Colonel Andrew Williamson, with a force of eighteen hundred men from South Carolina, joined Rutherford, but too late to take part in this attack. Williamson then pushed on to the lower towns, narrowly escaping complete disaster from an attack by Indians lying in ambush. Their route led them along the precipitous mountain heights and through forests where no trail had been cut. On the eve of the attack Rutherford's force came up, and the combined armies, after completely destroying the Indian settlements, returned to their homes. Colonel Samuel Jack had already led his force of two hundred Georgia rangers in a successful attack on some smaller Cherokee villages at the head of the Chattahoochee River.

On the first of October Colonel William Christian, with his army of Virginians, together with a small force from the Holston forts and four hundred North Carolinians, making a total of two thousand men, set out for the Overhill Cherokee villages.[1] These Indians, greatly inferior in numbers, were defeated, and with their outlying cabins and crops in ashes, gladly submitted to the terms proposed.

In the peace treaties of the following summer the Cherokee accepted the proposed boundaries whereby they surrendered some additional land. Tennessee settlements, for a time free from attack and increasing in numbers of inhabitants, furnished protection to immigrants along the eastern section of the Wilderness Road.

During November it was suspected that fifteen hundred Chippewa and Ottawa were rendezvousing with the intention of attacking Fort Pitt. Driven to desperation, backwoodsmen forsook their clearings and evacuated the country for 200 miles except where some of them forted.[2]

At the time the frontier defense was intrusted to one hundred men at Fort Pitt, one hundred at Big Kanawha, and twenty-five at Wheeling, all in the pay of Virginia. These numbers were far too meager for the purpose, much less were they adequate for any aggressive warfare. Messengers were dispatched to Congress and to Williamsburg, imploring an augmentation of the numbers in the garrisons and the formation of new posts having proper supplies of

[1] *Rev. on Upper Ohio*, pp. 175, 176.

[2] Morgan, *Letter Book*, August 31, 1776, Vol. II.

ammunition and provisions. Congress directed that a ton of gunpowder should be sent for this purpose. The militia of Westmoreland and West Augusta counties were called out. The county lieutenants of Hampshire, Dunmore, Frederick, and Berkeley were directed to collect provisions and hold their militia in readiness to march to Fort Pitt for immediate service.[1] A company of militia was ordered out as rangers for Fincastle County. But notwithstanding the defenseless condition of the frontier, apprehension was so widespread lest the savages should destroy their homes during their absence that the militia was gotten together only after great delay, many absolutely refusing the draft. Not until the 644 warriors and chiefs representing the Six Nations, Delawares, Munsee, and Shawnee assembled at Pittsburgh was it known for what purpose they came. The conference served to dissipate the widespread gloom, for these Indian envoys promised inviolable peace with the United States and neutrality during the war with Great Britain.[2] Twelve chiefs were induced to visit Philadelphia, where they were introduced to Congress. For a few months after the treaty all the other western tribes, with the exception of a few of the Mingo known as Pluggy's Band, seemed desirous of preserving peaceful relations.

With difficulty Colonel Morgan persuaded the Virginia authorities that an expedition against these banditti would tend to bring on general hostilities with the tribes, already jealous of the encroachments of Americans, who were settling on the Ohio below the mouth of the Kanawha. He thought it was more essential to restrain the frontiersmen and promote good order among them, to pacify leading chiefs by liberal donations, and in all respects treat the Indians with "Justice, Humanity, and Hospitality."[3]

[1] *Ibid.*   [2] *Ibid.*, November 8, 1776, Vol. I.
[3] *Ibid.*, April 1, 1777, Vol. I.

CHAPTER III

Organized Defense of the Frontier

THE year 1777 was long memorable as "the bloody year" in the annals of border history. Early in the year British authorities began to employ more aggressive measures with the view of distressing the frontiers of Virginia and Pennsylvania as much as possible and with the hope that the main American army would be weakened through the withdrawal of forces to meet this attack. September 2, 1776, Lieutenant-Governor Henry Hamilton proposed the employment of Indians for this purpose. The British government received the recommendation with favor, and orders were sent General Carleton directing him to employ every means "that Providence has put into his Majesty's Hands, for crushing the rebellion and restoring the Constitution."[1] Hamilton was commanded to assemble as many Indians as convenient, under suitable leaders, in the spring, to carry out this decree, or take them elsewhere as they might be most needed. Similar orders were sent to Lieutenant-Colonel St. Leger regarding the Six Nations. From the friendly disposition manifested by the representatives of many leading tribes at Detroit (June 17, 1777) Hamilton felt assured that one thousand warriors were ready to overrun the frontiers.[2] Although war bands were urged to act vigorously, they

[1] *Mich. Pioneer and Hist. Colls.*, IX, 347.

[2] Draper MSS, 49 J 13.

were ordered to act with humanity. But resolutions voiced by the chiefs to pay strict attention to the injunction that they should spare the blood of the aged and of women and children were idle. Special presents for proofs of obedience signified little.

The conduct of affairs at Detroit was left almost entirely to the judgment of Lieutenant-Governor Hamilton, and he was informed that the power of the sword was alone to be trusted.[1] By September, 1777, his authority was absolute. He reported in July that fifteen bands of savages had been sent to raid the frontiers, and in isolated localities, too remote for warning, men were killed or captured while at work in the fields or out hunting. Women and children were burned in the houses, or, as in other cases, the entire family were carried away as prisoners. Hard pressed by their pursuers, the Indians killed such prisoners as hindered their rapid retreat. Thus the tomahawk saved them from sharing the fate of their companions, which was frequently more cruel. Upon arrival at an Indian village, men prisoners were forced to satisfy the savage instincts of their captors by running the gauntlet or by being subjected to untold cruelties. Some of them were sold to British and French traders, and later effected their escape or were ransomed. Women were forced to become the wives or slaves of the warriors, and children were adopted into the tribe.

Although it cannot positively be proved that Governor Hamilton offered rewards for scalps, Americans generally believed him guilty of this crime. That scalps were paid for seems well established through the testimony of prisoners and of spies, disguised as traders, who visited Detroit. Among the goods listed at the post, which included blankets, kettles, knives, razors, and rum, were 150 dozen

[1] *Mich. Pioneer and Hist. Colls.*, IX, 469.

scalping knives. Hamilton's own dispatches indicate that the taking of scalps was by no means exceptional. In January, 1778, he wrote General Carleton that the Indians had brought in seventy-three prisoners and 129 scalps, and in a letter of September he says: "Since last May, the Indians of this district have taken 34 Prisoners, 17 of which they delivered up, and 81 scalps.[1] At the same time he asserted that it was customary to present a gift on "every proof of obedience they shew" in sparing the lives of such as are incapable of defending themselves.[2]

But charges of inhumanity cannot be brought against all British officials. Governor Abbott of Vincennes, in his appeal to General Carleton (June 8, 1778) to prevent the continuance of savage barbarities, declared that "it is not people in arms that Indians will ever daringly attack, but the poor inoffensive families who fly to the deserts to be out of trouble, and who are inhumanly butchered, sparing neither women or children."[3] Captain Henry Bird, one of the noted leaders of the British and Indians, offered the Wyandot chiefs four hundred dollars if they would spare the life of a certain prisoner. His harsh language to them on their refusal is said to have aroused the ill will of the savages toward him.[4] Major Arent DePeyster, who succeeded Hamilton at Detroit, was accustomed to pay more for prisoners than for scalps. William Pitt opposed the enlistment of Indians, "But who is the man," he declared in Parliament (November, 1777), "who has dared to authorize and associate to our arms the tomahawk and scalping-knife of the savage? . . . . What! to attribute the sanction of God and nature to the massacres of the Indian scalping-knife. . . . . They shock every sentiment of honor. They shock me as a lover of honorable war and a detestor of murderous

[1] *Ibid.*, p. 430.   [3] *Clark Papers*, p. 47.
[2] *Ibid.*, p. 465.   [4] *Penn. Archives*, VII, 524.

barbarity. These abominable principles, and this more abominable avowal of them, demand a most decisive indignation."[1] But Americans were not guiltless in this barbaric practice, for at least one governor and colonial council gave its sanction by the offer of premiums for the scalps of enemy Indians and Tories.[2]

Much time was consumed at Pittsburgh in the discussion on the character of aggressive operations to be undertaken. It was counseled that an expedition against Detroit was the only remedy against the incursions of Indians. No more telling reasons for an attack on Detroit and the probability of its success were formulated during the entire war than those submitted by Colonel George Morgan.[3] He urged, first, that the road was practicable; second, that the Delawares and Shawnee were disposed to remain quiet; third, that there were no powerful tribes near or on the road to Detroit to oppose such an expedition; fourth, that Detroit was at the time in a defenseless state; fifth, that it was from that post that the offending western Indians were supplied "in all their wants and paid for all their murders"; and sixth, that its possession would induce all the tribes, through fear and interest, to enter into an American alliance. He advised sending against that post from twelve to fifteen hundred regulars and as many volunteers as might be secured. He opposed all plans looking toward retaliatory expeditions which were then favored by Congress. Finding that his advice was unheeded, and confident that the policy then adhered to would

[1] The speech was made in reply to Lord Suffolk, who had declared that "there were no means which God and Nature might have placed at the disposal of the governing powers, to which they would not be justified in having recourse."

[2] *Frontier Retreat on the Upper Ohio*, ed. Louise P. Kellogg, *Wis. Hist. Colls.* (Madison, 1917), XXIV, 183, 184.

[3] Morgan to Daniel Brodhead, July 17, 1778, Morgan, *Letter Book*, III

produce a general Indian war, Morgan resigned his office as Indian agent.

Conspicuous among the defenders of Kentucky during this fateful year was George Rogers Clark. His presence and services were indispensable. Returning after his victory over Colonel Henderson, he proceeded to set in motion the machinery of government for Kentucky County, and in this way he established even more firmly his place as leader. Some form of organization was essential, for personal rights were about to yield to the assertion of individual might. "I'm afraid," John Todd, Jr., declared, "to lose sight of my house lest some invader should take possession." Absorbed in ceaseless political discussion, or lost in their dreams of the future greatness of this new country, the settlers neglected to make provision for adequate defense. "But why," Todd exclaims, "do I preach politicks? 'Tis a country failing . . . . I'm worried to death almost by this learned ignoramus set; and what is worse, there are two lawyers here and they can't agree."[1]

Harrodsburg was made the county seat. In addition to the county-lieutenant, colonel, and lieutenant-colonel, commissions had also been issued by the governor of Virginia to justices of the peace, who were to constitute the county court. A sheriff and a clerk were associated with this court, which was required to meet once a month. Two delegates were chosen to represent the county in the house of burgesses. Every free white man was an elector who one year prior to the date of the election was possessed of 25 acres of land "with house and plantation thereon," or 100 acres without these, and who either in his own right or that of his wife was possessed of the estate for life.

The need for military protection was even greater than that for the organization of government. Heretofore mili-

[1] June 22, 1776. Draper MSS, *Preston Papers.*

tary service had been voluntary. The pioneer, single-handed, defended his home, or in combination with his neighbors, under some leader chosen from their own number, carried on such retaliatory attacks against the Indians as were necessary for the protection of life and property. Armed with their long rifles and hunting-knives and with their pockets full of parched corn as a substitute for bread, they pursued the foe and fought him in savage fashion. It was a warfare in which many Kentuckians won reputations for individual prowess. But with the close of the year 1776 it was evident that attacks of Indian bands organized by the British called for further methods of defense.

To Clark, who was commissioned a major, was intrusted the organization of the militia. Associated with him as captains were Daniel Boone, James Harrod, John Todd, Jr., and Benjamin Logan, all of them noted as Indian fighters and possessing other qualities such as would win the affections of their stalwart backwoods associates. Compulsory military service was inaugurated, and every man, whether a permanent resident or not, was required to join one of the companies for an allotted time.

Preparations against a possible attack on the Virginia frontier settlements on the first day of 1777 were hastened by order of Governor Patrick Henry. County-lieutenants were warned to have the militia in readiness.[1] Magazines were directed to be erected in Ohio, Yohogania, and Monongalia counties, and ammunition was forwarded. Early in March some two hundred warriors crossed the Ohio with the design of cutting off the settlers gathered in the forts at Harrodsburg, Boonesborough, and Logan's Station. The number of men at these posts did not exceed 150. Such a stroke, it was hoped by Hamilton, would put an end to American control in Kentucky. The fury of the attack was

---

[1] *Rev. on Upper Ohio*, p. 223.

met with a resistance born of desperation. The posts were attacked in turn, and at times simultaneously, so that defenders might not be sent from one to the other. The service rendered by the women during these sieges was not less notable than that of the men. Some of them were skilled in the use of the rifle and took turns at the portholes. While off duty they assisted in loading the guns, cared for the wounded, cooked such scanty food as could be secured, and melted the pewter plates into bullets. Boone, Todd, and a number of other leaders were among the wounded.

Thus the days wore on into the summer which was described by Clark as follows: "Our conduct was very uniform, the defence of our forts, the procuring of provitions or when possible supprising the Indeans (which was frequently done) burying the dead and dressing the wounded seemed to be all our business." But he records elsewhere, April 19, 1777, "Two burgesses were elected"; July 9, "Lieutenant Linn married, great merriment"; and September 2, "Court held."[1] On the retaliatory expeditions Clark led the militia. While many were advocating the abandonment of Kentucky, he quieted their fears by assurance of succor from Virginia.

Making little headway at Harrodsburg and Boonesborough, the savages on the last of May appeared at Logan's Fort and began a siege which lasted until the second of September, when Colonel John Bowman, with a hundred Virginians, arrived just in time to rescue the heroic band of defenders from death by starvation or final surrender. Three weeks later forty-eight mounted men came from the Yadkin to Boone's relief, and in October one hundred expert riflemen came from Virginia. With these accessions the outlook for the wearied Kentuckians appeared

[1] *Clark Papers*, pp. 21, 23.

brighter, but their actual condition during the ensuing winter was still desperate. The greater part of their stock of corn had been burned, the growing crop was destroyed, and their cattle and horses had been stolen. Early in December Colonel Bowman wrote that their supply of bread would be exhausted within two months, and that of the two hundred women and children many of them were widows and orphans destitute of necessary clothing. Before the expiration of the period of enlistment for Bowman's men the fields were cultivated and stocks of provisions and ammunition were collected. Large numbers of immigrants entered Kentucky, and the feeling of security increased.

During April and May, 1777, small bands of Indians caused the utmost consternation on the Ohio frontier by committing numerous murders. Forts and blockhouses were hastily constructed in some localities, while in others the inhabitants sought safety in flight.[1] It was learned at Fort Henry through Cornstalk, noted chief of the Shawnee, that a general confederacy of the northwestern tribes was nearly completed, lacking only the addition of his tribe, and that hostilities were about to begin.

Informed of these hostile demonstrations, Congress resolved to send an experienced officer to take command at Fort Pitt, who was to embody the militia and plan for the general defense. This difficult task was intrusted to Brigadier General Edward Hand, who proceeded at once to Pittsburgh, arriving there June 1. To assist him in this mission Congress voted arms and ammunition for the use of the troops at that post and elsewhere on the frontier, and four thousand dollars for strengthening the works at Fort Pitt and for contingent expenses. Discretionary pow-

---

[1] *Rev. on Upper Ohio*, p. 256.

er was granted him to enlist one thousand or more militia for the defense of the frontier.[1] It was anticipated that the high opinion in which General Hand was held on the frontier, where he had served for four years, would cause the militia to respond at once. His appointment was welcomed by the borderers, for it marked the desire on the part of General Washington and the Continental Congress to furnish protection. Five companies of militia assembled at Point Pleasant with the object of invading the Indian country, and there awaited General Hand's arrival from Fort Pitt. Meantime, some mutinous soldiers murdered Chief Cornstalk, together with his son and two companions who were being held as hostages. Rewards were offered by the governor and council of Virginia for the apprehension and conviction of the murderers, but without avail, due to the excited state of public feeling. The Shawnee were thereafter the inveterate foes of the whites, and as a result the Indian war was renewed with greater vigor the following year.[2] Upon the arrival of General Hand with but a handful of regular troops and without provisions, the expedition was reluctantly abandoned and the militia returned to their homes. Messengers were then sent to the various isolated settlements recommending that they should be immediately abandoned and that the settlers should take shelter within the blockhouses, flee to the fortresses, four being accessible at strategic points, Kitanning, Forts Pitt, Henry, and Randolph, or retire east of the mountains. Notwithstanding the vigilance of scouting parties constantly traversing the woods, deeds of savage violence were almost daily occurrences.

General Hand learned through messages brought by runners from the Moravian towns that the Ohio settle-

---

[1] *Jour. Cont. Cong.*, VII, 247, 256.   [2] Draper MSS, 13 S 103, 144.

ments were soon to be attacked by a large force of Indians and British rangers from Detroit.[1] Settlers hastened to retire to the security of the forts. The first blow fell on Fort Henry, garrisoned by two companies of militia, forty men in all, under Colonel David Shepherd. Warned by General Hand of the approaching danger, Colonel Shepherd, early in August, assembled some four or five hundred of the militia for the defense of the fort. As the enemy did not appear, vigilance was relaxed and nine companies of the militia returned to their homes, leaving eight men as a guard for the fort. This fort, formerly called Fincastle, was an oblong stockade of squared timbers pointed at the top, with bastions and sentry boxes at the angles. Within the inclosure of half an acre were the barracks, a storehouse, a well, and a number of cabins. It stood on the bank of the Ohio near the mouth of Wheeling Creek, and was next in importance to Fort Pitt. Between the fort and the base of a steep hill was an open level space partly occupied by log cabins. The settlers were assured by scouts who had been watching the approaches that there was no immediate danger. During the night of August 31 between two and three hundred warriors hid themselves within a short distance of the village. Early next morning Andrew Zane and some companions, while searching for the horses, were surprised by six Indians and one of the whites was killed. The others escaped, Zane, it is said, having leaped from a high cliff. With the usual frontier rashness, although they were warned that the invaders numbered two hundred, fifteen men marched out to the attack. Discovering the main body of the Indians, they attempted to escape, but were all killed with the exception of two who were badly wounded but finally reached the fort. Another small party ad-

[1] *Frontier Defense on the Upper Ohio*, ed. Reuben G. Thwaites and Louise P. Kellogg (Madison, 1912), p. 55.

vancing to the relief of their comrades were in like manner shot down or butchered, one only escaping. The defense of the terror-stricken settlers, who meantime had fled for refuge to the fort, was dependent on thirty-three men. To their surprise, the Indians did not make an attack. After throwing up rude earthworks they killed all of the live stock within reach, set fire to the cabins, and then retreated across the Ohio. Many tales, mostly mythical, of the heroism of both men and women have been connected with this event. Some of these stories had their foundation in the siege of Wheeling, a year later.

On September 26 a scouting party consisting of forty-six men set out from Fort Henry. Returning the next day, they were attacked by Half King, chief of the Wyandot, who, with forty of his braves, was lying in ambush. Twenty-one of the whites fell in this affair, called in border history "the Foreman Massacre.[1] All efforts of General Hand to collect a force sufficiently large for making a general advance against the Indian strongholds were futile. His entire force, including the drafts of militia from the frontier counties, amounted to only eight hundred men. They were badly clothed, and with winter coming on General Hand distributed his force along the frontier so as to prevent the inroads of the savages and assist the inhabitants in securing their crops and other property. Contrary to their usage, the savages continued their depredations during the winter months when the borderers were off their guard.

Fearful lest these forays carried on at the instigation of British agents would lead to the depopulation of the Virginia and Pennsylvania frontiers, Congress, late in the year, appointed three commissioners who were to co-operate with General Hand in carrying the war into the en-

[1] Captains William Foreman and Joseph Ogle commanded the party. *Frontier Defense*, pp. 106–12.

emies' country.[1] They were empowered to extend their operations so as to include an immediate advance on Detroit and its dependencies, provided it was thought feasible at that season of the year and could be accomplished with a force not to exceed two thousand men, exclusive of Indian auxiliaries. Throughout the winter preparations were made for protection against the recurrence of the outrages of the preceding year. New forts were built and old ones were strengthened. The news of Burgoyne's surrender, interpreted as evidence of final colonial triumph, inspired the frontiersmen to renewed efforts and terrorized the western tribesmen. General Hand determined upon an aggressive policy.

During February, 1778, with a force of five hundred men, largely militia, he set out for Sandusky, a British trading and recruiting center. Because of the heavy rains and melting snow his advance was slow and the sudden rise of the rivers defeated his plans. After taking possession of some Indian towns almost deserted by their inhabitants the expedition was abandoned. Thus the first organized advance by Americans into the Indian territory of the Northwest was deemed a failure. It resulted only in the capture of a number of noncombatants and the affair was commonly known as the "Squaw Campaign." Disappointed at the outcome, which was not due to lack of ability on his part, "much pestered with the machinations" of the Tories, and believing that a new commander would receive better support, Hand requested to be recalled from Fort Pitt. His administration of affairs was noted for its efficiency, for during this critical period he had greatly strengthened the local garrisons and prevented

[1] *Jour. Cont. Cong.*, IX, 942, 944. November 20, 1777. The commissioners appointed were Colonel Samuel Washington, Colonel Joseph Reed, and Gabriel Jones.

the frontier from being pushed back on the colonies. His petition was granted by Congress and he was succeeded by General Lachlan McIntosh, who had entered the army at the opening of the war and whose military ability was highly esteemed by Washington.

Proclamations by Hamilton scattered along the trails promised generous rewards to frontiersmen in land and good quarters at Detroit if they would join the British. American disaffection increased because of these promises, and many secretly took the British test-oath. The ranks of the Loyalists increased also through the coming of numbers whose property had been confiscated and who had been driven from the older settlements. An act of the Virginia legislature, passed at the close of 1776, not unlike that of other states, provided a fine of twenty thousand pounds and imprisonment for five years for any who should openly defend the authority of the king or parliament of Great Britain. The law, however, was a dead letter in many sections. Appealing for more effective legislation, a frontier county official wrote toward the close of 1777: "The present Punishment is really a matter of Diversion to them. They bring no Suits, they never Elect, they dont attend Court; they can dispose of their arms and they dont want to purchase Land; by these means they entirely evade the force of the Law, to which I sincerely wish some amendments could be made to stop this growing Evil. They speak with caution therefore do not come within the Law for punishing certain offenses. In short they do as they please."[1] So considerable were the numbers of Loyalists in certain frontier communities that militia officers, in making arrests, were at times confronted with open rebellion. On occasion committees of safety called out skilful workmen whose duty it was to patrol the country, cap-

[1] *Frontier Defense*, p. 170.

ture those of suspicious character, and put to death any who refused to submit or give security for good behavior. In meting out punishment distinction was not always clearly made between horse-thieves, highwaymen, and Tories.

Conspicuous among the Tories at Pittsburgh who broke parole and as leaders of Indian bands became scourges of border communities were Alexander McKee and Simon Girty. McKee was a former crown officer, and Girty, who had been a captive among the Seneca, execrated for his duplicity and heartlessness, was an interpreter. Their escape, together with a number of companions, among them Matthew Elliott, was a significant cause for the resignation of General Hand.[1] On their way to Detroit, where they were received with favor by Hamilton, they visited the Delawares and the Shawnee and checked the progress which American agents were making toward gaining control over these tribes. Incursion of the savages, assisted by the Tories, upon the frontiers of New York, Pennsylvania, and Virginia were almost continuous during the spring and summer of 1778.

While these attacks were incited by the authorities at Detroit, many of the settlers themselves were not blameless. The borderers were characterized in a report of the Board of War as "a wild, ungovernable race, little less savage than their tawny neighbors; and by similar barbarities, have in fact, provoked them to revenge."[2] But the suffering of the innocent with the guilty made immediate relief a necessity. It appeared certain, however, that these forays were but the preliminaries to a general Indian war which threatened the devastation of the whole frontier.[3]

---

[1] For Hand's account of this episode, consult *Frontier Defense*, pp. 249–55.

[2] Washington Manuscript (Library of Congress), Box 35, No. 5.

[3] *Letters to Washington*, 1778 (Library of Congress), Vol. XXV, folio 86.

It was reported that sixteen hundred warriors from the Seneca, Cayuga, Onondaga, Mingo, Wyandot, and a few from the Ottawa, Chippewa, and Shawnee tribes, together with a number of British emissaries, were gathering for this purpose. All attempts to conciliate these tribes, and the threats of the American commissioners, no longer availed. The Indians were firm in the opinion, which had been assiduously inculcated among them, that the forbearance of the whites proceeded from their inability to revenge the outrages committed against them. Influenced by these considerations, and aware that Detroit was still in a defenseless condition, Congress determined to abandon the policy of a defensive war and to undertake immediately two expeditions.[1]

One of them was to have as its objective the capture of Detroit and the subjugation of such Indian tribes on the way thither as were enemies of the whites. The other expedition was to be organized for the purpose of carrying the war into the Seneca country and the conquest of such tribes of the Six Nations as were hostile. Another object of this expedition was to gain possession of Oswego. The expedition against Detroit was projected on so large a scale that its success seemed assured. An army of three thousand men, the majority of them to be furnished by Virginia, was to advance in two equal divisions, one by way of the Big Kanawha to Fort Randolph, where it was to be joined by the other division coming from Fort Pitt down the Ohio. Nine hundred thirty thousand dollars were appropriated toward providing for the expedition, but it was shown that with Detroit in American hands a much greater amount would be saved through the abandonment of the defensive policy.[2]

That the French at Detroit would render no assistance

[1] *Jour. Cont. Cong.*, XI, 588.

[2] *Ibid.*, p. 590.

to the English upon the approach of the enemy appeared certain.[1] Hamilton himself had knowledge of this disaffection. Writing General Carleton, he said: "When it is considered how many people in this settlement have connections with the Americans it will not be surprising if the Virginians should have notice of anything projected against them from this Quarter and tho a great deal if not everything depends upon secrecy I must not flatter myself 'twill be concealed (as it should) since an Indian for a Gallon of Rum may be engaged to carry letters or intellegence."[2]

General McIntosh set out in June for Fort Pitt with five hundred men, including the Eighth Pennsylvania Regiment under Colonel Daniel Brodhead, which had been ordered to the frontier by Washington, who was then at Valley Forge, and the Thirteenth Virginia Regiment under Colonel John Gibson. Commissioners sent by Congress assembled at Pittsburgh, and through the judicious distribution of presents among the Delawares, $10,000 having been appropriated for that purpose, obtained permission to traverse their territory. Meantime, Congress determined to defer the expedition against Detroit. This change of plan was due chiefly to the report that it was impracticable to secure the necessary men, horses, flour, and cattle within the time specified.[3] General McIntosh was directed to assemble fifteen hundred troops at Fort Pitt, proceed against the hostile tribes, and destroy their towns. As a step in fulfilment of this plan he built a fort (Fort McIntosh) at the mouth of Big Beaver Creek, 30 miles below Pittsburgh. This was the first fort built on the right bank of the Ohio, and although primarily intended as a refuge in case of defeat, it was well located to furnish as-

[1] Morgan, *Letter Book*, August 19, 1778, Vol. III.

[2] *Mich. Pioneer and Hist. Colls.*, IX, 431.

[3] *Letters to Washington*, 1778 (Library of Congress), folio 88; *Jour. Va. House of Burgesses* (July 7, 1778), p. 287.

sistance to the settlements, which had reached the Muskingum and extended a few miles up that river.

With a force of one thousand men, General McIntosh, toward the close of October, advanced westward. So slowly did he move on account of a herd of cattle which was driven along with the army for food and because of other obstacles that two weeks were taken in covering 50 miles. Having reached an elevated plain on the Tuscarawas River, 70 miles from Fort McIntosh, while waiting for his main supplies to come up, he began the erection of a stockaded fort. The construction of Fort Laurens completed, the season was then so far advanced, the time of enlistment of some of the soldiers had expired, and the difficulties in procuring provisions were so great that the forward movement was abandoned. Leaving Colonel Gibson in charge with a garrison of 150 men, McIntosh conducted his remaining force to Fort Pitt, where the militia was disbanded.

During the course of these events a plan was evolved which, like many another paper proposal, met with almost unanimous support in Congress. This comprehended the capture of Detroit and Niagara and also an attack on Quebec, in which American troops were to be supported by a French fleet and army under General La Fayette. Once more the far-sightedness of Washington prevented the enormous expenditure of money necessary for the equipment of these expeditions which must at the time have resulted only in failure and the possible destruction of American hopes for ultimate victory.[1]

The winter proved a trying one for the garrison at Fort Laurens. Late in January a party of fifteen men which had carried provisions to them was waylaid 3 miles from the fort, while returning to Fort Pitt, by a band of Mingo

---

[1] *Writings of George Washington*, ed. Jared Sparks (Boston, 1834–37), I, 311 ff. *Clark Papers*, Introduction, L.

and Wyandot led by Simon Girty. Other convoys of provisions failed to reach the fort because of attacks by Indians, and the garrison was on the verge of starvation. In February Captain Henry Bird, of the King's regiment, accompanied by Simon Girty and a few soldiers, led 120 savages against the fort itself. Colonel Gibson, who was aware of the presence of the enemy although they were in hiding, persisted in sending out eighteen men to bring in the horses belonging to the fort. Sixteen of the party were killed and the two others were made prisoners. For a month the fort was invested, the besiegers finally retiring for want of supplies. A few days later General McIntosh reached the fort with five hundred regulars and militia. He learned of their critical situation from an Indian who succeeded in stealing through the lines with a message from Colonel Gibson. The relief was timely, for the garrison had subsisted mainly on roots for nearly a week.

On his return to Fort Pitt, General McIntosh learned that his request to be relieved from the command of the western army had been granted and that Daniel Brodhead, a man well acquainted with conditions in the back country, had, on the recommendation of Washington, been appointed his successor. While little had seemingly been accomplished by these movements, nevertheless the British plans to gain possession of the West and thus lend assistance to their eastern forces had been foiled. The rumor that another expedition was to be sent from Pittsburgh in April not only frightened the officials at Detroit, but "greatly damped the spirits" of their Indian allies.[1] They were forced also to turn their attention to the more aggressive operations of George Rogers Clark, with whose coming a new phase of the war in the West was inaugurated.

[1] Draper MSS, 49 J 20, 58 J 32.

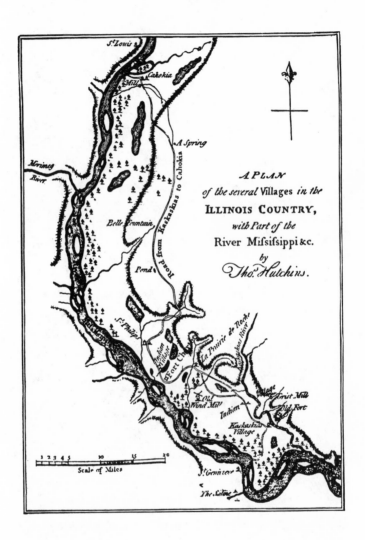

A PLAN
of the several Villages in the
ILLINOIS COUNTRY,
with Part of the
River Mississippi &c.
by
Tho. *Hutchins*.

CHAPTER IV
The Illinois Country

CLARK concluded that the surest defense against savage forays would be to capture the Illinois posts and win the friendship of the French inhabitants. As a first step thereto, in April, 1777, he sent Benjamin Linn and Samuel Moore as spies to Kaskaskia and Vincennes. What his designs were was a secret which he shared with no one.

The Illinois country included the territory extending from the Wabash and Miami rivers west to the Mississippi, and from the Ohio north to the Illinois. In the "American Bottom," averaging from 3 to 7 miles in width and stretching north 100 miles from the confluence of the Kaskaskia with the Mississippi, were some 300,000 acres.[1] The population of the four French villages within the area numbered, in 1778, between nine hundred and a thousand whites and some over six hundred Negro slaves. Kaskaskia was the largest settlement, with its eighty houses, five hundred white inhabitants, and nearly the same number of Negroes. The village was located on the Kaskaskia River, 6 miles above its mouth.[2] The river at this spot was 80

[1] Edmund Flagg, *The Far West; Early Western Travels*, ed. R. G. Thwaites, XXVII, 106 ff.

[2] During the year 1881 the Mississippi River cut through to the channel of the Kaskaskia and left the larger part of the village on an island. In 1899 most of the village was swept away by the river.

yards wide, with little current, and was deep enough to permit the loading and unloading of large bateaux from its banks at all seasons of the year.

Seventeen miles to the north, at the base of the limestone crags which rise to the height of 100 feet above the valley, was Prairie du Rocher, with a population of one hundred whites and eighty Negroes. The site of the village had been parceled out to the settlers from a grant which had been made by the Company of the Indies, Jean St. Theresa Langlois, the owner, retaining for himself certain seignioral rights according to the common law of Paris.[1]

Along the "King's Highway" 3 miles west of this village was Fort de Chartres, so named in honor of the son of the regent of France, the Duc de Chartres, which had been the center of civil government in the Illinois during the French régime. In 1720 a wooden fort had been completed on this site, one of the links in the chain of posts which was to reach from Quebec to the Gulf of Mexico—the dream of La Salle.[2] It was intended to be the chief seat, on the upper Mississippi, of the Royal Company of the Indies, center for trade and for the operation of the lead mines, and protection against the encroachments of both the Spanish and the English. This stronghold, rebuilt in 1756 at a cost of nearly 250,000 livres, an example of the engineering skill of the school of Vauban, was regarded as the most commodious and best-built fortification in America. The enveloping walls, 490 feet in length, 2 feet and 2 inches in thickness, and 15 feet high, were built of stone and plas-

---

[1] This grant had originally been conceded to the commandant, Boisbriant, the uncle of Langlois.

[2] Other French forts were Presque Isle, on the present site of Erie, DuQuesne, LeBoeuf, near Waterford, Pennsylvania, St. Joseph, Ouiatanon, Detroit, Michilimackinac, Fort Massac on the Ohio, and a fort on the Maumee. Juchereau's Post was begun in 1702 at the confluence of the Mississippi and the Ohio, but was soon abandoned.

FORT CHARTRES AS IT IS TO-DAY

tered over with mortar.[1] They were pierced with loopholes at regular intervals, and the four bastions had two portholes for cannon on each of their faces and flanks.

Here was stationed nearly a regiment of French grenadiers from which a company had gone down the Mississippi and up the Ohio in time to assist in avenging the death of Lieutenant Jumonville de Villers in the capture of Fort Necessity, July 4, 1754. Fort DuQuesne, cut off from Canada by the British, was provisioned by boat loads of flour and pork from Fort de Chartres, and reinforcements sent from this fort, under Charles Philippe Aubry, the last acting governor, aided in holding Fort DuQuesne for France until 1758, when he was forced to retire before a superior force led by General John Forbes. In November of that year Governor Aubry retreated to the Illinois, the French having burned the fort, and determined to abandon the valley of the upper Ohio. The Illinois country still held out for the King of France after Wolfe's victory on the Heights of Abraham (1759). By the fall of 1761 the French flag ceased to float north of the Ohio save in this district. Notwithstanding the surrender of New France to the British, the Illinois district was not abandoned by the French. A force of 132 soldiers was led through the wilderness from Michilimackinac by the Sieur de Beaujeu-Villemonde to strengthen the garrison at Fort de Chartres. It was to this stronghold that Pontiac, able chief of the Ottawa, after his unsuccessful attempt to capture Detroit, retired, still hoping to secure French aid in carrying out his plans for confederating the tribes of the Northwest. His request was rejected by Louis St. Ange, the commandant, who was left at the post with a detachment of forty men. This disappointment, together with the knowledge

---

[1] Philip Pittman, *Present State of the European Settlements on the Mississippi*, ed. F. H. Hodder (Cleveland, 1906), p. 88.

of the successful advance of Colonel Bouquet with 1,500 men from Fort Pitt to the upper Muskingum, where he made advantageous treaties with the Indians of that region, led Pontiac to see the hopelessness of his cause. In July, 1765, therefore, he set out to meet Colonel George Croghan, a successful trader who was skilled in dealing with the Indians. As deputy Indian agent representing Sir William Johnson, Croghan was advancing from Vincennes to the Illinois country accompanied by a large concourse of savages. Returning to the fort at Ouiatenon, where a great council was held, the humbled chieftain agreed to offer no further resistance to the British. Croghan then advanced to Detroit, where another important conference was held with the Indians during the summer of 1765. This resulted in a general peace with all the western tribes. The flag of the Bourbons continued to float over Fort de Chartres until October 10 of that year, when the veteran St. Ange, who for half a century had been a leader in the Northwest, surrendered the fort to Captain Sir Thomas Stirling, commander of the Forty-second Highlanders, of the celebrated Black Watch Regiment. Thus the empire of France in the New World ceased to exist.[1]

At Nouvelle Chartres, the village near the fort, which had originally contained forty families, only a few settlers lingered. The other inhabitants, following the lead of the French garrison, took refuge in St. Louis and Ste Genevieve, towns on the Spanish side of the Mississippi.[2] St. Philippe, five miles farther north, was founded by Philippe

[1] During the year 1914 the Illinois State Park Commission, of which the author of this volume was chairman, secured the site of this fort for the state. The original walls are easily traceable; the chief structures may be located; and the powder magazine shows only slightly the ravages of time. This remnant of Fort de Chartres is the oldest structure in the upper Mississippi Valley. It has now been partially restored.

[2] Pittman, *Miss. Settlements*, pp. 94, 95.

François Renault, who came there in 1719 with 250 miners, soldiers, and Negro slaves hoping to discover mines of gold and silver. He found wealth instead in the lead mines on the opposite side of the Mississippi, especially at Ste Genevieve. St. Philippe was likewise deserted by all but two or three families. Forty-five miles up the river was Cahokia with its fifty houses, three hundred white inhabitants, and eighty Negroes.

On the west side of the Wabash River, 262 miles from its mouth, was Ouiatenon, an important trading post with a stockaded fort, where a dozen French families resided.[1] Vincennes, with its eighty or ninety French families, on the east bank of the Wabash 150 miles from its mouth, was another strategic point on the trade route between the western posts and Canada. No British officer had been sent to take possession of the log fort which commanded this village until 1777. There were other French hamlets in the Northwest, at Peoria on the Illinois, at St. Joseph, Prairie du Chien, Green Bay, and Michilimackinac.

Near the French settlements in the American Bottom were the huts of the remnants of the four Illinois tribes of Indians—the Kaskaskia, Cahokia, Tamaroa, and Michigamea—numbering all told some four hundred warriors. In spite of the King's prohibitions and protestations of the missionaries, brandy had been furnished them by the French soldiers and traders and they were described as a poor, debauched, and dastardly people. There were a few Indian slaves, but their labor was unprofitable and the number decreased.

Travelers agree in writing of the superior fertility of the soil in the American Bottom and the valley of the Wabash, the former the terrestrial paradise, as it was called. In the

---

[1] Pittman, *Miss. Settlements*, pp. 97, 98; Flagg, *The Far West*; Thwaites, *Western Travels*, XXVII, 45.

forests along the rivers there grew the sycamore, oak, cottonwood, hickory, cedar, mulberry, persimmon, and black walnut trees. Maples, pecans, and cherries were also plentiful, and the thickets of wild plums, crab apples, and blackberries were matted together with the wild grape vines. From the grapes the French manufactured a wine which was very inebriating.[1] Buffalo and deer were still plentiful, and ducks, geese, turkeys, and pheasants abounded. The streams and small lakes teemed with fish.

So lavish was nature in her gifts and so prevalent was slavery that the inhabitants acquired habits of indolence. Most of the French had come originally with their families from Canada, and some of them had married Indian wives. English and French travelers agree with regard to the main features of society in these villages. Honesty and punctuality in their dealings, courtesy, politeness, and hospitality in their social intercourse, were general among all classes. They were cheerful and serene at all times, but lacking in enterprise.[2] Some of the French were well educated, but fully two-thirds of them could neither read nor write. The wives of the lower class, indolent and shiftless as their husbands, neglected their homes and spent the time gossiping with neighbors. In the early years of French occupancy marriages between *coureurs de bois* and Indian women were common, but the priests, by order of the government in 1735, were prohibited from solemnizing these marriages without the consent of the commandant.

The laborers wore pantaloons made of a coarse blue cloth or of buckskin, a colored cotton shirt, and a blanket-coat with a cape which could be drawn over the head.[3] The fringed, leather shirt and brightly colored cap made the

---

[1] Pittman, *Miss. Settlements*, pp. 97–98.

[2] C. F. C. Volney, *Travels* (London, 1804), p. 332.

[3] John Reynolds, *Pioneer History of Illinois* (Belleville, 1852), pp. 51 ff.

dress of the *voyageurs* conspicuous. As far as possible men and women of the well-to-do class took on the fashions in dress of New Orleans and Paris, including at times such luxuries as richly trimmed coats with "diamond" buttons, embroidered waistcoats, silk hose, and silver buckles. Moccasins and rude leather boots and shoes were worn by men and women, and in place of hats they commonly tied blue handkerchiefs over their heads, although home-made straw and fur hats were used. For the ballroom and church they dressed more neatly. While drinking and gambling were common, there was comparatively little drunkenness in these communities.

The almost nightly dance in the puncheon-floored cabins furnished amusement for all ages and all classes, for there was no distinction of wealth on such occasions. The village priest was frequently in attendance. The first of the year, too, was ushered in by a festival of dancing. During the carnival season, which began on January 6, the King's Day (Mardi Gras), and continued a number of days, balls with their cotillions, reels, and minuets were included as a part of the regular festivities of this occasion. *Voyageurs* and *coureurs de bois* lightened their burdens by measuring the strokes of their oars with songs, and around the blazing logs in the far-off wilderness danced gaily or accompanied the strains of the fiddle with the words of some old melody of love or of the chase.

Rarely did a festival of the calendar go unobserved, for the ceremony and discipline of the church laid a firm hold upon all and processions and festivals were important events in their lives. The church building was conspicuous in each village. The one at Kaskaskia, which was originally constructed of stone, was described by a traveler in 1835 as the aged Catholic church erected more than a century since upon the ruins of a former structure of similar character. . . . . It is a huge old pile, extremely awkward and ungainly, with its projecting eaves, its walls of hewn timber perpendicularly planted, and the interstices stuffed with mortar, with its quaint old-fashioned spire, and its dark, storm-beaten casements. The interior of the edifice is somewhat imposing, notwithstanding the somber hue of its walls which are rudely plastered with lime, and decorated with a few dingy paintings. The floor is of loose, rough boards, and the ceiling arched with oaken panels. The altar and the lamp suspended above are very antique. . . . . The lamp is a singular specimen of superstition illustrated by the arts.

One twenty-sixth of the produce of the farmers was collected for the support of the church, but it was necessary to supplement this contribution by donations from parishioners, gifts from the king and other persons in France. The income from lands held by the religious orders constituted the leading source of support for the churches.

Criminal offenses were almost unknown among the French. They readily acquiesced in the interpretation of the laws and customs made by judge or notary and submitted to the regulations of the district commandant or of the village priest. For seven years the regulations of the British government for the Illinois country were administered by military officers from Fort de Chartres. Each village maintained its own militia company. The captain was the chief citizen of the village, who represented the major commandant, put into execution the decrees of the judge, and performed functions similar to those exercised by an English justice of the peace.

During 1772 the Mississippi River began to undermine one of the walls of the fort and it was abandoned by the British, the garrison being transferred to Kaskaskia.

The fur trade, in one way or another, furnished means of employment to the majority of the inhabitants. In the villages were the merchants who on their own account, or

POWDER MAGAZINE, FORT CHARTRES

more frequently acting as agents or partners of Canadian merchants, furnished the supplies used in exchange for furs, such as hatchets, knives, kettles, blankets, ribbons, and glittering trinkets. At times, accompanied by *voyageurs* who propelled the canoes and carried the packs of goods and furs, they traded with the Indians in person. They outfitted, usually on credit, the *coureurs de bois*, who through love of adventure spent most of their lives in the woods. By twos and threes these wood-rangers sped along the waterways in their canoes or crossed the country to trade with distant tribes. At times they were to be found among the Indians on the headwaters of the Missouri and the Mississippi and as far as Santa Fé, journeys which meant months of privation and adventure. To most of them the restraints and privations of civilized life were unbearable. They were merry, patient, and industrious in the performance of tasks, usually faithful in meeting their engagements, and warm in their friendships; but revengeful toward an enemy and ready to take a mean advantage of him. Their lawlessness when among the Indians was proverbial, and disregarding the regulations of government and protests of missionaries they demoralized the Indians through furnishing them with brandy and rum. After months spent in a life of barbaric pleasure and hardship, toil and peril, with their cargoes of furs and game they returned to the villages, where they dissipated their energies and squandered their earnings in drinking and gambling, and then with new packs returned to the wilderness to repeat the same round of life over again.

Most of the *habitants*, or permanent villagers, spent their days in cultivating the fields, in hunting, fishing, and gossiping with their neighbors at the little wine shops of the village. In these villages were also men who were well to do. Some of them were of noble birth who had come from Canada or France as officials or to engage in trade, while others had risen to prominence as fur traders and were referred to as the gentry and men of ability, influence, and address. Besides these types there were some residents who followed the primitive mechanical arts, such as stone-masons, blacksmiths, and gunsmiths.[1]

The houses, placed close to the front of the lots, ranged along the narrow streets which ran at right angles to one another, were usually a story and a half high with a porch on one or more sides.[2] While a few of the more pretentious houses were built of stone, most of them were of wood set on walls of stone one or two feet in height. The interstices between the upright posts were filled in with "cat and clay," a mortar which was made of a mixture of common clay and finely cut straw. Thatched roofs were common, although shingles, which were attached by wooden pegs, were used. The puncheon floor and spacious fireplace and chimney completed the structure, whose exterior was whitewashed. Each dwelling was set in a yard which was surrounded by a picket fence five feet high. Within the inclosure were the peach, apple, pear, and other fruit trees and the flower garden and vegetable garden wherein were raised potatoes, melons, and squash. The houses of the more wealthy were comparatively well furnished, with "plate" on the sideboards and French mirrors on the walls, while a few men owned billiard tables.

French life, as in Canada, was centered in the village community, and the isolated farmhouse was rare. Adjoining the villages were the narrow ribbon-like strips of land, the "common fields" from one-half to a mile long and varying in width from ten to forty rods. The *habitants* cultivated these fields, which were plowed, sowed, and reaped

[1] Pittman, *Miss. Settlements*, pp. 102, 103.

[2] Reynolds, *Pioneer History*, p. 50.

according to rules agreed upon in the public assembly made up of all males of military age. It was at the door of the church, after mass, that the assembly met and the royal notary offered property for sale in a "high and audible voice," payments being made in silver, peltry, or slaves. All males over fourteen years of age were expected to attend the assembly. The syndic was the official elected to carry out the will of the assembly, and so long as the individual complied with the restrictions he was entitled to his land in fee simple. The "commons" was a tract set aside for pasturage and woodland. Each cultivator was required to build and keep in repair the fence along his farm which separated the common fields from the commons. After the crops were harvested, horses, cattle, and hogs were allowed to run in the common fields. By consent of the assembly, portions of the commons might be assigned as common fields to the indigent, to young married persons, and to newcomers in the community.[1] The time of plowing, harvesting, and other matters having to do with the crops, the upkeep of roads, and the building and repair of the churches were other items determined by the assembly.

While encouragement had been given by the French government to the settlers to develop the land, the ordinary villagers were at best but indifferent farmers. Work on the larger holdings was poorly performed by Negro or Indian slaves. Farm tools were of the crudest sort. Although the soil was capable of yielding large returns of wheat, corn, tobacco, hemp, flax, hops, fruits, and vegetables, the cultivation was so careless that wheat, for example, produced only from five- to eightfold.[2] Tilling the soil was burdensome when hunting, fishing, and trading yield-

---

[1] Flagg, *The Far West*; Thwaites, *Early Western Travels* (Cleveland, 1904), XXVII, 46.

[2] *Jesuit Relations*, ed. R. G. Thwaites (Cleveland, 1904), LXIX, 219.

ed a livelihood. Corn was raised only in small quantities as food for the stock. The cultivation of wheat was begun by the French in the Illinois country as early as 1687, and although wheat was grown, under orders from the Company of the West, as far down the Mississippi as New Orleans, the Illinois and Wabash settlements alone produced a surplus for the market. Lower Louisiana always counted on securing flour from this region, and in the year 1746, 800,000 pounds, which were sold at New Orleans, were produced north of the Ohio.[1] During the last ten years of French control the growing of wheat increased rapidly in upper Louisiana, at least three-fourths of the crop finding ready market at New Orleans and Detroit. After the transfer of Kaskaskia to Great Britain, M. Beauvais, with an estate on which he kept eighty slaves, furnished the King's magazine with 86,000 pounds of flour, representing a portion only of his harvest for a single year.

The agricultural methods were those of a century earlier, the clumsy wooden plows being drawn by oxen. There was no effort to renew the fields through the use of fertilizers. The farmers were well supplied with a hardy breed of cattle brought from Canada, and there were sheep and poultry; but their stock had degenerated in size for the want of proper care and food. Hogs in large numbers roamed the forests. The horses resembled mustangs and were noted for their strength and great endurance. The inhabitants traveled much on horseback or rode in the wooden carts, *charrettes*, with two horses driven tandem. There were a few horses of superior breed which were brought from the Pawnee Indians some 600 miles to the west, or from New Mexico.[2] In each village were water

[1] Henry M. Brackenridge, *Views of Louisiana* (Pittsburgh, 1814), p. 272.

[2] Clark to Patrick Henry, March 9, 1779. *Clark Papers*, p. 303.

mills for grinding corn and sawing boards, and grist mills which were operated with horse or water-power.

Besides flour, the Illinois posts sent peltry, tobacco, salted buffalo-meat, venison, tallow, and bear's oil to New Orleans in exchange for liquors, groceries, dry-goods, and articles used in the Indian trade. Goods were ordinarily sold at 100 per cent increase over prices in the Paris markets. The Missouri trade consumed annually European goods valued at 8,000 pounds. Three months were ordinarily required for the largest bateaux, usually covered, and some 40 feet long and 9 feet wide, with eighteen to twenty men at the oars, to ascend the river from New Orleans to the Illinois posts. The trip down the river consumed from twelve to fifteen days. Twice each year, in the early spring and during August, from seven to twelve of these boats, combining for protection against the Indians, constituting what was known as a convoy, made this voyage.[1] The piroque, made by hollowing out the trunks of trees, was likewise commonly used for down-river trade. Snags in the river and the caving in of the banks also made navigation dangerous. Trade relations were also sustained with Detroit and with Montreal, journeys requiring several weeks.

There was likewise travel overland, especially for the shorter distances. A roadway connecting the Illinois villages ran along the American Bottom from Kaskaskia to St. Philippe, and thence to Cahokia along the valley or by a second route on the bluffs. On the prairies the French found the trails of the Indians and the well-worn buffalo paths wide enough for two wagons to pass. These were later developed as roads by the government, one running from Cahokia to Peoria, and thence to Galena. Another

[1] Pittman, *Miss. Settlements*, p. 36.

ran to the mouth of the Tennessee, and there was also a well-known road from Peoria to Detroit.

Scarcely were the British in possession of Fort de Chartres when the agents of Eastern firms, chiefly from Philadelphia, inspired by the stories of wealth to be acquired through Indian trade and the acquisition of land, began to compete with the French for the control of the northwestern fur trade. The best known of these companies, and the first to extend its connections as far as the Illinois, was the one which operated under the name Baynton, Wharton & Morgan. It was on the advice of George Morgan, a graduate of Princeton, whom we have seen as Indian agent, that the firm established branch stores for trade and land speculation at Kaskaskia, Cahokia, and Vincennes. This company employed some 350 boatmen for the transportation of their merchandise (1767) down the Ohio to the Illinois country.[1] Morgan represented the company in these villages and was noted for his influence with the French. The information acquired by him on these expeditions formed the foundation for his plans for the conquest of the West at the outbreak of the Revolution, for he threw his whole soul into the patriot cause. The David Franks Company, of London and Philadelphia, and Bentley & Company were also among the well-known firms operating in the Illinois.

British traders bringing their goods by the Ohio route were able to undersell the French, who were forced to use the more circuitous routes by the way of the Great Lakes and the Wabash or up the Mississippi from New Orleans. In the fall of 1766 Baynton, Wharton & Morgan proposed to employ five boatmen for each boat constituting a convoy of sixty-five boats on the Ohio to be used in transport-

[1] Alvord, "Virginia and the West," *Miss. Valley Hist. Rev.*, III, 22.

ing their merchandise to the Illinois.[1] In a single year four convoys of boats were dispatched by this firm from Pittsburgh, one of them laden, it is said, with merchandise which had been transported from Philadelphia by six hundred pack horses and a large number of wagons. Five miles an hour was regarded as an average rate of rowing, and twenty days, without any mishap, was consumed in the trip down the Ohio. Among other articles listed in the shipments were clothing, ruffled shirts, silk handkerchiefs, shoes, blankets, looking-glasses, jew's-harps, black and white wampum, guns and munitions, brooches, earrings, silver arm and wrist bands, bells, medals, and vermilion.[2] Traders, together with agents and clerks, representing the companies came in such numbers that Morgan wrote in 1768 that an English militia company had been formed at Kaskaskia containing sixty members.[3] The ledger kept by Baynton, Wharton & Morgan for the three years preceding 1770 shows a list of 240 customers.[4] The profits from this trade were not as great as had been anticipated, for the investments were large, lists of goods shipped by this one company to Pittsburgh and the Illinois amounted to 401,000 pounds, Pennsylvania money. The expense of sending a single convoy of forty-five boats from Pittsburgh to Fort de Chartres with five men for each boat was some 5,000 pounds.

While goods could be shipped down the river, it was found to be too expensive to row boats upstream to Pitts-

[1] C. W. Alvord and C. E. Carter, *The New Régime*, *Ill. Hist. Colls.* (Springfield, 1915), p. 384.

[2] *Ibid.*, pp. 19–21.

[3] Alvord, *Kakaskia Records*, 1778–90, *Ill. Hist. Colls.* (Springfield, 1909), II, XXVIII.

[4] Alvord, *Miss. Valley Hist. Rev.*, IX, 236–41. Account of the Baynton, Wharton & Morgan Manuscripts.

burgh. Moreover, higher prices were paid for peltries at New Orleans than in the eastern markets. Appreciating these facts, General Gage wrote to Lord Shelburne on February 22, 1767:

> The Trade will go with the Stream, is a Maxim found to be true, from all accounts that have been received of the Indian Trade carried on in the vast Tract of Country, which lies on the back of the British Colonies; and that the Peltry acquired there, is carried to the Sea either by the River St. Lawrence, or River Mississippi, as the Trade is situated on the Lakes, Inland River and Streams whose waters communicate respectively with those two immense Rivers. The part which goes down the St. Lawrence we may reckon will be transported to Great Britain, but I apprehend what goes down the Mississippi will never enter British Ports; and I imagine that nothing but a Prospect of a Superior Profit or Force, will turn the Channel of the Trade contrary to the above Maxim.[1]

Boatmen were employed for a period of four months, since the usual way of returning was overland, a journey of 700 miles, or by boat from Pensacola. Seventy thousand dollars represented only in part the expenses of one of the smaller companies for two years.

Opportunity for speculating in land was scarcely second to the fur trade in attracting the attention of the men on the coast to the West.[2] Explorers and surveyors were sent out by companies to locate the best sites for colonies. The public, as usual, was eager to invest in such schemes.

---

[1] *The New Régime*, p. 506.

[2] In a letter (1768) discussing the possibilities of investment, especially in western lands, the writer says: "It is almost a proverb in this neighborhood [Philadelphia] that 'every great fortune made here within these fifty years has been by land.'" Alvord, "Virginia and the West," *Miss. Valley Hist. Rev.*, III, 21. "Washington, securing military bounty-land claims of soldiers of the French and Indian War, and selecting lands in West Virginia until he controlled over 70,000 acres for speculation, is an excellent illustration of the tendency." F. J. Turner, *The Frontier in American History* (New York, 1920), p. 124. Professor Turner cites a number of other illustrations (pp. 122, 123).

Financial backing and political influence were sought in Great Britain by promoters of these enterprises.

During the summer of 1763, notwithstanding the proclamation of 1763 forbade settlements in that region, the first company was formed for the purpose of planting a colony in the Illinois country. Thirty-eight well-known Virginians, among whom were George Washington, Richard Henry Lee, and William Fitzhugh, organized the "Mississippi Land Company" and petitioned the Crown for a grant of 2,500,000 acres of land on the Mississippi River which would include parts of the present states of Illinois, Kentucky, and Tennessee. Some of the arguments favoring the petition were: there would ensue an increase of agricultural population, an extension of trade and enlargement of revenue, and that it would serve as a buffer colony against the Spaniards.[1] George Grenville, then prime minister, held that this territory was imperial and that it could not be granted for exploitation to the citizens of a particular colony.

Among other colonial plans, one urging a grant of 1,200,000 acres in the Illinois country was sponsored by Sir William Johnson, William Franklin, the son of Benjamin Franklin, governor of New Jersey, and a number of prominent Pennsylvanians. Benjamin Franklin, who was greatly interested in the project, was constituted a special advocate for this memorial, and it met favor with Lord Shelburne, who advocated the establishment of colonies at Detroit, in the Illinois country, and on the Lower Mississippi. Franklin declared in a letter to his son, 1767: "A settlement should be made in the Illinois country—raising a strength there which on occasion of a future war might easily be poured down the Mississippi upon the lower coun-

[1] *Ibid.*, pp. 517, 518, 570–72, contains papers on the organization of the company and its purpose.

try and into the Bay of Mexico to be used against Cuba, the French Islands, or Mexico itself."[1] Owing to the reorganization of the ministry in 1768, whereby a new department in the Cabinet, secretary of state for the colonies, was created, with Lord Hillsborough in charge, the project failed.[2]

General Gage, in military command at New York, responding to the desire of the ministry that expenses should be reduced wherever possible, proposed that Fort de Chartres should be abandoned. As additional reasons for this policy it was urged that the site for the fort was not well chosen, offering no strategic advantages, and that it was in constant danger from the encroachments of the Mississippi River. Moreover, the location was unhealthful and the soldiers had suffered from numerous epidemics. George Morgan wrote in 1768: "There was but nineteen men capable of Duty at Fort Chartris, every Officer was ill at the same Time. . . . . The Groans and cries of the Sick Was the only Noise to be heard."[3] In December, 1771, General Gage was ordered to withdraw the troops from Fort de Chartres and Fort Pitt and to demolish both forts. Major Isaac Hamilton, the following year, in fulfilling these orders declared that "he has destroyed Fort Chartres in such a manner that at present it cannot afford the least shelter to an Enemy, and that he removed the stones which protected the banks of the river and opened drains to admit the waters, so that the Floods in the Fall will entirely wash away the front of the fort." Leaving fifty soldiers at Kaskaskia, Major Hamilton returned to Fort Pitt with the

---

[1] *Writings of Franklin*, ed. Smyth, IV, 141.

[2] For a more extended discussion of these companies, consult Alvord, "The Illinois Country, 1673-1818," *Centennial History of Illinois* (Springfield, 1920), I, 286-93; also, *Mississippi Valley in British Politics*, Vol. I (see Table of Contents).

[3] *Ibid.*, p. 297.

remainder of his force, and later to Philadelphia. Lord Dartmouth, who was Lord Hillsborough's successor in the ministry, favored a progressive policy of expansion to the West. The proposal of General Gage to abandon the Illinois country was negatived and he was instructed to leave the troops at Kaskaskia as a guard to the country lying along the Mississippi River, over which the Spanish and the French were exercising too much influence.

In keeping with the opinion advanced by prominent English lawyers that the Indian nations held the sovereignty over their lands, the Illinois Land Company in 1773 purchased from the Indians at Kaskaskia a large tract of land between the Ohio and the Mississippi rivers and another tract on the Illinois. During the fall of 1775 the Wabash Land Company, of which Lord Dunmore was a member, purchased from the Indians an extensive tract of land lying on both sides of the Wabash River.[1]

These transactions were carried on without the sanction of British officers, and their validity was denied by Captain Hugh Lord, commanding officer at Kaskaskia, who declared that any settlement of these lands would be expressly contrary to His Majesty's orders. Arguments in favor of the passage of the Quebec Act, 1774, whereby French law would be extended to the Northwest, were that it would serve as a deterrent to settlement by English colonists, and would therefore probably prevent the repetition of illegal purchases by land companies and would serve to regulate the fur trade.[2]

[1] *American State Papers, Public Lands* (Washington, 1833–61), II, 108 ff.

[2] The Illinois and Wabash Land companies united in 1780. Numerous memorials were brought before Congress asking recognition of these titles to land. Finally, in 1823, by a decision of the Supreme Court, it was determined that: "A title to land, under grant to private individuals, made by Indian tribes or nations, northwest of the river Ohio in 1773 and 1775, cannot be recognized in the courts of the United States" (8 *Wheaton*, 543–605).

Moreover, unfavorable reports on frontier society were constantly being sent to the government by both colonial and English writers. Until the passage of the Quebec Act the whole territory was under the direction of the commander-in-chief of the British forces with headquarters in New York. By this act the Northwest was included in the province of Quebec. A lieutenant-governor, or superintendent, was to reside at Kaskaskia, and a lower court of the King's Bench was to be established in that village. Like provision was made for Vincennes, Michilimackinac, and Detroit. This court in each of the four districts was "to be held at such times as shall be thought most convenient, with authority to hear and determine in all Matters of Criminal Nature according to the Laws of England, and the Laws of the Province hereafter to be made and passed; and in all Civil Matters according to the Rules prescribed by the aforesaid Act of Parliament."[1] A judge who should be a natural-born subject was to preside over each court. Appeals might be made from a district court to the governor and council, and in case of necessity to the king in council. The outbreak of the American Revolution prevented the carrying out of the provisions for civil government contained in this act.[2]

[1] Shortt and Doughty, *Constitutional Documents of Canada*, p. 423.

[2] The French language is commonly used by the villagers of Prairie du Rocher, and many eighteenth-century customs still survive.

CHAPTER V

Spanish Influence in the West During the First Years of the Revolution

ONCE in possession of the French posts of the Northwest at the close of the French and Indian War, British authorities sought to extend their supremacy over the entire Mississippi Valley. To accomplish this object Spanish influence must be overcome. The trade of the Missouri River centered at St. Louis. Notwithstanding the protests of English officials and the decrees of Spanish governors, traders from that post pushed their way up the Ohio, the Wabash, and the Illinois and trafficked with the Indians of the Wisconsin and the Fox rivers. French traders from the Illinois posts carried their packs of furs across the river to trade with their friends in St. Louis or transported them down the river, a trip of twelve days, to the New Orleans market. Even British traders from Fort Pitt and West Florida were drawn to New Orleans owing to the better prices paid there for furs than in the regular English markets. It was estimated in 1771 that peltries worth between 75,000 and 100,000 pounds sterling were exported annually from that port, chiefly to France.

At the time this trade was the one important factor in the development of the West. A British officer in a report of 1768 declared that a settlement "will never happen with any advantage to England until we can procure the Ideal Island of Orleans; . . . . Could we find passage for even small craft to go to the sea, the country of the Illinois would be worthy of attention, but had we the Island of Orleans, that country would in a very short time I believe be equal to any of our colonies."[1] But even with this obstacle to the establishment of English commercial supremacy the decade preceding the outbreak of the Revolution were critical years for Spanish interests in the Mississippi Valley.

Plans for the capture of these Spanish possessions in the event of war were fully discussed by British authorities. The two countries seemed on the verge of war in 1770 on account of the dispute over the Falkland Islands, and General Gage, commander of the British forces in America, was ordered to take steps preparatory to an attack on New Orleans.[2] With the ultimate capture of the entire province of Louisiana in mind, the mobilization of troops at New York was begun early in 1771. But the King of Spain, before hostilities were actually opened, acquiesced to the terms submitted by Great Britain.

The contest for the commercial control of Louisiana grew more intense during the years directly preceding the opening of the Revolution, with the odds greatly in favor of British traders. According to the report of a Spanish officer in 1776, the commerce of the colony amounted to $600,000 annually.[3] Only some $15,000 of this amount represented the commerce of the six or eight vessels operated by royal permission. In spite of the vigilance of the governor, Spanish planters secured their necessities from the

---

[1] C. E. Carter, *Great Britain and the Illinois Country*, 1763–64 (American Historical Association, 1908), p. 141, note.

[2] Arthur Hassall, *The Balance of Power* (London, 1898), pp. 327, 328. Secret dispatch of Lord Hillsborough to General Gage, and reply thereto.

[3] Carter, *The Illinois Country*, pp. 182–84. Don Francisco Bouligny, "Memoir concerning the Province of Louisiana," Alcée Fortier, *History of Louisiana* (New York, 1904), II, 24–47.

"floating stores" and the other ten or twelve English boats continually on the Mississippi. Influenced by this trade and by the coming of the Tories driven from the colonies, Manchac and Baton Rouge developed with such rapidity that they threatened to overshadow New Orleans and become a menace to Mexico. In order to offset this influence it was advised that Spanish merchants should be granted freedom of trade, as at an earlier period; that an army should be maintained which would be adequate, not only to defend Louisiana, but in case of necessity furnish reinforcements for Mexico and Havana; and that forts should be built on Spanish territory opposite the mouths of the rivers flowing into the Mississippi. The positive advantages accruing to Spain from the completion of these projects would be: the control of the navigation of the Mississippi, securing possession of Mobile and Pensacola, which were dependent on the returns from illicit commerce, and the consequent increase of income for the royal treasury.

The appeal for assistance in a letter of May, 1776, from General Charles Lee, who spoke for the Virginia Committee of Safety was therefore not unwelcome to Unzaga, who since August, 1770, had been the governor of Louisiana. The arguments presented were well calculated also to win favor from King Charles III and his advisers for the cause of America.[1] Should Great Britain succeed in subjugating the colonies, he wrote, her army and navy would be free at any moment to take possession of Mexico and Cuba. With America independent, Spanish possessions, it was maintained, need not fear attack. Great Britain alone would be incapable of raising sufficient troops for attempting such a conquest, and the superiority of her

[1] This letter of General Lee accompanied one sent by the Governor, dated September 7, 1776. *Archivo General de Indias*, Seville, Estante 87, Cajon I, legajo 6.

fleet would soon be reduced by the loss of America. Great Britain reunited to America would be more dangerous to Spain than one of the two if they remained separated. "Nor need there be any apprehension that the colonies having once established their independence would molest any other power for the genius of the people, their situation, and their circumstances engage them rather in agriculture and a free commerce which are more important to their interests and to their inclination." The Spanish were urged to furnish the American army with guns, blankets, and medicines, especially quinine.

A plan to secure gunpowder from New Orleans was conceived by Captain George Gibson, of the Virginia line. Bearer of the letter from General Lee, Captain Gibson, accompanied by Lieutenant William Linn and fifteen other men in the guise of traders, set out from Fort Pitt July 19, 1776. Arriving at New Orleans, the letter was intrusted to Oliver Pollock, who, acting as the unofficial agent of Virginia and later a friend indispensable to Clark, succeeded in concealing their identity from the numerous British spies.[1] To no other man could this mission have been intrusted with greater promise of success. As a trader in Havana for five years, he had become proficient in the use of Spanish and won the friendship of the leading officials, among them Don Alexander O'Reilly, governor-general of Cuba. During the year 1768 Pollock located in New Orleans. On August 17 of the following year Count O'Reilly, with three thousand troops, appeared before the city and demanded that the command should be surrendered by the French governor in conformity with the treaty of cession. The formal surrender took place with much pomp the next day. To capture a town of three

---

[1] Pollock, when twenty-three years of age, had come with his father from Ireland to Carlisle, Pennsylvania (1760). Two years later he went to Havana, where he engaged in mercantile pursuits.

thousand inhabitants with an overwhelming military force proved an easier task than it was to supply the troops with necessary provisions. Flour quickly rose to $20 a barrel and was obtained with difficulty at that price. Pollock possessed a boat-load of flour which he proffered to the General on his own terms. He was paid fifteen dollars a barrel for his flour, but for this mark of generosity he was granted freedom of trade in Louisiana as long as he desired.

In April, 1776, Pollock's efforts, with Governor Unzaga, to secure Spanish protection for some American vessels against their seizure by a British sloop of war on the plea that they were in a neutral port proved unavailing. To what extent the Governor was influenced by the contents of General Lee's letter can only be conjectured, but he finally permitted the sale of 10,000 pounds of powder to Pollock.[1] Pollock himself believed this changed attitude to be in part a result of the publication of the Declaration of Independence.[2]

Lieutenant Linn, with forty-three men, set out from New Orleans September 22 with a cargo of ninety-eight kegs of powder, 9,000 pounds, in barges. The expedition reached Wheeling the second of May, at a time when that post and Fort Pitt greatly needed the powder for protection and to further their dealings with the Indians.[3] In October Captain Gibson, who had been imprisoned by decree of the Governor in order to quiet the suspicions of the British Consul, was permitted to embark for Philadelphia on a vessel dispatched by Pollock. He took with him

[1] Eighteen hundred dollars were paid for the powder.

[2] "Letters and Papers of Oliver Pollock," *Papers of the Continental Congress*, October 10, 1776 (Library of Congress), pp. 51 ff.

[3] One means of gaining the friendship of the Indians was through the distribution of powder.

the remainder of the powder in carefully concealed pack-
ages.

Don Bernardo de Galvez, commander of a regiment at
New Orleans, who succeeded to the government of Louisiana in January, 1777, belonged to an influential Spanish
family. His father was the Viceroy of Mexico, and his
uncle, José de Galvez, stood high in court favor as secretary of state and president of the Council of the Indies.
He was twenty-nine years of age and was noted for his
ability, energy, and ambition. Governor Unzaga presented
Pollock to his successor as "a faithful and zealous American in whom he might repose implicit confidence."[1] Governor Galvez at once tendered his services to Pollock and
assured him that he would go every possible length for the
interests of Congress. He declared that the port of New
Orleans would be open and free to American commerce and
to the admission and sale of Portuguese prizes made by
American privateers. This was in keeping with the royal
order of October 23, 1776. A month earlier the British
Ambassador at Madrid had urged the Spanish court to
take action similar to that of Portugal whereby American
vessels were to be forbidden to enter her ports. Instead of
treating Americans as rebel subjects of a friendly power,
the King of Spain directed that American vessels should
be granted, in Spanish ports, any hospitality which might
be accorded to the French or the British. American trading vessels, upon arrival at the mouth of the Mississippi
River, were seized as Spanish property in order to protect
them against British vessels of war. Seizure of an American schooner provoked an order for the capture and confiscation of all British vessels "between the Balize and Manchac." Aid to American troops, in goods and money, was

[1] Oliver Pollock to the President of Congress, September 18, 1782, "Letters
and Papers of Oliver Pollock," Library of Congress.

tendered in the event of an expedition for the capture of Pensacola and the British posts on the Mississippi. Pollock urged action by the American government and suggested that blank commissions should be sent for enlisting troops in New Orleans.

Governor Galvez refused the demand made by the Governor of Pensacola for the surrender of Pollock and hastened to begin correspondence with Colonel George Morgan, who was in command at Fort Pitt. Morgan had already assured Galvez that it was the purpose of the United States, now free and independent, to maintain the closest relationship possible with Spanish subjects.[1] Very deftly he outlined the military operations of the Americans, the siege of Boston, the capture of New York, the surprise at Trenton and the hopeful outlook. "By stratagem and delay," he declared, "we shall gain the upper hand and shall establish our empire. This and the treaties of alliance and trade between Spain, France, and America will defeat Great Britain, for it can no longer be a question of reconciliation." Morgan submitted a plan for the conduct of the war in the West, should Spain and France make common cause with America against England, Portugal, and Russia. This comprehended the capture of Niagara and Detroit, and also, if transports and cannon could be secured for one thousand men to be embarked at Fort Pitt, the seizure of Mobile and Pensacola with all of their stores. Nothing came of the project, but the rumor that a large force of Americans were descending the river caused the Governor of Pensacola to strengthen the defenses of the post.

It was clear to Galvez, as it had been to his predecessor, that British plans contemplated an attack on Louisiana,

[1] George Morgan to the Governor of Louisiana, April 22, 1777. *Archivo General de Indias*, Seville, Estante 87, Cajon 1, Legajo 6.

and one of his earliest communications urged, as a means of defense, that the Indians should be won over to the side of Spain, which could, he thought, be easily accomplished because of their former subjection to France.[1] By means of gifts, friendly visits, and promises rapid progress was made toward the accomplishment of this object. Early in July, at a conference held at Mobile between English officials and the chiefs of the Creek, Choctaw, and Chickasaw tribes, on behalf of the twenty-five hundred warriors assembled, women and children accompanying them, the Indians declared they would remain neutral during the period of the war.[2]

Shortly after, Galvez requested that two frigates should be sent at once to defend the Spanish possessions against British aggression, which had reached "a point of intolerable insolence difficult to be borne by a man of honor."[3] Among the infinity of insults which could not be recounted he specifies the following: that the English had plundered Spanish dwellings along the river and fired on the inhabitants; that a Spanish and a French vessel had been fired on, and after capture were detained for periods of twenty-four and thirty hours, the communications under the seal of the Governor having been read; and that boats loaded with pitch at New Orleans had been seized as contraband. In meeting the demands of the inhabitants for reprisal, Galvez ordered the capture of vessels engaged in carrying on illicit commerce, and eleven were seized in one night.[4]

[1] Galvez to José de Galvez, January 28, 1777, *Archivo General de Indias*, transcript in the Ayer Collection, Newberry Library, Chicago. A year earlier Governor Unzaga had been directed to specify to the Spanish court what were his means of defense against an attack. In reply, he showed how inadequately Spanish possessions were protected by troops and fortifications and submitted evidence which seemed to point to a design on the part of the British to seize Louisiana.

[2] *Ibid.*, July 10, 1777. [3] *Ibid.*, May 6, 1777.

[4] Galvez to Torré, Captain-General of Cuba, May 6, 1777 (Ayer Collection).

British armed vessels appeared at New Orleans with the demand that the captured vessels and crews should be released. Hostilities seemed about to open, but the British withdrew when Galvez showed no disposition to yield.[1] Two of the vessels interned were owned by Americans, but they were released secretly upon the request of Oliver Pollock. The nine others were confiscated and their cargoes were sold as contraband. At that time, owing to a shortage in food, there was considerable sickness at Pensacola. Galvez sent 150 barrels of flour, as a gift, to relieve the distress, and this act of generosity settled the controversy.[2]

Although the immediate cause for dispute was adjusted, Galvez continued to call for armed vessels and means for strengthening the fortifications at New Orleans. Other causes for strained relations continued to develop. The English governor at Pensacola protested against the sending of arms and ammunition up the river under the protection of the Spanish flag.[3] A Spanish mail-boat was attacked while ascending the river, presumably by a British armed sloop. English subjects were forbidden to transact any business within the Spanish colonies, while French commercial relations were extended so much that two French commissioners stationed at New Orleans, in commenting on the concessions, declared that "the whole trade of the Mississippi is now in our hands."[4]

Meanwhile, Major Cruzat at St. Louis was directed to carry out the decree of the King whereby British influence

[1] "I received them with match-rope in hand in order to prevent any violence."

[2] Galvez to José de Galvez, September 15, 1777; December 30, 1777 (Ayer Collection).

[3] Governor Peter Chester to Galvez, March 7, 1777 (Ayer Collection).

[4] These commissioners were Villars and Farre d'Aunoy. Charles Gayarré, *History of Louisiana* (New Orleans, 1903), III, 118.

might be overcome through inducing Canadian families and other immigrants to found towns in Louisiana. To each of these families was to be assigned a plot of ground, the necessary utensils for tilling it, and supplies for the first year at the expense of the royal treasury, $40,000 a year having been appropriated for these purposes. As an added inducement to agricultural colonists the Spanish government agreed to purchase their entire crop of tobacco. By thus fostering the growth of tobacco the government hoped to accomplish two objects: Revenue could be secured through the duty imposed on the sale of this product in the Mexican province, and the monopoly of the tobacco trade held by the English and the Dutch in the French markets could be overcome.[1]

By July, 1777, the request embodied in the letter of General Charles Lee bore fruit and there were deposited at New Orleans, subject to the order of Virginia, two thousand barrels of gunpowder, a quantity of lead, and a large amount of clothing.[2] A year earlier the Duke de Grimaldi, Spanish prime minister, under the influence of Vergennes, induced Charles III to duplicate the secret loan of one million livres made by France to America. A continuation of the war would enable Spain, it was believed, to attack Portugal while Great Britain was unable to come to the rescue.[3] She awaited the opportunity also to take Gibraltar. The efforts of Benjamin Franklin won the favor of Count d'Aranda, Spanish Ambassador at Versailles, but King Charles III refused to declare openly for the American cause. On January 2, 1777, the Committee of Secret Correspondence notified Franklin of his appointment as

[1] Gayarré, *op. cit.*, III, 107.

[2] Stevens, *Facsimiles*, May, 1777, p. 151.

[3] Francis Wharton, *Diplomatic Correspondence of the American Revolution* (Washington, 1889), II, 282.

commissioner, by Congress, to negotiate a treaty of friendship and commerce with Spain.[1] Some days earlier Congress had instructed Franklin that the United States was prepared to assist Spain in an attack on Pensacola providing that port and the Mississippi River should be open to the Americans.[2]

Before receiving these messages, however, the American Commissioners in Paris had authorized Arthur Lee to go to Madrid to solicit an alliance with Spain.[3]

On February 18 Grimaldi had been succeeded as prime minister by the Count de Florida Blanca. With his advancement the outlook for open aid to America by Spain was greatly lessened. The new minister was forty-seven years of age. Not of the patrician class, he received a good education and devoted his life to diplomacy, in which, by his force of character, he had achieved marked success. He was a liberal, although his views were tempered by caution. He disliked England, was jealous of French ascendancy, and hated the spirit of revolution. To the new minister it was evident that should Spain assist in securing independence for the British colonies, Spanish rule in America would be likewise endangered. Spanish domination of trade with her colonies would be impossible with a vigorous nation developing as their neighbor. Moreover, alliance with America would mean war with Great Britain, and the Spanish navy, army, and treasury were in no condition to offer adequate defense against an attack by the greatest maritime power of the day. Assurances were giv-

---

[1] *Secret Journals of Congress*, II, 42.

[2] *Ibid.*, p. 40. This confirmed an act of Congress (December 30, 1776), *Jour. Cont. Cong.*, VI, 1057.

[3] Franklin was unable, because of his age, to undertake the journey. *Writings of Benjamin Franklin*, ed. Smyth, VII, 32. Stevens, *Facsimiles*, 269. A. Lee to Richard Henry Lee, October 4, 1777.

en the British authorities that no American representative
would be received at Madrid.

In keeping with this promise, Arthur Lee, before his
arrival at the Spanish border, received a message to the
effect that he should not proceed to Madrid, but that a
conference would be granted him at Burgos.[1] Here on
March 4 Lee was met by Grimaldi and was informed that
the Americans would find deposited at New Orleans and
at Havana stores of clothing and powder which their ships
might secure, that supplies were also being collected at
Bilbao for shipment to America.[2] In vain Lee argued that
the time was opportune for the immediate interposition of
Spain and France, for if Great Britain should again be
united to America by conquest or conciliation, he said,
she "would reign the irresistible though hated arbiter of
Europe." The reply setting forth the reasons for delay
seemed satisfactory to Lee, for he returned to Paris convinced of the sincerity and well wishes of the Spanish government.[3]

"You have considered your own situation, and not
ours," Grimaldi said: "The moment is not yet come for
us. The war with Portugal—France being unprepared,
and our treasure from South America not being arrived—
makes it improper for us to declare immediately. These
reasons will probably cease within a year, and then will
be the moment." Aid continued to be given surreptitious-
ly to the Americans by the Spanish government. The fate
of the West was largely dependent on the generosity of
Governor Galvez and the liberality of Oliver Pollock. By

[1] Jared Sparks, *Diplomatic Correspondence of the American Revolution*
(Boston, 1829–30), I, 400.

[2] Wharton, *Diplomatic Correspondence*, II, 279–80.

[3] *Ibid.*, pp. 282, 283.

the end of the year 1777 Galvez had aided the Americans by sending arms, ammunition, and provisions to the Mississippi posts and the frontiers of Pennsylvania and Virginia to the amount of $70,000.[1] The firm of Joseph Gardoqui & Sons, operating at Bilbao, served as the chief agents for assisting America. Funds were collected at Madrid by Diego Gardoqui and forwarded to Arthur Lee, who, in turn, gave his orders for goods to the firm at Bilbao. Transactions were on a cash basis, for the Gardoquis drew on Lee's bankers for payment.[2] During the year 1778 America secured in this way 18,000 blankets, 11,000 pairs of shoes, 41,000 pairs of stockings, and shirtings, tent-cloth, and medicines in great quantities.[3] Besides, an extensive private commerce was carried on by American merchants in Spanish ports, British representatives striving unsuccessfully to prevent this trade.

There can be no doubt that Spanish officials were prompted to this seemingly generous conduct through the hope of ultimate gain for Spain. Patrick Henry, then governor of Virginia, well understood what arguments would be most forceful. As the price of assistance he presented to the Governor of New Orleans the advantages which would accrue to Spain through the control of the trade of the southern states and the deprivation of their "ancient and natural Enemy the English of all those vast supplies of naval Stores and Many other Articles which have enabled them to become so powerful on the Seas." Again in possession of Pensacola and St. Augustine, they would be able, he thought, to enjoy a great part of the trade of our northern states. To facilitate intercourse by way of the

---

[1] Gayarré, *History of Louisiana*, III, 113.

[2] Wharton, *Diplomatic Correspondence*, II, 308.

[3] Edward Channing, *History of the United States* (New York, 1912), III, 284.

Mississippi he proposed to establish a post at the mouth of the Ohio.[1]

In acknowledging the aid already received, Governor Henry also pled with the Governor of Cuba for further assistance.

We are well acquainted, Sir [he wrote], with the Honour, Spirit, and Generosity of the Spanish nation and should therefore glory in an intimate Connection with it. For I suppose, I need not inform your Excellency, that the States are now free and Independent, capable of forming Alliances and of making Treaties. I think the Connection might be mutually beneficial, for independent, of the Beef, Pork, live Stock, Flour, Stores, Shingles, and several other articles with which we could supply your Islands, we have vast quantities of Skins, Furs, Hemp, and Flax which we could, by an easy inland navigation bring down the Mississippi to New Orleans from our back Country, in exchange for your Woolens, Linens, Wines, Military Stores, etc.[2]

The effects of a conquest by the Americans of the British posts east of the Mississippi River had already been considered by the Spanish government, and secret royal orders were sent to Galvez which defined the policy of that court.[3] In case the Americans seized these possessions and desired to deliver them to His Majesty, Galvez was instructed to receive them in trust. English officials were to be assured that they would be more secure under Spanish control than "under their enemies risen in rebellion." It is probable that Florida Blanca in this way hoped to complete the plan which was more definitely stated by him in his offer to mediate the following February. The United States was to be confined to the Atlantic seacoast; Great Britain was to be given the valley of the St. Lawrence; and Spain was to retain the Mississippi Valley as

---

[1] Letter of Patrick Henry, October 18, 1777 (Virginia State Library).

[2] *Ibid.*

[3] Orders of August 15, 1777. Galvez to José Galvez, December 30, 1777 (Ayer Collection).

far east as the Alleghany Mountains.[1] As a promise for the fulfilment of this scheme the attitude of Governor Henry must have been satisfying to Spanish officials. He wrote:

And were you once restored to the possessions you held in the Floridas (which I sincerely wish to see, and which I make no Doubt these States would cheerfully contribute to accomplish) the advantage to us both in a Commerical View would be greatly increased. The English, indeed insinuate that it would be impolitic in your nation to assist us in our present Situation, but you are too wise not to perceive how much it is their Interest that you Should be imposed upon by this Doctrine and how much more formidable they must be to you with the assistance of America than without it; and you must be too well acquainted with the Nature of our States to entertain any Jealousy of their becoming your Rivals in Trade, or, overstocked as they are with vast tracts of land, that they should ever think of extending their Territory.[2]

Three months later, however, in making application for a loan of 150,000 pistoles, Henry suggested that West Florida, embracing a large part of.the present states of Alabama and Mississippi, should be annexed to the United States.[3] Such a cession, he argued, would be the means of cutting off the supplies of lumber and provisions procured from the Mississippi region by the British West India settlements, and thus would prevent the progress of their rivalry to the Spanish colonies. These proposals were received with favor by Galvez, who submitted them to his government.[4] It cannot be stated definitely that Governor Henry

[1] Florida Blanca to Grantham, British minister at Madrid, February, 1778. Wharton, *Diplomatic Correspondence* (Introduction), 87.

[2] Patrick Henry to the Governor of Cuba, October 18, 1777 (Virginia State Library).

[3] January 14, 1778. Draper MSS, 60 J 363, 364. The pistole was a gold coin worth about four dollars.

[4] Galvez stated that he would be pleased to grant the request of Henry, but on account of loans to Pollock he was out of funds. He believed that Spain would be glad to see West Florida taken from the English.

contemplated carrying out this project through the expedition under George Rogers Clark, but it is certain that
Clark thought of it as an object to be accomplished. During the spring Galvez sent a special commissioner to Pensacola to demand prompt redress for the depredations
which British raiders were making on the Mississippi. He
welcomed, therefore, the arrival of Captain James Willing,
who set out from Pittsburgh early in January, 1778, in an
armed boat with a crew of twenty-nine men.[1]

Willing was commissioned to procure the supplies deposited at New Orleans and bring them up the river to
Fort Pitt. A further aim was to get control of the settlements in the Natchez district, where land had been acquired from the Choctaw along the river for a distance of
110 miles between the 31° and the mouth of the Yazoo
River.[2] The town of Natchez, where for three years Willing had been a merchant, contained in 1776 twenty log
and frame houses. During the preceding ten years also,
encouraged by English authorities, settlers from the Carolinas, Georgia, Virginia, and from New England and the
British West Indies came to Pensacola, Mobile, Manchac,
and other communities in the Lower Mississippi region.
In general these immigrants had no desire to take sides
in the Revolution. The number of inhabitants in the
Natchez district was increased in the fall of 1776 by the
coming of numerous Scotch-Irish from Pennsylvania, Virginia, and North Carolina who sought to escape the turmoil of divided sentiment prevalent in the back countries.

---

[1] Wilbur H. Siebert, "The Loyalists in West Florida and the Natchez
District," *Mississippi Valley Historical Proceedings*, VIII, 107. At the outbreak of the Revolution Willing was living in Natchez and was reputed to be
a man of wealth. He went to Philadelphia and offered his services to Con
gress.

[2] This strip of land was 40 miles in breadth at the lower end and 10 miles at
the upper.

Other immigrants to the region were Loyalists who had been driven from the frontier communities by their Whig neighbors. With his force increased to one hundred men, Willing captured Natchez and secured an oath of neutrality from the magistrates. Gaining additional recruits, French bateauxmen and a number of men from Natchez, Willing proceeded down the river carrying on a ruthless warfare by which the crops and stock of British planters were destroyed, houses burned, and slaves carried away. Most of the planters crossed the river and took refuge under the Spanish flag, but some of them were taken and held as prisoners of war.

Meantime, Pollock, after making arrangements with the Governor for the arrival of Willing, sent out a small armed boat which took Manchac, captured a British ship of sixteen guns which was fitted out as an American cruiser, and also captured a number of boats loaded with indigo, peltries, and Negroes.[1] Among the dispatches brought by Captain Willing was one which was gratifying to Pollock, for it contained his appointment, from the Committee of Secret Correspondence, as commercial agent for the United States.[2] He was authorized to purchase and ship forty or fifty thousand dollars' worth of blankets and other supplies for the United States Army. These goods were to be forwarded in fast-sailing vessels which he was directed to charter or buy. Two drafts amounting to $30,000 were sent in part payment, and the balance was to be met by a shipment of flour.[3] Four months later, however, Pollock

[1] The prizes were estimated to be worth £40,000. Oliver Pollock to a special committee of Congress, April 1, 1778.

[2] The commission was dated June 12, 1777, and was received by Pollock March 4, 1778. Pollock to Andrew Allen and Robert Morris, Committee of Congress, March 6, 1778.

[3] "Letters and Papers of Oliver Pollock," June 12, 1777, *Calendar of Documents*, Library of Congress, LVIII, Part I, 29–36.

was informed by the Commercial Committee that on account of the British blockade of the coast it was impossible to make the shipments of flour. But because of their necessities he was urged to forward the goods at once by sea, as transportation up the Mississippi was too slow and danger of capture by Indians was constant. Within a month Pollock was directed to send part of the goods up the river to Fort Pitt, where a quantity of flour had been sent to cover the cost.[1] These American attacks cut off the supplies of lumber and provisions which had formerly been shipped from the Mississippi posts to Jamaica and Pensacola.

Galvez was satisfied that he had performed his full duty as a representative of a neutral power in issuing a proclamation granting protection to the refugees. But toward the close of April three British armed sloops appeared before New Orleans and threatened to make reprisals on the town unless the prizes and all Americans were delivered to them. Certain of the inhabitants were warned by their friends in Pensacola to quit the colony in order to escape the storm which was about to break. Galvez replied to their demands that he could only refer their requests to his court.[2] At the same time he granted Pollock the liberty to dispose of all property taken from the English above Manchac. The captured posts, left unprotected by the Americans, were by the middle of May again in the possession of the British.

Heretofore large bateaux, under Spanish colors, propelled with twenty-four oars, managed to slip past Natchez

[1] The Secret Committee was reorganized as the Commercial Committee. "Letters and Papers of Oliver Pollock," October 24, 1777, *Calendar of Documents*, L, Part I, 37-39.

[2] Oliver Pollock to the Commercial Committee, May 7, 1778. "In this situation, he laughed at their Haughtiness and despised their Attempts and in short they returned as they came."

with goods sent by Pollock, and in eighty-five or ninety days arrived at the mouth of the Ohio and then continued to Wheeling or Pittsburgh. With a force of 40 British regulars and 60 rangers at Manchac, which was also defended by a sloop of war with a crew of 150 men and with Natchez protected by 200 men under arms, communication by the river after the first of May, 1778, was hazardous. Pollock ordered his boats to return and sent a warning to the Spanish commander at Arkansas Post to prevent any boats from descending the river. From this post the Americans were still able to secure supplies with bills drawn on Pollock. Assisted by Galvez, he fitted out a prize ship which he called the Morris, with a crew of 150 men, for the purpose of keeping the navigation of the river open. At the same time he urged Congress to send an expedition against Natchez, defended by a force of only two hundred men, and Manchac, with only one-half that number. The defense at Pensacola consisted of from eight hundred to one thousand men besides the Indians. A force of one thousand Americans would be sufficient, he thought, to clear the river of the enemy, and three thousand could capture Pensacola.[1] With the closing of the river Pollock continued to send vessels by sea loaded with taffia, sugar, and coffee. Securing these goods was made possible through a further advance of $6,000 by Galvez, although he had informed Pollock that he was not invested with such authority from his government, and that in case of a rupture with Great Britain all of his resources would be needed for defense of the colony.[2]

In May Pollock purchased a cargo of peltries and in-

[1] "Letters and Papers of Oliver Pollock," *Papers of the Continental Congress*, VI, 5 ff.

[2] Pollock to the Commercial Committee, April 1, 1778, May 7, 1778. Royal approval was granted August 25, 1778. Galvez to José de Galvez.

digo to the amount of $20,000, which he shipped under French colors to France, there to be exchanged for goods suited to the use of the Commercial Committee. The enterprise failed because of the seizure of the peltries by an agent of the United States stationed at Cape Francis on the claim that the government was indebted to him and that the cargo had been shipped by its agent. Exclusive of the supplies received directly from Galvez, Pollock's obligations on account of the government amounted to $50,000.[1] One item of expense was necessitated through providing for the support of Willing and his men. This, together with the spirit of insubordination prevailing among them which created enemies for the American cause, led to the demand by Pollock for their departure. By the middle of August the news of the success of George Rogers Clark in the Illinois country had reached New Orleans, and the men of Willing's party, led by Lieutenants Robert George and Richard Harrison, were ordered to join him.[2] Special permission was granted them by Galvez to march through Spanish territory. Galvez interpreted Clark's victory as a defeat for the British and their plans against the Spanish posts.

[1] Pollock to the Commercial Committee, May 7, 1778.

[2] Willing, carrying messages for Congress, embarked for Philadelphia. Draper MSS, 48 J 32. He was captured at Mobile and placed in confinement, but toward the end of the year was sent as a prisoner to New York. After three months he was permitted to go to Philadelphia on parole until exchanged. He is said to have been exchanged for Lieutenant Governor Hamilton (*Frontier Defense*, p. 193).

CHAPTER VI

Capture of the Illinois Country— Kaskaskia

UPON the withdrawal of the English troops from Kaskaskia in the spring of 1776, in order to save unnecessary expense, Captain Hugh Lord, to whom was given authority to select his successor, intrusted the administration of affairs to Phillipe François de Rastel, Chevalier de Rocheblave. During the French and Indian War Rocheblave won distinction as an officer in the French army along the Pennsylvania and New York borders. With many other Frenchmen, after the surrender of the Illinois country, he took refuge under the Spanish flag, where, in recognition of his ability, he was intrusted with the command at Ste Genevieve. Because of difficulties with Spanish officials he returned to the British side of the Mississippi River, where, after two years' service, he was employed, as Sir Guy Carleton wrote, "to have an eye on the proceedings of the Spaniards, and the management of the Indians on that side. His abilities and knowledge of that part of the country recommended him to me as a fit person."[1] The appointment proved to be a wise one, for Rocheblave, although quarrelsome and avaricious by nature, conducted affairs with a zeal which was commended by his superior officers.

By what means was Spanish influence to be overcome,

[1] Sir Guy Carleton to Rocheblave, October 28, 1776. E. G. Mason, "Rocheblave Papers," *Chicago Historical Society Collections* (Chicago, 1890), IV, 382.

at once demanded his attention and continued the chief problem during the two years he was in command. Experience with the Spaniards had developed in him a personal hatred for them, and his ambition also was quickened by the hope, confirmed by British officials, that he should be made governor of New Orleans in the event of a war between the two nations. "I shall in my correspondence with Mr. de Rocheblave," Hamilton wrote, "keep alive the hopes of his being Governor of New Orleans. A More active and intelligent Person is not to be found in this Country of ignorant Bigots, and busy rebels, and had he the means I doubt not of his curbing their insolence and disaffection."[1] He requested that all Spanish trade on the Ohio should be cut off, called attention to the aid which the American colonies were receiving from New Orleans, declared that Spanish agents were stirring up the tribes on the Illinois River to attack British posts, that English ships were the prey of Spaniards, and demanded during the summer of 1777, "Shall we make the first move or shall we permit it to be made?"[2] From the beginning his chief concern was the antagonism of certain of the English traders who operated in the French villages and were in sympathy with the cause of independence.[3]

As judge and acting commandant, offices which he had assumed, Rocheblave was in a trying situation in this community almost without the elements of established government. English merchants complained that he discriminat-

[1] Alvord, *Cahokia Records Ill. Hist. Coll.*, Vol. II, Virginia Series, Vol. I (Springfield, 1907), Vol. XXVI.

[2] Rocheblave to Lieutenant Governor Abbott, August 13, 1777. Mason, *Chicago Hist. Soc. Colls.*, IV, 394.

[3] For the growth of an American party in the Illinois country and its significance, consult Alvord, "Virginia and the West," *Miss. Valley Hist. Rev.*, III, 31 ff.

ed against them and favored the French, that he refused
the application of English law, that he was a trader buying and selling goods both wholesale and retail, and that
while the sale of liquor to the Indians had been forbidden,
he had himself exchanged rum with them for their beaver
and other skins. This antagonism to Rocheblave became
still more open when, in attempting to enforce the laws
of trade, he caused the arrest and imprisonment of numerous offenders. "If I were not a little crazed already,"
he wrote to Lieutenant-Governor Hamilton, "I believe
they would cause me to become entirely so."[1] Moreover,
this treacherous element, as Rocheblave described them,
corresponded with eastern leaders and carried on trade
with the rebels.[2] Glowing pictures of the advantages to be
gained through independence were alluring to their friends
among the French. An invasion of the Illinois villages was
openly talked about and supplies were collected for the
American troops when they should come.[3] Rocheblave,
who was aware of the depredations of Captain Willing,
besought his superiors to send troops and supplies sufficient to enable him to preserve the western country against
a similar invasion. "We are upon the eve of seeing here,"
he wrote, "a numerous hord of brigands who will establish
a chain of communication which will not be easy to break,
once formed." His requests for soldiers were unheeded,
and drafts against the government, beyond the amount

---

[1] May 8, 1777. Mason, *Chicago Hist. Soc. Colls.*, IV, 391. "At present," he
said, "one is obliged every day to imprison young men who demand if the English
law is favorable to them it should be followed; on another occasion the same
people will the very next day demand the old French laws which have always
been followed."

[2] For an account of this element, consult Alvord, *Kaskaskia Records*, pp.
xvi ff.

[3] *Ibid.*, p. 35.

of his small salary, were rejected. He was, as he said, left in charge of a great province without troops, without money, and without resources.

After an absence of two months, Linn and Moore, whom Clark, as we have seen, had sent to Kaskaskia and Vincennes, returned to Harrodsburg. Disguised as hunters, these young men succeeded in their mission, but evidently they did not get into communication with the American party, as would have been possible had they been aware of Clark's plans. They reported that there was no suspicion of an attack from Kentucky, that the fort at Kaskaskia was unguarded, and that while the French feared the American backwoodsmen, whom they regarded as desperadoes, they were lukewarm in their attachment to the British flag.

Guided by this report, Clark, in a letter to Governor Patrick Henry, gave a concise statement of the situation in the Illinois country and submitted a plan of action notable for its aggressiveness.[1] Kaskaskia, he asserted, was of the utmost importance, for from this center the British were able to keep control of the Indian tribes and send them against the Kentucky settlements; it furnished provisions for the garrison at Detroit, and controlled the navigation of the Mississippi and the Ohio, thus preventing the Americans from securing goods from the Spaniards with which to carry on Indian trade. He advocated sending a force to capture this post, for, he declared, "[We must] either take the town of Kuskuskies or in less than a twelve month send an army against the Indians on Wabash, which will cost ten times as much and not be of half the service."

He was aware that the task could not be accomplished unless the number of men which might be secured from

[1] Clark to Patrick Henry, *Clark Papers*, p. 30.

the Kentucky villages should be reinforced. On October 1, therefore, he started for Virginia to lay his plan before Governor Henry.[1] Two weeks earlier a company of forty-eight men had come to Kentucky, and this news, together with the report that one hundred fifty more were coming and that Howe had been defeated by Washington, led Clark to exclaim exultantly, "Joyfull News if true." Before setting out he displayed his shrewdness as a trader by purchasing a horse for 12 pounds sterling which he "swapped" with Isaac Shelby, receiving 10 pounds to boot. The further entries in his diary give an interesting account of the events of the journey. He joined a company composed of seventy-six men and a number of women and children who, fearing another outbreak of Indian outrages, were returning to their old homes. Progress along the Wilderness Road was still further delayed on account of the cattle which they drove along with them to be used for food. Their supplies were increased by some of the hunters killing three buffalo and a few deer. From 14 to 20 miles constituted a day's journey. The tenth day they met a company consisting of fifty men and two families on their way to Boonesborough. On the nineteenth day, having reached the region where it would be possible to spend a night at some cabin or frontier settlement, Clark rode on alone for a few days at a more rapid pace. He fell in with

---

[1] Clark, "Memoir," *Clark Papers*, p. 218. The leading sources for the history of the West from 1776 to 1779 are, Clark's "Memoir," Clark's "Journal," Clark's "Diary," "The Mason Letter," and Bowman's "Journal." These are all to be found in James, *Clark Papers*, *Ill. Hist. Colls.*, Vol. VIII. The value of Clark's "Memoir" as a historical document was first questioned by Theodore Roosevelt in *The Winning of the West*. Writers on the period have very generally accepted the view of Mr. Roosevelt. After a study of all the evidence obtainable on this point, it may be asserted with confidence, I think, that the "Memoir" must be accepted as a trustworthy supplement to each of the other documents named, and at times to all of them on a number of essential points in the narrative. For a presentation of the evidence, see Appendix I.

a Captain Campbell, who was his companion for a week. Once more he traded horses and sold his gun for 15 pounds and finally, on November 1, arrived at his father's house, having traveled 620 miles.[1]

The next day he pushed on to Williamsburg, where the people were greatly excited over the news of Burgoyne's surrender. For two weeks and a half he was forced to wait for an agreement by the state auditors to accept his accounts and those of the Kentucky militia. Meantime he mentions buying a ticket in the state lottery for 3 pounds and attendance at church on Sunday.[2] After a two weeks' visit at his old home he again returned to the capital to present his plan for the western campaign to Governor Henry. The favor of the Governor was won through Clark's power of persuasion, but he hesitated to order an expedition into a country so far distant. To lay the plans before the Assembly would deprive them of all secrecy and thus defeat the purpose. Thomas Jefferson, George Mason, and George Wythe, before whom the project was presented, advised that it should be carried out and promised to use their influence in securing 300 acres of conquered land, from the Assembly, for each man enlisting for the expedition, providing it should prove successful. On January 2 final action was secured in the Council which made the expedition possible. The consent of the Assembly had been gained through the general plea that it was designed as a defense for Kentucky.[3]

Clark was appointed lieutenant-colonel and was authorized to raise, anywhere in Virginia, seven companies of militia, each to contain fifty men.[4] He was advanced 1,200 pounds in depreciated continental currency and was

---

[1] Clark, "Diary," *Clark Papers*, p. 26.   [2] *Ibid.*

[3] Hening, *Statutes at Large*, IX, 375.

[4] Private letter of instructions, January 2, 1778, *Clark Papers*, p. 34.

given an order on General Hand, commanding officer at Fort Pitt, for the necessary boats, ammunition, and supplies. By the strict interpretation of his open letter of instructions Clark was to go to the relief of Kentucky. But in his private instructions he was directed to capture Kaskaskia. With no one, evidently, did he share his secret thought that after the conquest of the Illinois country he would march against Detroit.[1] So confident was he of the outcome that he entered into partnership with the Governor for securing possession of a tract of land.

Elated over the thought that it would soon be within his power to put an end to attacks by the Indians, Clark hastened to Redstone, the place of rendezvous. From the beginning his recruiting officers encountered difficulties in enlisting men. Virginians and Pennsylvanians were still contending for the control of the territory about Pittsburgh, and many leading men were opposed to making the sacrifice necessary to hold possession of Kentucky. Indian marauding parties were causing havoc among the settlements on the upper Ohio, and desertions from the garrison at Fort Pitt were frequent.[2] "I found my case desperate," wrote Clark when he learned that out of two companies enlisted by his captains, Joseph Bowman and Leonard Helm, two-thirds of the men had been persuaded not to serve. But no obstacle moved him from attempting to carry out his design. Besides, he had been assured that two hundred men from the Holston would join him in Kentucky. Finally, on May 12, with 150 frontiersmen together with a number of private adventurers and some twenty settlers with their families, he set out from Redstone.[3] After taking on stores at Pittsburgh and Wheeling,

<hr/>

[1] Clark's letter to George Mason, November 19, 1779, *Clark Papers*, p. 116.

[2] *Frontier Defense on the Upper Ohio*, pp. 278–80.

[3] "Mason Letter," *Clark Papers*, pp. 117, 118.

liberally granted by General Hand, representing in part, no doubt, the shipments of Oliver Pollock, they proceeded cautiously down the Ohio, not knowing when they might be surprised by Indian war parties. The mouth of the Kentucky, where they landed, was at first picked by Clark as a suitable spot to fortify as a protection for immigrants coming down the river. But the falls of the Ohio, while fulfilling this demand, would in addition furnish the site for a fort necessary to protect communication between the Kentucky settlements and the Illinois country. The flotilla of flatboats moved down the stream, reaching the falls of the Ohio on May 27, where Clark learned that instead of the four companies expected from the Holston, only part of a company would be available, and that only a small force of Kentuckians had arrived. But he did not waver in his purpose and worked more steadfastly to overcome this disappointment.

Throughout the Revolution Clark regarded the falls as a center for operations. This spot, when fortified, gave him control of the river traffic, for boats must there be first unloaded before they could be taken up or down the river, and it served also to hold in check the Indian tribes. At first he took possession of an island 70 acres in extent in the midst of the rapids in order the more easily to prevent desertions. Then, for the first time, he disclosed to his followers the real object of the expedition. The proposal was received with enthusiasm by officers and men alike. Some of the Holston men manifested fear at being taken on an expedition into the enemy's country and managed to escape to the mainland during the night. They were pursued by horsemen, but only seven or eight were captured.

Meantime, a small patch of land had been apportioned to each of the twenty families which had accompanied the

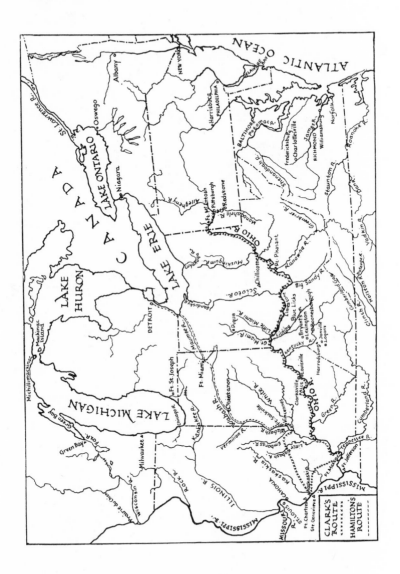

expedition.[1] They were to remain on the island in order to cultivate their crop of corn and defend the blockhouse where the provisions were stored.

Clark was the more eager to advance after he learned of the French alliance with the United States, news of which was brought to him by a messenger from Pittsburgh.[2] He counted on its effect over the Illinois inhabitants. On June 26, after a day given up to "amusements" between the troops who were to go on the expedition and those who were to remain for the defense of Kentucky, the little army of 175 men set off. The four companies commanded by Captains Joseph Bowman, Leonard Helm, William Harrod, and John Montgomery were made up of picked men, for all had been rejected who were thought incapable of withstanding the necessary hardships. The boats shot the falls during the time of a total eclipse of the sun, an omen which was variously interpreted by the men, but was regarded by the majority as favorable.[3] With oars double-manned they descended the Ohio to the mouth of the Tennessee, where final preparations were made for the overland march to Kaskaskia. Had the ordinary route down the Ohio to its mouth and up the Mississippi been selected they could not have escaped discovery by the scouts of the enemy. A boat descending the river which contained a party of American hunters was captured. As they had but recently come from Kaskaskia, Clark was able to gather from them the information he sought. Moreover, upon their request they were granted permission to accompany the expedition and serve as guides.

Dropping down the river 10 miles to Fort Massac, an

[1] There were about 7 acres on the island not subject to overflow.

[2] "Memoir," *Clark Papers*, p. 225.

[3] *Ibid.*, p. 224, note.

abandoned French stronghold where the boats were secreted, the expedition struck off on its march of 120 miles,
as the bird flies, through the wilderness toward the northwest. Each man carried only such equipment as was absolutely necessary. They marched single file in order to
make as little show of tracks as possible and thus excite
no suspicions in any who might cross their trail. Their
dress, which resembled that of the Indians, was common
among the borderers of the time.[1] The buckskin fringed
hunting-shirt covered the upper part of the body, reaching almost to the knees. This was girded about the waist
with a broad leather belt, much decorated, from which
hung the tomahawk. Leather breeches were worn by most
of them, while others preferred boots or leggings made of
coarse woolen cloth wrapped loosely and tied with garters
or laced on the outside. Moccasins were the usual covering for the feet. On the head was worn a broad-brimmed
felt hat or a cap made of squirrel skin or fox skin with the
tail dangling behind. Hanging over one shoulder was the
shot bag and powderhorn, and over the other a game bag
which was used also for provisions. Clumsy flintlock rifles
were carried by all.

For the first 50 miles they made their way through the
trackless forest with great effort. On the third day, having reached the stretches of level prairie, John Saunders,
who was serving as chief guide, lost his way and at once
there was the greatest confusion. Clark, fearful lest they
should be discovered by spies or attacked by Indians, suspected the guide of treachery and threatened, with great
anger, to put him to death unless he found the way that
evening. Within two hours he again got his bearings and the
march was resumed. On the evening of July 4 they came
to the Kaskaskia River, 3 miles above and on the opposite

[1] J. F. Smyth, *A Tour in the United States of America* (London, 1784), I, 179.

side of the river from the village of Kaskaskia. Six days had been consumed in the march. For two days they had been without food, but these days of hunger and fatigue did not weaken the resolution expressed by Captain Bowman that they were all determined to take the town or die in the effort.[1] At dusk they marched silently down the river to a farmhouse a mile or so above the town. The family were made prisoners, and from them Clark learned that Rocheblave, hearing rumors of a possible attack, had summoned the men to arms, but that his spies had returned without discovering any trace of an enemy and they were again off their guard.

Boats were procured, and within two hours Clark and his men had crossed the river.[2] So quickly did they move that no alarm was given. One division of the troops surrounded the town while Clark with the other division pushed on to one of the fort gates which was found to be open. Following John Saunders, who was still their guide, they advanced to the house of the commandant. Rocheblave, completely surprised, was found in an upper room and taken captive. The loud huzzas which followed were answered by shouts from the other divisions scattered in small squads about the town. Not a shot had been fired and within fifteen minutes every street was secured.[3]

Runners were sent throughout the town ordering the people, on pain of death, to keep close to their houses. By daylight all were disarmed and the villagers were in greatest confusion, for they had been told of the savage nature

[1] Joseph Bowman to George Brinker, July 30, 1778, *Clark Papers*, pp. 614–17.

[2] Joseph Bowman wrote, July 30, 1778, that they marched into town about midnight (*Clark Papers*, p. 615).

[3] The picturesque story which is told of the ball being given in the fort at the time of its capture is not supported by any contemporary testimony. See Roosevelt, *The Winning of the West*, II, 45, 46. Clark makes no reference to the influence of American sympathizers on the outcome.

of the Americans. They were shocked when they beheld the unkempt appearance of their conquerors, whose clothes, because of the hard march, were dirty and ragged. "Giving all for lost," wrote Clark, "their lives were all they could dare beg for, which they did with the greatest fervancy; they were willing to be Slaves to save their Families."[1] But instead of employing extreme measures, Clark was desirous of gaining their allegiance for he was well aware that with his small force it would be impossible to hold in subjection a town having a population of nearly one thousand who were closely allied with numerous tribes of Indians.

Moreover, he hoped to gain their assistance in carrying out the remainder of his plan. To the deputation of leading men, which he summoned, he explained the causes for the war, and informed them that although, by the laws of war, they were completely at his mercy, yet it was an American principle to free, and not to enslave, those whom they conquered. All who chose to become loyal citizens and take the oath of fidelity, he assured them, should have all the privileges of Americans. Complete liberty was granted to any who chose to take their families out of the country. This promise of liberty, together with the news of the French alliance and the influence of American traders who resided among them, won the adherence of the French. These Americans had shown marked hospitality for Clark and his followers.

Clark's generous conduct toward the church served still further to stir up French enthusiasm for the American cause. To Father Pierre Gibault, the village priest, who asked permission to conduct the usual services in his church, Clark replied that he had nothing to do with

[1] "Mason Letter," *Clark Papers*, p. 120.

churches except to protect them from insult, and that the Catholic church, under the laws of Virginia, would be granted as many privileges as any other. The effect of this conduct on the minds of the villagers was magical and was expressed by Clark as follows: "In a few Minutes the scean of mourning and distress was turned to an excess of Joy, nothing else seen or heard—Addorning the Streets with flowers and Pavilians of different colours, compleating their happiness by singing etc."[1] In this spirit they took the oath of loyalty to the American cause. Rocheblave, because of his harsh language, was imprisoned and later was sent under guard to Virginia, where he escaped after breaking his parole. His slaves were sold and the proceeds were distributed among Clark's troops.

Meantime Captain Joseph Bowman led thirty mounted men against the other Illinois towns. Prairie du Rocher and St. Philippe were surprised and captured. Reaching Cahokia, they rode straight to the house of the commander and demanded the immediate surrender of the town. Without parley he accepted the proffered terms, but the people requested that they be granted until the next day before returning an answer to the demand that they should take the oath of allegiance to America. That night, the third in which Bowman and his men had not slept, was passed in a stone house which served as a sort of fortification. In the morning, the reply being favorable, the oath was administered to more than one hundred of the inhabitants.[2] About the same time Gibault undertook to gain the support of the French at Vincennes for the American cause. While, as he expressed it, he had nothing to do with

[1] *Ibid.*, p. 121.

[2] Letter of Joseph Bowman to George Brinker, July 30, 1778, *Clark Papers*, p. 615.

temporal affairs, he assured Clark "that he would give them such hints in the Spiritual way that would be very conducive to the business."

The priest, accompanied by a Dr. Jean Laffont and a few companions, set out on horseback for Vincennes July 14. They took with them an address prepared by Clark for the inhabitants of that village and many letters to them from their friends in Kaskaskia which assisted materially in winning their favor. Every effort was to be made to disabuse them of any fears they might have of the conquerors of the Illinois posts. Becoming citizens of the States meant, they were informed, protection for their persons and property and greatly extended commercial privileges. On the other hand, by refusing the offer they would be forced to withstand the miseries of war.[1] The mission was completely successful, and early in August Gibault and Laffont returned bringing the news that the American flag was floating over that post. Captain Leonard Helm was then sent to take command of the French militia at Vincennes. Fort Sackville, which dominated the town, was a well-built wooden fort inclosing three acres of ground and located but a few feet back from the river. The four bastions, each surmounted by three guns, were built of solid logs and stood 12 feet above the level of the general wall, itself 11 feet in height.[2]

But would Clark be able to hold possession of the region he had conquered? His position was a perilous one, and removed hundreds of miles from the seat of authority, he was forced to act wholly on his own responsibility. Without reinforcements—and there was no promise of any— he could scarcely hope to deal successfully with the thou-

[1] *Clark Papers*, p. 54.
[2] *Ibid.*, p. 281. Clark Manuscript, Indiana State Library, Indianapolis.

sands of savages who were allies of the British. Much less would he be able to capture Detroit, the key to British power in the West. At no time in his career did he display greater talents and energy. With rare tact in developing the spirit of loyalty among the French, he took up the problems which caused two factions among them at Kaskaskia.

Gabriel Cerré, a well-to-do merchant, who was well spoken of by English officials and was virtually leader of the British faction, was absent from the village on a trading venture. His enemies, some of them of the American party, many of whom were in debt to him, preferred charges against him of a sort which were calculated to win favor for themselves with Clark. Cerré hastened his return, as demanded by Clark, in order to meet these criticisms, but his accusers, when in his presence, failed to repeat the charges. So diplomatically had this critical affair been conducted by Clark that he not only gained the confidence and support of a leader, but of his followers, who were among the chief men in the villages and upon whose generosity Clark was dependent for supplies for his men.[1]

Friendly relations between Clark and Fernando De Leyba, the Spanish lieutenant-governor at St. Louis, were begun immediately after the capture of Kaskaskia and became constantly more intimate, through correspondence, through the influence of Colonel Francis Vigo, trusted associate of Clark and partner in business with De Leyba, and through the visits of Clark at the home of the latter in St. Louis. "This gentleman," Clark wrote Governor Henry September 16, 1778, "interests himself much in favor of the States, more so than I could have expected. He has offered me all the force that he could raise, in case of an attack by Indians

[1] *Clark Papers*, pp. 47, 48, 228, 235.

from Detroit, as there is now no danger from any other quarter."[1]

That financial assistance for the expedition had received little consideration from Clark or Governor Henry is evident from the following statement by Clark. "The short notice I had of my destination, not more than ten days, having to settle my business in so short a time, I never thought of asking anything about it, I remember that his Excelly the Governor told me I could get what I wanted from Mr. Pollock."[2]

Without money for the support of his army Clark began after the capture of Kaskaskia to issue bills of credit on Virginia in exchange for supplies. These were satisfactory to the merchants and traders, for they were received and paid at their face value, in silver by Oliver Pollock, on whom they were drawn. In a letter of July 18 Clark wrote to Pollock; "I have succeeded agreeable to my wishes, and am necessitated to draw bills on the state and have reason to believe they will be accepted by you, the answering of which will be acknowledged by his Excelly, the Governor of Virginia."[3]

The capture of the Illinois posts was interpreted by Pollock as a step toward opening communication by the Mississippi and control of the river posts. This accomplished, Pollock counted on receiving adequate funds for meeting the demands of his creditors. In urging upon Clark the necessity for taking such a step before war should be declared between Great Britain and Spain he said: "The latter will save us that trouble and in conse-

---

[1] *Ibid.*, p. 69.

[2] Clark to De Leyba, December 17, 1778. There is only a *very questionable tradition* for the statement that Clark became betrothed to Therese, the sister of De Leyba. See Temple Bodley, *George Rogers Clark* (Cambridge, 1926), pp. 89, 161, 368, 369.

[3] *Clark Papers*, p. 55.

quence we will loose a valuable conquest which might now be easily obtained."[1] The task, he thought, could be readily accomplished, for Natchez was defended by a force of only one hundred men, and Manchac by eighty. He was instructed by the Commercial Committee of Congress to give all possible assistance to the expedition under Clark, to purchase goods on the best terms, to charter vessels, employ crews, or issue commissions to trustworthy persons for privateering. At that time Pollock was fitting out a vessel with which to attack a British sloop-of-war, used as a river patrol, manned by 150 men and mounting sixteen guns.

Full credit was given by Clark to Pollock for the aid given by which he was enabled to hold the Illinois country. Beyond the first bills of credit sent to New Orleans, amounting to $8,500, Clark asked that an additional $5,000 worth of supplies suitable for his soldiers should be forwarded to him by Pollock. Five hundred pounds of powder were sent at once in response to this request, but the demands of importers for silver money in exchange for their goods could not at the time be met by Pollock. He then granted Clark permission to take such articles as he needed from a cargo which had been sent up the river consigned to the agents of the general government.[2] During September, 1778, 2,000 pounds of powder and other supplies were sent by Pollock to Clark valued at $7,200.

Notwithstanding the insistent demands on the part of his creditors, Pollock succeeded in forwarding to Clark in January, 1779, 500 pounds of powder and some swivels. To meet his immediate obligations he was forced to dispose of some of his plantation slaves at a discount. By February, drafts were drawn on Pollock by Clark amount-

---

[1] Pollock to Clark, Draper MSS, 48 J 34.

[2] Draper MSS, 48 J 37.

ing to $30,000. Of this sum ten thousand dollars were paid by Pollock through contracting for the use of his slaves on the public works at New Orleans. In meeting the engagements imposed on him by the Commercial Committee he drew on Messrs. Delaps, of Bordeaux, to whom a cargo of goods had been forwarded. The Committee accepted these bills, but in due time they came back protested. Not only had the authorities of the United States and of Virginia neglected to provide Pollock the funds with which to meet their demands for goods, but they failed to advise him of the method by which such obligations would be covered.[1] This failure was due partly to the capture of Philadelphia and the confusion incident to the removal of government papers, and in part to the deranged condition of affairs in Congress growing out of the frequent succession of new members. Owing to the short crop of wheat in 1778 and the necessity of furnishing supplies, not only to the American army, but to the troops accompanying Count D'Estaing, the government was forced to put an embargo on all provisions. Moreover, not one of the vessels which had been dispatched by Pollock along the coast had reached its destination in safety.[2] The sloop on which Captain Willing embarked was captured and he was sent as a prisoner to New York. The vessel was recaptured and run ashore and thus a portion of the cargo was saved. The attitude of the new Commercial Committee which was appointed the middle of December gave promise of greater regularity in the conduct of affairs at New Orleans. They were empowered by Congress to exert every possible effort in making remittances to Pollock, and the unusual wheat harvest, "the finest crop that had been known for

[1] *Ibid.*, 48 J 4.

[2] Commercial Committee to Pollock, July 19, 1778, Virginia State Archives.

many years," gave assurance that the conditions would be fulfilled.

To still further win the loyalty of the French Clark pretended that it was now his intention of returning to the falls, since he had confidence in their ability to defend themselves. As anticipated, they were greatly alarmed lest the British should retake the posts, and besought him not to leave them. With seeming reluctance he yielded to their entreaties and consented to remain with his two companies. But they were assured that he would be able, at any time, to increase his force by additional men from the garrison at the falls. By presents and promises Clark induced one hundred of his troops to continue their enlistment for eight months. Young Frenchmen, also, joined the companies, and a regular system of military drill was begun, the good effect of which was described by Clark as follows:

Strict subordination among the Troops was my first object, and [I] soon effected it. Our troops being all Raw and undissipled You must [be] sensible of the pleasure I felt when harangueing them on Perade, Telling them my Resolutions, and the necessity of strict duty for our own preservation etc. For them to return me for Answer, that it was their Zeal for their Country that induced them to engage in the Service, that they were sencible of their situation and Danger; that nothing could conduce more to their safety and happiness, than good order, which they would try to adhere to, and hoped that no favour would be shewn those that would neglect it. In a short time perhaps no Garrison could boast of better order, or a more Valuable set of Men.[1]

Clark then gave his attention to the pacification of the Indian tribes. The task was a gigantic one. Impressed with the success of the French and Spaniards in dealing with this problem, he made a study of their methods and adopted them as his own.[2] The tribes in the vicinity of

---

[1] "Mason Letter," *Clark Papers*, pp. 129, 130. [2] *Ibid.*, p. 124.

Kaskaskia offered to treat for peace at once, and those near Vincennes showed a similar disposition. But at Cahokia a huge horde of savages gathered to hear what the Big Knives had to say. Some of them had come from villages 500 miles distant. Among them were chiefs and warriors from the Chippewa, Ottawa, Potawatomi, Sauk, Fox, Miami, and other tribes between the Mississippi River and the Great Lakes. Clark seemed to possess a complete understanding of their natures. While treating them with justice, he adopted an attitude as occasion demanded, either kind, conciliatory, or severe. He appeared confident, but was always on his guard and prepared for any emergency. While assuming an air of bravado, he confessed his apprehension "among such a number of Devils."[1]

During five weeks of August and September the councils continued. On the second night a party of warriors tried to force their way into his lodgings in order to capture Clark, but they were detected and were made prisoners by his guard. The townspeople, arming immediately, convinced the Indians that the French would support the Americans. Clark's decisive move at this point brought the Indians completely under his power. Among the prisoners who had been put in irons were some of the chiefs. They protested that they had sought in this way to learn whether the French would support the Americans, that they had acted on the advice of the English; and they besought Clark to spare their lives and take pity on their women and children. He refused to hear their pleas, treated the other chiefs, who sought to intercede, with indifference, and declared that his course would be the same whether they were friends or foes. All was confusion among the French and the Indians, but Clark remained unmoved. He refused to retire to the protection of the

[1] *Clark Papers*, p. 125.

fort, but as a precaution he directed the garrison to be prepared for action and concealed fifty armed men in a room adjoining his own. While the Indians were holding their council, Clark, as a further sign of his indifference, "assembled a number of Gentlemen and Ladies and danced nearly the whole night."[1]

In the morning all of the tribes were summoned to a general council. The captive chiefs were released in order that Clark might speak to them in the presence of their friends. After ceremonies, more than were usual on such an occasion, were gone through, Clark arose, and presenting the captives a war belt, urged them to behave as men and adhere to the cause they had espoused. While death would have been fit punishment for their act, he assured them that Americans did not thus stoop to revenge themselves. Instead, he offered them a safe conduct out of the village and declared that war against them should not be begun until three days had elapsed. Men under arms were alone to be attacked, but if they did not cease killing American women and children, he warned them, their own families would meet a like fate. Pointing to the war belt, he challenged them to begin hostilities. Even as enemies they were to receive provisions and rum while they remained, but he made it plain that he hoped for their early departure.

The other tribes, through their chiefs, in turn protested that they had been led astray by the British, and proclaimed that they would thenceforth be friends of the Americans. In reply Clark said that he came not to ask peace from any nation, but that he came as a warrior, not as a counselor, carrying in his right hand war and in his left hand peace.[2] If they chose war he would call on the

[1] "Mason Letter," *Clark Papers*, p. 126.

[2] "Memoir," *Clark Papers*, p. 244.

"Great Fire" for warriors in numbers sufficient to darken the whole land, and there would then be no sounds save that of the "birds that live on blood." They chose the peace belt and promised to call in all of their warriors from the warpath.

To their entreaties that the prisoners should be released, he remained obdurate, and spurned all approaches of the captive chiefs. Finally two young men were selected whose lives were to be offered as a propitiation for their act. Advancing to the center of the circle they sat down before Clark, and throwing their blankets over their heads, awaited the tomahawk. The suspense continued some time, when Clark broke the silence by ordering the young men to rise. He then assured them that influenced by their example he would grant peace and friendship to all their people. All then united in a feast which closed the council. For some time these ten or twelve tribes kept the chain of friendship unbroken, and American influence extended to other tribes. So skilfully had Clark dealt with the Indians at this critical time and so completely had he won their confidence that years afterward it was noted that when commissioners of the United States were endeavoring to treat with these Indians, if Clark were present he was the only man with whom they would speak.

CHAPTER VII
Capture of Vincennes

B Y AUGUST 6, 1778, Lieutenant-Governor Hamilton at Detroit, knew of Clark's success in the Illinois country, but supposed the attack had been made by a portion of the force under Captain Willing. While in expectation of a like report from Vincennes, he began preparing an expedition to regain the captured posts. Agents were sent at once among the Wabash, Miami, and Shawnee Indians with liberal presents to stir them up against the Americans. The Ottawa, Chippewa, and other tribes tributary to Detroit met in council, were feasted by British officials in the usual fashion, and told of the plans which were about to be executed. The commandants at Michilimackinac and St. Joseph were urged to co-operate through sending forces by way of the Illinois River. Hamilton was more confident of success because of conditions in the Illinois country described by him as follows: "The Spaniards are feeble and hated by the French, the French are fickle and have no man of capacity to advise or lead them, the Rebels are enterprizing and brave, but want resources, and the Indians can have their resources but from the English if we act without loss [of] time in the favourable cojuncture."[1] During the month of September provisions, artillery stores, and presents for the Indians were collected and forwarded in fifteen bateaux, each capable of carrying from 1,800 to 3,000 pounds.

[1] *Mich. Pioneer and Hist. Colls.*, IX, 478.

On October 7 some 175 white troops, two-thirds of them French volunteers and militia, and sixty Indians were drawn up on the commons, the Catholics receiving a blessing at the hands of the aged Father Pothier upon condition that they should strictly adhere to their oath of allegiance. Led by Hamilton himself they started on their journey of 600 miles which was to consume seventy-one days. Three objects, among others, it was hoped ultimately to accomplish by means of the expedition. These were: to erect a fort at the junction of the Mississippi and the Ohio which was to constitute a "bridle" on American trade; to get control of the mouth of the Missouri with the hope of underselling the Spaniards, and thus gain the favor of the Indians of that region; and by dislodging the rebels from the Illinois, to regain the Mississippi trade, which otherwise would be entirely lost. It was believed also that the expedition would contribute to the security of the Floridas.[1] Moreover, Governor Hamilton hoped in some measure to secure relief from the burdens of office. For three years, he had been forced to administer affairs of government under most trying circumstances in a community made up of French, Indians, British traders, and soldiers. To the Frenchmen, who grudgingly accepted British domination, his orders were deemed most arbitrary and intolerable. While collecting supplies for his expedition, the presentment of a grand jury in Montreal was being prepared in which he was held responsible for the acts of one of his officials who at various times "transacted divers, unjust and illegal, Terranical and felonious acts and things contrary to good Government and the safety of His Majesty's Liege subjects.[2]

---

[1] Haldimand to Clinton, November 10, 1778. Draper MSS 58 J 2.

[2] *Mich. Pioneer and Hist. Colls.*, X, 293, 294, 304, 336. One of the charges was that a Frenchman had been hanged illegally. Hamilton and the officer, named Dejean, were acquitted of the charge by the chief justice.

The traverse of 36 miles from the mouth of the Detroit River to the mouth of the Maumee was made with great difficulty. A gale during the night almost swamped the boats and forced the expedition to go ashore at a spot near the mouth of the Maumee. Because of the lowness of the water they proceeded slowly up this river until they reached a large Indian village on the portage to the head-waters of the Wabash, where conferences were held with a number of tribes. Having crossed the portage of 9 miles, they found the river so shallow that the boats could not have proceeded farther had the water not been deepened by a beaver dam 4 miles below the landing. A passage was cut in the dam and through this the boats passed. They were delayed by swamps, and twice dams had to be built in order that the boats might be floated across.

Meanwhile winter had set in and the ice cut the hands of the men as they were forced to drag the boats over the rocks. At times the stores had to be carried around the shoals. After a number of conferences at Indian villages they reached Ouiatanon, where they received the allegiance of a number of Wabash chiefs who had previously declared for the Americans. When within a few days' travel from Vincennes they captured some men who had been sent by Captain Helm as a reconnoitering party. Parties were ordered out to intercept any messengers who might be sent to the Illinois or the falls of the Ohio. Thus two men carrying a note from Helm to Clark, announcing the approach of the British, were made prisoners. Hamilton and his force, which had been increased to the number of five hundred by accessions from the Indians, entered Vincennes on December 17.[1]

Because of the capture of his spies Captain Helm was uncertain of the whereabouts of the enemy until they were

---

[1] Clark reported that Hamilton's force consisted of eight hundred ("Mason Letter," *Clark Papers*, p. 138).

within 3 miles of Vincennes. Panic seized the French inhabitants at the first sight of the British, and they deserted, leaving Helm but a single American soldier to guard
the fort. Resistance was impossible and Helm was forced
to surrender.[1]

The inhabitants, indifferent to both sides, numbering
621, when summoned to the church renewed their oath of
allegiance in the following words:

> We, the undersigned, declare and acknowledge to have taken the
> oath of allegiance to Congress, in doing which we have forgotten our
> duty to God and have failed in our duty to man. We ask pardon of
> God and we hope from the goodness of our legitimate sovereign, the
> King of England, that he will accept our submission and take us under
> his protection as good and faithful subjects, which we promise and
> swear to become before God and before man. In faith of which we sign
> with our hand or certify with our ordinary mark, the aforesaid day and
> month of the year 1778.

The militia seemingly manifested no reluctance in surrendering their American commissions. During the winter
the garrison consisted of ninety whites, the Detroit militia
having been sent home. Most of the Indians also returned
to their villages.

Had Hamilton pushed forward at once it is probable
he could likewise have regained control of the Illinois
towns; but to him the obstacles seemed insurmountable.
His stock of provisions was not adequate, he thought, for
a midwinter march which would be delayed by the flooded
country. Scouting parties were sent out, one to the mouth
of the Wabash to capture any boats on the Ohio, and others
toward the falls of the Ohio and Kaskaskia. Messages were

[1] The story of the loaded cannon related in Mann Butler, *History of the
Commonwealth of Kentucky* (2d ed., Louisville, 1834), p. 80, note, is not referred
to in the "Memoir" or in any of the other sources consulted. See Roosevelt,
The Winning of the West, II, 63, note, and R. G. Thwaites, *How George Rogers
Clark Won the Northwest*, p. 41.

forwarded to John Stuart, Indian agent among the southern tribes, urging him to prepare these Indians for a combined attack. Hamilton was confident of the complete success of his plan in a spring campaign in which he was to be aided also by troops from Pensacola. The people of the Illinois villages were warned to flee from the storm which was about to break and destroy the rebels and all who should support them.

Clark, shortly after the capture of Kaskaskia, was gratified to learn of the proposed march of General McIntosh from Fort Pitt against Detroit. Late in December, while in expectation of the news that this post had been captured, he was informed that the expedition had been abandoned. At the same time he learned of the expedition which had set out under Hamilton, presumably against Kaskaskia. Within a few days Clark proceeded to Cahokia to confer with some of the leaders regarding their conduct should the surrender of that post, which seemed inevitable, take place. Three miles out from Kaskaskia he and his guard of six or seven men and a few "gentlemen in chairs" narrowly escaped being captured by a party of forty Ottawa Indians under white leaders.

Ten miles farther on they arrived at the village of La Prairie du Rocher, where they expected to pass the night. While attending a ball given in their honor a messenger arrived with the report that Hamilton and his entire force were within 3 miles of Kaskaskia and preparing for an immediate attack. Clark's unconcern, as he ordered them to continue the dance until his horses were saddled, dissipated the general confusion of the company. Reaching Kaskaskia, he found the people in the greatest consternation over the attack, which they were convinced was imminent.

By morning the plan for defense was complete. Clark determined to burn that part of the town near the fort and prepare to withstand the attack. The villagers, confident of the success of the British, were at a loss how to act. Their resolution to remain neutral was quickly overcome upon seeing some of the buildings on fire. After he received the declaration of their allegiance Clark more completely won their favor through his kindly consideration for all their wishes. Captain Bowman arrived the next day with reinforcements from Cahokia. Their fears were lessened also when it was learned that "the great army" that gave the alarm consisted only of a small body of whites and Indians then making their retreat as fast as possible toward Vincennes. Clark now felt convinced that Hamilton was in possession of that post and that the attack on the Illinois posts was but a question of time.

While uncertain how to proceed, the information brought by Francis Vigo enabled him to decide at once on the course to be followed. Colonel Vigo, an Italian, who had favored the American cause from the time of the capture of Kaskaskia, was a partner of De Leyba in Indian trade. He was at Vincennes when it was retaken by Hamilton and was held as a prisoner. When released he set out for St. Louis, having agreed not to do anything injurious to the British interests on his way to that post. This agreement fulfilled, he hurried to Kaskaskia and on January 29 gave Clark "every Intelligence that I could wish to have."[1]

Clark's position was desperate when he resolved to forestall the enemy and risk all he had gained by at once taking the offensive and attempting the reduction of Vincennes. "It was at this moment," he declared, "I would have bound myself seven years a Slave to have had five hundred Troops." The wish was vain, for not only had he received no reinforcements from Virginia, but for nearly a

---

[1] "Mason Letter." *Clark Papers*, p. 138.

year he had not received, as he said, "a scrape of a pen" from Governor Henry.

His confidence that the expedition would be successful seemed to inspire his men, and "in a day or two the Country seemed to believe it, many anctious to retrieve their Characters turned out, the Ladies began also to be spirited and interest themselves in the Expedition, which had great Effect on the Young Men." With' this enthusiasm provisions and stores were soon collected. On the fifth of February the Willing, an armed row-galley, the first armed boat on the Ohio River, mounting two 4-pounders and four swivels, with a crew of forty men commanded by Lieutenant John Rogers, set off under orders to take station a short distance from Vincennes and prevent any boat from descending the Wabash, for it was surmised that in case of defeat the British would attempt to escape by this route. The following afternoon Clark, mounted on a handsome horse at the head of his small army of 172 men, nearly one-half of them French volunteers, Father Gibault having granted them absolution, marched out of Kaskaskia.[1]

The expedition thus begun was one of the most heroic and dramatic undertakings of the whole Revolution. From the outset they encountered trials which became steadily more extreme as they dragged themselves over the 180 miles to their goal.[2] The weather was mild, but the trail was miry on account of the frequent rains, and

---

[1] "Bowman's Journal," *Clark Papers*, p. 156. "Mason Letter," *Clark Papers*, p. 139. Here Clark states that the boats' crew and other men consisted of a little more than two hundred.

[2] Joseph Bowman to Isaac Hite, *Clark Papers*, p. 334. Clark had secured this stallion from New Mexico and intended to send him as a present to Governor Henry, who had expressed a desire that Spanish horses should be sent to him. Because of the high water Clark was not able to take the horse as far as Vincennes (*Clark Papers*, p. 303). In the "Mason Letter," Clark stated the distance as 240 miles.

in the lowlands and on the prairies the water stood several inches deep. With great effort Clark succeeded in keeping up the spirits of his men, who were worn out with fatigue. At night, with no tents for shelter, they gathered around the great camp fires and feasted on buffalo and other game, each company taking its turn in hunting and cooking. Singing, dancing, and other diversions followed. February 13 they reached the first branch of the Little Wabash. Vincennes was then about 20 miles distant, but the intervening country was almost completely under water. The two branches of the river, although a league apart, made a single stream 5 miles wide, with water 3 feet deep in the shallowest places. "This," wrote Clark, "would have been enough to have stop'ed any set of men that was not in the same temper we was." He ordered a canoe built to be used in ferrying men and stores across the main stream. A scaffold was built at the far side of the channel upon which to place the baggage until the pack-horses should be brought over and again loaded. This done, they marched on to the second branch, which was crossed in the same manner, and on the evening of the fifteenth they came to a high spot upon which they encamped "in high spirits." Clark states that through the acts of "a little Antick Drummer who floated on his drum" he was assisted in diverting the minds of his men.[1]

Their real trials now began, for provisions were scarce and all the game had been driven off by the floods. On the evening of the seventeenth they reached the Embarrass River, the waters of which were so high it could not be forded. Later in the evening they found a spot from which the water had but recently receded, and there, hungry and shivering with cold, they passed the remainder of the "drizzly and dark night." The next morning they heard the

---

[1] "Memoir," *Clark Papers*, p. 271.

morning-gun at the fort, then only 9 miles away. Still unable to ford the river, they marched downstream and early in the afternoon reached the Wabash. Here they remained during the two following days. Three unsuccessful attempts were made to get men across to the vicinity of Vincennes to gather information and to steal boats. Two men were dispatched in a canoe with orders to Lieutenant Rogers to bring on the Willing as fast as possible. The hungry, dispirited men were set to building boats which might be used in crossing the Wabash.

For two days they had been without food. Many of the volunteers were in despair, and Clark's energies were severely taxed to keep them from deserting.[1] Clark wrote George Mason: "If I was sensible that You would let no Person see this relation I would give You a detail of our suffering for four days in crossing these waters, and the manner it was done; as I am sure that You would Credit it, but it is too incredible for any Person to believe except those that are as well acquainted with me as You are, or had experienced something similar to it." Confident that his regular troops would not abandon the enterprise, Clark talked of the victory soon to be gained, laughed at their fears, and by his confidence gave courage to all the faltering. About noon of the twentieth, five hunters going down the river were captured. From them it was learned that Clark's approach had not been discovered and that the people of Vincennes sympathized with the American cause. The next night the troops were ferried to the eastern bank of the river and landed on a small hill. All thought of bringing the horses across was abandoned. Disregarding the warning of their French guides that Vincennes could not be reached, they plunged ahead 3 miles, with the water

---

[1] There is no reference, in any of the records consulted, to insubordination among Clark's men.

at times up to their shoulders, and reached another hill. There they encamped, and notwithstanding their sufferings, took comfort, as Clark said, "from the hopes of their Fatiegue soon being at an end and their wishes accomplish[ed] in getting in contact with the Enemy." On the morning of the twenty-second the march was resumed with shouts and favorite song, as ordered by Clark, who was in the lead. The canoes bore those who were unable to walk. "Had not the weather been warm," Clark says, "they must have perished." Before reaching the deepest water one of the men struck a path, and by following this with great care they finally came to a small area of ground covered with hard maples. This spot, which was comparatively dry, had been used as a sugar-camp. They were now 6 miles from Vincennes. The prisoners declared that any attempt to ford the water of greatest depth between them and the town would be extremely dangerous and utterly futile. The gloom of their situation was well expressed in the words of Colonel Bowman: "No provisions yet, lord help us."[1]

To add to their suffering the night was so cold that the water in quiet places was covered with ice one-half inch in thickness. Shortly after sunrise on the clear morning of the twenty-third Clark told his followers that within a few hours they might expect to see an end to their fatigue. He then plunged into the water, having given orders to Colonel Bowman, with twenty-five men, to close the rear and shoot any man who refused to march. His half-frozen famished followers, with a cheer, imitated the example of their leader.

In crossing the Horse-Shoe Plain, then a shallow lake 4 miles wide, they encountered their greatest trials. The hardships which they had undergone began to tell on the

[1] Bowman's Journal," *Clark Papers*, p. 159.

weakest, and as they fell in the ranks the canoes, by making several trips to an island about 10 acres in extent, saved them from drowning. Clark encouraged his men at every step and the strong lent assistance to their weaker companions. They came to a stretch of woods where the water was up to the shoulders of the tallest. Many were worn out, but clung to the trees and floating logs until they were rescued by the canoe-men. Others, as they gained the shore, fell exhausted with 'their bodies partly in the water. Fires were built and broth was made from a half-quarter of buffalo which was taken from some squaws who chanced to be passing in a canoe. Thus all were slightly refreshed, and cheered with warmth from the fires and the beauty of the day, they set out early in the afternoon with renewed courage. After crossing a deep, narrow lake in the canoes and marching a short distance they reached a small elevation of dry land covered with timber, known as the Warrior's Island. Here their hearts were gladdened by a view of the fort and the town scarcely 2 miles distant. A number of horsemen were seen shooting ducks on the pools which lay in the hollows between them and the town. From one of these Frenchmen, who was taken prisoner, it was learned that their coming was in no way suspected. He informed them also that the walls of the fort had been completed and that two hundred Indians had just arrived.

What was Clark to do at this critical time, for he was aware that the number of his troops was not one-fourth of the combined force of the enemy and their allies. If the attack were made without warning, a number of lives would probably be lost among the villagers and the Indians and this would serve to embitter the others. Knowing that some of the French were lukewarm in their allegiance to the British, Clark determined to announce his approach to the inhabitants, believing that a bold stroke at the time would encourage his friends and so confuse his opponents that they would manifest little hostility at his appearance. Accordingly, he prepared a letter to the villagers which was carried to them by the prisoners, who had been kept ignorant of the true numbers of the Americans.

Gentlemen [he wrote], Being now within two Miles of Your Village with my Army determin'd to take your Fort this Night and not being willing to surprize you I take this step to request of such of you as are true citizens and willing to enjoy the liberty I bring you to remain still in your house, and those (if any there be) that are friends to the King, will instantly repair to the fort and join the hair Buyer General and fight like Men and if any such as do not go to the fort, shall be discovered afterwards, they may depend on being well treated and I once more request they shall keep out of the streets for every person I find in arms on my arrival I shall treat him as an enemy.[1]

The people quickly gathered in the public square to hear this message. They were so surprised and appalled that none of them dared go to the fort to inform Hamilton. It was then about sunset, and Clark, having urged implicit obedience, ordered the march to begin with colors flying and drums braced. By marching to and fro, a slight elevation of land obstructing the view so that only the flags could be seen from the town, the impression was made that a force of one thousand men was approaching.[2] Darkness obscured their real numbers when at eight o'clock, guided by their five prisoners, they reached the town in two divisions, one led by Clark and the second by Captain Bowman. A few men were sent at once to fire on the fort. The surprise was so complete that Hamilton was not aware of the approach of the enemy and believed the rifle shots to have been fired by drunken Indians until one of his men was wounded by a shot fired through a porthole. An-

---

[1] "Bowman's Journal," *Clark Papers*, p. 159.
[2] "Mason Letter," *Clark Papers*, p. 141.

other party was sent to investigate the cause, but returned after the Americans were in possession of Vincennes.

With drums beating, the main division of Clark's force marched up the village street, the people greeting them joyfully. Some of the leading Frenchmen had secreted supplies of ammunition, and these were now freely presented to Clark, whose stock was well-nigh exhausted. The British-Indians fled at the approach of the Americans. A Piankeshaw, son of the chief of that tribe, tendered Clark the services of one hundred warriors, but the offer was declined.

Fifty of the Americans were detailed as a guard while the others, joined by a number of the Creoles, stormed the fort. The firing was almost continuous throughout the night. The British cannon and swivel were located 11 feet above the ground on the second floor of the blockhouses at each angle of the palisaded fort. Little damage was done by the cannon further than the destruction of a few houses. Two hundred yards in front of the fort gate the Americans threw up an intrenchment, but small squads of men, under cover of the houses and hastily constructed breastworks, advanced to within 30 yards of the walls. So accurate was the aim of the backwoodsmen and so constant their firing through the portholes that the cannon were silenced, a number of the gunners having been killed or wounded.

At daybreak a "very smart fire of small arms" was begun on the American works, and one man was slightly wounded. About nine o'clock Clark sent a messenger to Hamilton demanding the surrender of the fort. While awaiting the reply, his men took breakfast, which was their first regular meal for six days. Hamilton replied that they were "not disposed to be awed into action unworthy of

British subjects." The conflict was again resumed. At the end of two hours the firing ceased as Lieutenant Helm approached the American lines. He was instructed to say that the British were prepared to surrender under honorable terms. "Immediate surrender," was Clark's answer, and the acceptance of the proposal within thirty minutes; for it was with difficulty, he declared, that he restrained his men from storming the garrison. At the end of the time Helm returned bringing the proposal that there should be a three days' truce. This was likewise rejected by Clark, who again insisted on the unconditional surrender of the garrison. He stated his willingness to meet for a conference at the French church.

At this time a band of Indians led by a Frenchman, returning from a successful expedition against the frontier, with two prisoners and a number of scalps, marched triumphantly into town. In place of the welcome accorded at such times they were met by an attacking party which killed two of them, took six prisoners, and wounded several that escaped. Clark seized this occasion to show the Indians that the British were powerless to lend them aid, and ordered the prisoners tomahawked within view of the garrison. Their leader proved to be the son of one of Clark's volunteer lieutenants, and owing to the entreaties of his father and other officers his life was spared.

Hamilton, having agreed to a conference, proceeded to the church accompanied by Captain Helm and Major Hay, and was there met by Clark and Captain Bowman. Hamilton strove to secure a modification of the ultimatum, but Clark was obdurate. Toward evening the terms of the surrender were signed according to which Fort Sackville, together with all the stores, was to be delivered up and the garrison become prisoners of war. At ten o'clock on the following morning the garrison of seventy-nine men

Colonel Clark Compliments to Mr.
Hamilton and begs leave to inform
him that Col. Clark will not agree
to any Other Terms than that of Mr.
Hamilton's Surrendering himself and
Garrison, Prisoners at Discretion —

If Mr. Hamilton is Desirous of
a conference with Col. Clark he will

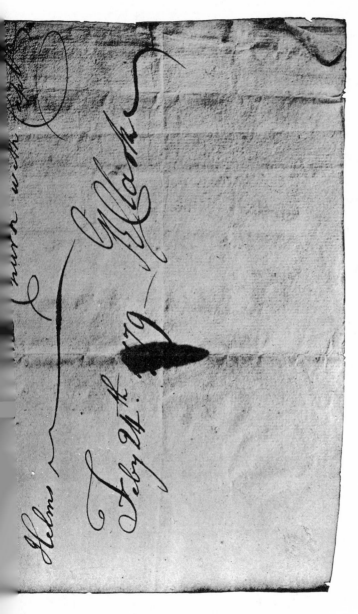

CLARK'S LETTER TO HAMILTON

Facsimile of the original in the Draper MSS, Wisconsin Historical Society. From Reuben G. Thwaites, *How George Rogers Clark Won the Northwest*. By permission of A. C. McClurg & Company.

marched out of the fort and were received at the gate by two companies of troops drawn up under Major Bowman and Captain McCarty. At the head of his other troops, Clark marched into the fort, hoisted the American flag, and gave the national salute of thirteen guns.

Clark was surprised to find that this fort, now renamed Patrick Henry, mounting twelve guns and well stored with ammunition, with a garrison of trained soldiers, had been given up so readily. This achievement marks the climax of one of the most heroic and notable achievements in history. The boldness of the plan, the skill with which it was executed, and the perseverance in overcoming obstacles seemingly insurmountable excited the admiration even of Hamilton himself.[1] Courage born of desperation was manifested by men and leaders alike, for all were fully conscious that failure would mean the loss, not alone of the Illinois country, but also of Kentucky.

The goods brought from Detroit by Hamilton and those taken from British traders were divided among Clark's followers, the officers receiving nothing except a few articles of clothing, the soldiers getting "almost Rich."[2] Besides the large quantities of military stores and Indian goods, the Americans were strengthened by coming into possession of a 6-pound brass field piece, two iron 4-pounders, and two swivels.

On February 26 Captain Helm, accompanied by fifty men, the majority of them French militiamen, ascended the Wabash in three armed boats with the object of intercepting a party of British sent by Hamilton to bring on the stores at Ouiatenon. Beyond making prisoners of forty men, seven boats heavily laden with provisions and In-

[1] Hamilton's report, July 6, 1781, *Clark Papers*, p. 207.

[2] In a letter from Joseph Bowman to Isaac Hite, June 14, 1779, he states that the goods captured amounted to 20,000 pounds sterling.

dian goods valued at $50,000 fell into his hands, and the booty was divided among his followers. Four days after the capture of Vincennes the Willing arrived. The crew were greatly disappointed that they had not been privileged to take part in the fighting. Aboard was a messenger from Williamsburg who brought to Clark and his men the thanks of the legislature for their part in the capture of Kaskaskia and the promise of some suitable reward.

Having almost as many prisoners as he had men, Clark sent Hamilton, seven of his principal officers, and eighteen other prisoners to the falls of the Ohio under guard of Captain Williams, Lieutenant Rogers, and twenty-five men. From there they were taken to Williamsburg, where Hamilton, because of his alleged cruelty to prisoners and incitement of the Indians to bring in scalps, was kept in close confinement until toward the close of the Revolution, when he was exchanged. The French volunteers who had accompanied th. British were paroled.

CHAPTER VIII

Results of American Successes and the Organization of Government in the Conquered Territory

IT IS probable that Clark, when he set out on the desperate undertaking to risk all in a single campaign against Hamilton, contemplated, in the event of victory, the capture of Detroit. By order of Governor Henry, the area of his activities had been extended beyond that defined in his original instructions so as to include the "Enemy's Settlements above or across," as he might think proper. He knew that with Detroit in his possession the whole Northwest would be under his control. He was informed that the British garrison at that post, numbering only one hundred men, without adequate supplies and subject to still greater distresses with the cutting off of the Illinois country as a source, might be overcome with ease. This desperate situation was expressed in a communication from Colonel Mason Bolton to General Frederick Haldimand at Niagara as follows:

Capt. Lernoult acquaints me that Detroit is capable in peaceable times to supply the Garrison with Provisions, but at this time the inhabitants are so much employed in Conveys & probably will continue so that they have not been able to thrash last years corn, and the great number of cattle furnished for Governor Hamilton's expedition as well as for Detroit with what have been consumed by Indians, have reduced the numbers so much that a pair of oxen cannot be purchased for less than 1,000 Livres & then reckoned a cheap bargain. . . . . Flour is 60 Livres a hundred & every article very dear.

Clark had, with Detroit in view, through his tact and liberal government succeeded in winning the friendship of the Illinois French, thirty citizens of Kaskaskia delivering to him by the last of August 54,600 pounds of flour for the use of his army. Lieutenant Bowman praised enthusiastically the generosity of the Cahokians who granted for the expedition one-fifth of their cattle and horses instead of the one-tenth demanded.[1]

The success of the expedition against Detroit, "in the execution of which," as Clark later expressed it, "my very soul was wrapt," was regarded as a certainty with the capture of Vincennes. The booty then secured, together with that captured by Captain Helm, furnished an added incentive to regulars and volunteers alike in their demands for such an expedition.

Again Clark showed excellent judgment in his treatment of the French volunteers who had accompanied the British troops. Instead of sending them to Virginia, as they had been led to expect, there to be held during the course of the war, they were discharged on taking the oath of neutrality. A few of them joined Clark's forces. Those returning to Detroit were provided with boats, arms, and provisions. The boats were to be sold upon arrival at their destination and the money therefrom was to be divided. This act, well calculated to promote Clark's interests among the French at Detroit, was successful. "I after this," Clark wrote, "had Spies, disguised as traders, constant to and from Detroit I learnt they answered every purpose that I could have wished for, by prejudiceing their friends in favour of America." He was informed that the French at Detroit celebrated for three days the news of his victory over Hamilton, and that the merchants were providing many necessaries which were to be given the

[1] *Clark Papers*, p. 327.

Americans upon their arrival. That the Americans would triumph was a wish openly expressed, and children in the streets, with cups of water, were accustomed to drink success to Clark. Clark fully counted on the capture of Detroit. He assured the paroled prisoners that he would be there nearly as soon as they, and sent by them a copy of the alliance between France and the United States. "I learn by your letter to Govr Hamilton," he wrote Captain Richard Lernoult, who was in charge at that post, "that you were very busy making new works, I am glad to hear it, as it saves the Americans some expences in building."[1] The spirit of such a message might easily be misunderstood by British leaders, and in referring to the letter, which he forwarded to General Clinton, General Haldimand wrote: "I send the latter because I think it curious from the impertinence of it's style."[2]

General gloom pervaded the garrisons at Detroit and Michilimackinac when it was learned that Hamilton had been captured and that two subordinate expeditions had likewise failed. Captain Charles Langlade, who had advanced as far as "Milwakee" on his way to assist Hamilton in an attack on the Illinois posts, was forced to return to Michilimackinac when his Indian followers refused to proceed farther. Gautier, also under orders from Hamilton to join him early in the spring, advanced with two hundred Indians over the Fox-Wisconsin waterway down the Mississippi as far as the mouth of the Rock River. Learning of Hamilton's capture, he made his way back to Green Bay. In anticipation of an attacking party of Americans expected from Pittsburgh, the British ordered a new fort

---

[1] Clark to Lernoult, March 16, 1779. *Clark Papers*, p. 306. The letter was sent by some inhabitants from Vincennes who went to Detroit accompanying the prisoners on parole.

[2] Draper MSS, 58 J 37.

built at Detroit, and carpenters were sent to repair the vessels. Urgent request was made that large reinforcements should be sent from Niagara for the completion of the fort and protection against Clark, who was daily expected.[1] Presuming on the weakness of the garrison, the French refused to assist in the project. Spades, shovels, and other tools necessary for carrying on the work were lacking. Provisions were scarce, owing to the large quantities consumed on the expedition to Vincennes. The Indians tributary to Detroit were panic stricken and demanded that detachments of troops with cannon should be sent to them at once as they were not able to contend unaided with the enemy. "So situated," wrote General Haldimand, "it will require great judgment and temper to preserve the Indians in our interest after so glaring and recent a proof of our want of strength, or want of conduct . . . . whenever they do quit us the valuable Fur Trade will immediately be lost to Great Britain."

British commanding officers in the Northwest were disheartened. Even before the capture of Hamilton the fears of the officials at Detroit were so much excited that they demanded his return. "The loss of Governor Hamilton is a most feeling one to me," said Captain Lernoult in a dispatch from Detroit: "I find the burthen heavy without assistance. It required, I confess, superior abilities, and a better constitution. . . . . I beg leave to repeat to you the necessity of a reenforcement being sent, as the consequences may be fatal." His position was made still more trying through the burning of the "Angelica," a boat being sent from Niagara with supplies for his relief. Major Arent de Peyster was convinced that Michilimackinac, defended as it was by an inadequate garrison poorly provisioned, would be doomed the moment Detroit surrendered

[1] *Ibid.*, 58 J 9.

although a single man should not be sent against it. Mystified by the report, purposely sent out by Clark, that he contemplated an advance on the post at Michilimackinac also, vigorous efforts were made to render it defensible.[1]

Clark was fully aware of the effects of his victory. "This stroke," he said, "will nearly put an end to the Indian War. Had I but men enough to take the advantage of the present confusion of the Indian Nations, I could silence the whole in two months."[2] The excitement incident to the capture of Vincennes over, many of his men succumbed to the effects of the campaign. Sickness among them increased, and recovery was retarded owing to the unusually stormy days at the beginning of March.

Clark did not at the time doubt the ultimate success of his plans to take Detroit, for in addition to his own men and the French militia, he counted on from two to three hundred troops from Kentucky. Moreover, the messenger from Williamsburg who arrived at Vincennes three days after the capitulation of that post brought the good news that five hundred men were to be sent at once from Virginia. To avail himself of these reinforcements, by which he would be able to overcome the opposition on the part of any Indian tribe, make a greater impression at Detroit, and also allow time for the collection of necessary supplies, the forward movement was deferred until June.

[1] De Peyster to Haldimand, May 13, 1779. "The Canadians who want to return to this Post have leave, on taking the oaths not to serve against the United States. Clark assures them that he will be here nearly as soon as themselves. . . . . I don't care how soon Mr. Clarke appears, provided he come by Lake Michigan, and the Indians prove stanch, and above all, that the Canadians do not follow the example of their brethren at the Illinois, who have joined the Rebels to a man." Hiram W. Beckwith, *Illinois State Historical Collections* (Springfield, 1903), I, 436.

[2] Clark to Colonel Harrison, March 10, 1779. *Clark Papers*, p. 305. He stated that three hundred men would have been an adequate number. Letter to the Governor of Virginia, April 29, 1779. *Clark Papers*, p. 172.

Meantime he took up the problems of the territory already secured. The Indians first claimed his attention. No man better understood how to win the favor of the savages. He awaited the coming of the chiefs, although he had not invited them to treat with him. In attendance upon their councils he gave due regard to Indian ceremonials, strengthened the chain of friendship by smoking the sacred pipe and exchanging belts of wampum, and when treaties were renewed provided taffia and provisions with which the Indians were to make merry at the frolic usual at such times.

In dealing with the Indians who had refused the advances of the British he "Extol'd them to the Skies for their Manly behavior and fidelity."[1] Very cleverly he disabused them of the thought which had been implanted by Hamilton that in the event of victory by the Virginians the lands of friends and foes alike would be taken:

I made a very long Speach to them in the Indian manner, told them that we were so far from having any design on their Lands, that I looked upon it that we were on their Land where the Fort stood, that we claimed no Land in their Country; that the first Man that offered to take their Lands by Violence must strike the tomah[k] in my head; that it was only necessary that I should be in their Country during the War and keep a Fort in it to drive off the English, who had a design against all People; after that I might go to some place where I could get Land to support Me.[2]

In conference with the Chippewa and other Indians who had accompanied Hamilton and came to sue for mercy, Clark was the complete master, for he said:

[1] *Clark Papers*, pp. 146, 163. Chiefs and parties from the Piankeshaw, Potawatomi, and Miami tribes waited on Clark March 15, to reassure him of their fidelity and to beg the protection of the Americans.

[2] *Clark Papers*, p. 146. The Indians presented Clark with a body of land two and one-half leagues square (July 16, 1779). After some time he refused to accept the gift.

Nothing destroys Your Interest among the Savages so soon as wavering sentiments or speeches that shew the least fear. I consequently had observed one steady line of conduct among them; Mr. Hamilton, who was almost deified among them being captured by me, it was a sufficient confirmation to the Indians of everything I had formerly said to them and gave the greatest weight to the speeches I intended to send them; expecting that I should shortly be able to fulfill my threats with a Body of Troops sufficient to penetrate into any part of their Country: and by Reducing Detroit bring them to my feet.

The messages sent the Indians directly tributary to Detroit were well calculated to neutralize any effort which might be made on the part of the English to stir them up for new expeditions. Whether they chose the peace belt or the war belt, they were told, was of little consequence, for the Big Knives' greatest glory was in war and they were in search of enemies since the English were no longer able to contend against them. Those nations which did not lay down their arms at once were threatened with extermination.

Preparatory to his return to Kaskaskia with the remaining prisoners, Clark carefully arranged for a satisfactory government at Vincennes by appointing the faithful Captain Helm to take control of all civil matters and to act as superintendent of Indian affairs. Moses Henry was made Indian agent. The garrison of forty picked men was left in command of Lieutenant Richard Brashears, assisted by Lieutenants John Bailey and Abraham Chapline. Letters were sent John Bowman, then county-lieutenant in Kentucky, urging him to begin collecting men and provisions for the proposed march on Detroit.

No victorious army ever returned with spirits more elated than the eighty men who on March 20 accompanied Clark. Within a year the authority of Virginia over the region stretching from the Ohio to the Illinois and 140 miles up the Wabash had been established by conquest. The danger that frontier settlements would be cut off by savages under the leadership of British officers was greatly lessened. These results had been accomplished against odds that would have completely overcome men not already inured to the harsh conditions incident to life on the frontier. The six boats pushed off down the Wabash amidst the rejoicing of the people who had assembled to wish them a "good and safe passage." A few of those, no doubt, who lingered to watch the boats until they were lost to view fully comprehended the results which had been attained. Their thought was expressed by one of their number as follows:

> Although a handful in comparison to other armies, they have done themselves and the cause they were fighting for, credit and honor, and deserve a place in History for future ages; that their posterity may know the difficulty their forefathers had gone through for their liberty and freedom. Particularly the back Settlers of Virginia may bless the day they sent out such a Commander and officers, men &c., &c., I say, to root out that nest of Vipers, that was every day ravaging on their women and children; which I hope will soon be at an end, as the leaders of these murderers are taken and sent to Congress.[1]

When the boats reached Kaskaskia "great Joy" was manifested by the garrison, then commanded by Captain Robert George, who had recently returned with sixty men from New Orleans. The villagers too were not less gratified at the return of Clark, for although they became at times restive under his stern discipline, he was the one American who had gained and continued to hold their love and confidence.

The problems and disappointments Clark was forced to meet during the succeeding three months were among the most trying of his whole career. Upon arrival he found the people excited over the recent conduct of a party of Delaware warriors. Learning also of depredations com-

[1] August 15, 1779. *Clark Papers*, p. 611.

mitted at Vincennes by another party, Clark, by way of warning to the other tribes, ordered a ruthless war against the marauders. In the attacks on their villages which followed, no mercy was shown except for the women and children. The Indians soon sued for peace.

By July, 1779, Oliver Pollock, who had contributed so much to the success of the war in the West, had so far exhausted his credit that in meeting a further order from Governor Henry for goods amounting to $10,000, he was forced to mortgage a part of his landed estate. At that time he had paid bills drawn on Virginia amounting to $33,000. The flour and meal which had been promised him had not been forwarded. At that date, although he had received no recognition whatever from the Governor of Virginia, he remarked with a spirit of optimism, "However, I hope there is a good time coming." To Governor Henry, Pollock wrote:

Being already drained of every shilling I could raise for the use of your's and the rest of the United States, I went first to the Governor of this place, and then to every merchant in it, but could not prevail upon any of them to supply said goods, giving for their reason the few goods they had here imported, would in all probability become double the value of what they were just now, particularly at this juncture as war between Spain & Great Britain was daily expected, and the little probability there was of geting paid from your Quarter in any reasonable time, by depending only on the Letter of Credit & Mr. Lindsay's Contract. In fine, finding it impracticable to obtain any by that means, and at same time being fearfull of the bad consequences that might attend your being disappointed in those goods, I have voluntarily by mortgaging part of my Property for the payment at the latter End of this year, purchased the greatest part of them from a Mr. Solomon: You have therefore Invoice & Bill of Loading amounting to 10,029 Dollars 1 Rial.[1]

Twenty-five thousand dollars in the bills drawn by Clark were under protest at New Orleans. Fully one-half

[1] Pollock to Henry, July 17, 1779. Draper MSS 49 J 60.

of these represented the expense incident to the fitting out of the expedition against Vincennes. They were issued in favor of a number of the inhabitants of Illinois, Francis Vigo being the leading creditor. These drafts had been received by the French merchants and traders in preference to the continental money which had recently appeared in small quantities. While borrowing money on his own credit, Pollock, in order to promote the shipment of arms, Indian goods, rum, and sugar to the Illinois country, to encourage cargoes in exchange made up of deer skins, beaver, otter, and flour, and at the same time keep up the credit of the continental currency, continued until July, 1779, to pay "Boatmen and Traders silver dollars for Paper Currency Dollar for Dollar."[1]

Continental currency had been used but little in the West previous to the expedition against Vincennes. Confidence of the people in the government, together with the efforts of Pollock, sustained this money at par when it had so far depreciated in the East as to be worth only twelve cents on the dollar. Traders from the East became aware of this situation and rushed to this region where goods might be procured with the certificates at their face value. They brought with them such large sums and distributed the money so liberally in trade, especially in engrossing the supply of provisions which they hoped to sell the army, that the inhabitants became alarmed and refused to receive it.

On returning to Kaskaskia Clark was not surprised to learn that his credit at New Orleans was exhausted. "I am sorry to learn," he wrote Pollock, "you have not been

[1] Pollock became possessed of $8,470 in continental currency, which he was forced to keep, as it did not pass at New Orleans. Pollock to the President of Congress, September 18, 1782, "Letters and Papers of Oliver Pollock," *Papers of Cont. Cong.*, I, 50 ff.

supplyed with funds as Expected your protesting my late
Bills has not surprised me. as I Expected it being surrounded by Enemies Mr. Hamilton & his Savages being
obligated for my own safety to lay in Considerable Stores.
I was oblidged to take every step I possibly could to procure them unwilling to use force." He was confronted also
with the problems growing out of a depreciated currency,
of which he says, in writing Governor Henry, "There is one
circumstance very distressing, that of our own moneys being discredited, to all intents and purposes, by the great
number of traders who come here in my absence each out-
bidding the other, giving prices unknown in this country
by five hundred percent., by which the people conceived
it to be of no value, and both French and Spaniards refused to take a farthing of it."

News of the American success in the Illinois country
reached Williamsburg the middle of November, 1778, and
Governor Henry promptly imparted the information to
the Virginia delegates in Congress. December 9 a bill
which must be regarded as an extraordinary state paper
passed the Virginia legislature establishing the county of
Illinois, which was to include the inhabitants of Virginia
north of the Ohio River. This type of government had
been brought into general usage by Virginia in her westward expansion. The act providing for the county of Illinois was to remain in force for a year and "thence to the
end of the next session of the assembly, and no longer."[1]
The establishment of some temporary form of government
was thought to be expedient, for, as stated in the act,
"from their remote situation, it may at this time be difficult,
if not impracticable, to govern them by the present laws
of this commonwealth, until proper information, by inter-

[1] Hening, *Statutes at Large*, IX, 552. Act of Establishment.

course with their fellow citizens, on the east side of the Ohio, shall have familiarised them to the same." The chief executive officer was the county lieutenant or commander-in-chief, who was appointed by the governor and council. He was to appoint, at his discretion, deputy commandants, militia officers, and commissaries. The civil officers, with which the inhabitants were familiar, whose duties were to administer the laws already in vogue, were to be chosen by the citizens of the different districts. Officers with new duties were to be maintained by the state; the others, by the people. Pardoning power was vested in the county lieutenant in all criminal cases, murder and treason excepted. In these cases, he was empowered to stay execution until such time as the will of the governor or, in case of treason, of the assembly should be ascertained. Provision was made for the protection of the inhabitants in all of their religious, civil, and property rights.

Clark was highly pleased when he learned that his friend, John Todd, Jr., with whom he had been intimately associated in Kentucky, had been commissioned county lieutenant of Illinois by Governor Henry. His undivided attention might thus be given to military affairs. The instructions issued by Governor Henry and the council December 12, 1778, to Todd and to Clark, who was to retain the command of all Virginia troops in the county of Illinois, showed a complete grasp of the situation. They were to co-operate in using their best efforts in cultivating and conciliating the affections of the French and the Indians. The rights of the inhabitants were to be secured against any infractions by the troops, and any person attempting to violate the property of the Indians, especially in their lands, was to be punished. All Indian raids on Kentucky were to be prevented, and the friendship of the Spaniards was to be maintained. As head of the civil department,

Todd was to have "Command of the Militia, who are not to be under the command of the Military until ordered out by the Civil Authority and act in conjunction with them." He was directed on "all occasions to inculcate on the people the value of liberty and the difference between the State of free Citizens of this Commonwealth and that Slavery to which Illinois was destined. A free and equal representation may be expected by them in a little time, together with all the improvements in Jurisprudence and police which the other parts of the State enjoy."

The document was carried by messenger across the mountains and was delivered to Todd in person at Vincennes shortly after the capture of that post by Clark. He set out for Kentucky in order to make the necessary preparations for assuming his new duties, and then proceeded to Kaskaskia, where he arrived early in May, 1779.

His coming was hailed with joy by the inhabitants, who, having experienced some of the harshness incident to military control, were enthusiastic for a change, no matter what the new form of government might be.[1] Indeed, the shouts for the French-American alliance were becoming feebler, and the enthusiasm at first aroused for the cause of liberty had begun to wane. The County Lieutenant was well fitted to fill his office acceptably. Beyond receiving a good general education, he had studied and practiced law for a time. Unable to resist the call of the frontier, he enlisted for service in Dunmore's War, and in 1775, when twenty-five years of age, went to Kentucky, where he was selected as one of the representatives to form a constitutional government for the settlement at Transyl-

---

[1] The first satisfactory account of the inauguration and history of the courts in the county of Illinois was written by Dr. Alvord in the Introduction to the *Cahokia Records* (Ill. Hist. Colls.), Vol. II, where fuller details than are here given may be found.

vania. In 1777 he was elected a delegate to the Virginia House of Burgesses from the county of Kentucky. The intimate friendship existing between Todd and Clark and their known ability and bravery promised a successful solution of the problems with which they were confronted.

The twelfth of May was notable among the villagers of Kaskaskia, for on that day Clark assembled them at the door of their church to hear the proclamation of the new government and to participate in the election of judges. The address prepared by Clark, who acted as presiding officer of the meeting, was well suited to the occasion:

> From your first declaration and attachment to the cause of the Americans until the glorious capture of the Post Vincennes, I doubted your sincerity; but at that critical moment I received proofs of your fidelity. I was so touched by the zeal which you there displayed that my desire at present is to make you happy, and to prove to you what sincere affection I have for the welfare and advancement of this colony in general and of each one of you in particular. The young people of this country have returned from Post Vincennes covered with laurels. I hope they will always continue so. Although there were some who did not take part in that glorious act, still I have no less esteem for them, hoping that they will take revenge, if occasion presents itself; for during my absence they have done their duty in guarding the fort with the greatest care.

He promised, as soon as it was within his power, that they should become partakers in the liberty enjoyed by Americans, and that a regiment of regular troops was to be sent for their protection. They were assured that the new government was one of such kindliness that they would bless the day they had chosen to favor the American cause. In presenting Colonel Todd he referred to him as his good friend and the only person in the state whom he desired to have take charge at that post. He spoke of the great importance of their meeting for the purpose of selecting the most capable and enlightened persons to judge their differences, and urged that only those most worthy of the offices should be chosen.

The brief response of Todd was likewise full of promise for the success of the new government which was to serve as guardian of their rights as citizens of a free and independent state:

Gentlemen, I am sent by the government of Virginia to exercise the duties of chief magistrate of this county. . . . .

The Republic of Virginia has had only noble motives in coming here. It was not moved by the love of conquest but has come to invite you to participate with her citizens in the blessing of a free and equal independence and to be governed and judged by officers who shall be placed in power by the people.

Your great distance from the Capital, gentlemen, does not permit you to send representatives to the assembly; but if in the future it happens that for your welfare or to avoid loss you prefer such representation, I have it in my instructions to assure you that it will not be refused you.

The purpose for which we have assembled you to-day, gentlemen, is that you may choose among you six of the most notable and most judicious to be judges of the court of Kaskaskia, conjointly with two others from Prairie du Rocher and St. Philippe. Each one with the right of voting can give his vote, either *viva voce* or by writing, to elect whomsoever he wishes to place in office.[1]

An election then followed whereby, for the first time within the territory of Illinois, the voters exercised their rights as citizens of a republic. There appeared at the top of a large ballot sheet, divided into squares, the names of the candidates for judges. On the side were placed the names of the voters as they gave their votes either in writing or by word of mouth. There was no evidence of the factional strife which prevailed during the last months of the British administration. The election resulted in the selection of those best fitted to carry out the provisions

[1] *Cahokia Records*, p. lix.

of the new constitution. At the head of the court was Gabriel Cerré, outstanding French leader, who had, as we have seen, won the confidence of Clark by his generous assistance in furthering the American cause. Two representatives of the court were also elected by the voters of Prairie du Rocher, and one at St. Philippe.

The personnel of the court being complete, Todd issued the commission, May 21, as follows:

> From the great Confidence reposed in your Judgment and Integrity by the good people of Kaskaskia and its dependencies and agreeably to an act of the general assembly of Virginia, you are hereby constituted and appointed Justices of the peace for the District of Kaskaskia and Judges of the Court of the said District in cases both Civil and Criminal. Any four or more of you are authorized to constitute a Court before whom shall be cognizable all actions and cases of which the Courts of the Counties of this commonwealth Respectively have Cognizance. Your Judgment must have the Concurrence of at least a majority and be entered with the proceedings previous and subsequent and fairly recorded in Books provided for that purpose.[1]

Todd had previously appointed a sheriff and a state's attorney. The court named its own clerk. One week earlier military commissions were made out. Some of the men given officers' commissions had been elected judges, and they were called upon to assume the duties of both offices. Elections of judges for the district courts of Cahokia and Vincennes took place shortly afterward and resulted, as at Kaskaskia, in the selection of Frenchmen.

At first there was an effort to hold court sessions each week, following the custom established in Clark's courts. This soon gave place to monthly sessions, with special meetings as required. The French law was retained, although it was slightly modified by the law of Virginia. Individual judges were given jurisdiction in cases involving not more than twenty-five shillings, as was customary in

[1] *Cahokia Records*, LXI.

other Virginia counties. Trial by jury was permitted and was probably required in criminal cases.

The harmony seemingly manifested during the inauguration of the new government was not real, however, for within a few days Todd was called upon to hear a recital of the grievances of the French inhabitants which had been formulated by the Kaskaskia justices. He was informed that a number of the oxen, cows, and other animals belonging to the petitioners had been taken and killed by the soldiers; that liquor was being sold to Indians, and trade carried on with slaves without the consent of their masters, both of which were contrary to French custom. An incident occurred during the summer of 1779 which illustrates the difficulties attending the organization of government. Captain Richard McCarty, up to the time of the capture of Kaskaskia, was an English trader from Canada. He accompanied Clark on the Vincennes expedition and was then placed in command of the small garrison at Cahokia. His live stock were permitted to run at large 6 miles from the village, as he claimed, and destroyed crops which were not inclosed. Some of the hogs were killed by the French, and McCarty made the following appeal to Todd for redress: "I don't see yet through the Designs of a few Despicable Inhabitants who say they are authorized by you to parade themselves in the fields Destroying My property when there is Numbers of other hogs in the Same place that are as fauctious as Mine. . . . . Indeed unless there is soon a change made for the Better me nor my Soldiers will have no Buissiness hear, neither can we stay half naked, what we are paid with call'd down by the Civil Power; with what can we get our necessaries of Life; Neither do I kno' the Laws you have Established."[1] At the same time he wrote a friend: "Colo. Todd's Residence

[1] *Cahokia Records*, pp. 614, 615.

here will spoil the people intirely for the Inhabitants no more Regard us than a Parcel of Slaves. . . . . I think it would be a happy thing could we get Colo. Todd out of the Country for he will possitively Sett the Inhabitants and us by the Ears."[1]

Antagonisms between these two types of people could scarcely have been averted, for both the troops and the French inhabitants were suffering from a lack of necessary food and clothing. At Kaskaskia and Cahokia the dissatisfied troops were daily deserting, and the garrison at Vincennes was without salt. Moreover, the French and the backwoodsmen differed in language, in manners, and in religion, and these fundamental differences would have produced clashes even in a better-organized society.

Colonel Todd's rôle was a most difficult one to fill. His salary was small and he feared that he would be forced to sell his property in Kentucky for his support. After serving three months he wrote the Governor: "I expected to have been prepared to present to your excellency some amendments upon the form of Government for Illinois, but the present will be attended with no great inconveniences till the Spring Session, when I beg your permission to attend and get a Discharge from an Office, which an unwholesome air, a distance from my connexions, a Language not familiar to me, and an impossibility of procuring many of the conveniences of Life suitable, all tend to render uncomfortable."[2]

To a man of his sensibilities the carrying out of certain decrees of the court must have been irksome. Within a month after assuming office he was called upon to execute a sentence pronounced by the Kaskaskia court upon a slave who evidently had been convicted of the imaginary

[1] *Ibid.*, p. 616.

[2] August 19, 1779, *Chicago Hist. Soc. Colls.*, IV, 319.

crime of "Voudouism," or Negro witchcraft. In such cases the commandant, according to the statute, was denied the privilege of granting a pardon. The entry in his record book reads as follows:

> To Richard Winston Esq., Sheriff in chief of the District of Kaskaskia. Negro Manuel, a Slave in your custody, is condemned by the Court of Kaskaskia, after having made honorable Fine at the Door of the Church, to be chained to a post at the Water Side and there to be burnt alive and his ashes scattered, as appears to me by Record. This Sentence you are hereby required to put in execution on Tuesday next at 9 o'clock in the morning and this shall be your warrant.[1]

Fearful lest there should be a repetition of the abuses under the Virginia land law as practiced in Kentucky, and that adventurers and speculators would get possession of the rich bottom lands, he decreed that no new settlements should be made on the flat lands "unless in manner and form as heretofore made by the French inhabitants." Americans coming to the region· paid little heed to this legislation, however, and there were instances within the next two years of its complete nullification. Adventurers, representing grantees residing in Philadelphia, London, and elsewhere, flocked to this region where grants of land from the Indians were easily procured, one of these containing a million acres.[2] County Lieutenant Todd complained that "some Land jobbers from the South side of the Ohio have been making improvements (as they call them) upon the purchas'd Lands on this side of the River, and are beyond the reach of punishment from me—with the arrival of New adventurers this summer, the same spirit of Land jobbing begins to breathe here."[3] The Illinois and Wabash Land Companies, organized as one com-

---

[1] June 13, 1779. *Chicago Hist. Soc. Colls.*, IV.

[2] *Clark Papers*, p. 357.

[3] Mason, "John Todd Papers," *Chicago Hist. Soc. Colls.*, IV, 188.

pany in 1780, saw in Clark's victories the opportunity for promoting their scheme and presented a memorial to the Virginia legislature announcing their intentions. In the reply it was declared that the right of pre-emption of all land within the limits of Virginia belonged to that commonwealth alone. The subscribers carried their appeal to the Continental Congress, but declared it to be their determination to defer action until the close of the war.

No problem proved more trying for Todd and Clark than the effects produced by depreciated currency. Complications were greater on account of counterfeit money, which in spite of the drastic legislation against it, was in circulation in all of the states. The Virginia legislature in November, 1778, made it a felony punishable with death without benefit of clergy to counterfeit the currency, or pass knowingly counterfeit money, or to have in possession instruments or material for the purpose of counterfeiting.[1] By the close of April the price of provisions in the West was three times what it had been two months previously, and Clark was enabled to support his soldiers only by the assistance of a number of the merchants and traders of Illinois.[2]

While in Kentucky, Todd learned that the issues of continental currency bearing the dates April 20, 1777, and April 11, 1778, had been ordered to be paid into the continental loan offices by the first of June, 1779, otherwise they would become worthless.[3] The British in New York

[1] Hening, *Statutes at Large*, IX, 541.

[2] Clark to Patrick Henry, April 29, 1779. *Clark Papers*, p. 173. Among the number thus sacrificing for the American cause, some of whom were later reduced to want, were: Daniel Murray, Richard Winston, Nicolas Janis, and Bienvenu, of Kaskaskia; Jean Girault, Charles Gratiot, and Richard McCarty, of Cahokia; J. M. L. LeGras and Francis Bosseron, of Vincennes; and Francis Vigo, of St. Louis.

[3] Todd to Clark, March 26, 1779, Draper MSS, 49 J 33.

had counterfeited these emissions and the country was flooded with this worthless paper. Todd hoped that time would be extended for the Illinois holders. Upon his arrival at Kaskaskia he found that the paper money had depreciated so that it was worth only one-fifth of its face value in specie. On June 11, therefore, with the desire of sustaining public credit, he addressed the court in the following letter:

The only method America has to support the present just War is by her Credit. That Credit at present is her Bills emitted from the different Treasuries by which she engages to pay the Bearer at a certain time Gold & Silver in Exchange. There is no friend to American Independance who has any Judgment but soon expects to see it equal to Gold & Silver. Some disaffected persons & designing Speculators descredit it through Enemity or Interest; the ignorant multitude have not sagacity enough to examine into this matter, & merely from its uncommon Quantity & in proportion to it arises the Complaint of its want of Credit.

Todd proposed to retire a portion of the bills through exchanging them for land certificates. Twenty-one thousand acres of land in the vicinity of Cahokia were set aside on which it was planned to borrow $33,000 in Virginia and United States treasury notes. The lender might demand, within two years, his proportion of the land or a sum in gold or silver equal to the original loan with 5 per cent annual interest. Land or money might be given at the option of the state. Large sums of money were exchanged for these certificates, but the project could not be carried further.

Discontent among the French grew steadily worse under these conditions. Colonel Todd refused to allow the exchange of peltries for provisions, as had been agreed upon, and the depreciated currency was almost worthless. Calling the people into council, he informed them that if they would not sell on the credit of the state they would be subject to military discipline.[1]

During the spring of 1780 Todd was elected a delegate from the county of Kentucky to the Virginia legislature. It was due to his exertions that aid secured from the legislature led to the founding of Transylvania University, the first institution of higher learning west of the Mountains.

In the summer of 1781 Todd was appointed by Governor Jefferson colonel of Fayette County, one of the three counties into which Kentucky County had been divided by the legislature. His relation to Illinois County seems only to have been nominal after 1780, and in his absence the discontent of the French under the exactions of military officers became constantly more extreme.

[1] *Chicago Hist., Soc. Colls.*, IV, 319.

CHAPTER IX

Clark's Problems in Extending His Conquests

BUT Detroit was uppermost in the minds of the two leaders, and preparations were rapidly made for the expedition which promised complete success. In this they were following the orders explicitly given by Governor Henry. The instructions to Todd read:

> The Inhabitants of Illinois must not expect settled peace and safety while their and our Enemies have footing at Detroit and can interrupt or stop the Trade of the Mississippi. If the English have not the strength or courage to come to war against us themselves, their practice has been and will be to hire the Savages to commit murder and depredations. Illinois must expect to pay in these a large price for her Freedom, unless the English can be expelled from Detroit. The means of effecting this will not perhaps be found in your or Col. Clarkes power. But the French inhabiting the neighbourhood of that place, it is presumed, may be brought to see it done with indifference or perhaps join in the enterprise with pleasure. This is but conjecture. When you are on the spot you and Col. Clarke may discover its fallacy or reality.[1]

Similar instructions were given Clark by the Virginia Council, as follows: "But you are to push at any favorable occurrences which Fortune may present to you. For our peace & safety are not secure while the Enemy are so near as Detroit.[2]

The fortifications at that post were still unfinished and the garrison consisted of only one hundred men. The population residing in the town and adjacent country numbered

---

[1] *Clark Papers*, p. 84.   [2] *Ibid.*, p. 80.

some 2,500, two-thirds of them being males.[1] A survey also enumerated 138 slaves, 413 oxen, 779 cows, 619 steers, 1,076 hogs, 664 horses, 313 sheep, and 141,500 pounds of flour. There were besides, in good quantities, wheat, Indian corn, oats, and peas.

Captain Daniel Maurice Godefroy de Linctot, a trader of considerable influence with the Indians, who had recently joined the Americans, was sent up the Illinois River with a company of forty men to secure the neutrality of the Indians and at the same time cover the design of the main expedition against Detroit. He reported on his return that peace and quietness was general as far as Ouiatenon.

Great enthusiasm was manifested on the part of officers, troops, and the French militia. On no occasion does Clark appear to a better advantage than in the appeal which he made for the support of the young men, many of whom had accompanied him on the expedition against Vincennes, returning, as he said, "covered with laurels." He assured them that their deeds and faithful conduct were well known throughout America. Not only were the villagers ready to enlist, some of the old men volunteering their services, but like enthusiasm was general at Vincennes among the people and American officers, and Clark was assured that not only the inhabitants at Ouiatenon and Miami but the garrisons also were ready to declare in his favor.

The arrival of Colonel John Montgomery from Virginia with 150 men, about one-third the number expected, was a keen disappointment to Clark. But he did not lose confidence, for he had been promised three hundred Kentuckians by Colonel John Bowman, their county lieutenant. On July 1 Clark, with a party of horsemen, reached

[1] *Mich. Pioneer and Hist. Colls.*, X, 327.

Vincennes, the place of rendezvous. Here he was joined by the remainder of the Illinois troops, with the exception of the company of mounted men dispatched under Captain Linctot to reconnoiter and to obtain permission of the Wea and Miami for Clark to pass through their country on his way to Detroit.

Before leaving Kaskaskia Clark learned that Colonel John Bowman had led the Kentucky forces against Chillicothe, a Shawnee town, and he was fearful of the effect on his Detroit plans. This expedition consisted of 296 men. The Indians fortified themselves so strongly in a few log cabins that the whites were repulsed. The greater part of the town was burned and Bowman retreated with a considerable amount of plunder. Influenced by Clark's victories, immigrants in large numbers entered Kentucky during the spring. Some of them returned to the older settlements for their families, and the others were scattered over such an extended area that to Bowman it seemed impossible to secure the number of men he had promised Clark by the time appointed, especially since the militia were so disheartened by the campaign against the Shawnee that only the most tried among them were ready to enter upon a new enterprise.

The arrival of only thirty Kentucky volunteers was a severe blow to Clark, and the capture of Detroit with his available force of about 350 men appeared at the time out of the question. Besides, most of his men were barefoot. Vincennes was able to supply scarcely enough provisions for its own inhabitants. All commerce with Detroit had ceased, and supplies could be gotten by the way of the Mississippi only with great difficulty owing to the attachment of the southern Indians to the British. "Never was a person more mortified than I was at this time, to see so fair an opportunity to push a victory; Detroit lost for want of a few men." In this way Clark expressed his sense of defeat at being forced to give up the expedition against that post.

Although abandoned, the influence of the preparation for the expedition proved of great significance. Threatenings from Vincennes led the British officials at Detroit to give up their plans for the recapture of that post.[1] A summer campaign of regulars and Indians against Fort Pitt was likewise abandoned. The British at Detroit and Michilimackinac were engaged in considering defensive operations and reinforcements were hurried to these posts. Notwithstanding the large expenditures for rum and presents for the warriors and food for the old men, women, and children, disaffection among the Indians became constantly more open. "Fear," wrote one of the officers," acts stronger on them than all the arguments that can be made use of to convince them of the Enemy's ill designs against their lands."[2] French and Indians were frightened over the report that an alliance between the French, Spanish, Germans, and Americans had been formed with the object of driving the English out of America.[3] De Peyster found excuse in the marked increase in expenditures as follows: "As the Indians are growing very importunate since they hear that the French are assisting the rebels—the Canadians, I fear are a great disservice to Government but the Indians are perfect Free Masons when intrusted with a secret by a Canadian, most of them being connected by marriage." The Menominee and the Sioux were alone counted upon to remain true to British interests.[4]

[1] Draper MSS, 49 J 41, 1 H 104, 58 J 37.

[2] Ibid., 58 J 39.

[3] Brehm to Haldimand, May 28, 1779. Mich. Pioneer and Hist. Colls., IX, 411, 417.

[4] De Peyster to Haldimand, June 1, 1779. Mich. Pioneer and Hist. Colls., IX, 382.

Lieutenant Thomas Bennett was sent from Michilimackinac (May 29) with a force of twenty soldiers, sixty traders, and two hundred Indians for the purpose of intercepting Linctot or to "distress the Rebels" in any other way. Captain Langlade was directed to levy the Indians at La Fourche and Milwaukee and join Bennett at "Chicagou." Indian scouts sent out by Bennett from St. Joseph's were frightened by reports obtained from other Indians and soon returned. Their fears quickly brought about a general panic. "We have not," wrote Bennett, "twenty Indians in our Camp who are not preparing for leaving us, I believe you will join with me when I say they are a set of treacherous Poltroons." The return to Michilimackinac was begun shortly afterward. In like manner a force of six hundred, chiefly Indians, led by Captain Alexander McKee was sent from Michilimackinac. Forgetting his boast that he would place a pair of handcuffs on every Rebel officer left in the country, he retreated from St. Joseph's upon hearing the report that Clark was marching toward Detroit.[1] Early in June Captain Henry Bird collected some two hundred Indians at the Mingo town. The account brought in by runners of the attack which had been made by Colonel Bowman on the Shawnee towns produced a panic among his followers. Some of the savages deserted in order to protect their villages against the American advance, which was momentarily expected.

Moreover, during August General John Sullivan, with the design of punishing the Iroquois for their raids and of lessening their control over the western tribes, led an expedition against the Iroquois villages of central New York which wrought great devastation among them. As originally planned by Washington, a force under Daniel Brodhead from Pittsburgh was to co-operate by striking a blow

[1] *Mich. Pioneer and Hist. Colls.*, p. 390.

at the Seneca or Mingo, the westernmost Iroquois tribe, whose villages were located on the upper Allegheny.[1] Although the orders for this flank movement were revoked, Brodhead, with Detroit in view, decided to carry out the original plan, since he had been granted permission to move in any direction he desired.[2]

With an army composed of six hundred regulars, militia, volunteers, and a few Delaware warriors, and with supplies for a month, Brodhead set out on August 11. Their route led "through a country almost impassible, by reason of the stupendous heights and frightful declivities, with a continuous range of craggy hills, overspread with fallen timber, thorns and underwood."[3] The advance guard encountered a party of Indians coming downstream and killed a number of them. Those escaping warned the villages and the inhabitants fled. Their houses and 600 acres of standing corn were burned and quantities of furs and other booty amounting to $30,000 were captured.[4] Having reached the towns near the present boundary of New York, they turned back because of the lack of a competent guide. This hazardous march of 200 miles and return was accomplished in thirty-three days without the loss of a single life.

These expeditions were successful because of their effects on the Iroquois and on British officers who were anticipating an attack on Niagara.[5] Brodhead found a delegation of Wyandot chiefs, one of the most powerful of western tribes, awaiting his return, for the spell of the Iroquois had been shattered and they sought an alliance whereby security would be gained for their villages, which

---

[1] *Frontier Retreat*, ed. Louise P. Kellogg, *Wis. Hist. Colls.*, Draper Series, V, 43 ff.

[2] *Ibid.*, p. 49.   [3] *Ibid.*, pp. 56, 57.

[4] This was sold and the money was divided among the troops.

[5] *Frontier Retreat*, pp. 50, 78.

lay on the route to Detroit. A branch of the Shawnee also came suing for peace and friendship. Accepting the promises of neutrality proffered by these tribes, Brodhead made provisional treaties with them.

The Wabash tribes had likewise made overtures to Clark. The effect of propaganda was again called into play, and Clark, "carefull to spread such reports as suited our interest," dispatched to Detroit a number of copies of the Articles of Alliance between France and the United States. "And do not doubt," he said, "but they will produce the desired effect."[1] He had been advised by Washington either to attempt the capture of Detroit during the winter when the Lake was frozen over or to delay until spring and meanwhile to collect supplies and information.[2] Colonel Brodhead had promised co-operation and was enthusiastic for such an expedition.

Before setting out for the falls of the Ohio, where he had determined to establish his headquarters, Clark issued orders to Colonel Montgomery and other officers left in command of the Illinois posts to begin collecting supplies for a campaign against Detroit the next spring.

Hunters were sent out to bring in a supply of meat, and officers sought to purchase provisions from the inhabitants. Failing in the attempt, they resorted to assessment, but this method likewise did not produce the supplies necessary for the army which Clark proposed. The French complained that they and their Negroes were naked, and refused to furnish supplies unless they should be given peltry in exchange instead of paper money, which was continuously depreciating in value. John Todd called them into conference and threatened, unless the demands were met, to hand them over to the military, and that he

---

[1] Clark to Patrick Henry, April 29, 1779, *Clark Papers*, p. 174.

[2] *Frontier Retreat*, p. 101.

would himself leave Illinois.[1] The French were seemingly unmoved, and in despair at accomplishing his aim through the operation of the civil government, Todd appointed Richard Winston as his deputy and then returned to Kentucky.

Under the military despotism thus introduced the *habitants* were forced to yield their goods through confiscation. Their principal leaders, among whom were Gabriel Cerré and Charles Gratiot, sought refuge in St. Louis, "an asylum where they find the protection which is due a free people."[2] Appeals to the government of Virginia brought no relief to those who remained. Protection by the courts, which were conducted by French officers of their own choosing, was of no avail since the primary object of these justices consisted in the use of official positions to further their private interests. Distrust and hatred continued to widen the breach between the French and the Americans.

During the late summer all was confusion at Detroit, for the harvests had failed and the British were expecting an attack from Vincennes or Fort Pitt. Conduct of the war in the East prevented the sending of reinforcements to Canada and the West as had been promised by General Clinton. Messages brought by couriers promised the coming of Clark with an army of two thousand well-armed Americans and French Creoles.[3] An officer who demanded that reinforcements should be sent wrote:

Every effort is making to strengthen and complete our new Fort, as we are not equal to oppose the passage of such numbers to this place. Our ditch and glacee will be in a very good state the end of this week. An abatte [abatis] is afterwards to be thrown round the barracks will be ready at the same time. I wish to God I could say the same of our

[1] *Kaskaskia Records*, p. 129.

[2] The year before, Father Gibault became the priest at Ste Genevieve. *Cahokia Records*, pp. lxxxiii ff.

[3] Letter of Captain Parke, July 30, 1779. Draper MSS, 58 J 46.

well; it is now upwards of 60 feet below the level of the river and no appearance of water. . . . . Could we only rely on the inhabitants or had they either the inclination or the resolution to defend their town, there would be nothing to apprehend on that Head as we might then take the field.

An attack on Detroit from neither quarter was at the time seriously threatened. In a letter to George Morgan, Brodhead said: "Why do you conceive, that 500 men are now equal to the task of carrying that place, which is rendered much stronger by men and works than it was two years ago, when 1,800 men were thought necessary. I conceive it to be next to an impossibility to carry on a secret expedition against that place, whilst the English have goods to engage the Indians in their interest, and we have nothing but words."[1]

When Clark reached the falls, about the middle of September, he found the work of settling on the mainland going forward rapidly. Influenced by the reports of Clark's victories and the stories of returning travelers that rich land might be easily acquired, immigrants in large numbers entered Kentucky, some descending the Ohio, others coming by the wilderness road. Glowing accounts describing this region as the "richest under the sun" continued to induce increasing numbers to enter Kentucky during the summer. The soil could not, it was said, be surpassed in richness; vast natural meadows furnished a range which seemed inexhaustible, and great herds of buffalo, elk, and deer were common.[2] So great was the impulse to secure lands in the West that people in certain parts of Virginia were reported to be "running mad" for Kentucky.

This interest was enhanced through an act of the Virginia legislature of May, 1779, by which on October 15 of that year land-office treasury warrants might be used in

---

[1] *Pennsylvania Archives*, XII, 160.   [2] Draper MSS, 23 J 164.

the purchase of vacant lands. From that day until the first of May following, when the first entries on these warrants were allowed, Kentucky was visited by large numbers of explorers who hoped to locate their warrants most advantageously. Upon the opening of the land office the rush was so great that for several days the time of three men was devoted entirely to receiving and receipting for these warrants.[1]

By order of the county court a regular government for the town, which received the name of Louisville, was established through the selection of seven trustees. June 5, 1780, by agreement of ninety-four men, a separate judiciary was established through the selection of six men who were empowered to elect magistrates, "to regulate the many Villanys and bring to justice all offenders." After taking the oath of office they elected a clerk and sheriff and appointed militia officers. The trial of cases by jury was also provided for.[2] In like manner trustees to be elected in each of the other Kentucky towns were given authority "to lay off the town with regularity" and prescribe rules for buildings. The plan of the town and proceedings of the trustees were to be returned to the county court. April 24, 1779, was the day set by the trustees of Louisville for drawing the half-acre lots to which each person was entitled. The drawing had been advertised in Harrodsburg, Boonesborough, and St. Asaphs, and it is probable some of the citizens of these communities took part in the lottery. One hundred sixteen assignments were made. Those who thus secured village lots agreed to clear off the undergrowth and begin the cultivation of the soil

[1] G. W. Stipp, *Western Miscellany* (Xenia, 1827), p. 52. The surveyor's office was opened at Wilson's Station, about 2 miles from Harrodsburg. Warrants of earliest dates were given the preference.

[2] Draper MSS, 50 J 45.

by June 10. By December 25 a "good covered house" 16 by 40 feet was to be built on each lot.[1]

The plan submitted by Clark to the surveyors engaged in laying off the town would, if adopted, have made Louisville, we are told, "the most beautiful city on the continent."[2] It provided for a reservation of land along the river front as a public park. Connected with the courthouse lot, which was to contain two whole squares, was to be a park half a square in breadth extending the entire length of the town. Clark constructed a new house which was notable at the time for a large room built of hewn logs on the inside and which had a good plank floor.[3] Upon invitation, men and women journeyed from the other settlements to take part in the ball and other festivities which marked its completion. The thrills incident to attendance upon such a social function were vividly portrayed by one who was present. Trabue wrote:

Some of us went from Logan's Fort, we went by Harrodsburg stayd all night in the morning Col. Harod & his Lady Col. Mc.Garry & several other jentlemen & ladys started about 20 men & about 6 Ladys when we had got about one mile from the Fort I Discovered Indians in the woods and running to get before us I told Mc.Garry of it, he halted the company and he went to examine the sign he came back said he saw the indians and said he was not able to fight them while we had these women and we retreted to the Fort a party of men went from the fort and found the Indians had gone away The next morning we set out again we had about 15 men & 3 ladies . . . . we got safe to the falls. . . . . He made a ball a number of Jentlemen & Ladies attended to it and when these Fort Ladys came to be dressed up they did not look like the same every thing looked anew. We enjoyed ourselves very much Col. Harrod & his lady opened the ball by Danc-

[1] Reuben T. Durrett, "Centenary of Louisville," *Filson Club Publications* (Louisville, 1893), VIII, 34.

[2] Draper MSS, 35 J 47. Letter of R. T. Durrett to Lyman C. Draper, April 19, 1883.

[3] "Trabue Narrative," Draper MSS, 57 J 23.

ing the first gig we had plenty of rum Toddy to Drink we stayed their some few Days.[1]

The ordinary one-story log cabins had clapboard roofs, puncheon floors, a small window, usually without glass, and a chimney carried up with "cats and clay" to the height of the ridge pole. The furniture was of the roughest sort, such as could be made with axe, saw, and auger. Wooden plates and bowls were commonly used, although for special occasions iron knives and forks and tin cups and occasional pewter plates and spoons were to be seen.

Settlers in the hamlets spent their days in cultivating the crops on the small clearings adjacent to the stockades, in tending the stock, and hunting—for deer and turkeys were plentiful, and buffalo were still to be gotten. At times some of the men stood guard while others cleared the ground for planting, and as they cultivated the fields the guns were always at hand. Turnips, beans, potatoes, pumpkins, and melons were grown, but corn bread and hominy constituted the chief articles of food. The corn was ground with great labor by hand mills or was pounded in the cavity of a stump by a pestle attached to a sweep. Parched corn made into meal and sweetened with maple sugar furnished a substitute for coffee. Toward the close of 1779 a log-dam was built at Harrodsburg and a pair of large hand-mill stones were placed in what was known as a tub-mill for grinding corn. Flax was grown, and the clothing made therefrom was in part substituted for that made from the skins of animals. A crude product manufactured from the fiber of the wild nettle mixed with buffalo wool was also used for clothes. Socks were made out of buffalo wool. Such trading as was carried on was done chiefly by barter, although furs were at times used for currency and there was some paper money.

[1] *Ibid.*

The routine of their lives was broken by hunting and shooting at a mark. Gatherings of the men for "raising" cabins and stables and for corn-husking were common. Among the usual pastimes were foot-racing, horse-racing, and wrestling. Fighting was also indulged in, and biting and gouging on the part of the combatants were carried to the extreme of brutality. Profanity and drinking were common, and coarse jocularities were not frowned upon. The militia musters offered occasions at the close of the day for all sorts of sports. Weddings were likewise the scenes of carousals and of mirth. Religious forms and usages other than teaching the catechism to children were generally neglected. The first organized church in Kentucky, the Presbyterian, was not started before 1783, but there was preaching in some of the communities at an earlier date. The Baptists, Methodists, Episcopalians, and Catholics also established places for worship about the same time.

Pulling flax and looking for wild plums were regarded as frolics by the young people. For young and old, dancing was the chief amusement. Evenings were spent also in listening to stories about the bold exploits and narrow escapes of noted Indian fighters, for they were naturally the heroes of greatest repute in these communities. The usual topics of conversation were connected with Indian wars, midnight butcheries, captivities, and horse-stealings. "Lie still and go to sleep or the Shawnee will catch you" was the expression commonly used to frighten children into quiet, and their troubled dreams included either the Indian or the copperhead snake, for both were common.

As settlements increased, confusion arose over conflict of titles to the land. Four commissioners were appointed by Virginia to adjudicate land claims and to grant settlement and pre-emption rights in the county of Kentucky.[1] Companies were organized through whose agency individuals prominent in the East and speculators were enabled to acquire possession of large tracts of land.[2] The abuse of such a system was set forth in the following letter to Clark:

And when I was with you I thought my acquaintance Mr. Randolph was likewise attached to the Interest of the Kentucky settlements but I am sorry to inform you that I have reason to believe the contrary for on looking over the books in the Land office I found a Certain Mr Bealls had taken out warrants to the amount of one hundred and forty thousand Acres of Land at least, part of which was enterd assigned to Mr N. Randolph now is this consonant with the doctrine he held when I was with you, and is it consistant with the Interest of that Country to assist a man (and a speculator too) in locating such a body of Land (& I suppose to of the Richest sort) when he will never see the Country or if he did, the portion is to large—no man can hesitate a moment to pronounce that it is not the Interest of the back Country. The evil tendancy will so fully appear to you that I will quit the subject & say nothing more about it.[3]

Actual settlers pled for relief from similar encroachments in a petition to the Virginia assembly. They declared:

[1] Hening, *Statutes at Large*, X, 43, sec. 8. The law under which they operated provided that each person who had prior to January 1, 1778, settled upon any waste and unappropriated lands on the western waters "to which no person hath any other legal title" was entitled to a settlement right of 400 acres. The state was to receive two dollars and a quarter for each 100 acres thus acquired. Besides, each person with a settlement right was entitled to acquire 1,000 acres adjacent thereto, known as a pre-emption, upon the payment of forty dollars in specie for each 100 acres.

[2] Draper MSS, 7 L 65. Letter of General Muhlenberg to Jonathan Clark, September 15, 1779. "I have just seen an advertisement in a Virginia paper of the 28th of August signed Isaac Hite, Abr. Bowman and J. Bowman, wherein they mention that they had entered into written articles with sundry persons relative to lands on Kentuckett and desire that all persons who have signed shall before the first day of October pay to Isaac Hite 40 besides fees for every 100 acres they have subscribed for otherwise they will not be bound by the articles. What think you of it? Have you any share or have you subscribed? or do you remember the conditions?"

[3] January 24, 1780. *Clark Papers*, p. 384.

A constant war for four years has reduced many of us so low that we have scarce cattle enough amongst us to supply our small families and many of us that brought good stocks of both horses and cows now at this juncture have not left so much as one cow for the support of our families. We have thought it proper to present you with a just estimation of our losses in settling and defending this extensive country. In the late act of the Assembly in opening and establishing a land office many of the petitioners are not able to get as much as one hundred acres. Unless there is some redress, this must be the unhappy event that we must lie under the disagreeable necessity of going down the Mississippi to the Spanish protection or becoming tenants to private gentlemen who have men employed at this juncture in this country at one hundred pounds per thousand for running round the lands.[1]

On October 4, 1779, the Americans suffered a disaster which strengthened the British and affected the decision of warring tribesmen. Early in the year 1778 Colonel David Rogers, accompanied by twenty-eight men, had been sent by Governor Henry with special dispatches to Governor Galvez. In addition to the loan of some $600,000 which Virginia hoped to obtain,[2] Rogers was to transport to Fort Pitt the blankets and munitions which had been deposited at New Orleans consigned to the use of Virginia.[2] Through the good offices of Oliver Pollock and the favor of Galvez, two boat-loads of goods were secured.[3] At the falls of the Ohio Clark detailed an escort for their protection up the river. Upon reaching a point a little beyond the present site of Cincinnati they were suprised by a band of Indians under Simon Girty. Thirteen men only of the seventy constituting the company escaped, and among the victims of the massacre was Colonel Rogers. In addition to the booty which the victors procured, important messages from Clark and John Todd were captured which revealed conditions in the West.

[1] Draper MSS, 14 S 31.

[2] *Archivo General de Indias*, Seville, Estante 87, Cajon 1, legajo 6. Copy in Virginia State Library.

[3] *Frontier Retreat*, pp. 83–93; *Clark Papers*, p. 39.

Kentucky leaders demanded a retaliatory expedition, but supplies could not be gotten, owing to the more aggressive policy of the enemy. Describing the situation, Clark wrote: "We set out on a plan of laying up this Fall great quantities of jerked meat for the ensuing season but as Detroit had pretty well recovered itself the Shawnees Delawares and other prominent Indian tribes was so exceedingly Troublesome that our hunters had no suckcess numbers being cut off and small skirmishes in the Cuntrey so common that but little notice was taken of them."[1]

By November, 1779, the inhabitants had so far lost their fears of Indian forays that they ventured to build cabins on their several tracts of land and again take possession. In a council at Louisville Clark took up the discussion with his officers of the preparation necessary for an expedition against Detroit. The reduction of West Florida, also a favorite topic with Clark, was likewise considered, for he had been assured that two-thirds of the people at Natchez were ready to declare in his favor.[2] It was agreed that at least one thousand troops would be necessary for the "long tedious fatiguing march through a hostile country" to Detroit. With no savages to encounter, with the inhabitants well disposed toward Americans, and with the certainty of an early breaking out of war between Spain and Great Britain, five hundred men were thought to be adequate to take possession of West Florida.

By this time winter, long remembered as the hard winter, had set in. For three months snow covered the ground and the rivers were frozen to the bottom. Most of the cattle and thousands of buffalo, deer, turkeys, and other animals perished. Settlers were reduced to the utmost ex-

---

[1] *Clark Papers*, p. 302.

[2] W. H. English, *Conquest of the Country Northwest of the River Ohio and Life of George Rogers Clark* (Indianapolis, 1896), II, 698 ff.; *Clark Papers*, p. 67.

tremity for want of bread, and numbers died of starvation and cold. "One johnny-cake was often divided into twelve equal parts twice each day." Corn rose from fifty dollars a bushel in November to two hundred dollars in March. "If we was only now in Old Virginia," one exclaimed, "we could have something good to eat and drink but here we have nothing to eat in this dreary wilderness and we dont know when we shall have." The suffering of many families on their way to Kentucky who were forced to pass the winter on the Cumberland River was even more extreme, their condition being described as follows: "Many in the wilderness frost bit. Some dead. Some eat of the dead cattle and horses when the winter broak the men would go to kill the buffaloes and bring them home to eat but they was so poore a number people would be taken sick and did actually Die for the want of food the most of the people had to go to the Falls of the Ohio for corn to plant."

By the end of February, a month of heavy rains, winter had disappeared and the tide of immigration to Kentucky again set in with increasing activity. The population of the western counties of Pennsylvania and of northwestern Virginia also showed notable gains in this movement. Three hundred large boats arrived at the falls during the spring months and a number of new settlements were begun.[1] It has been estimated that twenty thousand people entered Kentucky during the years 1779 and 1780, but this is doubtless an exaggerated statement. Large numbers came with land warrants, and after making their locations, returned to Virginia. With the advent of spring,

[1] The leading settlements by the close of the year 1780 were Harrodsburg, Boonesborough, Logan's, Bryans Camp, McAfee's, Licking, Elkton, Froman's, Sullivan's, Floyd's Spring, Hogeland's, Asturgis, Linn's, Cain, Boone's, and Lexington. Draper MSS, 49 J 89, 4 CC 89.

Kentuckians moved out to their clearings and planted corn and vegetables, which soon gave promise of an unusual crop. Apple trees were beginning to bear, and peach trees were loaded with fruit. In the midst of these flattering prospects for an unusual year the Shawnee appeared in the Beargrass settlements.[1] Settlers who did not take refuge in stations were cut off in the usual way. The utmost precaution had to be used to prevent surprises, and general gloom pervaded the settlements. The suffering at the Illinois posts, during the winter, equally severe, was described by Colonel Montgomery as follows: "Everything animate and inanimate groanes under a most unseportible Burden of a severe winter. Inhabitants has lost almost all their stocks for want of corn to feed them.[2] Notwithstanding their distress, the French at Vincennes, were ready to divide their slender stock of provisions with the troops in the garrison and render them every other assistance within their power."

In another section of the West the close of the year 1779 and the beginning of 1780 were notable months, for in the depth of the winter, pioneers under the direction of James Robertson began permanent settlements in the valley of the Cumberland. During the preceding ten years Watauga and adjacent settlements had prospered and increased in strength through immigration in spite of recurrent attacks by bands of warriors from the Creek, Chickamauga, and Cherokee tribes. These onsets were returned in kind by the borderers under such leaders as John Sevier, Evan Shelby, and William Campbell.[3]

---

[1] *Ibid.*, 4 CC 28. These six stations on Beargrass Creek had at the time six hundred men in their population.

[2] *Clark Papers*, Missouri Historical Society (St. Louis).

[3] For an extended account of these attacks, see Roosevelt, *The Winning of the West*, II, 295–323.

Playing a foremost part as military and civil leader, Robertson had likewise been notably successful in preserving peace with the Indians through his visits to the tribes. While serving as Indian agent for North Carolina, he was induced at the close of 1778 to accept the proposals of Judge Henderson for promoting colonization in the Cumberland Valley, which he believed lay within the bounds of North Carolina and was a part of the Transylvania purchase, a region which had become known through reports of hunters and explorers for its rich bottoms and choice springs. Early in February, 1779, Robertson, with eight companions, struck out along the Wilderness Road and through the wilderness of the Southwest to the great bend in the Cumberland River where they were to plant corn in preparation for the coming of the main body of emigrants. Selecting a site near the French Lick, where Nashville now stands, they built a few cabins. Here they were joined by Kasper Mansker and a company of hunters. Leaving three of their number to keep the "buffaloes out of the corn," the others returned to their homes in order to bring out their families and other settlers. Before returning to Watauga Robertson journeyed to Vincennes, with the object of conferring with Clark, who had entered, in the Virginia land office, in his own name, several thousand acres of land at the French Lick. They agreed that if this area should belong to Virginia—for the boundary had not been run— cabin rights should be procured from Clark. The following spring, however, surveyors established the line, which showed that the spot selected was within the bounds of North Carolina. Before returning Robertson purchased some "mares and tough pony horses" which he took with him to the Watauga settlements.

Late in the fall, 1779, two parties set out from the Holston for the "new settlement." Robertson led a company of men which reached the French Lick on Christmas Day. On New Year's Day they crossed the river on the ice to the spot where the cabins had been built. Other pioneers joined them, a few of them accompanied by their families. One man succeeded in bringing out twenty-one cattle and seventeen horses. The settlements on both sides of the river—for some of the newcomers remained on the east side—soon contained two hundred persons.

It was agreed that the second body of immigrants, under the direction of Captain John Donelson, whose daughter Rachel was to become the wife of Andrew Jackson, should make the trip by boat down the Holston River, the Tennessee, and up the Ohio and the Cumberland to the French Lick, a journey of nearly 900 miles. Setting out from Fort Patrick Henry on December 22, this flotilla, after it was joined by a number of other boats, consisted of some thirty flat-boats, dugouts, and canoes. These boats carried some two hundred persons comprising the immigrants and the families of the Robertson party. The expedition was not unlike many others of the period, but interest in it is enhanced because of the journal kept by Donelson in which he narrates a story of heroism descriptive of the dangers encountered and courage shown by these men and women conquerors of the wilderness during the four months required to reach their destination.[1]

Little advance was made, because of falling water and frosts, before the close of February, when they left the mouth of Cloud Creek. For an afternoon and a night the "Adventure," the flag ship of the expedition, lay on a shoal until a fortunate rise of the water floated it off. Another boat was driven by the current to the point of an island and sunk. The crew having been rescued, the boat was

---

[1] A. W. Putnam, *History of Middle Tennessee* (Nashville, 1857), pp. 69 ff.; J. G. M. Ramsey, *Annals of Tennessee* (Charleston, 1853), pp. 197 ff.

raised and bailed out and most of the cargo was recovered. They encountered their greatest dangers on reaching the Chickamauga Indian towns on the Tennessee River. At one of these villages the Indians showed signs of friendship, and two men set out in a canoe to go on shore. Having gone but a short distance they were met by a half-breed and some companions and were advised to put back. Several canoes filled with Indians then came out to the boats. The presents they received seemed to please the Indians, but while they were being distributed the whites observed a number of canoes approaching from the opposite side loaded with armed warriors painted red and black. Following the advice of the half-breed, the flotilla moved off at once and finally escaped its armed pursuers. Within a short time, believing all danger past, they approached another town. To protect themselves, having refused the invitation to land, the boats were driven too near the opposite shore and were fired on by Indians in ambush. One man was mortally wounded.

One of the boats, containing twenty-eight persons, was by mutual agreement some distance in the rear, for small-pox had broken out among her passengers. Defenseless when attacked by the Indians, they were all killed or captured. Retribution quickly followed, for the disease spread and made havoc among the Creek and Cherokee of that region. While passing through the narrows formed by Cumberland Mountain, Indians appeared on the heights and opened fire on the boats directly below them. Four persons were slightly wounded.

On the twelfth of March, arriving at the now famous Muscle Shoals, new fears were aroused among those unused to such navigation. "The water being high," Donelson wrote, "made a terrible roaring which could be heard at some distance among the drift-wood heaped frightfully upon the points of the islands, the current running in every possible direction. Here we did not know how soon we should be dashed to pieces. . . . . Our boats frequently dragged on the bottom, and appeared constantly in danger of striking." After three hours, having passed safely over the shoals, they encamped for the night.

A week later, arriving at the mouth of the Tennessee, they found the water in the Ohio high and the current rapid. The boat crews were exhausted from hunger and fatigue, for their provisions were almost gone. Here some of the boats departed for Natchez; others, for the Illinois Country; while the remainder, after two days of extreme labor on the part of their crews in stemming the current, arrived at the mouth of the Cumberland, and proceeding a short distance upstream, encamped for the night. A small square-sail placed in the bow of the Adventure gave much-needed assistance to the crew. They were without bread, but their hunters procured enough buffalo meat, which, though poor, kept them from starving. The only entry in the journal for one day was the following: "Set out again; killed a swan, which was very delicious." Herbs were gathered from which they made what they named "Shawnee salad." On the last day of March they were much rejoiced at meeting Colonel Henderson, who was engaged in running the line between Virginia and North Carolina. He assured them that a supply of corn which he had purchased was to be shipped from the falls of the Ohio to the Cumberland settlement. So slowly did they advance that three weeks more were consumed before they arrived at the settlement, where they were welcomed by Robertson and his companions (April 24).

Settlers in the stations on both sides of the Cumberland and at the French Lick suffered greatly from hunger and cold, but partial relief was afforded through the arrival of the supply of corn purchased by Judge Henderson. Nash-borough, built on the bluff under the direction of Robert-son, was regarded as the central post and place for general meetings.

As there were at first no signs of Indians, since the country belonged to no individual tribe, many settlers, disregarding the warnings of Robertson, quit the stockades and erected cabins on their own special claims. During April wandering bands of Delawares, Choctaw, and Chickasaw shot two or three men, whereupon the others hastened to take refuge within the defenses.

The first of May (1780) was notable, for on that day representatives from the eight stations met at Nashborough, and under guidance from Robertson and Henderson entered into a compact of government to "restrain the licentious and supply the blessings flowing from a just and equitable government." On May 13, after several important changes were made in the articles, 256 men ratified the work of their delegates by signing this document, which marked the inauguration of a pure democracy. By the terms of this association, affairs of the community were to be administered by a court of twelve judges, or "triers," who were to be elected within the eight stations by the freemen twenty-one years of age and over.[1]

Whenever the freemen of a station became dissatisfied with their judges they were empowered to call a new election for choosing others. Among other provisions, the court was given jurisdiction in cases arising over titles to land and for the recovery of debts or damages. In a suit where the debt or damage did not exceed $100, three of the judges might constitute a court; but for a larger sum,

---

[1] Three of these judges were to be elected by the settlers of Nashborough; two each by Mansker's and Bledsoe's, and one each by the other stations. The compact is given in Putnam, *Middle Tennessee*, pp. 94–100.

appeal might be made to the whole court. Decisions of the court were executed by persons whom they appointed.

The court had power also to punish all offenses against the peace of the community and all criminal acts, providing the enforcement of the decision did not affect the life of the criminal. A person accused of crime who was considered dangerous to the state was to be bound and sent under guard to some court having jurisdiction in such cases. Militia officers elected in the stations were empowered to call out the militia for protection and to inflict a fine on any who disobeyed their orders. Robertson was elected colonel and commander-in-chief of the military forces and also served as chairman of the committee of twelve judges.

The general assembly of North Carolina was petitioned to take these settlements under their protection and erect them into a county.[1] Judge Henderson, claiming control of the land under the Cherokee deed, opened a land office and disposed of land to the settlers at the rate of ten dollars for each 1,000 acres. Certificates were issued to the purchasers which were to be paid for when Henderson's claim was established. But the Transylvania Company was never able to secure a satisfactory title, and three years later North Carolina declared their purchase void.[2] Settlers thereafter procured their titles from the state in the usual way.

Returning to Clark we find that the year 1780 was the most significant of his career. At no time did he demonstrate in more varied and striking ways his ability as an organizer and leader of men under adverse conditions. Full power was granted him by Governor Jefferson either to en-

---

[1] But this was not accomplished until 1783.

[2] Two hundred thousand acres were then granted the Company in Powell's Valley.

gage in a campaign against Detroit, to lead an expedition against the Shawnee, or to construct a fort at the mouth of the Ohio. He declined to accede to the requests of the Kentuckians for a retaliatory expedition against the Shawnee, and declared to them if they were ready to furnish one thousand men and five months' provisions the capture of Detroit would be assured and that they would then have permanent peace. With the usual promises to pay, he engaged workmen to construct one hundred boats which were to be completed within two months. They were to be used to transport provisions on this expedition.

But to large numbers of the frontiersmen their dangers were immediate and promise of relief in an indefinite future was not satisfying. They interpreted what seemed a disregard of their petitions as further evidence of indifference on the part of Virginia toward their rights. Throughout the summer the desire grew for complete separation from the control of Virginia. The dissatisfaction growing out of the methods by which lands were acquired became more intense. This spirit was expressed as follows: "We have distressing news from Kentucky which is entirely owing to a set of Nabobs in Virginia taking all the lands there by office warrants, & Pre-Emption Rights—Hundreds of families are ruined by it. In short it threatens a loss of that county—Should the English go there and offer them Protection from Indians the greatest part will join—It is a truth that the people There publicly say it—Let the great men say they, who the Land belongs to come & defend it for we will not lift up a gun in Defense of it."[1] Others protested against being taxed while they were engaged in defending the country, and complained that it was dif-

[1] Draper MSS, 46 J59. Letter of Colonel George Morgan to Major Trent, July 24, 1780. Colonel Morgan asked that the members of Congress should be secretly informed of the facts.

ficult to get justice when they were from 600 to 1,000 miles from the seat of government. A memorial setting forth these facts, signed by 672 inhabitants, was presented to Congress, and the request was made that Kentucky and Illinois should be made into a separate state or that their government should be under the control of Congress.[1] Little attention was paid to the request, and Clark, by suppressing this movement, interfered with the success of his own project to establish a post near the mouth of the Ohio.[2] Writing his brother on August 23, 1780, he said: "The partizans in these Cuntries are again Soliciting me to head them as their Governor General as all those from foreign States are for a new Government but my duty obliging me to Suppress all such proceedings I consequently shall loose the Interest of that party."[3]

[1] Date of the petition, May 15, 1780. The petition is printed in Brown, "Kentucky," in the *Filson Club Publications*, VI, 59; also in Roosevelt, *The Winning of the West*, II, 398.

[2] His acts were fully sanctioned by Governor Jefferson, who wrote March 21, 1780: "I approve much of your most active endeavors to apprehend the guilty & put them into a course of trial. . . . . You seem to expect that writings may be found about them which will convict them of treason."

[3] *Clark Papers*, p. 453.

CHAPTER X
Need for Measures of Defense, 1780

TOWARD the end of September, 1779, Clark gave his reasons for locating a fort at the mouth of the Ohio. It would become at once, he thought, the key to the trade of the West, and in protecting this trade he had been forced to station an armed boat so as to command the navigation of both rivers. It would also constitute a post from which the Chickasaw Indians and the English posts on the Mississippi could be controlled. Tories and deserters in large numbers passing down the river might there be apprehended.[1] In 1777 Patrick Henry advocated building a fort at the same spot for the purpose of facilitating intercourse with the Spaniards at New Orleans.[2] Governor Galvez was in complete accord with this proposal, for freedom of trade on the Mississippi would in part make up for the loss of ocean commerce which had been greatly disturbed by British cruisers. At the time, however, the British held, and had fortified, Natchez and Manchac, and thus precluded the descent of American boats. In his secret instructions to Clark, Governor Henry again referred to the establishment of this post, which he

---

[1] Clark to Jefferson, September 23, 1779, *Clark Papers*, p. 364. The French, in 1702, desirous of keeping the English from the Mississippi, built a fort at the mouth of the Ohio. Three years later it was abandoned. Lieutenant-Governor Hamilton planned to build a fort at the same place.

[2] Governor Henry to Governor Galvez, *Archivo General de Indias*, Seville, Estante 87, Cajon 1, legajo 6.

thought might be fortified by the cannon secured at Kaskaskia. The establishment of some such stronghold was necessary, for during the spring (1780) the British were regaining their control over the Indians and were again about to attempt the recapture of the Illinois country.[1] As a check to such an expedition and to furnish a stronghold for the protection of the western country against the encroachments of the Spaniards, Clark and Todd agreed to concentrate troops at a fort to be built at the mouth of the Ohio.[2] The regular force available for defense of the several posts was not over 150 men. Owing to a failure of the crops the Illinois towns were no longer able to furnish supplies.

Moreover, the French, whose stock of provisions was depleted, chafed under the exactions of military officials. "It gives me great uneasiness," said the commissary-general at Kaskaskia, "to find the inhabitants put so little faith in Government that they even refuse the few soldiers who are here the necessary supplies of life, but I beg of you with advise of the court to furnish them with provision from day to day, otherwise you may rely on their taking it wheresoever they find it without the least respect to the owners and in my opinion will be justified in so doing."[3]

There was no hope of succor from Virginia. In his letter directing the establishment of the post at the mouth

[1] Clark to Harrison, October 18, 1782. "They Claime Fort Jefferson for being the Cause of the war between us but its notorious they had done a great deal of mischief for two years before and the building that post Actually Stopt a formidable Expedition Intended against the frontiers by them and their allies." *Clark Papers*, 1781–83, ed. James, *Ill. Hist. Colls.* (Springfield, 1926), XIX, 136.

[2] Clark to Todd, March, 1780: "I am not Clear but the Spaniards would fondly Suffer their Settlements in the Illinois to fall with ours for the sake of having the opertunity of Retaking Both. I doubt they are too fond [of] Territory to think of Restoring it again." *Clark Papers*, p. 404.

[3] William Shannon to Cerré, judge of the court, May 28, 1780, Shannon, *Orderly Book*, Virginia State Archives.

of the Ohio Jefferson wrote as follows: "The less you depend for supplies from this quarter the less will you be disappointed by those impediments which distance and a precarious foreign Commerce throws in the way for these reasons it will be eligible to withdraw as many of your men as you can from the West side of the Ohio leaving only so many as may be necessary for keeping the Illinois Settlements in Spirits."[1] His reasons for establishing a post at the mouth of the Ohio were: that it would facilitate trade with the Illinois and be near enough to furnish aid to that territory; that this fort, together with others to be established on the Ohio, would furnish a chain of defense for the western frontier and at the same time protect the trade with New Orleans. Commissioners, in keeping with an order from the Virginia Council, recommended that forts should be built at the mouths of the Guyandotte, Big Sandy, and Licking rivers, and one in Powell's Valley which should command the eastern end of the Wilderness Road.[2]

On April 14 Clark set out from Louisville for the purpose of building a fort which, after three weeks spent in exploration, was finally located 5 miles below the mouth of the Ohio, at the "Iron Banks," and was named Fort Jefferson.[3] Settlers were attracted to this location through the promise of 400 acres of land to each family at a price to be fixed by the general assembly.[4]

[1] Draper MSS, 29 J 8.   [2] *Frontier Retreat*, p. 51.

[3] Land on the south bank of the Ohio would doubtless have been selected had it not been subject to inundation. Clark proposed "banking them out as at New Orleans." But the arguments against such an undertaking were that it would prove expensive, that unusual floods might destroy the works, and the possibility that the enemy might, by cutting the levee, let in the water.

[4] This measure was recommended by Clark and adopted by Todd in order to secure men to assist in the building and in supplying food for the garrison. Clark to Todd, March, 1780; Todd to Jefferson, June 2, 1780, *Clark Papers*, p. 422.

The troops were withdrawn from Vincennes, and Fort Patrick Henry was garrisoned only by a company of French militia under Major Bosseron. Orders were sent Colonel Montgomery to retire most of the troops from the Illinois villages. But before the evacuation actually took place it was learned that an attack by the British was imminent. With the series of events thus introduced Clark was forced to forego the expedition to Detroit.

During the winter and spring of 1780 British authorities were engaged in carrying out a comprehensive plan for the conquest of the West, the only project by them for this purpose during the entire war which gave promise of complete success. This contemplated the capture of the Illinois country and the falls of the Ohio. Forts Pitt and Cumberland were then to be secured and garrisoned, and thus all communication between the East and the West would be entirely severed. Large numbers of British rangers and Indians would then be free to take part in the war on the Atlantic Coast. Attacks were also to be made on New Orleans and other Spanish posts on the Mississippi. To carry out this plan four simultaneous movements of forces were projected. Captain Charles Langlade, with a chosen band of Indians and Canadians, was directed to proceed from "Chicago and make his attack by the Illinois River."[1] Another party was ordered to "watch Vincennes and the other French posts. A much more formidable expedition was sent under Captain Henry Bird to "amuse" Clark at the falls of the Ohio.[2] Major DePeyster, governor at Detroit, lavished large sums upon the tribes which he assembled in order to satisfy their ever growing demands as rewards for their assistance. Eighty-four thousand thirty-five pounds sterling was declared, in the sharp reproof by

[1] *Wis. Hist. Colls.*, XI, 151.
[2] *Mich. Pioneer and Hist. Colls.*, X, 395.

General Haldimand, to be an "amazing sum" for this "overindulgence" of the Indians.

But immigrants were pouring into Kentucky in such numbers as to excite the apprehensions of the Detroit officials. On May 17 De Peyster wrote: "The Delawares and Shawnees are however daily bringing in Scalps and Prisoners . . . . those unhappy people being part of the one thousand families who to shun the oppression of Congress are on their way to possess the country of Kentucky where if they are allowed quietly to settle, they will soon become formidable both to the Indians & to the Posts."[1] So terrible was the havoc wrought by these scouting parties upon the defenseless families scattered through the woods of Kentucky that petitions from various communities were sent to Clark asking that he come to the rescue lest the whole country should become a "mere scene of carnage and Desolation." "If you could Assist us in that peticular," they said, and "Honour our interprize with your Presence and Command you would have the Consolation of redeeming from Destruction a Scattered divided and Defenceless People who have no other Probable source of defence but through your means."

But the contest for the control of the Mississippi was the salient feature of the plan. While British leaders since the early months of the war were partially aware of the attitude of Spain toward the colonists, they waited for some overt act.[2] "Though I have no doubt this minute of

<hr />

[1] *Mich. Pioneer and Hist. Colls.*, X, 396. De Peyster was commended for his foresight by General Haldimand (see *ibid.*, IX, 635).

[2] General Carleton, as early as October, 1776, was advised by Rocheblave of the correspondence between the colonists and the Spanish governor at New Orleans. Carleton urged Hamilton that care should be taken that nothing be pursued which may have a tendency to create a breach between the nations; that the Spanish side of the Mississippi must be respected upon all occasions (*ibid.*, IX, 344). Lieutenant-Governor Hamilton, February 13, 1779, wrote

the existance of a Spanish as well as a French war," Lieutenant-Governor Hamilton wrote on January 24, 1779, "yet I have, as yet, no accounts by which I may venture to act on the offensive against the subjects of Spain, which I ardently desire, as there would be so little difficulty of pushing them entirely out of the Mississippi." Three weeks later he wrote Governor Galvez protesting against the sale of gunpowder to the Rebels, and orders were to be enforced for intercepting at Natchez all supplies for Americans which were being sent up the river from New Orleans.

With Spain the prize ultimately sought was, not the trade of the Mississippi alone, so generously proffered by Governor Henry, but the possession of the entire valley. With this object in view, although it was not specifically stated, a treaty between France and Spain was agreed upon April 12, 1779.[1] The formal declaration of war against Great Britain quickly followed, and in July of that year Governor Galvez was authorized to attack Natchez and other British posts on the east bank of the Mississippi. "By beat of drum" on August 20 the independence of the American states was proclaimed at New Orleans.

On June 17, the day following the declaration of war by Spain, Lord George Germaine directed General Haldimand to order hostilities to begin immediately with an attack on New Orleans and other Spanish posts on the

---

Governor Galvez expressing a hope that the commerce in gunpowder with the Rebels would be prohibited. *Canadian Archives* (1882), p. 25. Captain Bloomer was stationed at Natchez engaged in intercepting supplies sent the American posts from New Orleans (*ibid.*, p. 26).

[1] The Spanish objects in entering the war as specified in the treaty were: to regain Gibraltar, acquire the river and fort of Mobile, Pensacola, and all the coast of Florida along the Bahama Channel, the expulsion of the English from the Bay of Honduras, and the restitution of the island of Minorca. F. A. Ogg, *The Opening of the Mississippi* (New York, 1904), p. 368, note 2.

river.[1] General John Campbell was ordered to proceed up the Mississippi to Natchez with an army and fleet. He was there to be joined by a force from the north, which was to capture St. Louis en route.

In spite of an adverse decision by his council, Governor Galvez determined, on his own authority, to attack at once the British posts.[2] He marshaled a force of 1,430 men made up of regular troops, militia, Indians, and volunteers, among the last being Oliver Pollock and nine other Americans. Although he was poorly equipped for offensive operations, Galvez led his force against Fort Bute at Manchac and captured it on September 8. Baton Rouge, a strongly fortified post, was the next object of attack. By clever strategy the Spaniards gained an advantage which led to a capitulation, September 21. Not only did they gain possession of this post with its five hundred defenders and thirteen pieces of heavy artillery, but the terms of surrender also included Natchez, 130 miles up the river. Galvez, returning to New Orleans made active preparations for an expedition against Mobile. Because of his successes no difficulties were encountered in securing a force of two thousand men, with which he set sail early in February, 1780. Mobile was surrendered without the necessity of an assault.

During the progress of these events General Campbell, with his army numbering less than one thousand men, one-third at least being made up of Pennsylvania and Maryland Loyalists, remained at Pensacola, seemingly making little effort to carry out the orders of his government, although it has been claimed that the vessels at his disposal were sufficient to carry only 250 men. Galvez

---

[1] Sinclair to Brehm, February 15, 1780, *Wis. Hist. Colls.*, XI, 145, 147.

[2] Gayarré, *History of Louisiana*, III, 122. The council recommended preparation for defense only.

made every preparation during the remainder of the year to go against this strongly fortified and well-garrisoned post. Under adverse circumstances he succeeded in marshaling a land force estimated at four thousand French and Spaniards. This army, in co-operation with the fleet, began a bombardment of Pensacola early in March, 1781, which continued with intermissions until May 9, when the capitulation occurred, "further resistance," as General Campbell said, on the part of his "handfull of gallant and intrepid officers and men" being impossible against "the multitude of foes."[1] With the surrender of Pensacola the province of West Florida also became a Spanish possession.

Meantime the British authorities at Michilimackinac and Detroit lost no time in carrying out their orders. A war party of Indians was dispatched by Lieutenant-Governor Patrick Sinclair of Michilimackinac to enlist the services of Wabasha, illustrious chief of the Sioux, who was attached to the British interests and could at the time muster two hundred warriors from his tribe.[2] Wabasha was to proceed with all dispatch as far down the river as Natchez, there to join General Campbell, having made as many intermediate attacks as possible.

Sinclair intrusted the command of an expedition against the Spanish and Illinois country—the conquest of which

[1] W. H. Siebert, "The Loyalists in West Florida," *Miss. Valley Hist. Assoc. Proc.*, VIII, 115.

[2] The Sioux were selected, for they were, as stated by Sinclair, "undebauched addicted to War, & Jealously attached to His Majesty's Interest" (*Wis. Hist. Colls.*, XI, 147). It is evident, according to Sinclair, then, that the surrender of Hamilton was having a telling effect on Indian constancy. He wrote February 15, 1780: "Lieut. Govr. Hamiltons disaster has nothing in it to make the Scioux and other nations far to the Westward, even to recollect the circumstance, many of them never heard of it" (*ibid.*, p. 144). Toward the close of 1779 the British secured the title to Mackinac Island from a Chippewa chief. During the winter work on the fort and stockade on the island went forward.

would be an easy task, as he believed—to a trader, Emanuel Hesse. On February 15, 1780, Captain Hesse was ordered to assemble for that purpose, at the portage of the Fox and Wisconsin rivers, the Menominee, Sauk, Foxes, and Winnebago. Accompanied by these Indians, and with a plentiful stock of provisions, Hesse descended the Wisconsin to the Mississippi, where he was joined by Matchikuis and his Ottawa braves.[1] To this chieftain, flattered with the title of general and with the privilege of wearing the scarlet coat and epauletts of the British, was given the chief command of the Indians.[2]

On May 2 the entire force, consisting of some 950 traders, servants, and Indians, set out on their 500 mile voyage for the attack on the Spanish and Illinois country.[3] While awaiting the Indian detachments at Prairie du Chien an armed boat from St. Louis with thirteen men was taken. An expedition dispatched to the lead mines succeeded in capturing seventeen prisoners and large quantities of supplies, and prevented the shipment of fifty tons of lead ore.[4] Various motives were adduced to stir up enthusiasm for the expedition. The northern Indians were incited through the opportunity thus offered to fall on their hereditary foes, the Illinois tribes.[5] Traders who should aid in

[1] *Wis. Hist. Colls.*, III, 232.

[2] Matchikuis it was, who, in 1763, surprised Michilimackinac. Under pretense of playing, he kicked a ball over the fort pickets, rushed in with his band, with arms concealed, and accomplished his purpose (*ibid.*, p. 224).

[3] *Wis. Hist. Colls.*, XI, 151. The number is based on the statement of Governor Sinclair that there were 750. With the 200 Sioux already mentioned, the entire force was probably about 950. The Spaniards estimated 300 regular troops and 900 savages (*ibid.*, XVIII, 416, 407). The force has been estimated also to consist of 1,500. Reported conversation between Benjamin Drake and William Clark. Draper MSS, 34 J 35.

[4] *Wis. Hist. Colls.*, XI, 151.

[5] Sinclair to Haldimand, *ibid.*, p. 151; *ibid.*, III, 150, 154, 157.

securing the Spanish posts were to be given the exclusive right to the Missouri trade for the ensuing winter.[1]

St. Louis was a town of 120 houses, chiefly of stone, and contained a population of about eight hundred, the majority of whom were French.[2] It was the capital of upper Louisiana and was in a flourishing condition due to the fact that it was a leading center for the fur trade. A number of villages on the Missouri and the Mississippi, such as Carondelet, St. Charles, and St. Ferdinand, had been settled from this center. The Spanish garrison consisted of fifty men under the command of Captain de Leyba.

The Americans at the beginning of the war were scarcely aware of the existence of such a village. They were ignorant of its location, as is manifest from the following incident. George Morgan in a letter of inquiry to Governor Henry early in the year 1777, wrote: "The County Lieutenant who is order'd to send 100 Men to meet Cap[t] Lynn with the Powder, is at a loss to know how far to proceed or where St. Louis on the Mississippi is—There being one place of that name 160 Miles above the mouth of Ohio—and no settlement or Fort less than 400 Miles below the Ohio. The nearest is at the River Arkansa."[3] In the absence of the Governor, John Page, acting governor, answered with splendid official agreeableness: "We are as much at a loss to know where St. Louis is, as you can be, but suppose it to be where you mention."[4]

[1] *Wis. Hist. Colls.*, XI, 152.

[2] The name by which St. Louis had been known among the inhabitants for years was "Pancore," abbreviated from Pain Court," meaning "without bread." Draper MSS, 8 J 55.

[3] Morgan, *Letter Book*, April 1, 1777, Vol. I. Upon the return of Captain Gibson to Virginia orders were issued that assistance should be sent to Lieutenant Linn. Linn did not meet this company, however, and succeeded in the enterprise as before indicated. For the orders, see *Rev. on the Upper Ohio*, pp. 226 ff.

[4] April 15, 1777. *Ibid.*, p. 248.

St. Louis was really discovered to the Americans by George Rogers Clark. It is not improbable, therefore, that Clark, who had intelligence early in 1780 of a projected attack on the Illinois country,[1] should have given timely warning to the Spanish commandant.[2] St. Louis was in no condition to offer defense when, at the close of March, it was learned from a trader that a large body of the enemy was descending the Mississippi for an attack.[3] Intrenchments were immediately thrown up, which during the attack were manned by a force consisting of 29 regulars and 281 villagers; orders were sent to the surrounding posts to send assistance;[4] a platform was erected at one end of the town upon which were placed five cannon; scouts were sent out; and cavalrymen were stationed to act as a picket guard. As indicated by the Spanish account,

The enemy arrived May twenty-sixth at one o'clock in the afternoon, and began the attack upon the post from the north side, expecting to meet no opposition; but they found themselves unexpectedly repulsed by the militia which guarded it. A vigorous fire was kept up on both sides, so that by the service done by the cannon on the tower where the aforesaid commander [Captain de Leyba] was, the defenders at least succeeded in keeping off a band of villains who if they had not opportunely been met by this bold opposition on our part would not have left a trace of our settlements. There were also to be heard the confusion and the lamentable cries of the women and children who had been shut up in the house of the commandant, defended by twenty

[1] Old inhabitants always spoke of "the Illinois" as including the settlements about St. Louis and those of Illinois, but it did not include Vincennes. Draper MSS, 8 J 55.

[2] Pierre Prevost, a Kaskaskian, who was engaged in the Indian trade on the upper Mississippi, wrote Clark February 20, 1780, of the efforts which were being made from Mackinac to stir up the Sauk, Fox, and Sioux tribes to make an attack on the "People of the Illinois." *Clark Papers*, p. 394. Governor de Leyba is said to have given no credit to the warning, politely declined all aid, and declared that the Indians were peaceable.

[3] *Mo. Hist. Colls.*, II, 45.

[4] Lieutenant de Cartabona hastened from Ste Genevieve with the local militia under Charles Valle and rendered signal service.

men under the lieutenant of infantry, Don Francisco Cartabona; the dolorous echoes of which seemed to inspire in the besieged an extraordinary valor and spirit, for they urgently demanded to be permitted to make a sally. The enemy at last, seeing that their force was useless against such resistance, scattered about over the country, where they found several farmers who with their slaves were occupied in the labors of the field. If these hungry wolves had contented themselves with destroying the crops, if they had killed all the cattle which they could not take with them, this act would have been looked upon as a consequence of war, but when the learned world shall know that this desperate band slaked their thirst in the blood of innocent victims, and sacrificed to their fury all whom they found, cruelly destroying them and committing the greatest atrocities upon some poor people who had no other arms than those of the good faith in which they lived, the English nation from now on may add to its glorious conquests in the present war that of having barbarously inflicted by the hands of the base instruments of cruelty the most bitter torments which tyranny has invented.[1]

So the Spanish account ends after reciting that the number of the killed and wounded was twenty-nine, and that twenty-four were made prisoners.[2]

In general, this narrative of Spanish zeal and courage satisfies the facts relating to the first repulse. No doubt also evidence existed for the declaration made by Lieutenant-Governor Sinclair, that the defeat was owing to the treachery of Calvé, an interpreter, and Ducharme, a trader who commanded companies of Indians; to the want of secrecy whereby the Spaniards had received timely notice of the projected attack; and to the backwardness of the Canadians.[3] But in addition to these three there was another, and it must be believed more potent, cause

[1] *Wis. Hist. Colls.*, XVIII, 407.

[2] Forty-six others were made prisoners on the Mississippi, according to the same account. According to a British report, seventy persons were killed, thirty-four taken prisoners, and forty-three scalped (see *Wis. Hist. Colls.*, XI, 156). Another report by Sinclair shows sixty-eight killed at St. Louis and eighteen made prisoners. *Mich. Pioneer and Hist. Colls.*, IX, 559.

[3] *Wis. Hist. Colls.*, XI, 154.

for the precipitate retreat which followed and the total defeat of the ultimate objects hoped for by British officials. That was the opportune appearance of Clark, who was supposed to be beyond striking distance at the falls of the Ohio.[1] As indicated, Clark had been engaged since April 18 in constructing a fort at the Iron Banks. Citizens of Cahokia, through Charles Gratiot, hastened to inform him of their alarming situation and urged him to come at once to their relief. "We are on the eve of being attacked," they said, "by considerable parties of savages, and cannot work at the cultivation of our grounds if we have not prompt succor. For this reason we take the liberty of addressing you, having confidence in the kindness and affection you have always manifested for us." With a small body of troops Clark set out May 13, receiving at the mouth of the Ohio other expresses from De Leyba and Colonel Montgomery, also urging his immediate presence. Twenty-four hours after his arrival at Cahokia the attack was begun, a short time after that at St. Louis. After a short skirmish the British withdrew.

The statement has often been made, and as frequently denied, that Clark, before the attack on Cahokia, crossed the river to St. Louis, and that it was his influence which caused the retreat of the British.[2] He claimed for himself

[1] It was known in Detroit by May 17 that Clark had gone to the mouth of the Ohio. Doubtless this was one reason for pushing forward Bird's expedition. *Canadian Archives* (1882), p. 35.

[2] "When Gen. Clark arrived at Coho he was informed that the number of men at St. Louis collected at Kaskaskia and other places was between 300 and 400. He went over to St. Louis to review the troops as well as the works of defence. The Spanish commandant at St. Louis, on the arrival of Clark, offered him the command of both sides; but Clark declined taking the command until he could ascertain where the assault would be made. He continued only about two hours in St. Louis when he returned to Coho" (Stipp, *Western Miscellany*, pp. 54 ff.). This writer prepared his sketches from notes given by General Clark and other pioneers.

Colonel Montgomery, February 22, 1783, said that Clark would have given

and his men the honor of having saved St. Louis and the rest of Louisiana for the Spaniards.[1] It may well be believed that the knowledge that he was in the vicinity caused the Indians to withdraw.

The main body of the attacking force retreated rapidly in two divisions—one by the Mississippi, the other directly across the country to Michilimackinac.[2] Langlade and his force escaped in two vessels and in canoes, thus preventing an attack on them by a force of two hundred Illinois cavalry which arrived at "Chicago five days after his departure." Clark at once organized a force of some 350 regulars, French volunteers from the Illinois posts, and Spaniards of St. Louis, which he sent under Colonel Montgomery against the Sauk and Fox.[3] Proceeding up the Mississippi and the Illinois in boats as far as Peoria, they marched to the Indian villages on Rock River, but the Indians had fled.[4] After burning the towns, Montgomery

the Spaniards assistance had not the strong winds prevented the signals from being heard. *Cal. Va. State Papers*, III, 443. Henry M. Brackenridge visited St. Louis in 1811 and had a good opportunity to learn of events which happened in 1780. He wrote: "In 1779 (1780) a combination of the Indian tribes prompted by the English, attempted a general invasion of the French villages on both sides of the river and accordingly descended in considerable force, but were checked by General Clark, who commanded the American troops on the other side. An attack was, however, made upon a small settlement commenced within a few miles of the town, and the inhabitants were nearly all butchered; others who happened to be out of St. Louis were killed or pursued within a short distance of the town. It is said that upwards of eighty persons fell victims to their fury" (Brackenridge, *Views of Louisiana*, p. 122).

[1] Clark to Genet, February 5, 1793. Draper MSS, 55 J 1.

[2] Sinclair to Haldimand, July 8, *Mo. Hist. Colls.*, II, 48.

[3] Draper MSS, 51 J 97.

[4] The failure of the expedition was attributed by the French to the "lack of management and bad conduct" of the Virginians. They were not in sympathy with the Americans at the time. "Memorial of Cahokians," in Alvord, *Cahokia Records*, p. 541.

returned to his boats. The retreat of 400 miles was accomplished after much suffering due to the almost total lack of provisions.[1]

Early in May, Colonel Henry Bird, accompanied by 150 whites and one thousand Indians, well armed, and with two pieces of light artillery, set out from Detroit. His route was by the way of the Maumee and the Miami rivers to the Ohio. His plan to attack the Americans at the falls was suddenly changed, due in all probability to the fact that he learned that Colonel George Slaughter had arrived from Virginia with reinforcements,[2] and he knew also that the British expeditions had failed. Besides, he feared the return of Clark.[3] Proceeding up the Licking, Bird attacked Ruddle's and Martin's stations, two small stockaded posts. Resistance was hopeless against the British cannon.[4] With no control over his blood-thirsty savages, Bird was unable to carry out the terms of the capitulation. Satisfied with his slight success, and laden with plunder, he set out for Detroit with about one hundred prisoners over the route by which he came.[5] Many of the women and children, unable to bear the strain of the march, were relieved from their sufferings through the use of the tomahawk. The cannon and shells were left at one of the

[1] *Wis. Hist. Colls.*, IX, 291.

[2] Major Slaughter, with one hundred men, was ordered to the falls of the Ohio. Jefferson to Clark, January 29, 1780. Draper MSS, 50 J 7.

[3] State Department Manuscript. Testimony by Knox and H. Marshall before the Board of Commissioners, December 7, 1787. Their information was obtained from Clark and they were themselves in Kentucky at the time of the attack.

[4] Bird's force of Indians was then reduced to eight hundred. Draper MSS, 29 J 25.

[5] Memorandum book of Captain John Dunkin captured at Ruddle's Station, *ibid.*, 29 J 25.

Miami towns, and were shortly afterward buried in order that they might not fall into the hands of the enemy.

Clark, having received intelligence of the British designs under Bird, showed that promptness and energy so characteristic of him at the time. On June 5, with a few men, he set out from Kaskaskia by boat for Fort Jefferson, barely escaping capture on the way.[1] Unmindful of the dangers, he struck off with two companions through the wilderness for Harrodsburg.[2] In order to deceive the lurking bands of savages they disguised themselves as Indians. On approaching the Tennessee River they were discovered by a party of Indians and narrowly escaped capture. They crossed the Tennessee and the Kentucky rivers on rafts which they made by binding logs together with grape vines. Harrodsburg was reached a short time before the news that Ruddle's and Martin's stations were captured by the British.

Clark began at once the organization of a retaliatory expedition. With characteristic decision he ordered the land office closed until he should return from the expedition, and then proceeded to enlist volunteers from the crowd eagerly awaiting the opportunity to get an assignment of land. This order provoked general discontent on the part of speculators, but the call for volunteers was cheerfully met by the people in general, and one thousand men were soon under arms.[3] So eager were they to deal a blow to the Shawnee, who had been their most persistent enemy, that in some cases only the boys and old men and

---

[1] By Indians above the island just above the fort. He found that three men had been murdered near the fort and that two more were missing. Draper MSS, 26 J 14.

[2] Major Josiah Harlan and Captain Herman Consola.

[3] Clark's account of the expedition, August 22, 1780, *Clark Papers*, p. 451.

women were left to guard the stations. The mouth of the Licking was appointed as the place of meeting, and by August 1 all was in readiness. Clark had come up the Ohio with a small company of regulars from the falls. Colonel James Harrod, with a force of two hundred men in canoes and hastily repaired boats, came over the same route. Their food on the way was partially provided through sending out hunting parties. One of these squads, under Captain Hugh McGary, having crossed to the north bank with the hope of finding game more plentiful, was surprised by Indians and a number of whites were killed. Colonel Benjamin Logan, who acted as second in command to Clark on the expedition, led his regiment, which was enlisted at Boonesborough and adjacent towns, across the country to the place of rendezvous. Besides the leaders mentioned there were Boone, Levi Todd, and William McAfee.

When the limited supplies were divided each man received a pound and a half of meal, nine quarts of parched corn, and a small amount of buffalo meat. On the second of August they crossed the river, and leaving a company of forty men to guard the boats, began the march toward Old Chillicothe, the Indian capital. Four days were taken for the march of some 70 miles to this Indian center. Warned of the approach of Clark, the Indians fled, making good their escape. After burning the town and destroying the crops the army pushed on to Piqua, a few miles distant on the Big Miami.[1] This town was composed of well-built log cabins located along the river, each surrounded by a strip of corn. At the lower end of the town was a strong

[1] Clark's account says the town was burned by his order. *Clark Papers*, p. 452. Another account of the expedition says it was burned by the Indians (*ibid.*, p. 497).

blockhouse. Several hundred Indian warriors, aided by Simon Girty and his brother, had collected for its defense.[1] Two divisions of the troops under Colonel Logan were sent to approach the town from above and prevent any escape in that direction. Clark himself, at the head of the two other divisions, forded the river and began a rapid movement toward the lower end of the town. A body of Indians hidden in some woods began the attack and the action quickly became general, with savage fierceness on both sides. The fighting was continuous over the broken plain of a mile and a half to the town. Driven from the wooded elevation, the savages escaped from one field of corn to another until they finally took refuge under the protection of the fort and nearby cabins and waited for the assault. Within half an hour Clark renewed the attack, bringing into use for the first time the small cannon which had been brought on the back of a pack-horse. The rifle shots from the Indians, owing to the distance, were of no effect, whereas their stronghold was shattered by the cannon. At sundown, unable longer to resist the attack, the savages left their fort. In escaping, some of them came so close to Clark's lines that the fighting was renewed at close range. At this time Joseph Rogers, a cousin of Clark's, who for two years had been a prisoner among the Indians, made his escape, and running toward the Americans, shouted to them not to shoot him, for he was a white man.[2] He was mortally wounded, however, and Clark reached

---

[1] Wilson's account says 1,500 warriors, *ibid.*, p. 481. Clark stated that the Indians had been making preparations for ten days; that the day before his arrival there were 300 Shawnee, Mingo, Wyandot, and Delawares; and that several reinforcements arrived during the day.

[2] Joseph Rogers had been a prisoner for two years. December 25, 1776, he was captured when, with John Gabriel Jones, he attempted to bring the powder Clark had hidden while on his way to Kentucky (see Clark's "Diary," 1771–81, *Clark Papers*, p. 20).

his side but a short time before he died. Logan's wing had been delayed so much in crossing the stream that they came upon the scene as the last of the savages retreated. The heaviest loss was on the side of the Indians, and had Logan been present the defeat would have been a decisive one.[1] As it was, this campaign of a month, during which time Clark led his forces 480 miles, had been so effective that the Kentucky settlements were free from serious molestation for the remainder of the year.

No effort was made to pursue the scattered force of the enemy. Without provisions for his troops, Clark gave up his plan to march against the Delaware towns. After the destruction of Piqua, with its cornfields, he returned to the mouth of the Licking and disbanded his army.[2] The return march was marked by the usual suffering incident to frontier campaigns. Their supply of solid food was exhausted, and the short rations of green corn and vegetables alone saved them from starvation.

Evidence points to the fact that Clark's victory over the Shawnee would have been more complete had the Indians not been warned by the French at Vincennes of the advance of the American force. This disaffection from the American cause, due in the main to the exactions of military officers, became more apparent with the coming to the Illinois country, during the summer, of a French officer, Augustin Mottin de la Balme, a friend of La Fayette. During the year 1776, with recommendations from Benjamin Franklin and Silas Deane, he had come to America and offered his services to Congress. The commission, inspector-general of cavalry, which was assigned him proved

---

[1] Clark states that his losses were fourteen killed and thirteen wounded, and that the enemy lost triple that number.

[2] Clark stated that there were 800 acres of corn which had been cultivated by white labor.

unsatisfactory, for he aspired to command a division of the army, and after a few months he resigned his commission.

During June, 1780, he came West, apparently with the authorization of Luzerne, the French minister, to arouse the French to make an attack on Detroit. This was in keeping with the project which had been conceived by Washington and approved by La Fayette and Luzerne, namely to induce the Canadians to join with the Americans and the French in the general effort to win independence.[1]

Arriving at Fort Pitt, he joined Linctot in an appeal to the friendly Indian chiefs, in council, to avert a threatened Indian war. It was the wish of the French King, he urged, that they should, together with the French, adopt the cause of the United States and Spain.[2] Arriving at Vincennes in July, he was enthusiastically welcomed by the French, being "received by the Inhabitants as the Hebrews would receive the Messiah."[3] Here and at Kaskaskia and Cahokia he won their support through the promise of assistance from France. In recognition of their antagonism toward the Virginians he declared that the troops of that colony had carried out the western expedition in spite of the protests of the United Colonies, which were in alliance with France and Spain.[4] While keeping aloof from the Americans, he attempted to gain the favor of the French for the expedition against Detroit, which, as he said, "will win the confidence of the honorable Congress

---

[1] For this plan, see *Washington's Writings*, ed. Sparks, VIII, 44, 72. Evidence on La Balme is presented in *Cahokia Records*, Introduction, p. lxxxix. It has been suggested that this expedition was undertaken for the purpose of giving France control in the trans-Alleghany country as a part of the plan to regain their colonial possessions in America. See Turner, "Policy of France towards the Mississippi Valley," *Amer. Hist. Rev.*, X, 255.

[2] In his report to Luzerne he claimed that the Indians had promised complete obedience to the French. *Kaskaskia Records*, pp. 163–68.

[3] *Ibid.*, p. 196.   [4] *Ibid.*, p. 182.

and convince the King of France of the real interest which you take in a cause for which he has already made great sacrifices and which will procure for you in a little while all imaginable assistance from him."[1]

With difficulty La Balme enlisted a small company of some eighty French and Indians, and in October, following the French flag, they set out for Detroit. The Miami post, on the site of Fort Wayne, was captured and plundered. A few days later the traders and Indians, rallying, attacked the expedition and dispersed it. La Balme and a number of his associates were killed. Another detachment which he had sent from Cahokia captured St. Joseph, a trading-post, having a population of forty-eight.[2] On their return march they were overtaken near Chicago by a company of traders and Indians, and all but three were killed or made captive.[3] This outcome went far toward destroying French influence over the Indians, and for a time restored English prestige which had been lost through the capture of Hamilton.

During Clark's absence Fort Jefferson had been attacked by a force of Chickasaw and Choctaw warriors led by Colbert, a Scotchman. The erection of the fort and village was merely another cause for the hatred of the Indians for the whites who were continuously encroaching upon their hunting grounds.[4] Besides, the instructions of Governor Jefferson that the site for the fort should be purchased had for some cause been disregarded.[5] The at-

---

[1] *Kaskaskia Records*, p. xcii.

[2] Located near the site of Niles, Michigan.

[3] *Mich. Pioneer and Hist. Colls.*, XIX, 592.

[4] The village was named Clarksville. Trustees were elected and they petitioned for a separate county government. *Clark Papers*, 1771–81, p. 425.

[5] Jefferson to Major Martin, Indian agent, January 24, 1780. *Clark Papers*, p. 385. "But the ground at the Mouth of Ohio in the South side belonging to the Cherokees we would not meddle with it without their leave." Martin was

tack continued six days and nights, and during this time savage onslaughts were met with a courage born of desperation. Not more than one-half of the garrison of thirty men under Captain Robert George were fit for service on account of sickness. Their supplies of food, water, and ammunition were almost exhausted when the Indians withdrew. Within a few hours reinforcements which had been sent from Kaskaskia in response to an appeal arrived.

Sickness was prevalent among the inhabitants of the village, and many died; their crops were destroyed, and their stock lost. A few only could be induced to remain at the settlement, some of them going down the river and others to the Illinois country, an event of importance, for it marks the coming of the first considerable group of American settlers to Illinois.[1]

The year 1780 was likewise a critical year for the settlements on the Cumberland. Indian bands, jealous of the encroachments of white hunters, early made their appearance and drove outlying settlers to the protection of the stockades. These attacks were continuous throughout the year.[2]

The successes of British leaders in the South during the summer of 1780 threatened to offset the effects of Clark's

---

authorized to secure goods from New Orleans amounting to 3,000 pounds sterling with which to purchase the land.

[1] James Piggott was one of the trustees at Clarksville, but was not in command at the time of the siege, as has frequently been stated. It is said that because of the petition to Governor St. Clair, in 1790, signed by Piggott and four other residents of Piggott's Fort at Grand Ruisseau, Congress passed the act granting to every settler on the public land in Illinois 400 acres and a militia grant of 100 acres to every man enrolled in the militia of that year. John Reynolds, *My Own Times* (1855), 59 (see Alvord, *Cahokia Records*, p. 190, n. 1, for an account of his earlier career).

[2] For an account of these hostilities, see Roosevelt, *The Winning of the West* II, 348 ff.

drive against the Shawnee, and likewise endangered American control over Kentucky and Tennessee. Georgia had been reconquered during the previous year, and with the capture of Charleston in May, 1780, and the total defeat of General Horatio Gates at the battle of Camden, August 16, South Carolina was also reduced to submission. Cornwallis then proceeded northward with his main army, gaining accessions to his force from Tory militia and bands of Creek and Cherokee warriors.

The task of crushing out any' remaining rebellious tendencies and of recruiting the Loyalists, mainly Highland Scotch, of Georgia and the back country of South Carolina was intrusted to Major Patrick Ferguson, a Scotchman. He had won a notable reputation as an able partizan leader and frontier fighter. The terror of his name was general throughout the back country. Loyalist militia in large numbers responded to his call. Moving rapidly, he succeeded in bringing South Carolina and large parts of North Carolina under British control. Their leaders were confident of the early conquest of Virginia.

From the eastern base of the Blue Ridge Mountains, Ferguson sent a message to the "Back-water Men" warning them that if they did not cease their hostilities he would cross the mountains, hang the leaders, and destroy their settlements with fire. Far from being frightened at such a threat, Isaac Shelby, who was the first leader to read it, rode with all haste from the Holston to Watauga in order to consult John Sevier. Preparations were being made for a barbecue and horse race, but drawing aside from the crowd of merrymakers the two leaders agreed to Shelby's plan for uniting the western forces and making an attack on Ferguson.[1]

[1] The best extended account of the following events is to be found in Lyman C. Draper, *King's Mountain and Its Heroes.*

Their troops, together with four hundred Virginia rifle-men from the Holston under Colonel William Campbell, and the refugees of Colonel Charles McDowell's force which had been driven across the mountains, mustered at Sycamore Shoals on the Watauga on the morning of September 26. They numbered a thousand men mounted on wiry horses. Their uniforms consisted of long loose hunting-shirts girded at the waist with a beaded belt, breeches, leggings, and moccasins. On their coon-skin caps were fastened buck-tails or sprigs of evergreen. Each carried a spiral grooved rifle having a barrel some 30 inches long. "With the sword of the Lord and of Gideon," an invocation uttered by their preacher, still ringing in their ears, they set out over the mountains to smite the enemy whenever they should come upon him.[1]

They were joined by a force of 350 North Carolina militia under Colonel Benjamin Cleveland, a well-known Indian fighter who, because of the mistreatment of his foes, was known as one of the most brutal of frontier leaders. Without executive authority for the expedition and with no single commanding officer, it was determined to forget all personal rivalries by adopting the suggestion of Shelby that to Colonel Campbell of Virginia should be given the chief command, since the four other leaders were North Carolinians.

Living chiefly on ears of corn which they stripped from the fields, Campbell, with his followers augmented to between fifteen and eighteen hundred, pressed forward on the heels of Ferguson, who had been warned of their approach and was marching to join Cornwallis at Charlotte, North Carolina. Ferguson's army probably did not exceed eleven hundred men. Messengers were dispatched to Cornwallis for reinforcements. On the evening of October 6 he

[1] For the advance of the Backwater men, see *ibid.*, pp. 216 ff.

reached King's Mountain, about a mile and a half south of the North Carolina line and some thirty-five miles from Charlotte, where Cornwallis was encamped. On a table land at the summit of this plateau, 600 yards long and from 60 to 120 yards wide on the summit, rising some 60 feet above the surrounding country, he pitched his camp to await the coming of reinforcements. His position was well protected from an enemy by the dense forests on the sides of the ridge and the rocks on top.

Meantime the frontiersmen had reached the Cowpens, where they learned of Ferguson's route and his plans. In a council of the officers it was decided to push forward with a force consisting of the best mounted and best armed troops and attack Ferguson before his reinforcements should arrive. A force of nine hundred men set off in the rain at night, leaving the others to follow as rapidly as possible.

Having reached the forest at the base of the hill, they dismounted and crept up the ascent under protection of the trees. The numbers of men constituting the two forces were about equal.[1] The American approach was not discovered until they were within a quarter of a mile of the British outposts, but with remarkable energy and skill Ferguson formed his troops in battle array before the attack was actually begun. The battle was one of the most desperate encounters of the whole war. With hundreds of his men dead or disabled, Ferguson, in attempting to break through the American line with some of his officers, was killed. The survivors, led by De Peyster, continued the hopeless conflict for a brief period but were forced to surrender.

King's Mountain may be regarded as one of the decisive battles of the Revolution. The Loyalist spirit in the

[1] Draper, *King's Mountain*, p. 238.

Carolinas was crushed. Patriot zeal, which languished after the defeat of Gates, was renewed, and the victory was fatal to the expedition of Cornwallis. The tide of the war in the South was turned.

Returning farther West, we find that early in January, 1781, St. Joseph, which was regarded as a British post of importance, was captured by an expedition sent against it from St. Louis.[1] One of the objectives of Spain in entering the war, as we have seen, was to secure for herself the territory east of the Mississippi River. This desire was not unknown to Americans, for Clark had urged the construction of a fort at the mouth of the Ohio as protection against the encroachments of the Spaniards.

It seems evident, however, that Francisco Cruzat, Spanish governor at St. Louis, who was responsible for the expedition against St. Joseph, undertook it primarily as a retaliatory stroke against the British, for plans were then under way for another attack on St. Louis in 1781.[2] In proposing such an expedition in the depth of winter Governor Cruzat was influenced no doubt by the example of Clark in his march against Vincennes, and was spurred to action also by the successes of Governor Galvez.

Captain Don Eugène Pourée, in command of the detachment consisting of fifty militiamen from St. Louis, a dozen more from Cahokia, and sixty Indians, proceeded by boat up the Illinois River until their advance was pre-

---

[1] Clark planned to capture this post in September, 1779, on account of the stores deposited there, which were used to keep the friendship of the Indians. Volunteers could not be secured for the expedition, it was claimed, on account of the lack of shoes for the troops. *Clark Papers*, p. 366.

[2] Frederick J. Teggart, "The Capture of St. Joseph, Michigan, by the Spaniards in 1781," *Mo. Hist. Rev.*, V, 214–28; C. W. Alvord, "The Conquest of St. Joseph, Michigan, by the Spaniards in 1781," *Mo. Hist. Rev.*, II, 195–210. Professor Alvord maintains that the attack on St. Joseph was undertaken by Cahokians with some assistance from St. Louis to avenge the loss of their friends in the La Balme expedition.

vented by the ice. They then marched overland to St. Joseph. Having gained the neutrality of the Potawatomi Indians at the post through the promise that one-half the booty should be theirs, the surprise attack was begun at daybreak and the post was immediately surrendered. For a period of twenty-four hours the Spaniards were in possession, but fearing a counter-attack by the English, they set out for St. Louis. Before retiring, Pourée and his officers drew up a document taking possession, by right of conquest in the name of the King of Spain, of St. Joseph and its dependencies and of the rivers St. Joseph and Illinois."[1] The expedition was highly commended by the King, and the officers taking part were advanced in rank. In the negotiations at Paris the following year this "conquest" was made the basis for claims to territory north of the Ohio.

The policy of Spain toward the trans-Alleghany region has already been defined.[2] The terms of a possible treaty with that nation drawn up by Congress September 17, 1779, provided, in the event that Spain should continue to be active in the war against Great Britain, that the King of Spain should not be precluded from regaining the Floridas. To the United States was to be granted the right to the free navigation of the Mississippi River, "into and from the Sea."[3] John Jay, who at the time was serving as president of Congress, was selected as minister plenipotentiary to carry on negotiations with Spain. These provisions were made a part of Jay's instructions, and he was also particularly to endeavor to obtain some convenient fort or forts below the thirty-first degree of north latitude, on the river Mississippi, for all merchant vessels, goods, wares, and merchandises belonging to the inhabitants of these states. The distressed state of our finances and the great depreciation of our paper money inclined Congress to hope that his Catholic majesty, if he shall conclude a treaty with these States,

---

[1] *Mo. Hist. Rev.*, V, 217.   [2] See *ante*, pp. 102, 103.

[3] Wharton, *Diplomatic Correspondence*, III, 326.

will be induced to lend them money. You are therefore to represent to him the great distress of these States on that account, and to solicit a loan of five millions of dollars upon the best terms in your power, not exceeding six per centum per annum.[1]

There was little prospect of success for this mission when, on account of the presence of English cruisers, Jay was forced unexpectedly to disembark at Cadiz, January 22, 1780. "Very disagreeably circumstanced," as he expressed it, he was without letters of credit or recommendation to anyone in the city, and had no money except what had been loaned him by two of his fellow-passengers.[2]

William Carmichael, his secretary, was sent at once to Madrid, instructed by Jay, as follows: "In speaking of American affairs, remember to do justice to Virginia and the western country near the Mississippi. Recount their achievements against the savages, their growing numbers, extensive settlements, and aversion to Britain for attempting to involve them in the horrors of an Indian war. Let it appear also from your representations that ages will be necessary to settle those extensive regions. . . . . It would be advantageous to know whether Spain means to carry on any serious operations for possessing herself of the Floridas and banks of the Mississippi."[3] On April 4 Jay arrived at Madrid prepared to open negotiations with Count Florida Blanca.

At no time during the two years he remained was he given official recognition, and he was as a result excluded from the court and studiously neglected by nobles and officials. His embarrassment was the greater for the Com-

---

[1] *Ibid.*, pp. 344, 353.

[2] Johnston, *Correspondence and Public Papers of John Jay*, ed. H. P. Johnston, I, 254.

[3] *Ibid.*, pp. 266, 268.

mittee of Foreign Affairs had drawn on him before his arrival in Spain for 100,000 pounds sterling.

Writing of such a policy, he said: "I would throw stones with all my heart, if I thought they would reach the committee without injuring the members of it."[1] In an extended conference, May 11, 1780, Florida Blanca assured Jay that it was the intention of Spain to give America all assistance within their power, but that a loan was not then possible.[2] In fulfilment of promises made him, Jay was finally able to secure as the result of his efforts a loan of $150,000. The one obstacle in the way of making a treaty arose, it was intimated, from "the pretensions of America to the navigation of the Mississippi." The United States, Florida Blanca asserted, had at one time relinquished all right to the use of the Mississippi and was now making it an essential point of a treaty. Jay replied that many of the states were bounded by the river and were greatly interested in its navigation. It was made clear to Jay, however, that "this was an object that the King had so much at heart that he would never relinquish it."[3] At a conference held in September Florida Blanca took the same position, and, as expressed by Jay, "with some degree of warmth" declared "that unless Spain could exclude all nations from the Gulf of Mexico they might as well admit all; that the King would never relinquish it; that the minister regarded it as the principal object to be obtained by the war; and *that obtained*, he should be perfectly easy whether or no Spain procured any other cession; that he considered it far more important than the acquisition of Gibraltar; and that if

[1] Sparks, *Diplomatic Correspondence*, VII, 304, 305.

[2] A complete account of this conference is given in Johnston, *John Jay*, I, 316-26.

[3] Wharton, *Diplomatic Correpondence*, III, 724.

they did not get it, it was a matter of indifference to him whether the English possessed Mobile or not. . . . ."[1]

A few days earlier Jay had expressed, in a conference with Don Diego Gardoqui, member of a wealthy firm at Bilbao, the view which in general prevailed among American leaders and no doubt prompted the statement by Florida Blanca.[2] It was stated by Gardoqui that "aids" would no doubt follow an offer by Jay to surrender the navigation of the Mississippi. To this Jay replied

that the Americans, almost to a man, believed that God Almighty had made that river a highway for the people of the upper country to go to the sea by; that this country was extensive and fertile; that the General, many officers, and others of distinction and influence in America were deeply interested in it; that it would rapidly settle; and that the inhabitants would not readily be convinced of the justice of being obliged either to live without foreign commodities, and lose the surplus of their productions, or be obliged to transport both over rugged mountains and through an immense wilderness to and from the sea when they daily saw a fine river flowing before their doors and offering to save them all that trouble and expense, and that without injury to Spain.

Franklin, at Paris, congratulated Jay on the stand he had taken and wrote (October 2, 1780): "Poor as we are, yet as I know we shall be rich, I would rather agree with them to buy at a great price the whole of their rights in the Mississippi than sell a drop of the waters. A neighbor might as well ask me to sell my street door."[3]

Luzerne, French minister in Philadelphia, was using his influence to further the Spanish position. He declared before a committee of Congress that Spain would not consent to an alliance unless Congress should concede that the United States had no right to territory west of the line

[1] Johnston, *John Jay*, 424, 425.

[2] September 3, 1780. Gardoqui represented Florida Blanca in this conference.

[3] Johnston, *John Jay*, I, 433.

established by the Proclamation of 1763, and should yield their claim on the right to the free navigation of the Mississippi to the sea.

While some members of Congress were prepared to abandon the position taken on the free navigation of the Mississippi, new instructions which were drawn up for Jay's guidance (October 4, 1780) manifested no disposition to yield to Spain's demands. It was provided: "that the Minister adhere to his former instructions, respecting the right of the United States of America to the free navigation of the river Mississippi into and from the sea; which right, if an express acknowledgment of it cannot be obtained from Spain, is not by any stipulation on the part of America to be relinquished."[1]

Alarmed at the success of the British in the South during the summer of 1780, delegates in Congress from Georgia and South Carolina urged that a proposal be made Spain to yield the exclusive navigation of the Mississippi below the thirty-first parallel as the price of an immediate alliance. January 2, 1781, the Virginia delegates were instructed by their state legislature to favor such an action, but they were to endeavor to secure free ports for American traders near the mouth of the river.[2] In keeping with this recommendation Congress (February 15, 1781) issued instructions to Jay to recede from the demand for the free navigation of the river below the thirty-first parallel. He was also to yield on the issue of free ports, "provided such cession shall be unalterably insisted upon by Spain."[3]

Americans were convinced that this spirit of liberality would lead to an early treaty with Spain, with many at-

---

[1] *Ibid.*, pp. 435, 449. It must be acknowledged, however, that there were no principles of international law upon which a nation was justified in laying claim to the free navigation of a river whose mouth was held by an alien.

[2] *Ibid.*, II, 208.   [3] Johnston, *John Jay*, I, 46.

tendant advantages. Samuel Huntington, the president of Congress, wrote Jay: "You will not only be able without further delay to conclude the proposed alliance with his Catholic Majesty, but that the liberality and friendly disposition manifested on the part of the United States by such a cession will induce him to afford them some substantial and effectual aid in the article of money."[1] Robert Morris, recently appointed superintendent of finance, was hopeful that Spain would be prepared to relieve the financial stress by granting large sums of money, either as loans or subsidies, $5,000,000 being suggested as an amount sufficient for "our present emergencies."[2] As compensation for such generosity Spain might anticipate, on the return of peace, in addition to repayment of the loan and protection of Spanish-American dominions, a large increase in exports to America of wine, oil, fruit, silk, and cloth, and remittances in return, of wheat, corn, fish, and naval stores. America, he urged, would never be a dangerous neighbor, for "the attention of this country for a century past has been, and for a century to come most probably will be, entirely turned to agriculture and commerce. . . . . Mutual benefits and the reciprocation of good offices will endear a connexion between them, and their interests require that this connexion should be of the closest kind."

In attempts at negotiation, continuing for months, Jay's patience was to be sorely tested; as he expressed it "delay is their system."[3] Florida Blanca declared that he

[1] May 28, 1781, *ibid.*, II, 35.

[2] July 4, 1781. Morris to Jay (*ibid.*, II, 40–51). Jay spoke of this letter as excellently well calculated for being shown entire to the Spanish minister, and it was later submitted to him (*ibid.*, pp. 102, 103, 107). This wish was a vain one, even if a most satisfactory treaty had been arranged, for Jay two months later stated that the Spanish treasury was low, and that "much of the money for the expenses in this war costs them between thirty and forty per hundred, by mismanagement and want of credit (*ibid.*, p. 73).

[3] *Ibid.*, p. 131.

was "too sick or too busy," and Del Campo, his secretary, who was named as his successor in the negotiation, claimed that he was without instructions and much indisposed. In fact, Jay was not informed of the change of negotiator until three months after the appointment had been made.[1] Moreover, Jay's instructions were common knowledge before they were received by him. His letters passing by post were uniformly opened, kept back for a period, and were at times entirely suppressed.[2] His instructions of February 15 became known to him after the lapse of three months through the letter of a friend.[3] On May 19 Jay waited on the Minister but was unable to make advance toward securing a treaty. Efforts at negotiation, equally fruitless, continued until early October, when Jay made an extended report to Congress.[4]

The reply to Jay's arguments uniformly took the form already reiterated, that the "King had always been accustomed to consider the exclusive navigation of the Gulf of Mexico as a very important object to Spain, more so indeed than even Gibraltar, and he was persuaded that his Majesty would never be prevailed upon to change his ideas on that subject."

While using his best effort to carry out instructions, it is evident Jay was not in sympathy with the proposal on the navigation of the Mississippi, which he styled "ungenerous concessions on the part of Congress,"[5] for, as he said: "The cession of this navigation will in my opinion render a future war with Spain unavoidable, and I shall look upon my subscribing to the one as fixing the certainty of the other."[6] Jay's advances during the remainder of the

---

[1] Johnston, *John Jay*, II, 235, 238.
[2] *Ibid.*, p. 20.   [3] *Ibid.*, p. 79.
[4] Florida Blanca to Jay (*ibid.*, pp. 75–97).
[5] Wharton, *Diplomatic Correspondence*, IV, 381.
[6] Johnston, *John Jay*, II, 86.

year 1781 were continuously met with evasion and delay
on the part of the Spanish representative; as he expressed
the situation February 6, 1782, "I have not been able to
obtain anything more than excuses for procrastination."[1]
As a fitting return for such a dilatory policy, Franklin declared: "If I were in Congress, I should advise your being
instructed to thank them for past favors and take your
leave."[2]

Finally a letter from Jay, April 28, 1782, was convincing in its evidence that nothing could be expected from
Spain.[3] Congress then adopted the significant resolution
that "the American Minister at Madrid be instructed to
forbear making any overtures to that Court or entering
into any stipulations in consequence of overtures which he
has made; and in case any propositions be made to him by
the said Court for a treaty with the United States, to decline acceding to the same until he shall have transmitted
them to Congress for approbation."[4] Convinced that nothing was to be gained at Madrid, Jay, upon receiving an
urgent message from Franklin that the American commissioners needed his assistance in negotiating for peace with
Great Britain, set out for Paris, reaching that city on the
twenty-third of June.[5] Carmichael, secretary of legation,
remained in Spain, but Florida Blanca instructed Count
d' Aranda, Spanish minister to France, to continue negotiations with Jay.

[1] *Ibid.*, p. 176.

[2] Franklin to Jay, January 19, 1782. Wharton, *Diplomatic Correspondence,*
IV, 120.

[3] This report was addressed to Robert R. Livingston, who had been elected
secretary of foreign affairs (*ibid.*, IV, 336–77).

[4] August 7, 1782. Johnston, *John Jay*, II, 209.

[5] *Ibid.*, p. 311.

Chapter XI

Renewal of Plans to Capture Detroit

A T THE close of the campaign against the Shawnee Clark was free once more to develop plans for the capture of Detroit. He was aware that the only assistance to be furnished him from Virginia would be a single regiment under Colonel Joseph Crockett. But he was assured that an important expedition under his command was to be undertaken the ensuing year, 1781. The presence of Patrick Henry, Richard Henry Lee, George Mason, and other Virginia leaders in the House of Delegates promised a more aggressive policy in the West. Governor Jefferson, with full appreciation of the significance of the capture of Detroit, had appealed to Washington to furnish powder for the expedition, the burden of which was otherwise to be borne by Virginia.[1] Jefferson was aware that prompt action was necessary, for there was unmistakable evidence that a British expedition would be sent against Kentucky in the spring. Clark proceeded to Richmond to consult over the means possible for checking this formidable invasion.

By December 25 full instructions were drawn up under which Clark was to advance with two thousand men into the hostile territory at the earliest practicable moment

---

[1] Jefferson to Clark, December 25, 1780. *Clark Papers*, p. 485. At the time there was a powerful British army in the South which had but recently defeated General Gates.

after the opening of navigation. The ultimate object of the expedition was to be the reduction of Detroit and the acquisition of Lake Erie.[1] Such a movement was intended to place the British on the defensive. If no check were given their advance, it was feared that militia would ultimately have to be withdrawn from the South to be sent against them.

The effects which were expected to follow the reduction of Detroit were stated by Jefferson as follows:

If that Post be reduced we shall be quiet in future on our frontier, and thereby immense Treasure of blood and money be saved, we shall be at leisure to know [turn] our whole force to the rescue of our Eastern country from subjugation, we shall divert through our own country a brand of commerce which the European States have thought worthy of the most important struggles and sacrifices and in the event of peace on terms which have been contemplated by some powers we shall form to the American Union a barrier against the dangerous extension of the British Province of Canada and add to the Empire of Liberty an extensive and fertile country, thereby converting dangerous enemies into valuable friends.[2]

Frontier militia, "well armed with arms suitable to western service," together with a battalion under Colonel Crockett, were ordered sent to Fort Pitt by the first of March.[3] They were to be commanded by Clark. By March 15 the Kentucky militia were to rendezvous at the falls of the Ohio, and ammunition and provisions for the entire force were to be collected at the same place.[4]

[1] Jefferson's Letter Book, December 25, 1780, 1781 (Virginia State Library), pp. 10 ff.

[2] Draper MSS, 51 J 13.

[3] Orders were issued to the county lieutenants of Monongalia and Ohio counties to furnish one-fourth of their militia. Hampshire was to furnish 255 men; Berkeley, 275; Frederic, 285; and Greenbrier militia were to act as escort for three hundred pack horses to be sent forward with powder and lead.

[4] The counties of Fayette, Lincoln, and Jefferson, together, were to furnish five hundred militia.

The promise for success was greater when it was known that Washington was ready to answer the appeal for assistance. "I have ever been of opinion," he wrote Jefferson, "that the reduction of the post of Detroit would be the only certain means of giving peace and security to the whole western frontier, and I have constantly kept my eye upon that object. . . . . I shall think it a most happy circumstance, should your State, with the aid of Continental stores which you require, be able to accomplish it."[1] In keeping with this promise he ordered Colonel Brodhead at Fort Pitt to give the enterprise every possible assistance by furnishing, upon Clark's order, the supplies asked for and a detachment of Continental troops, including a company of artillery, as large as could be spared. "I do not think," Washington wrote, "the charge of the enterprise could have been committed to better hands than Colonel Clark's. I have not the pleasure of knowing the gentleman; but, independently of the proofs he has given of his activity and address, the unbounded confidence, which I am told the western people repose in him, is a matter of most importance."[2]

In order that any question of rank might not interfere with complete exercise of power by Clark, Jefferson urged that a continental commission should be bestowed upon him by Washington. This was not possible under the established rule which forbade the granting of such a commission to officers in state regiments. On January 22, however, Clark was made brigadier-general, by Jefferson, "of the forces to be embodied on an expedition westward of the Ohio."[3] This act completed an effective military

[1] *Writings of Washington*, ed. Sparks, VII, 341.

[2] *Ibid.*, p. 345.

[3] Draper MSS, 51 J 18. The commission was granted under authority of Jefferson with the advice of the council of state evidently on account of some

organization in the West. The preceding November, on account of the rapid growth of the population in the county of Kentucky, the legislature of Virginia divided it into the three counties of Fayette, Jefferson, and Lincoln.[1] John Todd was appointed county lieutenant and colonel of militia for Fayette County, having Boone for his lieutenant colonel. John Floyd occupied the same position in Jefferson County, and Benjamin Logan in Lincoln. Clark, as superior officer, was to supervise the work of these three.

For some time Clark had been engaged, under the direction of Baron Steuben, in carrying on a defensive movement against Benedict Arnold. The day following the receipt of Washington's approval for the western expedition Jefferson directed Clark to secure his release in order that he might set out for the frontier.[2] But Clark was not well on his way to Fort Pitt before Jefferson was made aware of difficulties which must be overcome if the enterprise were to succeed.

The issue of orders for the drafting of the militia of Berkeley County to go immediately to the falls of the Ohio served to demonstrate that extreme measures would be necessary to induce men to enlist. The Recruiting officers wrote,

We beg leave to represent to your Excellency, that we have seventy men on duty from this County, now in the Southern army,

---

misgivings on the part of Clark relative to his relations to continental officers of the same rank as his own. Clark to Jefferson, January 18, 1781. *Clark Papers*, p. 495. The wording of the commission was due to the fact that according to the laws of the state a general officer might be appointed only for a *special* purpose.

[1] In general, Fayette County extended east from the Kentucky River, comprising the northeastern portion of the present state of Kentucky. Jefferson extended from the Kentucky River south to the Green River; and the remaining territory was called Lincoln.

[2] Jefferson to Clark. *Clark Papers*, p. 491. January 22, Clark started for Fort Pitt.

which with the 68, we are to raise for the army and the 275 now ordered into service will make nearly one-half of the militia of this Country fit for duty—From these circumstances and the immense distance from here to the falls of the Ohio, being by way of Fort Pitt, little less than a thousand miles, we are sorry to inform your Excellency that we have the greatest reason to believe that those whose Turn it now is from this County will suffer any punishment rather than obey our orders for their march. So general an Opposition to orders of Government from such a number we think of too much consequence at this crisis, for us to proceed without informing your Excellency of the difficulties with which the execution of those orders will be attended.[1]

The drafting in Frederick County served to show similar aversion to the undertaking. By the report of the county lieutenant not more than twenty guns were available for the 280 men to be equipped. Officers of Greenbrier County, in answer to entreaties from the inhabitants, who were fearful of the dangers to which they would be exposed upon the withdrawal of so large a force, requested that their quota for the continental army should not be demanded until the return of the militia about to leave for the West.[2] Attempts to collect provisions and men in Hampshire County resulted in the actual mutiny of some seventy men. With a lax military law, and fearful lest the attempt at enforcement of his orders would lead to open disobedience, Jefferson adopted the suggestion of the county officials and issued a call for volunteers.[3]

Moreover, the men constituting the regiment of regular

[1] *Clark Papers*, p. 501.

[2] Draper MSS, 51 J 33. March 21, 1781. Within two months Cornwallis was retreating, pursued by Greene, who was aided by Campbell with two thousand militia from the back counties of Virginia, and by Sumpter with the militia of the Carolinas.

[3] *Calendar of Va. State Papers*, II, 40. Governor Harrison, as late as May 30, 1785, asked for a remedy for this defect in citing the case of sixteen men who were ordered to defend a jail and stores. Ten of them refused to obey the order. Benjamin Harrison Letter Book, 1783–86 (Virginia State Library), p. 143.

troops under Colonel Crockett, then marching to Fort Pitt, were suffering for want of suitable clothing and were without shoes.[1] In this extremity Clark did not lose confidence, and declared, "I begin to fear the want of men, but the idea of a disappointment is so disagreeable to me that if the Authority and Influence that I have with every Exertion that can be made will Carry my point I shall certainly do it without your orders for the Enterprise is Countermand[d] or a failour in the supplies I am to Receive which I hope will not be the case."[2] The prospect of assistance from the remaining counties was still promising. By February 13 Baron Steuben, upon request of Jefferson, had ordered Colonel John Gibson, with his regiment consisting of two hundred regulars, to be added to Clark's command.[3]

The artillery company ordered to accompany Clark from Fort Pitt was lacking in the quota of officers and men necessary for that service, and the equipment in cannon, shells, shot, and other stores was inadequate.[4] Accumulation of supplies for the expedition was so much delayed that the time of setting out from Fort Pitt was extended to June. After three weeks' deliberation Congress agreed to grant the request of the Board of War for supplies. Three weeks longer were necessary for their collection, owing to

[1] *Cal. Va. State Papers*, I, 572. Crockett to Jefferson, March 14, 1781. At this time the distress of the regular army in Virginia was likewise extreme, as is shown in the following letter: "I found upon my return hither [Chesterfield], that all the troops that marched from hence upon the arrival of the enemy, had by order of Baron Steuben come back to this Station, from their utter inability to keep the field, from want of almost every species of Cloathing. Many . . . . are dependent upon others for a part of a blanket to shelter them at night from the cold. The want of shirts and shoes is another distressing circumstance. . . . . They [the men] are not able to do anything in the field and near 60 of them too naked to do anything."

[2] Clark to Jefferson, *Clark Papers*, p. 505.

[3] Jefferson to Clark, *Clark Papers*, p. 508. Gibson was to be second in command.

[4] Draper MSS, 51 J 31.

the lack of both men and money.[1] The kegs in which the powder was being forwarded from Philadelphia were so poor that a delay of two weeks was necessary at one point in order to make new ones.[2]

During this period of waiting Clark learned of the abuses incident to the conduct of public affairs in the West. Instances were cited in which goods belonging to the state were used in carrying on private trade with the Indians. Laborers in public employment were accused of performing only one-tenth as much work as those who were engaged on tasks of their own.[3] Reports of the subordination of public interests to private gain were not, however, confined to any one section. It was a period when sheriffs in Virginia were accused of misappropriating large sums of county money with which to invest in land-office warrants.[4] A proclamation was issued by the council of Pennsylvania against "forestalling," by which individuals gained control of flour and other necessities on the market and thus enhanced the prices.[5] State assemblies were called upon by Congress to put a stop to "criminal commerce" with the British, and it was recommended that the furnishing of provisions and military supplies to the enemy should be treated as a capital offense.[6] Two years earlier Washington declared that "want of virtue . . . . is infinitely more to be dreaded than the whole force of Great Britain, assisted as they are by Hessian, Indian, and Negro allies. . . . . To make and extort money in every shape that can be devised,

---

[1] *Ibid.*, 51 J 46.   [2] *Ibid.*, 51 J 33.

[3] Colonel Slaughter to Thomas Jefferson, January 14, 1781. *Clark Papers*, p. 493.

[4] Report concerning sheriffs (November 17, 1779) by a special committee of the House of Delegates.

[5] State regulation of prices followed. Neville B. Craig, *The Olden Time* (Cincinnati, 1876), II, 322.

[6] *Executive Papers* of December, 1780, in Virginia State Archives.

and at the same time to decry its value, seems to have become a mere business and an epidemical disease, calling for the interposition of every good man and body of men."[1] In fact, these lapses in public morals are not wholly surprising when the commanding officer at Fort Pitt makes the following proposal to the governor of Pennsylvania: "Should our State determine to extend its settlements over the Alleghany River I should be happy to have an early hint of it because it will be in my power to serve several of my friends."[2] That he surrounded himself with favorites who imitated their leader in subordinating public office to private gain and thus produced destitution among the troops has been well established. Among the numerous charges which were brought against Brodhead and finally caused his recall were land-jobbing and speculation with public funds.[3] As stated in a petition of four hundred men who demanded his removal from office, "Colonel Brodhead is actuated by motives, selfish and interested and his views are totally confined to Land, Manors, and Millseats.[4] But the reply of President Joseph Reed came as a well-calculated rebuke to all such suggestions. "At present," he wrote, "my Station will prevent my engaging in pursuits of that nature lest it might give offense and give Reason to a censorious world to suppose I had made an improper use of my publick Character."[5]

Clark's confidence in some of his former associates was misplaced and he poured out his resentment as follows: "Its supprising to me that Maj[r] Slaughter as an officer of the State would suffer those persons to persevear in their

---

[1] *Writings of Washington*, ed. Sparks, VI, 91.

[2] Colonel Brodhead to President Reed, February 28, 1780. He proposed to form a company of proprietors, of which Governor Reed should be one, to purchase land. *Pennsylvania State Archives*, VIII, 121.

[3] *Frontier Retreat*, pp. 356 ff.   [4] *Ibid.*, p. 365.   [5] *Ibid.*, p. 150.

Villany was he as he hints truly sensible of ye principal that actuated them you know my sentiments Respecting Sev^{rl} persons in our Imploy. those he accuses are gen^{ly} men of fair Characters. I have long Since determined to Conduct myself with a particular Regour towards every person under me. . . . . But to Reflect on the steps I have been obliged to make use of to prosecute a war for these several years there is an indignity in it that often Hurt me."[1]

Early in May Clark suffered his greatest disappointment upon learning that Colonel Brodhead had refused to allow the regiment under Colonel John Gibson to accompany him. The surprise and disappointment was the greater for Brodhead had already given assurance of his complete co-operation.[2] By the middle of March Brodhead regarded his own condition as desperate. He feared an attack from Detroit and Niagara, and in that event he believed that large numbers of the inhabitants would aid the enemy. Besides, he was aware that the revolt of the Delawares that were not under Moravian influence was about to lead to a general Indian war.

A delegation of their chiefs had visited Detroit and agreed upon terms with the commandant. This defection was especially serious for the frontiersmen, for the Delawares, because of their proximity, were familiar with the strength of the garrisons. Brodhead determined to strike the first blow, and with a force of 150 regulars and as many

---

[1] Clark to Jefferson, March, 1781. *Clark Papers*, p. 516. The particular charges made by Colonel George Slaughter against William Shannon and others were examined by four commissioners and found not to be true. Slaughter to Jefferson, January 14, 1781 (*ibid.*, p. 493). Evidence against John Dodge and his associates for dishonest practice seems to have been established. *Cahokia Records*, p. xcviii.

[2] Brodhead to Clark. *Clark Papers*, p. 509. "You may rely on every supply I am authorized to afford to facilitate your expedition."

volunteers he proceeded down the river to Wheeling, with his Moravian Indian guides, to the Delaware towns on the Muskingum. The Indians were completely surprised and routed. After destroying the towns, the volunteers refused to go farther, and the expedition returned with a number of prisoners and booty which was sold for 80,000 pounds.[1]

That volunteers joined this expedition in order to avoid accompanying Clark cannot be definitely asserted, but it is certain his enlistments were materially affected thereby. It seems probable, however, that Clark's project was defeated because of the covert opposition of Brodhead. Colonel Brodhead now sought some argument which would excuse his policy of opposition to Clark, for he was of the type which is incapable of co-operating with anyone. "I shall not be surprized," he wrote, "to see his Expedition fall through for it is clear to me, that wise men at a great distance, view things in the western Country very differently from those, who are more immediately acquainted with Circumstances and situations."[2] Moreover, he was desirous of winning laurels for himself and a number of times had appealed to Washington for permission to organize an expedition against Detroit and Natchez and for assistance in carrying it forward.[3] Brodhead convinced himself that he was well within his instructions in refusing to grant Clark's request for a regiment. His orders read: "You will likewise direct the officers with the company of artillery to be ready to move, when Colonel Clark shall call for them; and, as it is my wish to give the enterprise every aid, which our small force can afford, you will be pleased to form such a detach-

[1] *Frontier Retreat*, p. 399.

[2] *Pennsylvania State Archives*, VIII, 787.

[3] Washington to Brodhead, January 4, 1780. Washington stated that from the estimate he made of the garrison at Detroit, the men in garrison at Fort Pitt, together with the militia, would not be adequate to make the attempt, and that the same was true of Natchez.

ment as you can safely spare from your own and Gibson's regiments, and put it under the command of Colonel Clark also. I should suppose, the detachment cannot be made more than a command for a captain or major at most. . . . . Your good sense will, I am convinced, make you view this matter in its true light."[1] Clark interpreted Jefferson's dispatch to mean that by the consent of Baron Steuben and Washington he was to be accompanied by Colonel Gibson's regiment and Heath's company.[2]

Both men appealed to Washington. "From your Excellencies letters to Col° Brodhead," Clark wrote, "I conceived him to be at liberty to furnish what men he pleasd. . . . . If you should aprove of the troops in this department Joining our forces tho they are few the acquisition may be attended with great good consequences as two Hundred only might turn the Scale in our favour." The next day he appealed again for assistance, saying: "For in part it has been the influence of our posts on the Illinoise and Ouabash that have savd the frontiers and in a great measure baffled the designs of the Enemy at Detroit. If they get possession of them they then Command three times the number of Valuable warriors they do at present and will be fully Enabled to carry any point they aim at Except we should have a formidable force to oppose them."[3]

Clark assumed that his request would be granted. Regular officers and soldiers were desirous of going on the expedition, which was supposed to be aimed against the Indians.[4] While awaiting Washington's reply, boats were

[1] Washington to Brodhead. *Writings of Washington*, ed. Sparks, VII, 343.

[2] Clark to Washington, May 20, 1781. *Clark Papers*, p. 551. Gibson agreed with Clark in this interpretation.

[3] *Clark Papers*, p. 553.

[4] Draper MSS, 51 J 57. See *Clark Papers*, p. 550. President Reed wrote Clark, May 15, 1781: "But from common report we learn, that an expedition

completed and provisions collected. Notwithstanding the desire of President Reed, of Pennsylvania, to render all the assistance within his power, volunteers were secured only after the use of extreme measures, due chiefly to the dispute over the boundary.[1] A general draft was finally resorted to.[2] Enforcement of the order in Monongalia County brought on a riot.[3]

Among other problems demanding Clark's attention besides the suppression of this mob[4] was the difficulty of securing supplies with a currency which steadily depreciated in value.[5] "I am sorry to have to inform you," an officer wrote, "that a set of Rascals have Begun to depreciate the Virgᵃ money now in Circulation, and some of them have even gone so far as to refuse taking it, in particular Smith the Brewer has refused to take it in payment for Beer, I am much afraid it will reach the Country and of Course retard your proceedings." Findings of the general court-martial were reviewed by Clark in which such questions were considered as the legality of drafting, punishment of horse-thieves, and embezzlement of public property.[6]

---

under your command is destined against Detroit. We are very sensible of its importance to this State, as well as Virginia, and there is no Gentleman in whose abilities and good conduct we have more Confidence, on such an occasion. After this it seems unnecessary to add, that it will give us great satisfaction if the inhabitants of this State chearfully concur in it."

[1] Draper MSS, 51 J 49, 56.

[2] *Ibid.*, 30 J 91.

[3] *Ibid.*, 51 J 58.

[4] *Clark Papers*, p. 568. "We the subscribers being Accessary to a Riot in Supressing a draught in this country on the 12th Inst Being Sensible of our Error and as a security of our future good conduct do hereby Engage to Serve Ten months in the continental Service in case we should be guilty of the like misdeminor."

[5] *Ibid.*, p. 561.

[6] James Thomson, convicted of horse theft and desertion, was forced to run the gauntlet through the brigade (*ibid.*, p. 577).

Clark's problems were still more complicated because of a dispatch from Washington by which he was informed that Colonel John Connolly was about to join forces with Sir John Johnson and come by the way of Lake Ontario against Fort Pitt and other western posts.[1]

In the midst of these preparations social life at Fort Pitt was not lacking. "We have heard," wrote Colonel Gibson, "that the Gentlemen and Ladies of Stewarts Crossing's intend paying us a visit tomorrow, in Consequence of which a grand Bower is erected in the Orchard, a Barbacue is preparing for tomorrow and a Ball in the Evening at Col Gibson's Room." The celebration of the "Aniversary of our Glorious Independance" also received due attention.[2]

While the necessary supplies had been collected by the first of June at a cost approaching $2,000,000, the weeks wore on with Clark still hoping to secure the requisite number of volunteers.[3] His appeals to Washington that Colonel Gibson's regiment might be permitted to accompany him failed. Drafts were of slight avail, and finally, early in August, despairing of accomplishing his designs in the face of deep-seated opposition on the part of the officials of the western counties of Pennsylvania, he set out for Louisville with four hundred men.[4] This number was

---

[1] Connolly, recently exchanged, had proceeded from New York to Quebec. *Writings of Washington*, ed. Sparks, VII, 25. "I doubt Sir," Clark wrote Jefferson relative to Connolly's expedition, "we shall as utial be obliged to play a desperate gaim this campaign. If we had the 2,000 men first proposed such Intelligence would give me pleasure" (*ibid.*, p. 559).

[2] Draper MSS, 51 J 65.

[3] *Cal. Va. State Papers*, II, 140. Clark, in a letter to Jefferson, August 4, 1781 (*Clark Papers*, p. 578), says he had given Colonel Harrison £126,581 to enable him to collect stores. £300,000 had already been forwarded to Colonel Harrison. Jefferson to Clark, April 20, 1781. Jefferson's Letter Book, 1781.

[4] *Cal. Va. State Papers*, II, 345. In a letter to Colonel Davies, W. Croghan declared that the reason Clark was able to get so few men at Fort Pitt was "owing

little more than adequate to guard the boats which contained supplies for fully two thousand men. Clark still hoped his force would be reinforced in Kentucky and that he might accomplish his object, or at least make some demonstration against the disaffected Indians. Before setting out he was forced to draw on his supplies in order to relieve the distressed condition of the garrison at Fort Pitt. Plans were outlined whereby Colonel Gibson was to lead an attack against the Wyandot September 4, and Clark was to march at the same time from the mouth of the Miami upon the Shawnee villages.

Clark's preparations had served as a defense for the frontier. Efforts were redoubled to put Detroit in condition to withstand an attack. Demands for presents made by the Indians in council at that post increased "amazingly."[1] By the end of May the fears of the British and their allies were increased by the report that Clark was descending the Ohio with one thousand men and that this number would be increased by a like number from Ken-

---

to the dispute that subsists here between the Virginians & Pennsylvanians respecting the true bounds of the Latter. And the General being a Virginian was opposed by the most noted men here of the Pennsylvania Party. The people here bleam Virginia very much for making them & their lands (which beyond a shadow of a doubt is far out of the true bounds of pensylvania) over to pennsylvania." Draper MSS 16 S 54 ff. The force accompanying Clark was composed of Colonel Crockett's regiment of Virginia state troops and Captain Craig's company of artillery, together with volunteers and militia. Clark was represented by some of the leading men opposed to him as a flour merchant, and again as a trader and land-jobber, for the state of Virginia (*ibid.*, 52 J 18). James Marshall, county lieutenant of Washington County, and County Lieutenants Cook and Davis, were named by Clark as his main opponents. Marshall advised the people to pay no attention to the drafts ordered for Clark and offered protection to those who refused. He had told Clark that while he could do nothing for the expedition as an official, that as a private person he would give every assistance within his power. *Pennsylvania Archives*, IX, 318.

[1] *Mich. Pioneer and Hist. Colls.*, X, 465.

tucky.[1] Their confidence was restored through a dispatch from General Haldimand contradicting this rumor and assuring them that Detroit and the Indian country were in no danger. They were ordered to act at once in order to prevent the further strengthening of the frontier settlements. Such an order meant war on combatant and noncombatant alike.

While a force of one hundred rangers under Captain Andrew Thompson and three hundred Indians under Captain McKee were advancing to the Ohio to waylay Clark, Captain Joseph Brant, at the head of a force of one hundred whites and Indians, surprised a body of 107 Pennsylvania volunteers under Colonel Archibald Lochry which was descending the Ohio to join Clark.

This company of picked men from Westmoreland County reached Fort Wheeling a few hours after Clark's departure. On August 16 eight men were sent forward with a letter to Clark. Five of them were captured, and from the letter Brant learned that Lochry was coming down the river. His plan of attack was completely successful. The Americans, having reached a point 10 miles below the mouth of the Big Miami, landed to cook breakfast and to cut grass for their horses. They were attacked by the Indians. Attempting to escape across the river, they were surprised by another party; one-third of their number were killed and the remainder made prisoners.[2] A number of the prisoners, including Colonel Lochry, were afterward murdered. After marching with their prisoners a few miles up the Miami, the victors met the forces led by Thompson

---

[1] Simon Girty to Major de Peyster. *Mich. Pioneer and Hist. Colls.*, X, 478. This rumor was started on account of the expedition against the Delawares by Colonel Brodhead.

[2] *Ibid.*, p. 530. An account of this expedition is given in *Indiana Historical Society, Pamphlets*, No. 4 (1888). See also Anderson's "Journal" in English, *Conquest of the Northwest*, II, 725.

and McKee. The Indians were satisfied with what had been accomplished and believed that their villages would now be safe. With great difficulty they were persuaded that security from invasion lay only in attacking Clark. On September 9 they were within 25 miles of the falls. Scouts came in with two prisoners from whom it was learned that Clark could not with his small force undertake an expedition. But the Indians were not disposed to attack him, and numerous small bands deserted, some returning to their villages while others scoured the country, burning cabins and stealing horses. The rangers were without food and insisted on retreating toward Detroit.[1]

All the posts anxiously awaited Clark's return. The new fort at the falls had been completed as he had directed.[2] For months, however, the garrison had suffered through a lack of clothing and food. Early the previous winter Captain Slaughter declared: "My men have no shirts, hats, blankets, or Breeches, not having drawn Cloath for that purpose, shoes, Stockings, moccasons, so that they are totally unfit for duty."[3] For three years these troops had received no pay; they were without adequate food, and none was obtainable without money, since the credit of the government was gone. Numbers of the best men were deserting daily. Supplies were no longer obtainable in the Illinois country on credit or for continental currency.

Without suitable goods which might be used in exchange for provisions the distress of the troops at Fort Jefferson became constantly more acute. Their melancholy condition in October, 1780, was described by Captain Leonard Helm as follows: "Sitting by Capt. George's fire with a piece of Light wood and two Ribs of an old Bufaloe

---

[1] *Mich. Pioneer and Hist. Colls.*, X, 516.

[2] Fort Nelson, so named in honor of the governor of Virginia.

[3] Draper MSS, 50 J 79.

which is all the meat we have seen this many days, I congratulate your success against the Shawanahs but this never doubt when that brave Col. Clarke Commands we will know the loss of him at the Illinois. . . . . Excuse Hast as the Lightwood just out and mouth watering for want of the two ribs."[1] Settlers at the post, harrassed by bands of Indians and the consequent loss of crops and stock, shared in these distresses. Desertions among the soldiers and inhabitants became more frequent, some becoming traders and others going down the river, and finally, in June, 1781, the fort was evacuated.[2]

Conditions elsewhere in Kentucky were little, if any, better. Preparations for the promised expedition against Detroit had been made by frontier officials under adverse conditions, for the credit of Virginia was exhausted, as illustrated by the following typical communication to Clark: "I prepared the Canoes ordered by Governm[r] and am liable for the Price of most of them, having on the faith of the Governors Letter promised to pay for them long since, & he promised to send me money by the first opportunity to defray the Expense which is about L40000. I have received no money on that Account nor have I any of my own to advance I should therefore be glad you cou'd contrive to have it sent out if possible People have been so long amused with promises of paying off Expenses long incurred that the credit of the State is very little better here than in Illinois."[3] "At present," one of Clark's officers wrote, "in great want of Flour, whiskey, and Linen for the soldiery as every person who has any to dispose of seems much against crediting the State. Send down supply

[1] *Clark Papers*, p. 466. Addressed to Colonel George Slaughter. Captain Robert George was then in command at Fort Jefferson.

[2] *Ibid.*, p. 585.

[3] *Ibid.*

especially Linen as the officers and soldiers are nearly all naked and not one pound of flour for either."[1]

Large quantities of beef which had been collected were unfit for use.[2] During the winter and spring a succession of Indian raids well-nigh devastated Fayette and Jefferson counties.[3] Ammunition and provisions were scarce, and the settlers sought the protection of the forts or fled panic-stricken to the stronger settlements. "There is scarce one fort in the county but once a month seems upon the eve of breaking for want of men to defend it," John Todd wrote in April. "Such residents," he continued, "as had most property and Horses to remove their effects, having retreated to Lincoln. One half of the remainder are unable to remove. We have no tax Commissioners in the County & almost nothing to tax."[4]

John Floyd, county lieutenant of Jefferson County, declared that forty-seven inhabitants had been lost in that county by Indian attacks between January 1 and the middle of April, whole families having been sacrificed, regardless of age or sex; that their food consisted mainly of wild meat which could be gotten only with great labor and danger, and that the county was not wholly desolate was due to the confidence of the people in Clark's vigilance, enterprise, and military virtue and to their inability to escape.[5]

[1] Falls of the Ohio, April 28, 1781. Colonel George Slaughter to Clark. Clark MSS, Missouri Historical Society.

[2] Colonel Floyd to Clark, April 26, 1781. Out of 150,000 pounds of beef, all but 16,000 pounds spoiled.

[3] *Clark Papers*, p. 540.

[4] Todd to Jefferson, April 15, 1781. John Todd was at the time county lieutenant in Fayette County and was stationed at Lexington. *Cal. Va. State Papers*, II, 44.

[5] *Clark Papers*, p. 530. Letter of John Floyd to Thomas Jefferson, April 16, 1781. On April 24 Floyd again wrote Jefferson as follows: "Indigent Widows and Orphans make up a great part of the Inhabitants of this county who are

Dissatisfaction with American rule on the part of the inhabitants of the Illinois villages prevailed. Avarice, prodigality, and petty strife among the officers were continuous. Moreover, with the coming of La Balme the animosity of the French toward the Virginians increased, for they had been aroused by the hope of French aid in their behalf. In a memorial sent to the Governor of Virginia they declared that no more troops would be received by them except those sent by the King of France. Memorials were likewise drawn up addressed to Luzerne, which set forth in detail their grievances against the Virginians.[1]

The situation at Vincennes was similar. Oliver Pollock, as already noted, had been unable to meet the bills drawn on the treasury of Virginia. Colonel Le Gras stated the situation as follows: "I beg you if you can to send me in place of this same bill of exchange one of the same amount as those which are sent you from the treasury of Virginia for 1752 dollars in order to produce me some means of ministering to my pressing wants."[2] Continental money had been accepted by the Frenchmen in good faith following the assurance by American officers that it was equal in value to silver. Refusing to accept it in payment for provisions, they were commanded by public order to receive it or become subject to punishment.

During February a detachment of regular troops had been sent to Vincennes from Fort Jefferson, and their exactions were intolerable to the French. In a memorial to the Governor of Virginia they recited all their grievances

---

bereaved of their Husbands and Fathers by Savages and left among strangers without the common necessaries of life" (*ibid.*, p. 541).

[1] *Cahokia Records*, p. xciv. The messengers who carried these petitions, together with the papers of La Balme, were captured.

[2] *Clark Papers*, pp. 435, 469. La Gras to Clark, August 1 and December 1, 1780.

since the time Clark left them. "They have perpetrated others," they relate, "of a more serious character by killing our cattle in the fields and our hogs in our yards, taking our flour from the mills, and the corn in our garners, with arms in their hands threatening all who should resist them, and the destruction of the fort we built at our own cost. . . . . If it be thus you treat your friends, pray what have you in reserve for your enemies?"[1] Exhausted through repetition of these abuses, the French settlers finally retaliated. Captain John Bailey, in charge of the garrison, declared: "I must inform you once more that I cannot keep Garrison any longer without some speedy relief from you my Men have been 15 days upon half allowance, there is plenty of provisions here but no credit, I cannot press being the weakest party some of the Gentlemen would help us but their Credit is as bad as ours therefore if you have not provisions send whiskey which will answer as good an end."[2] The troops were shortly after withdrawn from Vincennes and the Illinois villages were also evacuated by the end of the year 1781, a few spies only remaining.

What was to be done by Clark in this crisis? His own force had been greatly depleted by desertions, and the time of enlistment for the majority of the regular troops at Louisville was about to expire. The loss of Colonel Archibald Lochry and his men was a cruel blow to Clark. Kentucky settlers were waiting impatiently to learn what was to be done for their protection against the assaults of the Indians, for the tribes north of the Ohio were in general revolt against Americans, and rumors of expeditions to be sent against them from Detroit were continuous.[3] By order

[1] *Clark Papers*, pp. 430 ff. See *Kaskaskia Records*, pp. 189 ff., for petition of the Kaskaskians.

[2] Letter to Colonel Slaughter, August 6, 1781. *Clark Papers*, p. 581.

[3] Draper MSS, 15 CC 35. A small tribe of the Kaskaskia Indians were still firm in their allegiance.

of the assembly the expedition directed against Detroit was again postponed.[1]

The three county lieutenants, together with three other field officers, constituted a council called by Clark. At their meeting in Louisville September 7, placing the situation squarely before them, he appealed for their co-operation in carrying on a general expedition and stated the influence of the western department on the Revolution. "But I know and always knew," he wrote, "that this Departm^t was of more real Service to the United States, than half of all their Frontier Posts, and have proved of great importance by engaging the attention of the Enemy that otherwise would spread Slaughter & Devastation throughout the more Interior Frontier, deprived them of giving any assistance to our Eastern Armies, and more than probable, the Allegany would have been our Boundary at this time." He called attention to the evacuation of Fort Jefferson, the probability of similar action at Vincennes, and the consequent loss of influence over several thousand warriors. Of the two routes which seemed open for an expedition—that by the Miami against the Shawnee and Delawares, or up the Wabash—Clark preferred the latter. This would bring them at once against the greatest bodies of Indians; but he was prepared to risk all in a single stroke, since their condition as well as his own appeared desperate. He saw in this expedition, if successful, the possibility of carrying his operations against Detroit. "I wait as a Spectator," he said, "to see what a Country is determined to do for itself when reduced to a State of Desperation; I am ready to lead you on to any Action that has the most distant prospect of Advantage, however daring it may appear to be. . . . . Some stroke of this sort might probably save your Country Another Season From

[1] *Cal. Va. State Papers*, II, 156, 177. June 21, 1781.

some late Occurrences I am apprehensive this will be the last piece of Service that I shall have in my power to do for you, in the Military line and I Could wish it to be as Compleat as possible My situation being desperate; similar conduct would be agreeable."[1]

While expressing confidence in Clark inasmuch as they were prepared to promise five hundred men, two-thirds the entire military strength of the three counties, and secure necessary provisions for any expedition he might undertake, the council advised against any offensive operations, or at most favored half-heartedly a small expedition up the Miami.

In keeping with the recommendation of the assembly, they advised the construction of forts at intervals along the Ohio, and especially one at the mouth of the Kentucky, which should be well garrisoned. They objected to maintaining the chief fort at the falls, since by so doing their strength would be needlessly divided, and opposed Clark's statement that it was a post of first importance. "To say that the falls is the Key to this country," John Todd, who was one of the council, declared, "seems to me unintelligible. It is a strong rapid which may in an age of commerce be a considerable obstruction to the navigation, but as we have no Trade we neither need nor have any keys to Trade."[2] They assumed that the fort, which they recommended, would be constructed and garrisoned by regular soldiers. But when it was ascertained that these burdens were to be borne by themselves, they refused to acquiesce, giving as their reasons the necessity of securing their crops, the want of money and intrenching tools, and constant fear of attacks by the Indians, which necessitated the militia's remaining at home.[3]

[1] *Clark Papers*, p. 598.
[2] *Cal. of Va. State Papers*, II, 562.   [3] Draper MSS, 51 J 93.

In a council of the officers of the department held the next day it was agreed that an expedition which should consist of only seven hundred men, the number of regulars and militia available, was impracticable. While insisting that the garrison at the falls should be maintained, they likewise recommended that a fort should be built at the mouth of the Kentucky, and urged the assembling of a strong force for the reduction of Detroit the next spring.

British officials were now giving greater attention to border affairs. Savage favor was maintained through the expenditure of larger sums for presents.[1] "I cannot," Haldimand wrote, "help expressing my surprize not only at the astonishing amount of those Bills, so soon following the last, but at so great expence being incurred at all." A continuous succession of attacks by small parties kept the frontier inhabitants from Illinois to New York in perpetual terror.[2] The brunt of these attacks fell on the Kentucky settlements. Even while Clark was in council with his officers, Brant and McKee were, as already related, marching toward Louisville with their victorious savages. Refusing to attack Clark, two hundred Mingo and Huron were with great difficulty kept together and led southward in order to attack some of the Kentucky forts or infest the roads.[3] Besides the constant fear from the Shawnee and other tribes north of the Ohio, reports were general that an attack on Kentucky by the Cherokee and Creek was soon to be expected.

The spirit of general despondency was portrayed by Colonel Floyd in the following letter: "The frontier of this

---

[1] General Haldimand to Major de Peyster, October 6, 1781. *Mich. Pioneer and Hist. Colls.*, X, 524.

[2] "It would be endless and difficult to enumerate to Your Lordship the Parties that are continually Employed upon the back Settlements." General Haldimand in a report to Lord George Germain, October 23, 1781 (*ibid.*, p. 530).

[3] *Mich. Pioneer and Hist. Colls.*, X, 517.

County [Jefferson] along the Ohio River is 227 miles by computation and the Inhabitants greatly dispersed & cooped up in small forts without any ammunition. The most distressed widows & Orphans perhaps in the world make up a great part of our Inhabitants."[1] Numerous appeals were made to the Virginia authorities for assistance. A thousand men, in addition to the available militia, would be able, they were informed, not only to secure Kentucky, but at the same time offer protection to the other back settlements on the New River as well as those on the Upper James and Roanoke. Without such assistance, and the consequent sacrifice of Kentucky, six thousand Indian warriors would be free to lay waste the whole frontier from Pennsylvania to South Carolina.

Clark still advocated an expedition up the Wabash against the Indian nations among which the English power was most strongly intrenched. He saw in such a movement, if successful, the capture of Detroit, control of the savages and preservation of the Kentucky settlements, retention of power over the Illinois, both Spanish and American, and ultimate influence on the terms of peace. It is probable he had in his possession at that time the message from Colonel Arthur Campbell, written nearly a month before, in which he stated that peace would probably be declared within a few months. "I wish," he wrote, "we could carry our arms to the banks of Lake Erie before a cessation would take place. . . . . altho' every true American must acknowledge, the advantages that would accrue, could Canada be added to the Union."[2]

---

[1] Letter to Governor Nelson, October 6, 1781. Clark MSS, Virginia State Archives. He reported that eighty-four of the inhabitants had been killed within six months. The number of militia for Jefferson County was then three hundred. Ninety-seven persons were killed in the region of the falls from February 6 to the end of the year 1781. Draper MSS, 16 CC 36.

[2] *Clark Papers*, p. 595.

The situation was, to Clark, full of discouragement when he declared: "But I would not wish to trouble your Excellency with my remarks. I have lost the object that was one of the principal inducements to my fatigues & transactions for several years past—my chain appears to have run out. I find myself enclosed with few troops, in a trifling fort, and shortly expect to bear the insults of those who have for several years been in continual dread of me."[1]

[1] *Clark Papers*, p. 608, October 1, 1781. Thomas Nelson was then governor of Virginia.

Chapter XII
The Last Year of the Revolution in the West

AFTER Yorktown the Revolution east of the mountains was really at an end. The instructions issued to Sir Guy Carleton on April 4, 1782, as he was setting out to take command in America, contain evidence of this fact. He was directed to transfer the garrison at New York to Halifax, even at the price of "an early capitulation," and the garrisons of Charleston and Savannah were to be similarly treated. During the last months of 1781 and for upward of a year thereafter the control of the West was still in the balance, and British and American leaders in that region continued to exercise their greatest military and diplomatic powers.

Early in December, 1781, the numerous recommendations from western officials were considered by the Virginia legislature.[1] While the members were fully aware of the critical situation, they were powerless to assume the burdens of an offensive warfare with an empty treasury and with paper money depreciated to the ratio of 1,000 to 1.[2] "Our paper money is at an end," wrote Governor Benjamin Harrison, "and from the redundancy of that baneful medium which has hitherto circulated amongst us, the credit of the State is at a very low ebb."[3] Legislative regu-

[1] *Journal of Virginia House of Delegates* (December 11, 1781), p. 35.

[2] Draper MSS, 51 J 98.

[3] Governor Harrison to the President of Congress, January 21, 1782. Harrison Letter Book, 1781 (Virginia State Archives), p. 31.

lation and the imposition of heavy taxes were resorted to
with the hope of restoring their lost credit. But contributions to the support of the army under General Nathanael
Greene and the campaign against Lord Cornwallis had
drained the state of its resources. The extended territory
from which collections were to be made rendered immediate relief through taxation impossible. Governor Harrison
was forced to answer the appeal of General Greene for relief as follows: "The credit of the State is lost and we have
not a shilling in the Treasury. The powers formerly given
to embody and march the militia of the State are no longer
continued to us, nor can we impress what may be necessary for you or even for ourselves. Invasion has nearly
drained us of our Stock of Provisions and Refreshments
of all kinds necessary for an army. As this is not an exaggerated but a true state of our situation I leave you to
judge whether any great Dependance can for the present
be placed on this State."[1]

The hopes of the leaders in the West were revived for
a time by the report of the successes of Greene in the South
and the capture of Cornwallis; but failure to carry out the
expedition under Clark and Colonel Gibson aroused their
fears lest they should now be attacked from Detroit.[2] Discontent became more prevalent during the winter months.
Fort Pitt was described as a heap of ruins. The combined
garrisons at this post and at Forts McIntosh and Wheeling
numbered 230 men. Military stores were almost exhausted; provisions were scarce, owing to the lack of public
credit, although at the time it was stated that at least 300
tons of flour were being held at Pittsburgh for shipment

[1] January 21, 1782. Harrison Letter Book, 1781, p. 32.
[2] Washington Manuscript (Library of Congress), Box 24, pp. 255, 256 ff.
Clark and Gibson were to combine in an attack on Detroit.

to Kentucky and New Orleans at the opening of navigation.[1]

The boundary line between Pennsylvania and Virginia had not been settled, and neither civil nor military authority could be enforced. There was an outcry against taxation of every form. Large numbers of the inhabitants of Westmoreland county, because of Colonel Lochry's defeat, were threatening to retire to east of the mountains.[2] A day was set upon which other settlers were to assemble at Wheeling for the purpose of acquiring lands on the Muskingum and founding a new state which must ultimately come under British control. Desertions were common among the troops.[3] For two years and three months they had received no pay. Forced to live in cold open barracks with little fuel and without adequate clothing, officers and men alike were incapable of performing the routine of garrison duties. "I never saw troops cut so deplorable, and at the same time despicable a figure." "Indeed, when I arrived," so wrote General William Irvine, the successor of Brodhead, who, in September, had been ordered to surrender his command to Colonel Gibson, "no man would believe from their appearance that they were soldiers; nay it would be difficult to determine whether they were

---

[1] General Irvine to General Washington, April 29, 1782. "Since I came up, I have given permits to ten boats for New Orleans and Kentucky Loaded with flour. I believe none of them carried less than thirty tons. I am informed ten or twelve more are to be down in one fleet of a much larger size." C. W. Butterfield, *Washington-Irvine Correspondence* (Madison, 1882), p. 202.

[2] James, "George Rogers Clark and Detroit," *Miss. Valley Hist. Assoc. Proc.*, III, 314.

[3] "Though nothing like general mutiny has taken place, yet several individuals have behaved in the most daring and atrocious manner, two of whom are now under sentence and shall be executed tomorrow, which I hope will check these proceedings." Butterfield, *Washington-Irvine Correspondence*, p. 111.

white men."[1] The Pennsylvania assembly seemed to disregard all appeals for frontier relief, and the commanding officer was forced to beg assistance from local authorities.

By order of the Governor of Virginia, Clark was directed to garrison the falls of the Ohio, the mouth of the Kentucky, the mouth of the Licking, and the mouth of Limestone Creek. Two gunboats were to be built for each post which should be used to patrol the Ohio and prevent any Indian bands from crossing.[2] This defense, it was argued, would enable the inhabitants to protect themselves against the incursions of the enemy and occasionally to attack them.[3] These garrisons were to be manned by regulars and militia consisting of one hundred men at the falls and sixty-eight at each of the other posts. The carrying out of these measures was dependent upon the generosity of the people themselves, supported by the promise that any debts contracted for the purpose should be met by the first means available and that there was every expectation of punctuality.[4] The troops under Clark were poorly prepared for the service they were expected to render. For two years many of them had served without receiving any pay, and during that time had been given neither shoes, nor stockings, nor a hat.[5] For a like period others had received no clothing of any sort from the state.[6]

[1] *Washington-Irvine Correspondence*, p. 75.

[2] Harrison Letter Book, 1781, pp. 13-15.

[3] *Jour. Va. House of Delegates* (December 15, 1781), p. 35.

[4] Harrison Letter Book, 1781, pp. 82, 83.

[5] Captain Robert Todd to the Virginia Council, December, 1781, *Executive Papers*, Virginia State Library. Captain Todd was the paymaster of Clark's regiment.

[6] "Our distress for the want of clothing cannot be otherwise than apparent when you reflect sir that for more than a year and a half we have not in this particular experienced the bounty of our country but have been left to struggle through a complication of difficult and distressful circumstances upon our own

Forced to live on half-rations, they conceived themselves totally neglected, while the main army, as they firmly believed, lacked nothing and was even supplied with luxuries. But the hardships in the camps of the continental army were quite as extreme. Because of a lack of the ordinary means of transportation, provisions collected in one county were unavailable for the use of the troops in an adjoining county. At that time Virginia troops at Cumberland Old Court-House had received no meat for fourteen days, and a state regiment at Portsmouth was reported to be in need of bread, meat, and salt.[1]

Once more Clark's preparations, his evasive answers to their inquiries, and messages to the enemy exerted a marked effect upon British plans and Indian acts. Typical of Clark's reports was one sent to the court of Kaskaskia early in December, calling for the thorough enforcement of the laws and asserting that peace was shortly to be expected, since Cornwallis with his entire army had surrendered and Clinton had lost three thousand men. "Charleston," he declared, "is besieged, and I think by this time it has surrendered with all the English troops; so that there will scarcely remain an Englishman on the Continent except those who are prisoners." More than one-half the Indian tribes made overtures to him for peace.[2]

During the fall and winter British authorities strove to gain control of all the northwestern tribes. Immense treasure was bestowed upon them and discipline was relaxed, for, as stated by one of the officials, Indians must

slender means" (Joseph Crockett to Governor Harrison, April 3, 1782, Clark MSS, Virginia State Library). Crockett accompanied Clark on the expedition.

[1] Harrison Letter Book, 1781, p. 37.

[2] *Wis. Hist. Colls.*, "Shane Papers," 16 J 37. It was estimated that twenty-seven of the fifty tribes were prepared to treat with Clark.

be used to prevent the inroads of the Virginians, and must be "delicately managed to prevent their favoring those rebels."[1] In January a company of Indians was sent to drive off some traders at "Chicagou" who were using their influence among the Indians in behalf of the Americans. Late in February chiefs of the Shawnee, Wyandot, Delaware, and ten other tribes assembled at Detroit.[2] They were instructed to make no attack, particularly on Kentucky, until toward spring. As a feint, small parties were sent forward to steal horses and commit minor depredations, thus keeping settlers off their guard until the coming of the main expedition which was to capture Fort Nelson and the other posts and at a single blow lay waste the whole frontier. Promise for the success of the plan was greater because of the arrival at Detroit of Rocheblave, Lamothe, and other captured leaders, all anxious to retrieve their former disasters by capturing the Illinois country and Vincennes.[3] Early in February the most exposed settlements of Kentucky and Virginia were surprised, a number of prisoners were captured, cabins were burned, and stock killed.

The outlook was still gloomier, for Clark had tendered his resignation to the Governor. Power to draw bills on the state had been intrusted to Clark alone, but large quantities appeared drawn by Colonel John Montgomery, Captain Robert George, and others. It was suspected that there was collusion between the drawers and those to whom the bills were made payable because of the large amounts and the fact that most of them were for specie, when it

[1] *Mich. Pioneer and Hist. Colls.*, X, 548.

[2] Butterfield, *Washington-Irvine Correspondence*, pp. 90, 91; *Mich. Pioneer and Hist. Colls.*, X, 546, 547.

[3] For the plan submitted by Lamothe, see *ibid.*, pp. 569, 572.

was common knowledge that there was no specie available in the state.[1] By an act of the assembly five commissioners were appointed to investigate the conduct of all officers, agents, contractors, and other persons who had disbursed public money in the West belonging to Virginia, and, if thought desirable, to appoint others to their places.[2] Clark interpreted the act as a reflection upon his conduct of public affairs. Free from military service, he planned to give attention to his land holdings, for, as he said, he possessed an "unprecedented Quantity of the finest Lands in the western world." At that time, immigration to the West was so extensive that the rise of land values was "amazing." Not only was his request to be relieved from service refused, full confidence in him having been expressed by the Governor, but his powers were made more extensive.[3]

Fully aware that the task was the most difficult he had ever undertaken, Clark pushed his preparations vigorously for foiling the main attack of the enemy, which it was understood would be directed against Fort Nelson.[4] "If we should be so fortunate as to repel this invasion without too great a loss to ourselves," he wrote, "the Indians will all

[1] Draper MSS, 46 J 69.

[2] Harrison Letter Book, 1781, pp. 41, 42. The Commissioners named were William Fleming, Thomas Marshal, Samuel McDowell, Daniel Smith, and Granville Smith. Any three of them might constitute the Commission. The "Journal of the Western Commissioners" is to be found in *Clark Papers*, 1781–83, ed. James, *Ill. Hist. Colls.*, Vol. XIX, *Virginia Series*, Vol. IV (Springfield, 1924), pp. 290–464.

[3] Clark MSS, Virginia State Library, Clark to Governor Harrison, February 18, 1782. "I am Satisfy'd Respecting the verbal message alluded to in your finding that it was not aimed at me, I wish those who see the Resolution may not think so as its known that most publick transactions in the Western Department pass's thro my hands, such an idea must be painfull to me well knowing the exertions I have used to save the publick monies."

[4] "But I doubt it will be out of my power to save this infant country from these impending strokes that now hover over it." Clark to Jonathan Clark, February 16, 1782. *Clark Papers*, 1781–83, p. 39.

scatter to their different Countries and give a fair opportunity for a valuable stroke to be made among them." In reply to his appeal for armed boats to prevent the incursions of Indians south of the Ohio Governor Benjamin Harrison wrote: "I am sorry to inform you that we have but four shillings in the treasury, and no means of getting any more."[1]

Assuming a part of the expense himself, Clark gave special attention to the construction of four armed galleys with the design of using them to control the navigation of the Ohio at the mouth of the Miami. Spies and scouting parties were constantly engaged on the various trails leading to the settlements in order to prevent possible surprise.[2] Early in July one of the boats, with a 73-foot keel, was completed, having bullet-proof gunwales 4 feet high and false gunwales which could be raised in case of attack.[3] When completely equipped it was to be manned with 110 men and was to carry a six-pounder, two fours, and a two-pounder. The obstacles encountered in carrying out defensive measures were continuous. Militia ordered on duty at Fort Nelson refused to march,[4] and a company of thirty-eight men serving on the row-galley deserted, even after unusual concessions had been granted them.[5] The regiment of state infantry promised for western defense could not be sent for it was found that their services would be necessary to guard the coast.[6] Added to the general confusion

---

[1] April 22, 1782. [2] Draper MSS, 52 J 2.

[3] The expense was met in part by the sale of flour from the general storehouse. "Take all the pains you can to find out and encourage Boatbuilders and good workmen to repair to this place immediately they shall have good wages, in hard money, if you can find experienced ship carpenters that come immediately he shall have almost what wages he will ask." Clark to Joseph Lindsay, March 5, 1782.

[4] Draper MSS, 52 J 2.

[5] *Ibid.*, p. 25. [6] Harrison Letter Book, 1781, pp. 82, 83.

and lack of discipline incident to the fear of attack there was a spirit of insurgency on the part of certain leaders born of the desire to form an independent state and "calculated on purpose for disaffection & an evasion of duty."[1]

Clark's preparations were, in the usual fashion, greatly magnified by the authorities at Detroit. It was asserted that he was about to march with four thousand men for the capture of that post. According to another report which was current, a force of one thousand French and Spaniards were to join Clark on this expedition. To add to their alarm and confusion, the first news reached Detroit early in April of the surrender of Cornwallis, and it was rumored that the Iroquois were about to make peace with the Americans.[2] There was no hope for assistance from Montreal, for the British authorities were in expectation that such troops as they could spare would be needed to make a diversion in favor of Sir Henry Clinton, who was defending New York. While directing that an effort should be made to render Detroit safe from assault, General Haldimand, in anticipation of the importance of holding that post should peace ensue, ordered the collection of sufficient provisions to enable the garrison to withstand a formidable assault

The advance of Colonel William Crawford from Fort Pitt at the head of 480 mounted men was regarded as the advance guard of this American army. His force was made up of Pennsylvania and Virginia frontiersmen, some of whom had been guilty of taking part in the Moravian Indian massacre two months earlier. The outcome of Crawford's expedition can be fully understood only in its relation to this massacre, or the "Gnadenhuetten affair," as it has been called. No other deed narrated in the annals of the

[1] April 8, 1782. *Clark Papers*, 1781–83, p. 54.
[2] *Mich. Pioneer and Hist. Colls.*, **X**, 565, 566.

frontier gives such evidence of a lapse into revolting brutality on the part of the borderers.

Early in the year 1772, David Zeisberger and John Heckewelder, Moravian missionaries who had labored faithfully among the Delawares in western Pennsylvania, responded to the appeal of the Delaware nation in Ohio and led their followers of Christian Indians to a site which was granted them by the Delawares on the Tuscarawas River about 100 miles from Fort Pitt. Here they founded three settlements, Salem, Gnadenhuetten, and Schönbrunn, where for a number of years they lived undisturbed as prosperous farmers. Their cabins were well built; they were governed by published laws; and their children received some schooling. At the outbreak of the Revolution their leaders declared they were to remain neutral, an impossible rôle, living as they did on the warpath between Fort Pitt and Detroit. Both sides were suspicious of them, for at times some of their young men joined the war parties of the enemy Indians, and there is evidence of a secret correspondence between them and the Americans at Pittsburgh. That a stricter watch might be kept on them, a band of 250 British and Indians under the renegade Captain Matthew Elliot, during September, 1781, appeared at their settlements and forced them to accompany him to the upper Sandusky River. Their leaders were taken to Detroit, but as no evidence was obtainable relating to their sympathy for the Americans, they were permitted to return to their followers. Their suffering at the hands of their Indian captors and because of hunger and cold was extreme. Before the opening of spring a company of about a hundred Christian Indians was permitted to return to the deserted villages to harvest the corn which still stood in the fields.

Early that spring there was great consternation in the region of Fort Pitt because of Indian atrocities, and it was supposed the enemy was occupying the deserted Moravian Indian towns. Colonel David Williamson, with a force of some three hundred militia, was sent against them.[1] Disregarding the warning sent them, the Christian Indians made no effort to escape, and the entire company of men, women, and children, about ninety in all, was captured. For three days the captors deliberated, and then, as determined by the majority, all of the Indians were put to death in a "most cool and deliberate manner," one boy only escaping.[2] Denounced by the leaders on the frontier as an act disgraceful to humanity and productive of dangerous consequences, they demanded that the perpetrators should be brought to punishment. But nothing further than the condemnation of the act resulted from the investigation by the assembly of Pennsylvania. Some of the guilty, however, soon met a just fate as members of the expedition under Crawford, for the Delawares, especially, sought to avenge the loss of their relatives.

Colonel William Crawford, who was a personal friend of Washington, saw service at the Battle of Brandywine in charge of a West Augusta regiment. He had served also in the West under General Hand and General McIntosh, and was reported to be a brave and active officer. But he was not the leader for a retaliatory expedition against an Indian enemy, and only one hundred of his troops were veterans in this kind of warfare.

On May 25 they set out in four columns from the Mingo Bottom, a day's journey from Fort Pitt, in the direction of the Wyandotte and Shawnee towns on the upper Sandusky. These Indians, having some five hundred warriors,

---

[1] General William Irvine to Washington, April 20, 1782. *Washington-Irvine Correspondence*, p. 99.

[2] Major William Croghan to Colonel William Davies, July 6, 1782. *Clark Papers*, 1781–83, p. 71.

constituted the most inveterate foes of the whites, and, according to General Irvine's instructions, they were to destroy them "with fire and sword by which we hope to give ease and safety to the inhabitants of this country." Colonel Crawford planned to move rapidly, as directed, and effect a surprise, but scouts reported his plans at Detroit before the advance was actually begun, and Indian spies followed their every movement.[1]

Owing to the rough route and to what seems a lack of foresight, three days more were consumed in the march than were actually necessary. By a forced march the attack might have been made according to orders, which were "to make the last day's march as long as possible and attack the place in the night." But, confident of success, they encamped ten miles from the first Sandusky town and set out leisurely at seven in the morning after firing a volley from their rifles.

In the meantime, the commandant at Detroit, while keeping careful watch for Clark's coming up the Wabash, dispatched Captain William Caldwell with a company of rangers, volunteers, and Lake Indians to the defense of the Sandusky villages.[2] "It will, however, not be prudent," Colonel De Peyster wrote, "to weaken this garrison much more till I am satisfied that Mr. Clark is not meditating a stroke at this settlement." After accessions of bands of Wyandotte and Delaware warriors, this force of some three hundred, two-thirds of them Indians, encountered the Americans on the early afternoon of June 4. The battle which ensued lasted until dark, with little advantage gained on either side, notwithstanding the superiority of the Amercans in numbers.

At daybreak the following morning the firing was re-

---

[1] *Mich. Pioneer and Hist. Colls.*, X, 574-77.

[2] May 14, 1782, *Mich. Pioneer and Hist. Colls.*, X, 575.

sumed and was kept up at long range during the greater part of that day. The Americans had lost their advantage, for in the early afternoon a force of 140 Shawnee joined the Indians. Believing that the force of the enemy was now superior, American officers determined to retreat. In the darkness they forced their way through two divisions of the enemy. Discipline was impossible, and driven along by the Indians in close pursuit they finally fled in great confusion. At daybreak the main body, together with straggling parties, a force of about three hundred men in all, had reached a spot 5 miles from the scene of action. Colonel Crawford was among the number missing, and Colonel David Williamson, who was second in command, directed the retreat. So closely were they pursued by a force of rangers and Indians that they were forced to defend themselves in an open plain. In this action the enemy was repulsed, the Americans entered the woods, and the retreat was continued without further molestation. On June 13 they recrossed the Ohio, and the next day were disbanded. The losses of the British were inconsiderable. Fifty of the Americans were killed or missing. Most of those who fell into the hands of the Indians were put to death after extreme suffering. Colonel Crawford, with Dr. Knight, who served as surgeon on the expedition, together with nine others, were separated from the main body of troops and were captured by the Indians. Taken to an Indian town, they were stripped of their clothing, their bodies were blackened, and they were forced to run the gauntlet, men, women, and children beating them with sticks and clubs. All of the prisoners save Crawford and Knight were put to death at once, but these two were selected for torture. Knight was compelled to witness the sufferings of his companion, who, with a rope around his body, was led to a stake. He was then forced to walk barefoot over burning coals while his tormentors poked burning sticks against his naked body, while Crawford appealed, in vain, to Simon Girty to end his suffering by shooting him.[1] Knight was informed that he was to receive similar treatment at a neighboring town. On his way thither he was guarded by only one savage. The Indian, wishing a fire, unbound his prisoner and ordered him to collect the wood. Having found a good "chunk," Knight felled his guard with it and escaped into the forest. After twenty-one days of suffering through want of food, he finally reached Fort Pitt. The Delawares justified their fiendish performances as a retaliation for the cruelties of the Moravian massacre, and asserted that not a single prisoner should in the future escape torture.

In the midst of the general consternation caused by Crawford's defeat, the savages, incited by their victory, appeared in large numbers on the upper Ohio and advanced as far as Hannastown, some 30 miles beyond Pittsburgh along the old Forbes Road.[2] This settlement was burned and twenty of the inhabitants who were unable to gain the fort were made prisoners or killed. Isolated settlers were cut off in the usual fashion and settlements were burned. The inhabitants who did not escape to the forts were murdered or held as prisoners, crops were destroyed, and stock driven off by bands in the New River region and upon the other back settlements of the Carolinas.

Frontiersmen who had sustained the greatest losses through Crawford's defeat urged retaliation and besought General William Irvine to lead them on such an expedition. They offered to raise one thousand militia and equip them with horses and provisions. In arranging for another campaign against the Sandusky villages, General Irvine, who

[1] *Clark Papers*, 1781–83, p. 72.

[2] *Washington-Irvine Correspondence*, pp. 171, 250, 383, 391, note.

lacked confidence in volunteers, proposed to send one hundred regulars as a nucleus for the force of nearly a thousand men. He was the more confident of success since Clark had promised co-operation by advancing against the Shawnee.

General De Peyster early received intelligence of this movement, which he rightly interpreted as a concerted plan for the capture of Detroit. The defenses were strengthened and a gunboat was ordered to be stationed at the mouth of the Miami River.[1] Messages were forwarded to Captains Caldwell and McKee, who were at Sandusky, and to Captain Joseph Brandt, who intended to attack Wheeling, directing them to act solely on the defensive. But by the end of July the Kentucky settlements had received a staggering blow. Eleven hundred Indians, the greatest single body mustered during the entire Revolution, were brought together by Caldwell and McKee for an attack on Wheeling. While marching in that direction they were overtaken by Shawnee messengers imploring them to return for the protection of their villages against an attack by Clark. The alarm had grown out of the appearance of the armed rowgalley at the mouth of the Licking. Most of the savages declined to go farther, but the leaders, not content with a fruitless expedition, determined to invade Kentucky. With a small body of rangers and three hundred Wyandotte and Lake Indians they crossed the Ohio and on the night of August 15 appeared before Bryan's Station. This post, situated 5 miles to the northeast of Lexington, was the northernmost settlement of Fayette County. These two, together with Boone's, McGee's, and Stroud's, were the only settlements north of the Kentucky River. At the time, Bryan's Station was a palisaded post of forty cabins occupied by ninety men, women, and children. The in-

[1] *Mich. Pioneer and Hist. Colls.*, X, 625-27.

closure, which was 200 yards long and 40 yards wide, was surrounded by a wall 12 feet high. At each of the corners was a blockhouse two stories high with the upper story projecting 2 feet beyond the lower.[1] Its defense was dependent on forty-four men, heads of families, hunters, and surveyors.

The excitement during the night of August 15 was intense, for the settlers had been informed that a band of Indians which had been committing depredations had defeated a small company of militia sent in pursuit of them from a neighboring station. Some of the defenders of Bryan's were preparing to leave the fort to join those from other settlements in cutting off the retreat of the savages when evidence of their own danger was discovered. With such secrecy had the Indians advanced that "no spy or scout gave warning of the storm."[2] By daybreak the fort was surrounded. Before sunrise a few spies were sent forward to draw the garrison outside the gate, but through bad management this movement failed and the whole plan was detected.

Work of defense was immediately begun and two messengers were sent to Lexington praying for assistance. The spring which supplied the fort with water lay at the foot of the hill within easy reach of the ambushed enemy. To deceive the savages, the women and girls volunteered to go, as usual, to secure a supply of water. So cheerfully did they leave the fort gate and descend the path that the Indians took it for granted they were ignorant of the presence of an enemy. They reasoned if they captured the women the fort could not be surprised. Consequently, they allowed the pails to be filled and permitted the women to return unmolested. Shortly afterward a small body of

[1] *Filson Club Publications*, XII, 23, 24.

[2] *Executive Documents*, August 31, 1782, Virginia State Archives.

Indians was sent to open fire on the fort from the side nearest the Lexington road. Such an attack, it was believed would draw out a force from the stockade in pursuit and thus leave the others defenseless against the attack of the main body. Simon Girty and the other leaders were themselves deceived. Thirteen men rushed out of the gate toward Lexington, firing as they ran, as if in hot pursuit, but they returned as quickly. Believing that their ruse was successful, the main force of the Indians ran whooping toward the western gate. The defenders, fully prepared for such a stroke, opened fire on the approaching savages and drove them back in confusion. Before retreating they set fire to some cabins outside the stockade, but a contrary wind blew the sparks away from the fort and it was saved.[1] The enemy returned to the assault, no longer in the open, but from behind trees and stumps tried to direct their fire through the portholes. The settlers strove to pick off any warrior who exposed himself. This irregular firing was kept up until early afternoon with but inconsiderable losses on either side. At that time a rescue party of some forty men under Colonel Levi Todd appeared. The two horsemen from the fort overtook Colonel Todd, who was a short distance out from Lexington on his way to cut off the retreat of a band of savages which had been committing depredations south of the Kentucky. He set out at once for Bryan's. To reach the fort along the Lexington road they were compelled to pass by a field of tall corn in which the enemy was hidden. Warned by shots from the fields, seventeen mounted men, who were in advance, pushed on at top speed, and screened by a cloud of dust succeeded in entering the fort in safety. Colonel Todd, with the remainder of the force, mainly footmen, seeing that there was no

[1] Canadian Archives, *Haldimand Papers*, Series B, CXXIII, 308. Stipp, *Western Miscellany*, p. 185.

hope to reach the gate, fled toward Lexington, escaping from their pursuers with the loss of two men killed and two wounded.

Despairing of reducing the fort before the coming of other rescue parties, Girty, from a position in which he was protected, called on the garrison to surrender. He promised protection if they capitulated, but declared that none might hope for mercy if the siege were continued, for reinforcements were hourly expected bringing artillery with which the fort could be blown to pieces. But the defenders were familiar with the fate of Ruddle's and Martin's stations, and were not to be won by an empty promise of protection. A young man of the garrison, Aaron Reynolds, is said to have met the proposal in true backwoods style. He assured the renegade leader that he was well known and despised by all of them; that they had no fears of his artillery; and that if any of his followers entered the fort they would not deign to use rifles to oppose them, but would drive them out with switches. He dared Girty to remain another day, for by that time their own reinforcements were promised, and then not a single one of his followers should escape. The attack was continued throughout the night and ineffectual attempts were made to set fire to the fort. In the morning Girty and his associates, convinced that the siege was hopeless, withdrew. They destroyed growing corn, potatoes, and hemp, killed the cattle, sheep, and hogs, and took with them most of the settlers' horses. The retreat was conducted with deliberate slowness, and two days were consumed in covering the 40 miles to the Licking River. No effort was made to disguise their route, and when they encamped at the Blue Licks on the evening of the seventeenth, spies were stationed in expectation that a pursuing force would soon overtake them.

Shortly after the Indians retreated from Bryan's,

armed forces from Lexington, Harrodsburg, Boonesborough, and the smaller stations, in answer to the messages calling for assistance, began to arrive at that post. One hundred thirty-five militia from Lincoln County, without orders from Colonel Benjamin Logan, their county lieutenant, who was absent, led by Colonel Stephen Trigg and Majors Hugh McGary and Silas Harlan, hurried to the rescue. They were joined by the Fayette County militia, led by Colonel John Todd and Colonel Daniel Boone. After a hurried council it was determined to begin the pursuit at once, for they were eager to avenge the losses caused by this invasion. Besides, they were assured that the numbers of the enemy were inconsiderable, and that they might safely be attacked by the force then available.[1] On the morning of August 18 Trigg rode rapidly along the buffalo trace on the trail of the enemy. He led a force of picked men, well armed and noted for their skill in the use of the rifle. The morning of the nineteenth, having reached the Lower Blue Licks, they discovered a few Indians moving leisurely up the rocky ridge on the north side of the river, three-quarters of a mile away. The Kentuckians halted and held a council. Colonel Boone, the most experienced Indian fighter among them, when called on for his advice urged delay until they should be joined by the troops under Colonel Logan who were known to be coming to their assistance. All were then aware that the force with which they were confronted was probably superior to their own, and the officers in command were ready to accept Boone's views. But the more impetuous were opposed to delay of any sort. They believed that their numbers were but slightly inferior, and declared that a fierce attack would so confuse the enemy that their defeat would be assured. The headstrong McGary, still smarting under the

[1] Draper MSS, 52 J 37.

taunts of cowardice with which he was shortly before accused by his companions, was outspoken for an immediate attack, and spurring his horse into the river, exclaimed: "Delay is dastardly; let all who are not cowards follow me, and I will show them where the Indians are."[1] The challenge was accepted and the whole force dashed precipitately through the stream. On the farther side a single line of attack was formed, with Colonel Boone in command on the left, Colonel Trigg on the right, and Major McGary in charge of the center. They rode rapidly to within 60 yards of the enemy, where they dismounted and the battle was begun with a heavy fire from both sides.

Neither had the advantage of position, for the ground was favorable to both and the timber good. The attack by the left wing was so fierce that the Indians were driven back 100 yards; but the right wing, outflanked, was forced to give way. The center, attacked from front and rear, was forced back on the left, and the whole line quickly broke and fled in greatest confusion. The entire action lasted only about five minutes. The retreat became a mad panic as they neared the ford. "He that could remount a horse was well off," wrote Levi Todd, "and he that could not had not time for delay." The Kentuckians suffered their greatest losses in crossing the river. Their retreat to the ford was partially intercepted by a force of Indians, and many were tomahawked as they swam the stream. Benjamin Netherland was among the first to cross. Accused of cowardice for urging delay before the battle, he assumed command at this critical moment and rallied those who had crossed the river to the protection of their struggling companions. By a vigorous fire they forced the Indians to withdraw far enough to enable the remaining whites to cross in safety. Then the flight was resumed, and did not

[1] Stipp, *Western Miscellany*, p. 92.

cease until the fugitives met the force of volunteers under Colonel Logan which was advancing to co-operate in the attack and had reached a spot 6 miles beyond Bryan's Station. More than one-third of the Kentuckians, about seventy, including Colonels John Todd and Trigg, Major Harlan, and a number of other officers, were killed, and some twenty more were captured or badly wounded. The losses of the victors were so slight, a Frenchman and six Indians killed and ten Indians wounded, that they were ready to withstand a retaliatory stroke, and even delayed their retreat a day in expectation of such an attack. Three days later Colonel Logan, having gathered a force of 470 mounted men, marched to the field of battle, but the enemy had gone. After burying the dead, Colonel Logan led his troops back to Lexington, where they were disbanded. On the second of September the inhabitants of Jefferson County were likewise frightened by the sudden appearance of a band of one hundred Indians. Kincheloes Station was surprised and thirty-seven of the settlers were captured. The savages escaped after committing the usual depredations.

There was general despair in all of the frontier communities after the disaster at the Blue Licks. A similar stroke, it was believed, would not only lead to the destruction of the Kentucky settlements, but would bring the savage forces in larger numbers against the more interior counties of Virginia and the Carolinas. "The Ballance stands upon an equilibrium," one of the leaders wrote, "and one stroke more will cause it to preponderate to our irretrievable wo, and terminate in the Intire Breach of our country, if your Excellency is not concerned In our Immediate safety."[1] Numbers of young men, as usual in time of great danger, hastened to return to the older

[1] Andrew Steele to Governor Harrison, August 26, 1782. *Clark Papers*, p. 97.

settlements. Men with families threatened to leave the country unless protection should be sent them. Numerous petitions to the Governor and legislature of Virginia, describing the general calamity, called for intervention on their behalf. Others petitioned Congress to be taken under the protection of the general government. Criticism of Clark was widespread for failing to establish other fortified posts in addition to Fort Nelson, which was held to be so far to the west that it offered no protection against the inroads of the enemy.

Stirred by these messages, Governor Harrison rebuked Clark for failing to communicate with him for several months and for his neglect in carrying out orders for the establishment of additional posts, which would have prevented, he said, such a disaster.[1] But Clark held himself blameless for the situation in the West. The falls of the Ohio, he insisted, must first be fortified, and the completion of Fort Nelson had, he believed, saved the western country. Despairing of capturing so formidable a post, the enemy had divided his forces and sent one expedition against Wheeling and another to fall on the Kentucky settlements. That these posts had been surprised, he maintained, was due to a lack of foresight in not keeping scouting parties constantly employed, as had been ordered. The conduct of the leaders at the Blue Licks he characterized as "extremely reprehensible," due in large part to an attempt to offset their former neglect of duty. Plans had been made by Clark to put into operation the complete plan for fortifications. After strengthening Fort Nelson, he proposed to construct a fort at the mouth of the Kentucky and another at the mouth of the Licking. County officials refused their

[1] *Ibid.*, p. 134.

assistance in furnishing the necessary men and supplies, and his own force, growing weaker each day because of desertions due to the failure to provide them with necessary food and clothing, was too small to garrison the additional posts. Another advance by the enemy which was expected would, Clark asserted, make their labors useless.

Early in September Captain Caldwell was again at the upper Sandusky, where he awaited the coming of the expedition from Fort Pitt. Runners were dispatched to Detroit and to the other posts urging that reinforcements should be sent at once to his relief. At the time, owing to sickness among the rangers, his defense was dependent almost wholly upon the Indians. Detroit officials, anticipating that Captain Caldwell would be forced to retreat before so formidable an enemy and that the Shawnee would be unable to withstand an attack by Clark, prepared a second defense which would cover the retreat to Detroit.[1] As usual, Major De Peyster, overcome with fear at the approach of the enemy, was ready to sacrifice his allies, and wrote Captain McKee as follows:

By the accounts of their force in the present sickly state of the Rangers and the Indians being so much distressed I fear you will be obliged to retreat at least till you are joined by the Miamies. I have sent all the Indians I could muster particularly the Ottawas of the Miamie River. . . . . You must be sensible that my soldiers are little acquainted with would [wood] fighting and Ill equipped for it withall. I have therefore only ordered them to take post where they can secure the ammunition and provisions and support you in case you are obliged to retreat which I hope will still not be the case.

During September and October preparations continued for the co-operative campaign, in which General Irvine was to advance with twelve hundred men, militia and regulars, against Sandusky, and Clark was to attack the Shaw-

[1] Major De Peyster to General Haldimand, September 29, 1782. *Mich. Pioneer and Hist. Coll.*, X, 651.

nee strongholds. Nine hundred men were also to be sent against the Genesee towns.[1] Kentuckians responded at once to Clark's call for a retaliatory expedition.[2] Parched meal, buffalo meat, and venison were quickly collected, but other supplies were gotten together with great difficulty. The credit of the state was worthless, and creditors who had already advanced all of their property were at the time beseeching Clark to aid in the adjustment of their claims. His own available resources were exhausted. "I have already taken every step in my power to get the creditors of the state paid to no effect," he wrote Oliver Pollock, "Except what the state owes me am not worth a Spanish dollar. . . . . if you could point out the means [to pay the debts] nothing would give me such pleasure, and fully Recompense all the uneasiness I have suffer'd on account of those persons, many whom I know have advanced all they had on the faith of government."[3] He finally exchanged 3,500 acres of his own land for the flour necessary for the expedition.

By November 1 the two divisions of Kentucky troops reached the mouth of the Licking, the appointed place of rendezvous. Colonel Floyd, in charge of one division consisting of regulars from Fort Nelson and militia from the western stations, ascended the Ohio with the artillery, while the other section, commanded by Colonel Logan, marched from the eastern settlements.[4] On the fourth of November 1,050 mounted men, with Clark in command, set out for Chillicothe, the main Shawnee stronghold. Rigid discipline was maintained during the march of six days.[5] A plan of attack had been worked out by Clark in

[1] *Washington-Irvine Correspondence*, pp. 181, 182.

[2] Clark to Governor Harrison, October 22, 1782. *Clark Papers*, p. 140.

[3] October 25, 1782. *Ibid.*, p. 144.

[4] Draper MSS, 52 J 52.　　　　[5] *Ibid.*, 11 J 24.

minute detail. Three miles from the town, Colonel Floyd was sent forward with three hundred men to make the attack. But his approach was discovered, and warned by the alarm-cry, the inhabitants made good their escape with the loss of ten killed and ten who were taken prisoners. Chillicothe and five other Shawnee towns were burned, and 10,000 bushels of corn and large quantities of provisions were destroyed. Colonel Logan, with a detachment of 150 men, captured the British trading-post at the head of the Miami and burned such stores as they were unable to carry away with them. After vainly attempting for four days to bring on a general engagement, Clark returned with his troops to the mouth of the Licking, where the divisions again separated.

By this blow Clark had not only saved the frontier settlements from danger of attack, but he had offset the designs of British authorities to bring about a union of the northwestern and southwestern tribes. This plan, closely akin to that of 1781, was well calculated to win the support of the Indians, for it promised the advance of a large force from Detroit against Fort Pitt, the capture in succession of that post, Fort Nelson, and other Kentucky posts, and the retaking of the Illinois country. In this manner Kentuckians, it was said, would be driven across the mountains and "the other inhabitants into the sea." Clark had extended the radius of menace toward Detroit and had thrown the enemy into utmost confusion. The Indians were panic-stricken at this evidence of strength. Their winter supplies were destroyed, and the policy of retrenchment on the part of British officials, due in part to the high prices fixed by monopolies, cut down the quantities of Indian presents.[1] In fact, further demands by the Indians

[1] *Mich. Pioneer and Hist. Colls.*, I, 320, 321. General Haldimand in a letter to Thomas Townsend, November 9, 1782, wrote: "I flatter myself, that the

for protection from Detroit were denied. So effectively had Clark carried out his policy of intimidating the Indians that, as stated by Boone: "The spirits of the Indians were damped, their connexions dissolved, their armies scattered and a future invasion [was] entirely out of their power."[1]

This testimony was corroborated by British officials, one of them declaring: "I am endeavoring to assemble the Indians, but find I shall not be able to collect a number sufficient to oppose them, the chiefs are now met here upon that business who desire me to inform you of their Situation requesting you will communicate it by the inclosed strings to their Brethren the Lake Indians, without speedy assistance they must be drove off from their country, the Enemy being too powerful for them."[2]

Sickness still pervaded the ranks of the rangers, and regular soldiers, it was claimed, were not suitable, nor were they equipped for a winter campaign. "The few Rangers at this Post," Major De Peyster wrote, "prevents my doing anything essential for the relief of the Indian Villages, it is therefore to be hoped that when the enemy have done all the mischief possible they will retire."[3] He was aware that the road to Detroit was open, and he fully expected an attack would be made by the Americans in the spring.[4]

King's Ministers, must be convinced of my attention to Diminish the Public Expense. I have now to acquaint you Sir, that a spirit of monopoly, pervaded this Province, a combination has been made and succeeded, in engrossing, into a few hands, the Rum, Brandy and other spirituous Liquors which have been imported."

[1] Testimony of Daniel Boone before a Committee of Investigation, December 20, 1787.

[2] Captain McKee to Major De Peyster, November 15, 1782. *Haldimand Papers*, Series B, CXXIII, 336.

[3] De Peyster to Haldimand, November 21, 1782. *Mich. Pioneer and Hist. Colls.*, XI, 321, 322.

[4] Captain McKee to Major De Peyster, November 15, 1782. "Whatever their Intentions may be, the Road I am afraid will be open for them to Detroit."

Indian leaders were again ordered to act solely on the defensive. In demanding reinforcements, De Peyster declared: "Light troops are therefore what we want, and believe me there will be amusement for a good number of them the ensuing campaign without acting on the offensive."[1]

Messengers sent by General Irvine had informed Clark that the expedition against Sandusky was assured.[2] But as they were about to set out from Fort McIntosh, the place of rendezvous, letters were received from the Continental Secretary of War countermanding the order for the expedition. Washington had been assured, on British authority, that all hostilities were suspended and that the savages were to commit no further depredations. Reports were still sent out by Irvine that he was about to march with a large force toward Sandusky. These were well calculated to deceive the Wyandotte and prevent their co-operation with the Shawnee against Clark.[3]

With the return of Clark's victorious troops, the feeling of confidence among Kentuckians was restored. Their numbers had been perceptibly increased during the summer months by the coming of large numbers of immigrants. That Kentucky was the land of promise is well shown in a letter of James Monroe. At that time he was a member of the Virginia Council, but evidently contemplated removal to the West.[4] He expressed his admiration for the spirit of enterprise which had been manifested by Kentuckians, and inquired specifically about the increase of settlements and their ability to protect themselves, the progress of society, the resources of the country in products and trade relations,

[1] *Mich. Pioneer and Hist. Colls.*, XI, p. 321.

[2] The Wyandotte center. This message was received by Clark November 2. *Washington-Irvine Correspondence*, p. 398.

[3] *Ibid.*, pp. 400, 401.

[4] Confidential letter to Clark, June 26, 1782. *Clark Papers*, p. 68.

and the prospect for setting up an independent government. Settlers with land warrants crowded the offices of the surveyors. So keen was the rivalry to secure choice locations of land that the commissioners sent by Virginia to adjust the military accounts were with difficulty able to secure attendance upon their meetings.[1]

Clark took up at once with the commissioners the problem of establishing forts, for the letters from Governor Harrison specified that the original plan should be carried out. But obstacles were still insuperable. By disposing of some of his own lands, the credit of the state being worthless, Clark had, as we have seen, supplied the necessary stores at Fort Nelson.[2] Herds of buffalo were exterminated or had retreated so far beyond the settlements that the expense of hunting them was prohibitory.[3] A specific tax was in vogue in Fayette County alone. Men were not available for the performance of garrison duties, and the artillery was inadequate. As Clark expressed it: "There is not a sufficiency of cannon for a Block hous, instead of mounting four or five forts." It was not difficult for the commissioners, when confronted by actual conditions, to understand how utterly futile would be the attempt to enforce the instructions of the Governor.

Steps must be taken, however, to protect immigrants who should enter the country by the Ohio and through Cumberland Gap, and also insure safety to the river trade. Fort Nelson, the commissioners agreed, served as a shield to trade and as protection for the inhabitants of Jefferson County.[4] Three of the commissioners favored the establish-

---

[1] *Executive Papers*, Virginia State Archives, Lincoln County, December 23, 1782. Meetings of the three commissioners were held at Harrodsburg and Lexington prior to December 23. Messengers were sent to Kaskaskia and Vincennes demanding that creditors and officers appear before them at Louisville.

[2] *Ibid.*, November 30, 1782. *Clark Papers*, p. 161.

[3] *Ibid.*, p. 168.   [4] Draper MSS, 60 J 261.

ment of a post at the mouth of the Kentucky. The mouth of the Limestone was advocated by the fourth commissioner as a suitable site for a fort which would afford protection to Fayette County and at the same time would induce immigrants to locate between the Ohio and the settlements already established.[1]

Combatant and noncombatant alike at Detroit and all of the Kentucky settlements awaited the passing of winter with anxious foreboding. British officials fully expected the coming of the Americans at the earliest possible date with the design of extending their frontiers in the Northwest as far as possible, and thus, in the event of peace, to get control of the fur trade.[2] Clark's threats to march against the other enemy Indians as he had against the Shawnee kept the tribes in continual turmoil. They were already restive under the restraints of British leaders and looked upon the policy of retrenchment in supplying them with presents as a step toward their complete abandonment to the conquerors.[3]

Clark likewise beheld the coming of spring with apprehension. Messengers were dispatched to the Chickasaw and Creek nations to induce them to enter into treaty relations and to secure their lands, which would naturally come within the Virginia boundaries, if they could be acquired, as advocated by Clark, at moderate rates.[4] Although he was confident that no formidable Indian advance was probable before fall, Clark appealed to the com-

----

[1] The mouth of the Licking and Limestone were opposed by the three commissioners on account of their location so far up the river that it would be impracticable to supply them with provisions.

[2] *Mich. Pioneer and Hist. Colls.*, XI, 351.

[3] *Ibid.*, p. 336.

[4] December 19, 1782. Virginia in this manner was to establish her right to charter boundaries and counteract the claims set up by some of the states of sovereignty by purchase.

missioners to assist him in strengthening the defenses against Indian hostilities which still occurred from time to time. Again he urged the importance of Fort Nelson as the key to the country. As a protection to the eastern Kentucky settlements he once more advocated the construction of one or more garrisons farther up the river. To complete his plan for foiling the enemy he urged the mustering of fifteen hundred troops who were to march against the Indian stronghold at the head of the Wabash. In this way he proposed to convince the Indians that their very existence depended upon peace with the Americans.[1] A garrison of regular troops was to be stationed at Vincennes, with supplies adequate to equip a force which might be brought together at any time for the purpose of penetrating "into any Quarter of the Enemy's Country at pleasure."

No further effort was made to carry out these plans, for by the middle of April the official announcement of the signing of the peace preliminaries at Paris and the cessation of hostilities had been sent to the frontier settlements.[2] The proclamation of a general peace soon followed.[3]

By the terms of the definitive treaty of peace, concluded at Paris September 3, 1783, the Old Northwest was ceded to the United States.[4] No reference is made in the diplomatic papers to the conquest by Clark as a factor in reaching a final agreement. The question has been a mooted one, therefore, as to how far Clark was in military control of this territory, and two views have been advanced. One

---

[1] *Executive Papers*, Virginia State Archives, February 25, 1783.

[2] Preliminary articles were signed at Paris, November 30, 1782.

[3] Harrison Letter Book, April 9, 1783. The cessation of hostilities was agreed to at Versailles, January 20, 1783. Some five hundred prisoners were released by the Detroit authorities. *Mich. Pioneer and Hist. Colls.*, XI, 367.

[4] For the events leading up to the definitive treaty and the terms agreed upon, see Edward Channing, *History of the United States*, III, 346-73.

of these is fairly presented in a letter of Governor Benjamin Harrison to Clark, July 2, 1783, in which he states that since an offensive war against the northwestern Indians has been given up, Clark's services in that region will no longer be necessary, "But before I take leave of you," he wrote, "I feel myself called on in the most forcible manner to return my thanks and those of my council for the very great and singular services you have rendered your country in wresting so great and valuable a territory out of the hands of the British enemy, repelling the attacks of their savage allies, and carrying on successful war in the heart of their country." John Pierce, representing the United States, as one of three commissioners appointed to adjust the claims of Virginia for debts contracted in carrying on the Revolution in the West, maintained "that by leaving the territory with his forces, Clark relinquished the defense of it, and he cannot, I think be said to have maintained or defended a country beyond him in which he retained no garrison and from which he was at such a distance as to afford no immediate assistance."[1]

In general, historians have advanced similar views, of which the following may be taken as fairly illustrative. "Clark would have pushed on to capture Detroit also but want of sufficient reinforcements compelled him to be content with holding Vincennes, Cahokia, and Kaskaskia. These posts, however, were sufficient to insure the American hold upon the Northwest until, in the peace negotiations of 1782, the military prowess of Clark was followed by the diplomatic triumph of Jay."[2] "Jay and Franklin could have found no footing for their contention, had Clark not been in actual possession of the country. It certainly

[1] Report of the Commissioners.

[2] Claude H. Van Tyne, *American Revolution*, American Nation Series, IX, 284.

was a prime factor in the situation."[1] "We were in reality," Theodore Roosevelt asserted, "given nothing more than we had by our own prowess gained; the inference is strong that we got what we did get only because we had won and held it."[2] The second view is summarized in the following statement: "The summer of 1779 marked the zenith of Virginia's power north of the Ohio; from that date, there was steady decline. . . . . For a year more there were a score of soldiers in those posts, acting as scouts; but even these were recalled in the following winter, and the villages were left to shift for themselves. . . . . Virginia had really only weakened the hold of the mother country on a small corner of the disputed territory."[3]

But the fact that Clark concentrated his available force at Fort Nelson after 1779 does not prove that he relinquished the defense of the Northwest. His own testimony points to an opposite conclusion, for he wrote: "I see but one probable method of maintaining our Authority in the Illinois which is this by evacuating our present posts and let our whole force center at or near the mouth of the Ohio."[4] Moreover, if Clark's position at the close of the campaign against the Shawnee is considered, a more satisfactory interpretation of the influence of his efforts becomes apparent. We have seen that this stroke marked the final aggressive movement in his offensive-defensive policy.[5] It demonstrated the wisdom he dis-

[1] Reuben G. Thwaites, *How George Rogers Clark Won the Northwest*, p. 72.

[2] Roosevelt, *The Winning of the West*, II, 381.

[3] Alvord, "Virginia and the West," *Miss. Valley Hist. Rev.*, III (1916, 1917), 34.

[4] He refers to the construction of Fort Jefferson, but the same argument obtained relative to Fort Nelson.

[5] For a more extended discussion, consult James, "To What Extent Was George Rogers Clark in Military Control of the Northwest," *Report American Historical Association* (1917), 313–29. See also, *Clark Papers, Ill. Hist. Colls.*, XIX, Introduction (lv–lxv), and documents.

played in selecting Fort Nelson as a base for such operations. At no time were the British prepared to reduce this post, although they were well aware it constituted the key between the East and the Illinois country, that it dominated western trade and was the center for operations against Detroit. From this base it was possible for Clark to reach Vincennes or Kaskaskia in a much shorter time than it could have been accomplished by the British from Detroit, and the knowledge of any advance by the enemy was quickly imparted to Clark.[1] Moreover, the warriors of the tribes on the Scioto and the Miami, especially the Shawnee, "the first in at a battle, the last at a treaty," chief dependence of the British, could not be induced to engage in any expedition which would leave their villages exposed to attack by an enemy so readily brought against them. These facts regarding Clark's military control must have been patent to the negotiators of the peace terms, and served no doubt to confirm Lord William Shelburne in his decision to yield to the demand the American Commissioners were instructed to make that the Mississippi and the Great Lakes should constitute the boundaries.

The appeal made to Shelburne by Franklin, that generosity on the part of Great Britain would regain the love of the Americans, was no doubt effective. Fifteen years later (1797), after the British troops were withdrawn from the posts on the Great Lakes, Shelburne wrote a friend in America: "I cannot express to you the satisfaction I have felt in seeing the forts given up, I may tell you in confidence what may astonish you, as it did me, that up to the very last debate in the House of Lords, the Ministry did not appear to comprehend the policy upon which the boundary line was drawn, and persist in still considering it as a measure of necessity not of choice. However it is indif-

[1] Opinion of Colonel Knox.

ferent who understands it. The deed is done: and a strong foundation laid for eternal amity between England and America."[1]

[1] Lord Edmond Fitzmaurice, *Life of William, Earl of Shelburne* (London, 1875–76), II, 202, note. I cannot agree with the statement of Dr. Alvord, however, "that the basis for the success of American diplomacy had been laid, not by the victory of the arms of Virginia, not through the boldness of George Rogers Clark in winning the Old Northwest for the United States, but in the liberal principles held by a British statesman." Alvord, "Virginia and the West," *Miss. Valley Hist. Rev.*, III, 38. See Louise Phelps Kellogg, "Review of George Rogers Clark Papers, 1781–83," *Ill. Hist. Colls.*, Vol. XIX, *Miss. Valley Hist. Rev.*, XIV (1927), p. 83.

Chapter XIII

Western Problems at the Close of the War

B Y THE middle of April, 1783, when general peace was proclaimed, Clark, under orders from the Governor of Virginia, had set out for Richmond. The investigation of his conduct, which had been under way for some months, pertained not alone to the unauthorized bills drawn by his inferior officers but to the charges of lack of discipline and want of economy in the conduct of western affairs.

Governor Harrison declared that he thought the charges false. Clark acknowledged that many errors had been committed, but that they were incidental to the management of the extensive and varied business of the western department. The "little men" sometimes sent to the seat of government from the West were, he insisted, the originators of false impressions.

Jealous of their importance, [he wrote] they embrace that declamatory principal so very agreeable to such bodies, supposing by striking at the principal characters of their Country, that Strangers will view them as men of consequence. The credit that is given to such characters near the helm of affairs, I can assure you Sir hurts the Interest of the State greatly. The expences in this department hath been considerable, but had it not been for them and the consequential service, we should have been obliged before this to have spent five times as much in defence of our frontiers, and except some expences that have proved unnecessary, as a citizen, I am satisfied with the propriety of the Whole.[1]

[1] Clark to Colonel William Davis, October 19, 1782. *Clark Papers*, p. 139.

These criticisms were characterized, after the findings of the Western Commissioners were made public, as groundless and nothing more than the "production of Envy and Cankered Mallice thrown out by little narrow minded Malitious Persons."[1] In fact, so carefully had Clark preserved vouchers for articles purchased and so trustworthy was his testimony that in the final adjustment of his accounts the Virginia Assembly authorized the auditors "to admit his oath for disbursements" to the amount of $11,599.[2]

Clark explained the seeming lack of efficiency in the conduct of western affairs as follows:

After you consider the Various circumstances attending the Command I was intrusted with you could not suppose it strange that only memorandums should be taken of some of them and many totally neglected which I doubt will prove Ruinous to my private Interest as the great Variety of other publick business solely Engaged my attention and Required all the address I was master of to superintend the publick Interest to advantage not only the Civil Government of the people of the Illinois to attend to Recruiting and disposing of troops that was difficult to support etc. But numerous tribes of Indians that had Ingagd in war against us that Required great and constant attention as well as Considerable sums of money to support.[3]

He was unwilling to attempt the defense of the West and at the same time be compelled to cope with the disaffection toward the state which was manifested by the adherents of the general government.[4] Congress, as represented by Virginia officials, was determined to seize the conquered territory without making adequate returns for the expense connected with its capture and defense.[5]

[1] William Clark, cousin of George Rogers Clark. Draper MSS, 3 M 18–25 (March 16, 1783).

[2] July 5, 1785. Department of State, Bureau of Indexes and Archives. Clark to Oliver Pollock, October 25, 1782.

[3] *Clark Papers*, p. 242.

[4] Clark to Governor Harrison, March 8, 1783. *Ibid.*, p. 214.

[5] James Monroe to Clark, January 5, 1783. *Ibid.*, p. 180.

Discontinuance of general hostilities in the West rendered the regular military organization unnecessary, and Clark was voted out of commission. When imparting the content of this resolution the Governor concluded his letter as follows: "But before I take leave of you, I feel myself called on in the most forcible manner, to return to you my thanks, and those of my council, for the very great and singular services you have rendered your country in wresting so great and valuable a territory out of the hands of the British enemy, repelling the attacks of their savage allies, and carrying on a successful war in the heart of their country. This tribute of praise and thanks so justly your due, I am happy to communicate to you, as the united voice of the executive."[1] In retiring, Clark manifested no spirit of bitterness. He expressed an appreciation for these words of approbation and offered his services whenever the state might call upon him for its defense.

Clark now gave his attention chiefly to the Indian problem in the West. He knew better than any other man of his time the policy which would prove successful. He opposed terms which were gotten through the bestowal of presents, for this would be interpreted by the tribes as a sign of fear. Treaties secured in this manner, he declared, would merely incite young warriors to greater greed and bring on renewed attacks when the tribe itself might be ready to sue for peace. He advocated complete military control, and if his plan had been put into operation it is probable that the losses in the later Indian wars would have been largely avoided.[2]

To prevent attacks on the settlements and convince the Indians of their inferiority, he proposed sending an army of two thousand men into the heart of their country. With

[1] July 2, 1783. *Clark Papers*, p. 246.
[2] *Ibid.*, p. 229. Clark to Governor Harrison, April 30, 1783.

such a force, easily enlisted from all the frontier settlements and equipped by the state, a vigorous campaign of three months would suffice to secure the obedience of the Northwestern tribes. A part of the expense was to be met through the confiscation of Indian lands. While there were to be no infringements on the treaty by the whites, the breaking of its terms by a single tribe would lead to war against the offenders and the seizure of territory sufficient to cover all the expenses.[1]

But the economic condition of Virginia was such that an offensive war was impossible. Some months earlier Governor Harrison declared: The credit of the State is lost and we have not a shilling in the Treasury. . . . . Invasion has nearly drained us of our stock of Provisions and Refreshments of all kinds necessary for an Army.[2]

Four days after the preparation of this plan, Clark appealed to Governor Harrison for assistance in meeting his personal needs. "I can assure you, sir," he wrote, "that I am exceedingly distressed for the want of necessary clothing, etc., and I don't know of any channel through which I could procure any except of the executive." At that time the state was in his debt 3,400 pounds on account of the flour furnished the garrison at Fort Nelson and for his pay during a period of more than five years in which he served as colonel and as brigadier general.[3] The sum thus due him as an officer amounted to 2,193 pounds.

Under such circumstances Clark was forced to accept military certificates for a portion of the amount due him and warrants on the military fund for the remainder. He had, as noted, become responsible also for supplies gotten in the name of Virginia for which he had been unable to pay. His liability for many of these state bills brought

---

[1] *Clark Papers*, p. 238.   [2] Harrison Letter Book, 1781, p. 32.
[3] Report of Commissioners, July 1, 1783. *Clark Papers*, p. 244.

him before the courts, and his appeals for equitable adjustments continued during the remainder of his life.

This picture of distress is a sad one, and especially when it portrays the condition of a leader who by his fortitude, courage, and shrewdness had accomplished tasks which appeared well-nigh impossible. Many times in the course of the narrative we have seen his little half-starved army forced to live on meat which had spoiled because of lack of salt. Often, on the march, they were barefoot and distressed for lack of clothing and blankets. Boats, horses, wagons, powder, rifles, and cannon, necessities for a military expedition, were totally inadequate. But Clark's daring, foresight, and tactfulness were nowhere more manifest than in the Indian councils, where their demands were to be met from inadequate stores of vermilion, taffia, blankets, and tobacco.

But victory in the West was due not alone to the sacrifices of soldiers. Clark and his officers were ready on all occasions to give credit to civilians, such as Francis Vigo and Gabriel Cerré, for their assistance in procuring the bare necessities without which their plans must have failed. The one man who stood out as Clark's chief support was Oliver Pollock. That he secured the powder necessary for the advance on Kaskaskia, dispatched supplies from New Orleans to the Illinois country under circumstances the most adverse, and sustained Clark's credit during those critical days of 1778 and 1779 have already been noted. The personal sacrifices of Pollock in meeting these demands as well as similar ones on behalf of Virginia and of the United States have never been given adequate recognition. To him the title Financier of the Revolution in the West may with aptness be applied. "The invoice Mr. Pollock rendered upon all occasions, in paying those bills," Clark wrote (1785), "I considered at the time and now to be one of the happy circumstances that enabled me to keep possession of that Country."[1] As agent at New Orleans for the United States, and impliedly of Virginia—for that state later protested that his formal appointment had never been confirmed—he made advances during the war to the amount of $300,000. In reply to his appeal for remittances to the secret committee of Congress, consisting of Benjamin Franklin, Robert Morris, and Richard Henry Lee, they wrote, July 19, 1779, that while they recognized his claims, his sacrifices, and his faithfulness to duty, they were unable to make good any promises.

His claim against Virginia for advances made to Clark and his officers amounted in January, 1782, to $139,739, and according to his testimony, in July of that year he was in debt at New Orleans for the sum of $92,199 for money borrowed to support Virginia troops in the West. For months he was a suppliant before the assembly of that state, asking in vain for relief from a situation defined by him as follows: "When I undertook the Agency of the United States and conceived it my Duty to Act for Virginia also, my credit was extensive, my fortune equal to 100,000 Dollars. At this Day my credit as a merchant is injured, my fortune annihilated, and my numerous family become Pensioners on the Bounty of my Friends."[2]

In his distress he besought the assistance of Clark:

It may not be amiss to observe that before I could leave New Orleans, or be permitted by my creditors to Depart this Country, I was obliged to sell my Dwelling House, Plantation Slaves, Stock, Furniture, Store Goods, and part of my wife's Domesticks, to distribute their proceeds among my much injured creditors,—Creditors Sir made

[1] Department of State, Bureau of Indexes and Archives. *Miscellaneous Letters*, January–April, 1791. It is my plan to bring out a volume of the letters of Oliver Pollock under the auspices of the Chicago Historical Society.

[2] Pollock to Governor Harrison, July 16, 1782, *Executive Communications to the General Assembly*. There were six children in his family.

from the most virtuous motives, the desire of serving a country I loved, in distress, in a Cause my Judgment approved. The feeling human Heart will readily Conceive, the Anguish of my Tortured Soul, at parting with my wife and numerous family, Whom I reduced to Extreme misery and distress by Unprudently giving these Tortures to serve a Country, Whom Gratitude and Justice I had *too much* confidence in. I am too Conscious of the Rectitude of my Conduct, and feal too sensibly the suffering which have arose from a zeal, perhaps more warm than prudent, to apprehend a longer Delay of such Justice to which Effort Sentiment from an Honest Heart must proclaim me entitled.

My fortune which was respectable when you Sir by your address found the way to draw it from me, is now exhausted and I would be contented if it were not worse, I have extended my Credit for the Service of Virginia and borrowed for the same purpose 100,000 dollars from different people at New Orleans and now Sir when I appeared here with my accounts in hopes of finding Government disposed to pay, and to pay me with gratitude, assurances of which I have had from you, I find they are as destitute of inclination as of the means of paying me. . . . .

Step fourth rescue your Country from the Eternall Disgrace that must attend their iniquitous reward of my exertions, as you have by exertions when on the Mississippi Saved and preserved that valuable Country for the State you Serve.[1]

"I am heartily sorry," Clark replied, "that you should meet with such disappointments in the settlement of your accounts, ... If I was worth the money I would most chearfully pay it myself and trust the state, But can assure you with truth I am entirely Reduced myself by advancing Everything I could Raise, And Except what the state owes me am not worth a Spanish dollar, I wish it was in my power to follow your proposition to step forth and save my country from the disgrace that is like to fall on her."[2]

Examples of self-sacrifice on the part of leaders during the Revolution and of the utter inability of the governments, both state and federal, to meet their obligations are nowhere else more clearly portrayed.

Indeed, in a communication of Pollock to the President

[1] Draper MSS, 52 J 26.

[2] *Clark Papers*, p. 144.

of Congress there is to be found an appeal that the real patriot will appreciate as long as our nation endures:

It has not been my fortune to move on a splendid Theatre, where the weary Actor frequently finds in the applause of his Audience, new motives to Exertion. I dwelt in an Obscure Corner of the Universe alone and unsupported. I have laboured without ceasing, I have neglected the road to affluence, I have exhausted my all, and plunged myself deeply in Debt to support the Cause of America. In the Hours of her Distress, and when those who call'd themselves Friends, were Daly deserting her, But these things I do not Boast of, What I do boast of is, that I have a Heart Still ready (had I the means) to bear sufferings, and make new sacrifices. I pray your Excellency to submit this Narrative to the indulgences of Congress, I am in their judgment, and in their Justice I repose the fullest Confidence.[1]

That Congress was helpless but not oblivious to his appeals is seen in the reply: that Pollock had exerted himself with much zeal and industry as commercial agent of the United States at New Orleans; and that he had advanced large sums of money and had contracted large debts in the service of the United States and Virginia. It was recommended that all of the balances should be paid or security given for payment whenever the state of the public funds should make it possible. To this end they urged the adjustment of his accounts by Virginia with as much dispatch as practicable in order that a settlement with the United States might be agreed upon.[2]

With a keen sense of disappointment at his failures to secure relief, with humility because of his inability to secure the release of his attorney, who was being held as a hostage in New Orleans by Spanish creditors, Pollock was cheered by the hope (1783) that by becoming commercial agent at Havana, an office tendered him by the federal

[1] September 18, 1782. "Letters and Papers of Oliver Pollock (Library of Congress), L, Part I, 1-14.

[2] *Papers of the Continental Congress*, L, 25, 26. The report of the Committee was agreed to by Congress October 22, 1782.

government, he might be enabled to discharge his debts. Permission was granted him by Spanish officials to trade in flour and provisions, with seeming promise of handsome profits. Pursued with the bills of his New Orleans creditors, which he was unable to satisfy, he was arrested and held in custody, the subject "of many indignities from the officers of justice and the arrogance of other Spanish officers."[1] His wife and family were permitted to go to Philadelphia bearing the appeal, addressed to the Financier General, that the interest due on his accounts should be paid to Mrs. Pollock, since she had no other means of support.

His letter to the Governor of Virginia some months later was of like intent. "I hope," he wrote, "Your Excell'y will in turn pay the same honor to my signature as I have done to yours at the *critical moment* for a much larger sum, for which and my other advances for your State, I and my family are reduced to implore as a charity what is due by common justice."[2]

"With Respect to this Gentleman's application for money," Robert Morris wrote, "I found my hands tied up by an act of Congress; and therefore neither his Services nor Sufferings nor a view of those Distresses to which a helpless Family are reduced, could induce me to grant that Relief which Justice and Humanity did equally demand. I persuade myself, however, that it will be among the earliest objects calling for the attention of Congress to alleviate Sufferings which in their Causes and in their attending Circumstances are equally severe and extraordinary."[3]

[1] "Letters and Papers of Oliver Pollock, L, Part II, 445–47.

[2] Havana, March 5, 1785. *Cal. of Va. State Papers*, IV, 14.

[3] Robert Morris, to the President of Congress, September 30, 1784. Draper MSS, 43 J 132, 133.

Early in 1785 his friend during revolutionary days, Galvez, came to Havana as governor of Cuba. Through his influence Pollock was released and after eighteen months characterized by him as "the gloomy confinement and tedious detention of my person," he was granted permission to embark for Philadelphia.[1] He gave bond that all of his obligations to Spanish subjects, which he had incurred, should be paid in full.[2]

Still virtually a prisoner on parole, Pollock continued to petition the President of Congress and the Virginia Assembly that at least small pittances should be advanced on his account which might be used for the support of his family.[3] Finally (December, 1785) he was awarded the sum of $90,000 by Congress, but the treasury was empty and he was not paid for another six years. Meanwhile, securing funds on his credit, he fitted out a vessel, loaded it with flour, and after disposing of the cargo in Martinique, took on another and sailed for New Orleans. Here he was received with favor and was permitted to carry on his trading ventures. His success was such that by the summer of 1790 he had met all of his financial obligations in that city.

Confirmatory of this remarkable financial recovery, Governor Stephen Miró wrote Governor Randolph:

Altho' he disposed of all his Estate, real and personal in this Country, at a great disadvantage, for the purpose of fulfilling his engagements with his creditors in this Province, Mr. Pollock has since his late arrival here, very honorably and to the entire satisfaction of his creditors in this Province, discharged all his remaining debts here, to a considerable amount, which he owed on account of the United States

[1] Draper MSS, 43 J 158.

[2] November 21, 1785. Pollock to his representatives in Richmond. *Clark Papers*, Bundle 1, Virginia State Archives.

[3] New York, August 1, 1785; September 22; September 28. "Letters and Papers of Oliver Pollock," L, Part II, 503, 507.

and the State of Virginia. The great integrity evinced by this Gentleman in the faithfull discharge of his engagements entered into for the service of his country, strongly interests me in his favour, and induces me to pray you will have the Goodness to take him under your protection.[1]

Adjustments between Virginia and the United States having finally been made, Pollock's claim, to the amount of $108,605, was assumed and paid by the federal government. His other accounts with Virginia were eventually paid by that state.[2]

Clark's interest in the West was not relaxed, and as chairman of the committee of officers of the Illinois Regiment his attention was given to securing from the assembly bounty-land legislation similar to that enacted for the regular continental line. As we have seen, men were induced to enlist in Clark's first campaign because of the assurance that, if successful, in addition to their regular pay, 300 acres of conquered territory would doubtless be granted to every common soldier, and to the officers, amounts commensurate with their rank.[3] In keeping with this recommendation, the Virginia legislature on January 2, 1781, adopted a resolution setting aside 150,000 acres of land for this purpose, to be located on the northwest side of the Ohio at some place designated by a majority of the officers.[4] But, as passed, the act provided that soldiers or

[1] July 27, 1790. Miró to Edmund Randolph, *Cal. Va. State Papers*, V, 182.

[2] In 1792 Pollock bought an estate, Silver Springs, near Carlisle, Pennsylvania. Active in civic affairs, he received the nomination for Congress three times (1797, 1804, 1806), but was not elected.

The "necessary and reasonable expenses incurred by Virginia" were finally agreed upon by three commissioners (May 15, 1788), and $500,000 was fixed as the amount due by the federal government to Virginia.

[3] *Clark Papers*, p. 37.

[4] A meeting of the majority of these officers was held at Louisville, February 1, 1783. Clark was chosen president of the board and also chairman of the com-

officers later incorporated into the regiment were to be granted equal bounty rights. Thus, in the final allotment only 108 acres each were assigned to the common soldiers, and grants to officers were proportionately reduced.[1] Clark and his associates petitioned the legislature for a grant of land selected by them opposite Louisville, extending from a spot below the falls up the river such a distance as would suffice to make the length not to exceed twice the breadth.[2]

Reasons urged for this particular location were: that settling these lands would serve as protection to the Kentucky settlements against Indian attacks; that it was well situated for trade, and as the Indians of the Wabash and the Miami were induced to bring their products to this center for trade, to that degree would they be transformed from inveterate enemies into firm friends. To further these ends it was urged that trustees should be appointed who were to select the site for, and plan, a town at the most suitable spot on the river, reserve a desirable landing place, and erect warehouses for storing tobacco, hemp, and other products. The main lines of these recommendations were followed by the Assembly, and a board of ten commissioners, six of them officers in the Illinois Regiment, was appointed to carry out the provisions of the act. All claims were to be submitted to this board.

In the meantime, Clark and William Croghan were named as principal surveyors of the public lands which had been set aside for the men who served in the Virginia state line. Having passed an examination acceptable to the president and faculty of William and Mary College,

---

mittee of five deputies who were to represent the board when a general meeting was impracticable.

[1] Hening, *Statutes at Large*, X, 585.

[2] *Legislative Petitions*, May 21, 1783. Clark MSS, Virginia State Archives.

and provided a bond of 3,000 pounds, the two were ready to assume their duties.[1]

While Clark was nominally in control of this survey until 1788, he probably gave but little personal attention to the performance of the duties connected therewith, for his time was taken up with other problems.[2]

At no time in his whole career did he manifest greater enterprise than during these years. He served as a member of the board of Commissioners, much of the time acting as chairman, which supervised the allotment of lands in the Illinois grant and promoted improvements.[3] Governor Harrison acknowledged the necessity of consulting Clark on the subject of Indian affairs along the Ohio and securing the quota of Indian boys for William and Mary College.[4]

Upon his arrival at Louisville about the middle of April Clark found the northwestern tribes greatly disturbed over the fact that peace had not been offered them by the American government, being apprehensive, as he said, "that something fatal to them is on the carpet."[5] Representatives

---

[1] They were to receive three shillings for each 1,000 acres surveyed. One-sixth of the fees were to go to William and Mary College. Clark and Croghan were to provide for the pay of their four assistants at the rate of three shillings a day.

[2] Croghan was in control of the office, but corresponded with Clark and took directions from him.

[3] After the organization of this board, February 1, 1783, there were meetings at irregular intervals, usually a number of times each year until December, 1816. *Record of Proceedings of the Illinois Officers.* William Clark, cousin of George Rogers Clark, was appointed chief surveyor. He also served as one of the commissioners. For his services in the Illinois Regiment Clark finally received 8,049 acres, and as brigadier general in the state line he was given a warrant for 10,000 acres.

[4] Harrison Letter Book, January 22, 1784, Virginia State Library.

[5] Clark to Thomas Mifflin, president of Congress, April 26, 1784. *Papers of the Continental Congress,* Letters C, 78, 6, folios 231–34.

of the Shawnee had sought to interview him, and chiefs of the other tribes, he supposed, would follow this example. His plan, formulated on his own initiative, aimed to keep the Indians in suspense until the general policy of the government should be known, and by messages to the different tribes warn them that unless they ceased their hostilities a general treaty would not be possible and they must then expect to be the greatest sufferers. Once more he advocated that the tribes should be forced to make all overtures.

Not before March 1, 1784, did Virginia finally complete the cession to the United States of her right and title to the territory northwest of the Ohio River. This claim was based on her charter of 1609 and also on the conquests made by Clark. New York had maintained that on account of various treaties she had become the lawful successor to the western lands formerly claimed by the Iroquois.[1] Massachusetts, under the charter of 1629, and Connecticut, under a charter of 1662, likewise laid claim to strips of land west of the New York boundary. South of the Virginia line, the Carolinas and Georgia claimed the territory lying west of their borders, extending to the Mississippi. The six landless states maintained that this territory had been gained through a war in which there had been common sacrifice, and therefore that the individual states should surrender their claims. Maryland, in 1779, refused to ratify the Articles of Confederation unless first assured that these lands were to become the property of the United States. The other states had ratified the Articles by February, 1779. But Maryland feared the future power of her

---

[1] A summary of the controversy over the validity of claims to western lands is well stated in Justin Winsor, *The Westward Movement* (Boston, 1897), pp. 205–8.

neighbors, inasmuch as Virginia planned to pay off her soldiers by grants of western lands, while Maryland could meet this obligation only through taxation. Congress, on September 6, 1780, made a noteworthy appeal to the states in which it was suggested that they should cede their unappropriated lands to the general government to be disposed of for the common benefit of the United States. Coupled with this was the resolution, passed a month later, which offered to reimburse the *reasonable expenses* which any state had incurred in subduing the British posts. New York had previously decided to give up her claims; Virginia, in January, 1781, promised, under certain conditions, to take similar action; and on the second of February the Maryland legislature empowered her delegates in Congress to subscribe to the Articles of Confederation.

Virginia offered to cede her claim to territory north of the Ohio River on condition that Congress guarantee to her the possession of Kentucky. This proposal was vigorously opposed in Congress, and during the next three years great pressure was brought to bear on Virginia to secure the surrender of her claims unconditionally. The isolation of Virginia was manifest to her leaders, and James Madison declared, early in 1782, that on account of the enemies' claims and calumnies which these claims formed against her it was desirable to preserve her military contingent on a respectable footing.[1] James Monroe, who had invested in Kentucky lands, declared in a letter to George Rogers Clark, October 18, 1783, that it would be for the best interest of Virginia that an independent state should be formed to the westward, which dominated by Virginia traditions, would give the Old Dominion added strength in the federal councils.

[1] *The Writings of James Madison,* ed. Gaillard Hunt, I, 185, 187.

Meantime, Kentuckians were petitioning Congress for permission to set up as an independent state.[1] An increase of states in the federal Union, they argued, would promote the strength and dignity of that Union, "for, it is as possible that one State should aim at undue influence over others as that an individual should aspire after the aggrandizement of himself." An increase of states would lessen this danger. In answer to the objections raised because of their inferior social conditions they replied: "Some of our fellow citizens may think we are not yet able to conduct our affairs and consult our interests; but if our society is rude, much wisdom is not necessary to supply our wants, and a fool can sometimes put on his clothes better than a wise man can do it for him. We are not against hearing council; but we attend more to our feelings than to the argumentation of others."[2] As proof that such a move would promote the material interests of Virginia, they say: "Our nearest seaports will be among you, your readiest resources for effectual succour in case of an invasion will be to us; the fruits of our industry and temperance will be enjoyed by you, and the simplicity of our manners will furnish you with profitable lessons. In recompense for these services you will furnish our rustic inhabitants with examples of civility and politeness and supply us with conveniences which are without the reach of our labour." With the understanding that Kentucky would soon be admitted into the Union as an independent state, Virginia ceded to the United States her title to the territory north of the Ohio.

Massachusetts surrendered her claims in 1785. Con-

[1] *Ibid.*, p. 229.

[2] Frederick J. Turner, "Western State-Making in the Revolutionary Era," *American Historical Review*, I, 252.

necticut, in her cession of the following year, reserved a tract of land 120 miles long on the shore of Lake Erie, now known as the "Western Reserve." Not before 1800 did Connecticut grant to the United States complete jurisdiction over this Reserve containing some 3,250,000 acres.

There can be no doubt about the importance of these cessions. A series of inevitable controversies over conflicting claims were thus fortunately escaped. From that time this western territory was regarded as the property of the Confederation, to be used for national purposes. Here was the beginning of our national domain.

The confidence in Clark and the friendship always manifested toward him by Thomas Jefferson were especially marked at this period. In retirement, Jefferson studied the shells and the seed, the bones and tusks of the mammoth in his private museum which had been forwarded to him by Clark. Before departing for Europe he wrote Clark, November 26, 1782:

> I received in August your favor wherein you give me hopes of your being able to procure for me some of the big bones—a specimen of each of the several species of bones now to be found is to me the most desirable object in natural history. Elk-horns of very extraordinary size, petrifications or any thing else uncommon would be very acceptable . . . . any observations of your own on the subject of the big bones or their history or on anything else in the western country, will come acceptable to me, because I know you see the works of nature in the great and not merely in detail. descriptions of animals, vegetables, minerals, or other curious things as to the Indians, information of the country between the Mississippi and waters of the South Sea etc., etc., will strike your mind as worthy being communicated. I wish you had more time to pay attention to them.

To what degree the mind of the statesman, on western affairs, was molded through his relations with the soldier cannot be definitely stated. The Mississippi and the Great Lakes were the boundaries to be secured during the Revolution through their mutual endeavor. Both were deeply interested in the problems of Kentucky and the West. In days of gloom the messages of Jefferson were to strengthen Clark for new endeavor. Toward the close of 1782 he wrote:

I perceive by your letter that you are not unapprised that your services to your country have not made due impression on every mind. that you have enemies you must not doubt, when you reflect that you have made yourself eminent. if you meant to escape notice you should have confined yourself within the sleepy line of regular duty, when you transgressed this and enterprized deeds which will hand down your name with honour to future times, you made yourself a mark for malice and envy to shoot at. Of these there is enough both in and out of office.

December 4, 1783, Jefferson made a proposal to Clark especially noteworthy in its relation to the task accomplished some twenty years later by Meriwether Lewis and William Clark, the youngest brother of George Rogers Clark. In this letter Jefferson said:

I find they have subscribed a very large sum of money in England for exploring the country from the Mississippi to California. they pretend it is only to promote knowledge. I am afraid they have thoughts of colonising into that quarter. Some of us have been talking here in a feeble way of making the attempt to search that country but I doubt whether we have enough of that kind of spirit to raise the money. How would you like to lead such a party? tho I am afraid our prospect is not worth asking the question.

Nothing came of the offer, however, for the definitive treaty was presented to Congress and served to remove Jefferson's fear for the ascendancy of Great Britain in the trans-Mississippi territory.[1] Moreover, the problems incident to the organization of the Northwest, the formation of western states, and the commercial relations with Great Britain occupied his mind.

Early in the year 1784 Jefferson succeeded in securing

[1] *Writings of Thomas Jefferson*, ed. W. C. Ford, III, 351.

Clark's election by Congress as one of the five commissioners who were to treat with the Indians of the Northwest.[1] Beyond the service Clark would render as member of such a commission, the leading motive of Jefferson in securing his appointment was to bring Clark "forward on the continental stage."[2] Full powers were granted the commissioners to hold conventions with the Six Nations and all other Indians to the northward and westward of them and as far south as the Cherokee within the limits of the United States. Besides receiving them into the "favour and protection" of the United States, boundary lines were to be established between the Indian hunting grounds and villages and the territory open to settlement by white men. Had some such line of action been instituted a year earlier, much trouble and bloodshed would have been averted.

The preceding September Congress issued a proclamation against the unlawful occupation of Indian lands, but this was of little effect. In spite of the vigilance of the commanding officer at Pittsburgh, boats frequently passed down the Ohio bearing parties whose outspoken designs were to encroach upon the Indian country. Some of these were fired upon and captured, but numbers escaped.[3] Descriptive of the situation, Washington wrote, November 3, 1784:

Such is the rage for speculating in, and forestalling of lands on the No. West of the Ohio, that scarce a valuable spot, within any tolerable distance of it, is left without a claimant. Men in these times talk with

---

[1] Jefferson to Clark, March 4, 1784. Virginia State Archives.

[2] The other commissioners appointed were Oliver Wolcott, Nathanael Greene, Richard Butler, and Stephen Higginson. Nathanael Greene and Stephen Higginson declined to serve, and Benjamin Lincoln and Arthur Lee were appointed to their places. Philip Schuyler was appointed, but he and Benjamin Lincoln also declined to serve. Arthur Lee was appointed to take the place of Clark, who had returned to Kentucky. Samuel Hardy, John Francis Mercer, and Arthur Lee to Governor Benjamin Harrison, May 13, 1784.

[3] *Mich. Pioneer and Hist. Colls.*, XI, 385, XX, 175.

as much facility of fifty, an hundred, and even five hundred thousand acres, as a gentleman formerly would do of one thousand. In defiance of the proclamation of Congress, they roam over the Indian side of the Ohio, mark out Lands, survey and even settle on them. This gives great discontent to the Indians, and will unless measures are taken in time to prevent it, produce a war inevitably with the western tribes. . . . . Declare all steps heretofore taken to procure land on the Northwest side of the Ohio, contrary to the prohibition of Congress, to be null and void—and that any person thereafter, who shall procure lands, shall not only be considered as outlaws, but fit subjects for Indian vengeance. If these or similar measures are adopted, I have no doubt of Congress's deriving a very considerable revenue from the western territory.[1]

For the purpose of carrying out the policy of Congress three of the commissioners, Oliver Wolcott, Richard Butler, and Arthur Lee, together with representatives from Pennsylvania, met in conference at Fort Stanwix chiefs and warriors of the Iroquois and a few representatives from the Delaware and the Shawnee tribes. In these councils, which took place during the month of October, 1784, Cornplanter, chief of the Seneca, and Captain Aaron Hill, chief of the Mohawk, assumed to represent the cause, not alone of the Six Nations, but also of all the tribes west to the Mississippi.[2] The words of advice by La Fayette during the first day of the council went far to prepare the Indians to accede to the terms submitted to them, for he spoke as a representative and great warrior of the French nation as well as a leader and general among the Americans.[3]

The governor of New York disregarded the invitation

[1] *Writings of George Washington*, ed. W. C. Ford, X, 417, 418.

[2] Minutes of the treaty are given in Craig, *The Olden Time*, II, 406–30.

[3] La Fayette's supposed speech is given in Craig, *The Olden Time*, II, 429. He spoke of the alliance between the French and the Americans and the entrance of the Indians into that alliance after peace with the Americans had been consummated. This would entitle them to receive the manufactures of France in trade. *Report of Canadian Archives* (1890), p. 146.

to join in the conference, insisting on the right, denied by the United States, of a state to treat separately with the Indians. He had already submitted terms of peace to the Iroquois, and his agents strove in various ways to frustrate the efforts of the commissioners.[1] According to the terms finally agreed upon, the Iroquois surrendered their title to the lands north and west of the Ohio.[2]

But the western tribes were not prepared to have their rights disposed of so cavalierly, and accused the Iroquois of breach of faith.[3] Consequently, invitations were forwarded to these tribes to attend a conference at Fort McIntosh, and toward the close of November, George Rogers Clark, Arthur Lee, and Richard Butler, accompanied by a guard of artillery under Colonel Harmar, proceeded to that post. Commissioners from Pennsylvania were also in attendance.

Very slowly the chiefs and warriors of the Chippewa, Ottawa, Wyandotte, and Delaware tribes, accompanied by their women and children, gathered for the conference. With difficulty their demands for provisions, ammunition, kettles, blankets, and rum were complied with.[4] The commissioners and soldiers themselves, housed in a dilapidated fort in the depth of winter, suffered for want of sufficient clothing. On January 21, 1785, agreement was reached, the first in a long series of treaties, by which the United States gained the territory northwest of the Ohio River.

[1] Craig, *The Olden Time*, II, 408–19.

[2] In the treaty at Fort Stanwix, 1768, the Ohio was fixed as the boundary line. By the treaty of 1784 a tract 6 miles square around Fort Oswego was reserved to the United States. The Iroquois also ceded to Pennsylvania all territory claimed by them within the bounds of that state. Craig, *The Olden Time*, II, 499.

[3] Arthur Lee, "Journal," published in Craig, *The Olden Time*, II, 337.

[4] *Ibid.*, p. 341. Orders were issued later that no rum should be furnished the Indians.

In exchange for the goods to be distributed among the tribes, the Indians surrendered their title to the lands, retaining possession of an area in the northwestern portion of the present state of Ohio. The boundary line of this reservation ran from Lake Erie up the Cuyahoga River and down the Tuscarawas to a spot above Fort Laurens. It then extended west to the portage between the Big Miami and a branch of the Maumee, then along the latter river to Lake Erie, and thence to the starting-point.[1] This cession of territory, estimated at 30,000,000 acres, was far greater than had been anticipated.[2] Certain places within this territory which were to be under the control of the United States were reserved for the establishment of trading-posts.[3]

The Shawnee, the most warlike of the Ohio tribes, were not present at Fort McIntosh. Because of their ascendancy over the other tribes, no agreement could be lasting without their assent. At this time there were clear signs of the neutralization of the efforts of the American commissioners on the part of the British agents.[4] In fact, the leading features of the British policy relative to the Northwest which obtained during the succeeding ten years were then becoming manifest.[5]

[1] *American State Papers*, Vol. V, *Indian Affairs*, I, 11.

[2] *Writings of George Washington*, ed. Ford, X, 447.

[3] An area six miles square was reserved at the mouth of the Maumee, six miles square on the portage between the St. Mary and the Big Miami, six miles square on Sandusky Lake, and two miles square on each side of the lower rapids of the Sandusky.

[4] Craig, *The Olden Time*, II, 486.

[5] For an excellent account of the British Policy, see Andrew C. McLaughlin, "The Western Posts and the British Debts," *Yale Review*, II, 408–24; IV, 58–79. See also Samuel F. Bemis, "The Frontier Crisis," *Jay's Treaty*, pp. 161 ff.

CHAPTER XIV

The British Continue in Control
of the Northwest

UPON the announcement of the provisional peace, officials at Detroit and Mackinac were alarmed at the Indian problem with which they were confronted. "Heavens!" exclaimed Colonel De Peyster, "If goods do not arrive soon what will become of me—I have lost several stone wt. of flesh within these twenty days."[1] In communicating the treaty to his subordinates, General Haldimand warned them to keep the terms from the Indians as long as possible. But reports of the treaty soon spread throughout the Indian country.[2] The inhabitants of entire villages journeyed to the posts, impatiently demanding what was to become of them and their lands and requesting supplies of blankets, paints, feathers, rum, and other goods which had been promised.[3] Agents were dispatched to the various tribes to prevent the coming of greater numbers.[4]

That peace had come seemed no less agreeable to the Indians than to the whites, but they were gravely concerned over the rumored boundaries to their lands. "They look upon our conduct to them as treacherous and cruel,"

[1] *Mich. Pioneer and Hist. Colls.*, XI, 369.

[2] *Report on Canadian Archives* (1886), p. 64.

[3] For a list of Indian presents at Detroit, see *Mich. Pioneer and Hist. Colls.*, XI, 382.

[4] *Ibid.*, pp. 379, 407.

wrote a British representative who had conferred with the
chiefs of the Six Nations.

> They told me they never could believe that our King could pretend
> to cede to America what was not his own to give, or that the Americans
> would accept from him what he had no right to grant. . . . . They
> still insisted that the King had no right to give away Forts built in the
> heart of their country, without consulting them, but leaving them to
> the mercy of their Enemies and his Enemies, a conduct that was scan-
> dalous and dishonorable to the English. . . . . I do from my soul Pity
> these People, and should they commit outrages at giving up these Posts,
> it would by no means surprize me.[1]

By the end of June there was evidence of an interpretation of the terms of the treaty which was very early to become a settled policy on the part of British officials. While
Detroit was acknowledged by General Haldimand to be
within the limits of the United States,[2] Colonel De Peyster
declared before an Indian Council: "I tell you the World
is now at Peace and you have saved your Lands, but had
you not defended them agreeable to my desire, the Americans would have taken them from you."[3] The fact that he
had not received the "particulars of the peace," and in
part, no doubt, fear of Indian wrath, may have induced De
Peyster to interpret liberally the terms of the treaty. But
Sir John Johnson could neither plead ignorance nor fear
for his speech to the Six Nations when he said:

> Although the King your Father has found it necessary . . . . to
> conclude a long, bloody, expensive and unnatural war, by a Peace

---

[1] Letter of Brigadier General Maclean to General Haldimand, May 18, 1783.
Ibid., XX, 117–21. The letter was sent to Lord North.

[2] Letter to Lord North, June 2, 1783. *Mich. Pioneer and Hist. Colls.*, XI,
365. While British officers could not deny the validity of the treaty, they did
deny its effect so far as it concerned the Indians. Haldimand wrote Johnson
that he did not consider any of the Indian territory within the United States
was ceded by a line drawn to define the southern boundary of Canada. *Report
on Canadian Archives* (1886), p. 420.

[3] Council at Detroit, June 28, 1783. *Ibid.*, p. 371.

which seems to give you great uneasiness on account of the boundary line agreed upon between His Majesty's Commissioners and those of the United States: yet you are not to believe, or even think that by the Line which has been described, it was meant to deprive you of an extent of country, of which the right of Soil belongs to, and is in yourselves as sole Proprietors, ... Neither can I harbour an idea that the United States will act so unjustly or impolitically as to endeavour to deprive you of any part of your country under the pretext of having conquered it.[1]

These first statements of British officials relative to lands of which the cession was taken for granted by Americans were still further emphasized in a communication of General Haldimand. On November 27, 1783, he wrote Lord North: "I already hinted to your Lordship my wishes that their orders will be to withdraw the Troops and stores from the posts within a certain time, and to leave the Indians and Americans to make their own arrangements.[2]

Favor with the Indians was to be maintained, and General Haldimand and other British officials, in various ways, strove to quiet their discontent. Should they be dispossessed of their lands they were to be compensated by receiving territory on the north shore of Lake Ontario.[3] Although the plan appealed to Joseph Brant and other Indian leaders, only a small number of the Iroquois availed themselves of the offer. Efforts were not relaxed to convince the tribes that their alliance with Great Britain was still firm, and increased supplies were clear proofs of the assertion.[4] Another feature of the British policy was to cement more strongly the elements of confederation among

[1] These instructions were likewise imparted to the Northwestern tribes in a council at Sandusky, September 6, 1783. *Ibid.*, XX, 176–77.

[2] For the distinction between the *transfer* of the posts and their *evacuation*, see A. C. McLaughlin, "The Western Posts and the British Debts," *Yale Review*, IV, 65.

[3] *Mich. Pioneer and Hist. Colls.*, XX, 123, 124.

[4] *Ibid.*, pp. 124, 139, 177.

the tribes which had been developed during the years of the Revolution. The personal influence of Alexander McKee among the Detroit Indians, of Simon Girty on the Wabash and the Ohio tribes, and of Joseph Brant as special messenger from the Iroquois to the Creek and Cherokee went far to produce this unification in the minds of the savages.[1] Numerous official communications bear evidence that British plans looked toward maintaining peace among the tribes and restraining them from committing hostilities against the Americans. It was insisted that they were to act only on the defensive, and failure to comply would lead to the withdrawal of all assistance.

Among the motives back of this policy, which ultimately led to the determination to control the Northwest through retention of the posts, none was as prominent as the monopoly of the fur trade.[2] When the terms of the provisional peace were announced and the surrender of the fur trade south of the boundary line seemed inevitable, there was a movement in favor of the establishment of new forts north of that line. Canada, it was maintained, would furnish furs superior in quality to the area surrendered.[3] For over a century agents of the Hudson's Bay Company had extended the field of their operations beyond Forts York and Churchill on Hudson's Bay until they exercised a monopoly of trade over an area of unknown extent.[4] It was suggested that the trade of this company might be thrown open to all traders upon payment of a small tax for the support of the necessary fortifications.[5]

[1] *Ibid.*, pp. 164, 174, 176, 179, 183; XI, 467, 470.

[2] See *Yale Review*, IV, 60–63.

[3] Hansard, *Parliamentary History*, XXIII, 465.

[4] This company was organized under a charter granted to some London merchants by King Charles II in 1669.

[5] Lord Sheffield, *Observations on the Commerce of the American States*, p. 115 (2d ed., p. 102). Parliament was to purchase the chartered rights of the Company.

But the men who profited through trade within the American lines were not to be won by future promises.

British control over the Indians of the Northwest was materially strengthened also by the formation of the Northwest Company in 1783. During the preceding twenty years French traders and *voyageurs* in the employ of independent British traders came each spring to Detroit, Mackinac, Sault Ste Marie, and Grand Portage with their fleets of canoes laden with peltries secured in trade with the Indians. To these posts returned at the opening of the season from Montreal, headquarters of the adventurers, brigades of bateaux, each boat of about four tons burden navigated by eight or ten men. In these boats were transported the woolen and cotton goods, hardware, and trinkets imported from London for use in the trade. Competition and at times open warfare between the independent traders finally produced complete disorganization of the trade.[1] At the close of 1782 twelve large operators remained in the territory. The following year a majority of them united their interests and formed a stock corporation, the Northwest Company. The other independent operators joined this union in 1787.

At the outset the Northwest Company stretched its arms over the northwestern lakes, aided by Canadians, half-breeds, *voyageurs*, and Indians, as well as by Scotch agents occupying Detroit, Mackinac, and the other posts which had formerly belonged to the French along the line of the Great Lakes and the Mississippi. Their operations soon expanded to Lakes Winnipeg and Athabaska, to Great Slave Lake and the Pacific Ocean.[2] Within a year after its

---

[1] *Report on Canadian Archives* (1890), p. 50.

[2] Freeman Hunt, *Merchants' Magazine and Commercial Review*, III, 193. Frederick J. Turner, "The Character and Influence of the Indian Trade in Wisconsin," *Johns Hopkins University Studies*, IX, 51.

organization this company was employing five hundred men in its transportation service alone and had entered upon the policy of contesting the field with the Hudson's Bay Company.[1]

Grand Portage was their chief operating headquarters in the Northwest, and canoes from this center, navigated by four or five men, carried goods to the interior posts more than a thousand miles beyond.[2] The estimated value of the furs and outfits belonging to the Company at this post, in 1785, was £50,000.[3] Here at the opening of each season two or three of the proprietors from Montreal met the partners from the interior to discuss the affairs of the company. The festivities on these occasions were baronial in character. A vivid description of this life has been given us by Washington Irving.

Indeed, the partners from below considered the whole dignity of the Company as represented in their persons, and conducted themselves in suitable style. They ascended the rivers in great state, like sovereigns making a progress; or rather like Highland chieftains navigating their subject lakes. They were wrapped in rich furs, their huge canoes freighted with every convenience and luxury, and manned by Canadian *voyageurs*, as obedient as Highland Clansmen. . . . .

These grave and mighty councils were alternated by huge feasts and revels, like some of the old feasts described in Highland castles. The tables in the great banqueting room groaned under the weight of game of all kinds; of venison from the woods, and fish from the lakes, with hunter's delicacies, such as buffaloes' tongues and beavers' tails, and luxuries from Montreal, all served up by experienced cooks brought for the purpose. There was no stint of generous wine, for it was a hard-drinking period, a time of loyal toasts, and bacchanalian songs, and brimming bumpers. While the chiefs thus revelled in the hall, and made the rafters resound with bursts of loyalty and old Scottish songs, chant-

[1] The Company finally consisted of twenty-three partners and had two thousand persons in its employ. Washington Irving, *Astoria*, p. 12.

[2] *Report on Canadian Archives* (1890), p. 51.

[3] *Ibid.*, p. 53.

ed in voices cracked and sharpened by the northern blast, their merriment was echoed and prolonged by a mongrel legion of retainers, Canadian *voyageurs*, half-breeds, Indian hunters, and vagabond hangers-on who feasted sumptuously without on the crumbs that fell from their table, and made the welkin ring with old French ditties, mingled with Indian yelps and yellings.[1]

But Grand Portage, according to the terms of the treaty, was south of the boundary line. Memorials asking for the retention of this key to the trade of the Northwest could not have been disregarded by Lieutenant-Governor Hamilton and General Haldimand, representatives of the Crown resident at Quebec. "If the late treaty of Peace is adhered to respecting the cession of the upper Posts," one of these messages reads, "the United States will also have an easy access into the North-West by way of the Grand Portage. From these circumstances your Memorialist is humbly of opinion, that this branch of trade will soon fall a prey to the enterprizes of other nations, to the great prejudice of His Majesty's subjects, unless some means is speedily used to prevent it."[2]

Detroit and Mackinac constituted the trade head-

---

[1] Irving, *Astoria*, pp. 11–19. This account portrayed the life at Fort William, the post to which the British trade was transferred from Grand Portage.

[2] Memorial of Peter Pond, a member of the Northwest Company, to Lieutenant-Governor Hamilton, April 18, 1785. *Report on Canadian Archives* (1890), p. 53. "It, therefore, becomes necessary for Government to protect and encourage the North-West Company in order that trading posts may be settled and connections formed with the natives, all over the Country, even to the Sea Coast; by which means so firm a footing may be established as will preserve that valuable trade from falling into the hands of other powers; and under proper management it may certainly in a short time be so extended as to become an object of great importance to the British nation and highly advantageous to this mutilated Province." The memorial refers also to the establishment of a trading-post on the Pacific by some Russians.

During the summer of 1784 trade northwest of Lake Superior was made accessible through the discovery of a new route. *Mich. Pioneer and Hist. Colls.*, XX, 221. *Ibid.*, XI, 462.

quarters for the territory between the Great Lakes and the Mississippi. Moreover, they were essential to the life of the trade at Grand Portage. Boats from Montreal were compelled to secure additional supplies from these posts or change the character of their cargoes, then made up of two-thirds goods and one-third provisions. A letter to Hamilton declares: "Should the United States be put in possession of the Posts, their situation will be still more precarious, as the Americans will have it in their power to injure or Ruin every man from this part of the Province, who depends on receiving his Provisions from that Settlement."[1] Fears were also expressed lest, with the transfer of these posts, British resident traders would elect to become American citizens.

Year by year the territory within the American lines contributed furs amounting to not less than 100,000 pounds sterling to the Canadian merchants.[2] Traders outfitting at Detroit carried annually into the Indian country goods of British manufacture amounting to more than one half that amount.[3] In these figures may be seen a partial interpretation of the policy of statesmen which was evolved under pressure from the commercial classes. "Not thinking the naked independence a sufficient proof of his liberality to the United States," exclaimed a member of the House of Commons who opposed the peace terms, "he has clothed it with the warm covering of our fur-trade."[4]

London merchants demanded legislation which would

[1] May 2, 1785. *Report on Canadian Archives* (1890), p. 55.

[2] During the year 1785 furs valued at £100,000 sterling were received from the Detroit and Mackinac traders. In 1786 the estimated amount was £160,000 sterling. *Mich. Pioneer and Hist. Colls.*, XI, 462, 473, 474.

[3] It was estimated in 1788 that £60,000 sterling of British manufactured goods were sent into the Indian country from Detroit alone. *Ibid.*, p. 631.

[4] Opposition to the peace preliminaries. Hansard, *Parliamentary History*, XXIII, 457.

prevent the loss of this trade. A document of July 22, 1781, well illustrates this influence. In this appeal the merchants say:

Furs have been sent hither from the first settlement of America and upon exportation Bonds were given that they should be imported into Great Britain; affected as this Trade is expected to be in its Circuit by Canada a great Part of what heretofore came that way will most probably be now inverted into New England and New York, in which States as well as in Pennsylvania much Beaver was manufactured and even exported to the West Indies; . . . . The French it is to be feared will rival us in the manufacture of Furs; It is therefore presumed that Beaver Skins and other Furs should be received Duty free, as the only means to render Great Britain the port for these articles, or should they still continue subject to any Duty, the whole should be drawn back on Exportation. It will moreover be necessary for the better security of this Trade that all the carrying places, Lakes, Rivers and other Waters and all ways and passes by land be open to his Majesty's subjects to pass and repass freely to and from the Indian Country, as well as to the Indians in like manner from and to the Province of Quebec.[1]

The problem demanded settlement, for during the summer of 1783 enterprising Americans, regardless of congressional decree, were pushing into the Northwest. Washington early recognized the significance of the refusal to surrender the posts. "Bribery," he wrote, "and every address which British art could dictate have been practiced to soothe them, to estrange them and to secure their trade."[2]

Instructed by Congress, Washington prepared a communication to General Haldimand which was delivered to him August 11, 1783. Baron Steuben, who acted as special

---

[1] For the document and an account of its discovery and significance, consult *American Historical Review*, XVIII, 769–80.

[2] *Writings of Washington*, ed. Ford (November 3, 1784), X, 420. "But it is now more than twelve months since I foretold what has happened and I shall not be surprized if they leave us *no posts* to occupy."

messenger, was given full power to arrange for taking possession of the posts occupied by the British forces.[1] He was kindly received by British officials, but was informed by General Haldimand that since he had received no notification of the ratification of peace, he was not warranted in complying with the request.[2] With like decision he declined to permit General Steuben to visit the posts on the lakes in order to ascertain what measures would be necessary for their proper garrisoning.[3]

To what degree other Canadian officials were cognizant of the purpose of Haldimand cannot be stated, but that they fully appreciated its significance and contributed to its strength cannot be questioned. A few days before the demand made by Washington was prepared, General Maclean gave a clear statement of the situation. Fearful of the "designing knavery" of Americans, he wrote: "The Indians get this day from the King's Stores the bread they are to eat tomorrow, and from his magazines the clothing that covers their nakedness; in short, they are not only our allies, but they are a part of our Family; and the Americans might as well (while we are in possession of these Posts) attempt to seduce our children and servants from their duty and allegiance as to convene and assemble all the Indian Nations, without first communicating their intentions to His Majesty's Representatives in Canada.[4]

Another objection brought against the treaty in Parlia-

[1] *Mich. Pioneer and Hist. Colls.*, XX, 141.

[2] *Ibid.*, pp. 167–68. Reply to Washington, *ibid.*, p. 165.

[3] *Ibid.*, pp. 165, 168.

[4] July 8, 1783. *Ibid.*, p. 139. The letter was addressed to Colonel De Peyster. "For I do not believe the world ever produced," he said, "a more deceitful or dangerous set of men than the Americans: and now they are become such Arch-Politicians by eight years practice, that were old Matchioavell alive, he might go to school to the Americans to learn Politics more crooked than his own; we therefore cannot be too cautious."

ment, besides the total and absolute loss of the fur trade, was "that all faith was broken with the Indians," and that as a consequence "the province of Canada was rendered insecure."[1] That Haldimand was, in part, dominated by this fear of savage retaliation when he refused to treat with Steuben is manifest in the letter explanatory of his conduct. "To prevent such a disastrous event as an Indian war," he wrote Lord North, "is a consideration worthy of the attention of both nations, and cannot be prevented so effectually as by allowing the Posts in the Upper Country to remain as they are for sometime."[2]

On March 19, 1784, Governor George Clinton, of New York, sent Colonel Fish as a special messenger to ask that he be informed when arrangements might be made for the transfer of Niagara and other posts within that state.[3] Haldimand maintained that since the treaty had been made with the United States it would not be permissible to treat with a single state. In May Governor Chittenden, of Vermont, made a similar request relative to posts on Lake Champlain.[4]

Colonel William Hull was sent by General Knox, on behalf of the United States, to demand the precise time when the posts were to be given up. The message was delivered on July 12, 1784, Hull proposing that they enter into negotiations for the transfer. But Haldimand refused to accede to the request.[5] At that time he had received

[1] Hansard, *Parliamentary Debates*, XXIII, 381, 383. "Having given up the forts which awed the Indians, we could no longer be protected from their ravages. Their lust of plunder, their revenge for our shameful and unpardonable treatment of them, would give rise to scenes of cruelty, from which the civilized heart must revolt with abhorrence: and the sufferers would be our own innocent fellow-subjects."

[2] *Report on Canadian Archives* (1885), p. 574.

[3] *Mich. Pioneer and Hist. Colls.*, XX, 215.

[4] *Report on Canadian Archives* (1885), p. 367.

[5] *Mich. Pioneer and Hist. Colls.*, XX, 238.

instructions written by Lord Sydney on April 8, 1784, more than a month before the ratifications were exchanged. Refusal to give up the posts was approved and their evacuation was to be delayed "till the Articles of the Treaty of Peace are fully complied with."[1]

Resulting from this delay, Haldimand saw the opportunity for traders in the interior to withdraw their property and for the Indians to make more advantageous terms with the Americans.[2]

By the middle of August definite orders were given to discontinue work on the new fortifications on the Canadian side of the line.[3] In November, while the possibility of the evacuation of the posts was still suggested, there was evidently greater concern about the enforcement of decrees against American traders who were persistent in their efforts to become masters of the northwest trade, which was then yielding unusual returns.

[1] *Report on Canadian Archives* (1884–85), p. 286.

[2] Haldimand to Johnson, June 14, 1784. *Report on Canadian Archives* (1886), p. 431.

[3] *Mich. Pioneer and Hist. Colls.*, XX, 243.

CHAPTER XV

Efforts of Americans to Gain Possession of the Northwest

URING the summer of 1785 the Americans were still in doubt as to the real designs of Great Britain.[1] Since British officials continued their marks of friendship toward the Indians and of encouragement to emigrants from the American territory, it was conjectured that they would not give up the posts.[2]

Meantime, immigration to the west increased steadily. The income from the land office of the Kentucky district in 1783 amounted to some 400 pounds, and during 1784 the fees from this office exceeded 2,000 pounds. The estimated population of Kentucky in 1783 was thirty thousand.[3] Twelve thousand more came during the year 1784. Fleets of boats setting out from Pittsburgh and Wheeling for Kentucky loaded with families, household goods, slaves, and stock were a common occurrence. These water craft

---

[1] John Adams was then in London in the capacity of special commissioner striving to ascertain the reason for the non-fulfilment of the terms of the treaty, but no definite answer to his inquiries was brought to the consideration of Congress before November 1, 1786.

[2] *Writings of John Jay* (Ed. Johnston), III, 214. As Secretary of the Department of Foreign Affairs, Jay submitted a report to Congress on the charges made by Great Britain. *Secret Journals of Congress, Foreign Affairs*, IV, 185 ff. Jay wrote Adams, November 1, 1786: "The result of my inquiries into the conduct of the States relative to the treaty is, that there had not been a single day since it took effect, on which it had not been violated in America by one or other of the States."

[3] Draper MSS, 11 J 43.

were of many varieties, from the piroque hollowed from a large tree or from two trees united, dug-outs, made from smaller trees, and canoes, to the flatboats capable of carrying 20 to 70 tons, and keel boats, long, slender, and easily propelled over shallow waters.

"And by the numbers which pass," a traveler wrote in 1785, "seems as if the old states would depopulate, and the inhabitants be transported to the new."[1] It was estimated that a thousand boats descended the Ohio during the year. At the opening of navigation in 1786 a thousand people, it was said, went to Kentucky by boat within forty days. A regular emigrant service was established between Pittsburgh and Louisville, the trip, except in the season of low water, lasting from a week to ten days. There were keel boats bound for Natchez and New Orleans to engage in a trade which was very profitable to those persons who had been granted permission to engage therein by Spanish officials. Barge canoes loaded with furs from Kaskaskia and Vincennes were rowed upstream, a difficult task, to Pittsburgh. The voyage down the river was full of hardships and dangers. Boats were damaged and frequently destroyed, with a consequent loss of life, because of the sand bars, rapids, sunken logs, and sudden squalls of wind.[2] At times they were fired upon by bands of Indians, but notwithstanding the dangers the spirits of the emigrants were buoyed up by the prospect which was to open in the fields to which they were bound.

It has been stated that the numbers of immigrants traveling over the Wilderness Road were as large as those coming by water.[3] Families from the same neighborhood often journeyed together over the poor roads on horse-

[1] Craig, *The Olden Time*, II, 499.

[2] *Ibid.*, pp. 433, 449, 452, 453.

[3] Draper MSS, 11 J 43.

back, with pack trains, and driving their flocks and herds. Before leaving the last settlements they usually waited until there were enough riflemen in the company to furnish protection against any Indian band which might obstruct their advance.

Immigrants came from North Carolina, Virginia, Maryland, Pennsylvania, a number of other states, and from various European countries. There were among them the industrious and the shiftless, speculators and criminals fleeing from justice as well as actual settlers—farmers, stock-raisers, mechanics, soldiers of the Revolutionary armies—seeking thus to better their fortunes under a new environment.

Some of the settlers, by blazing a tree and marking it with the date and the number of acres, established what was known as the "tomahawk claim" to the land. Others, by clearing a few acres and planting them, set up what was known as the "corn title." These possessions had frequently to be defended from seizure by other settlers who came with land patents from the Virginia legislature. Patents were of three sorts, namely, pre-emption rights, military grants, and warrants from a land office. Warrants were issued in such large numbers that the litigation growing out of the adjustment of conflicting claims and the land jobbing which ensued retarded agricultural development for some years.

Under a Virginia law every man who raised corn in Kentucky during the year 1780 was granted 400 acres and an additional 1,000 acres by pre-emption. Speculation in land was common, and many men acquired as much as 100,000 acres. Clark was among the number who held large areas of fertile wild land, but was "land poor" because there was no opportunity of converting his holdings into money.

Travelers wrote of the indolence of Kentucky farmers, due in part to their extensive land holdings and the frequent incursions of savages.[1] A report to the Secretary of War in 1790 states that during the preceding seven years, 1,500 Kentucky settlers had been killed by the Indians, and that 20,00 horses and property amounting to 15,000 pounds sterling had been carried away by these marauders.[2]

Indian corn, used chiefly for bread, was the leading crop, but tobacco, wheat, rye, oats, hemp, and flax were produced. Cabbages, pumpkins, turnips, beets, and peas were also grown. Agriculture was of the crudest sort. The ground was broken with the wooden mold-board plow, and the seed was sown by hand. Grain was cut with a reaphook or a cradle and was beaten out with a flail or the feet of horses. Hand mills were in common usage for grinding the grain, and the flour was sifted through a coarse linen cloth. Flax and wool were spun on wheels and woven on looms. Travelers wrote of the excellent breed of horses raised, and of other stock in abundance, especially of the droves of hogs. These were usually allowed to run at large, gaining subsistence in the woods. The cows fed on the cane. Salt was obtainable by boiling water from the salt springs, 120 gallons of water yielding, on the average, one gallon of salt. A love for horse-racing was general, and a racecourse was laid out at Harrodsburg as early as 1783. In May of that year Hugh McGary was tried by the court, was found guilty, and pronounced an infamous gambler for betting a mare, worth 12 pounds, on a race run over this course.

Log schoolhouses were built in the stations and villages, the same structure frequently serving for school and for

---

[1] "Diary of Major Erkuries Beatty, 1786," *Magazine of American History*, I, 1, 310.

[2] Brown, "The Centenary of Kentucky," *Filson Club Publications*, VII, 46.

church purposes. The teaching was done by the minister, by the chance traveler with a smattering of knowledge, or by a surveyor out of work for the time. Instruction in these log schools did not go beyond the primer, spelling-book, and elementary arithmetic, but a few select schools were established. As early as 1780 the Virginia legislature, chiefly through the influence of Colonel John Todd, Jr., a delegate from Kentucky County, passed an act which became the foundation for higher education in the West. It provided that 8,000 acres of land, formerly owned by British subjects, should be donated by Virginia for the purpose of erecting a "seminary of learning" in the county of Kentucky as soon as the state of its funds should permit. Three years later the provisions of the act were made more specific, and to the board of trustees of Transylvania Seminary, composed of William Fleming, William Christian, Benjamin Logan, George Rogers Clark, and fifteen other men whose names were well known in the West, was granted such powers as those exercised by any board of governors of a college or university within the state.[1] Up to 20,000 acres of land, held or purchased for the use of the Seminary, were to be free from taxation. Professors, masters, and students of the institution were to be exempt from militia duties. The first teacher, James Mitchell, who had been a tutor in Hampden-Sidney College, was appointed in the autumn of 1784, but the Seminary was not opened for the instruction of pupils until February, 1785.[2]

Travelers returning from Kentucky praised without measure the "Eden of the West," where were to be found

[1] The other trustees were John May, Levi Todd, John Cowan, Edmund Taylor, Thomas Marshall, Samuel McDowell, John Bowman, John Campbell, Isaac Shelby, David Rice, John Edwards, Caleb Wallace, Walker Daniel, Isaac Cox, Robert Johnson, John Craig, John Mosby, James Speed, Christopher Greenup, John Crittenden, and Willis Green.

[2] Mitchell had also served as a Presbyterian clergyman.

the finest soil and climate in the world. One, with prophetic insight, exclaimed:

Here are the finest and most excellent sites for farms, cities, and towns. Here may the industrious and broken-hearted farmer, tired with the slavery of the unfortunate situation in which he was born, lay down his burthen and find rest on these peaceful and plenteous plains; here may Iberia, Britain and Scotia, pour out their superabundant sons and daughters, who with cheerful hearts, and industrious hands, will wipe away the tear of tyrannic toil, and join the children of America in the easy labors of comfort and plenty, and bless the providence of that power who hath directed them to such a land.[1]

The range was declared to be inexhaustible. Forests containing ash, walnut, oak, hickory, sugar-maple, and other varieties of trees furnished timber in abundance, and buffalo, elk, deer, turkeys, and other game were seemingly inexhaustible.[2] Fish, such as bass, cat fish, and perch, were plentiful in the rivers. Clark and John Saunders, his Kaskaskia guide, together with Alexander Skinnor, a physician, entered into an agreement to supply meat to the settlement at Louisville. Saunders, with three men secured by his partners, and equipped also by them with a pack horse, ammunition, and salt, was to spend the winter and spring of 1784 and 1785 in hunting. In return he agreed to be "assiduously industrious" in procuring buffalo beef, bear's meat, and vension, which he was to forward to the falls to be disposed of by Skinnor.[3]

Pittsburgh seemed to promise little as the site for a future city, owing to the encroachment by the rivers on their banks. The little log houses were occupied chiefly by Scotch and Irish. Money was scarce, but barter in wheat, flour, and skins was common. At the beginning of the year

---

[1] Richard Butler, "Journal," Craig, *The Olden Time*, II, 446, 447.

[2] Draper MSS, 44 J 45.

[3] By December 5, 1785, travelers reported that Saunders and his hunters had procured 3,000 pounds of buffalo meat.

1785 there were four attorneys in the town, two doctors, but no clergyman.[1] The *Pittsburgh Gazette*, the first newspaper west of the Alleghanies, was set up the following year.

Louisville, with a population of three hundred living in the fifty to sixty log and a few frame houses, notwithstanding its superior location, was making but slow progress, owing chiefly to extravagance in wages and the indifference of tradesmen. Such articles as nails and calico, axes and broadcloth, silks, furniture, bonnets, hats, sugar, medicine, whiskey, tea, and books constituted the stock of the general stores. Tobacco, beef, pork, and corn were brought in to be exchanged for these articles. Beef, flour, and other produce were cheap, but all goods brought from New York or Philadelphia sold at an advance of 500 per cent over the original cost. Much time was consumed by all classes in card-playing, drinking liquor, and speculating in land and town lots.[2] The first distillery for making whiskey out of corn was erected in 1783. Brandy distilled from peaches, fermented grape juice, and beer made from the persimmon were common beverages, and Madeira wine and Jamaica rum were also to be found on the tables of those who could afford them. May day and the Fourth of July were the leading holidays. The celebration on the first of May consisted of dancing in a circle around a pole decorated with flowers, followed by drinking and carousing and firing guns in honor of St. Tammany, the patron of the festival.[3]

Social and economic conditions in the other villages, such as Bardstown, Danville, and Lexington, with its ninety to one hundred log houses, were the same as those

[1] Arthur Lee, "Journal," in Craig, *The Olden Time*, II, 339.

[2] Butler, "Journal," Craig, *The Olden Time*, II, 494.

[3] Joseph Buell, "Journal," in S. P. Hildreth, *Pioneer History*, p. 143.

to be found in Louisville. Owing to the lack of good water, fever and ague, especially in the summer months, was the common disease from which the settlers suffered. Opening of the veins of the patient and liberal doses of calomel were the usual remedies employed for various ailments by the pioneer doctor, who carried his "drug store "in his saddle bags.

Federal garrisons, as they were established, became centers for social life. An officer at Louisville wrote of "a very elegant dinner" which was served by Clark to a "number of gentlemen." After the dinner they walked to the dancing-school, where there were twelve or fifteen young misses, "some of whom had made considerable improvement in that polite accomplishment and indeed were middling neatly dressed, considering the distance from where luxuries are to be bought and the expense attending the purchase of them here."[1]

The act of the Virginia Assembly, setting aside bounty land for the soldiers who were engaged in the conquest of the Northwest, as interpreted by Clark and his associates on the board, sanctioned an immediate survey of the lands reserved to them and conveyance of the several portions to the claimants. He gave particular attention to the plans for a town on the 1,000-acre tract at the falls of the Ohio, which had been reserved for that purpose.[2] Clarksville, it was anticipated, would become an important city, since the location was thought to be superior to that of Louisville. To Clark was granted a site and the right to erect the first saw and grist mill.[3]

Following a protest by the President of Congress that

[1] "Diary of Major Erkuries Beatty, 1786," *Magazine of American History,* I, 1, 241.

[2] Richard Butler, "Journal," in Craig, *The Olden Time,* II, 495.

[3] *Record of Proceedings,* August 7, 1784, Virginia State Archives.

the carrying out of this plan invited war with the Indians since title to the lands had not been confirmed by treaty, Governor Harrison sent the following rebuke to Clark:

You must excuse me for saying that there is a degree of cruelty in the proceedings to your Country which was never expected from General Clark, as he must well know it would involve us in a most bloody and expensive war, which we are at this time not in any degree able to support. True it is the act vests the Lands in the Trustees for the use of you and your corps but as the same Act cedes the remaining country to Congress it is a very fair conclusion to suppose that the legislature never meant that Lands should be possessed or entered on till Congress should have obtained them from the Indians either by treaty or purchase. . . . . I request of you Sir to reflect on what you have done and the distress you will bring on your country by persevering in your plan which if you do I am persuaded you will immediately recall the settlers and wait for a more favorable opportunity to carry your intentions into execution.[1]

As authorized by the assembly, the Governor suspended the act permitting the survey. Almost three years were to elapse before the passing of a new act gave the commission authority to resume the survey and allottment of the lands.[2]

Since the year 1779, in spite of the efforts to prevent them, trespassers had been taking possession of lands on the Indian side of the Ohio between Fort McIntosh and the mouth of the Muskingum. Such settlements existed 30 miles up some of the tributaries of the Ohio.[3] The completion of each treaty opened a new field for land-jobbers and speculators, who were characterized as "prowling about like wolves in many shapes."[4]

The commissioners at Fort McIntosh, early in 1785,

[1] Draper MSS, 53 J 14.

[2] Hening, *Statutes*, XI, 447, January 25, 1787.

[3] *Ohio Archaeological and Historical Society Publications*, VI, 135.

[4] *Writings of Washington*, ed. Ford, X, 447. Timothy Pickering, later secretary of state, in a letter to Elbridge Gerry (March 1, 1785) wrote: "If they [Congress] mean to permit adventurers to make a scramble for them [lands west

gave the following instructions to Colonel Josiah Harmar, who was in command of the troops on the Ohio.[1] "Surveying or settling the lands not within the limits of any particular State being forbid by the United States, in Congress assembled, the commander will employ such forces as he may judge necessary in driving off persons attempting to settle on the lands of the United States."[2] Two months later Ensign Armstrong, with a small force, was sent by Colonel Harmar to dispossess these intruders. The order was executed from Pittsburgh to a point opposite Wheeling.[3]

Armstrong's report showed that unless early action was taken by Congress to prevent trespassing on lands west of the Ohio, "that country will soon be inhabited by a banditti whose actions are a disgrace to human nature."[4] He declared that there were then six hundred families settled on the Hockhocking and the Muskingum rivers and fifteen hundred persons living on the Scioto and the Miami. So determined were these adventurers to hold and govern their possessions that they issued a call for an election of members to a convention which was to frame a constitution.[5] This was another assertion of squatter sovereignty which had been proclaimed so frequently by communities west of the Alleghanies during the preceding five years.[6]

---

of Alleghanies] it will behove us to engage seasonably with some enterprising but confidential character to explore the country and make locations. But I would rather suppose Congress would fall on a more regular plan. . . . . But if there must be a scramble we have an equal right with others" (Papers of Rufus King, 1785–87, New York Historical Society Collections).

[1] January 24, 1785: *St. Clair Papers*, II, 3, note 1.

[2] This proclamation probably originated with Arthur Lee. Craig, *The Olden Time*, II, 340.

[3] *St. Clair Papers*, II, 3, 4.   [4] *Ibid.*, p. 4, note.

[5] *Ibid.*, p. 5. March 12, 1785.

[6] See "Western State-Making in the Revolutionary Era," *American Historical Review*, I, 70–87, 251–68. "I do certify," the last paragraph of the advertisement for the elections declared, "that all mankind, agreeable to every constitu-

Congress determined, even before the cessions of western lands were completed, to sell them, and thus partially provide for the payment of the national debt. It was estimated that 10,000,000 acres could be placed on the market at one dollar an acre, and that subsequent treaties with the Indians would yield 20,000,000 acres more. In this way the bulk of the domestic debt would be provided for.[1] Alarmed at the "excessive rage" for possessing western lands, Congress, by the ordinance of May 20, 1785, provided for the survey and sale of the lands northwest of the Ohio River which had been acquired from the Indians. This fund was to be applied toward extinguishing the public debt.

In the survey of the lands, what is known as the rectangular system was used. This plan was suggested a year earlier by a committee of which Thomas Jefferson was chairman. The unit of survey was to be the township, 6 miles square and divided into thirty-six sections each one mile square. Section 16 of every township was to be set aside for the support of the public schools. Land was to be sold at auction at a minimum price of one dollar an acre plus the cost of the survey. Congress (1785), having created the office of geographer of the United States, elected to that position Thomas Hutchins, who inaugurated the first systematic survey west of the Alleghanies.

Some satisfactory system for governing the territory was also essential. As early as 1780 it had been proposed to make new states out of it, and in pursuance of this plan, Thomas Jefferson, in 1784, submitted a report which pro-

---

tion formed in America, have an undoubted right to pass into every vacant country, and there to form their constitution, and that from the confederation of the whole United States, Congress is not empowered to forbid them, neither is Congress empowered from that confederation to make any sale of uninhabited lands to pay the public debts, which is to be by a tax levied and lifted by authority of the Legislature of each State."

[1] *The Letters of Richard Henry Lee*, ed. J. C. Ballagh, II, 349, 362, 379.

vided for the division of the land north of the thirty-first parallel and south of the forty-fifth into fourteen or sixteen states. Each was to have a name, such as Metropotamia, Polypotamia, Illinoia. They might adopt constitutions like those of any of the original thirteen states and become members of the confederation. The ordinance was adopted by Congress when the clause abolishing slavery "after the year 1800" was removed, but the names suggested for the states were rejected. The ordinance remained practically a dead letter, but it is of interest, for it was the forerunner of the famous Northwest Ordinance adopted for the government of the Northwest Territory three years later.

Early in June, 1785, a report sent by Colonel Harmar to the Secretary of War showed clearly that order could with difficulty be preserved in this region. While the intruders had been driven off for a distance of 70 miles below Pittsburgh, he declared that the number beyond was "immense," and that unless "Congress entered into immediate measures" it would be impossible to prevent an extension of these settlements.[1] Besides, British agents and traders from Detroit were keeping alive the spirit of resentment among the Indians against the American advance. "They know," a council of the tribes proclaimed, "their [United States] intention was to draw near, so near that in bed they could hear the sound of axes felling the trees."[2]

To make their demands more effective and at the same time protect the surveyors of the public lands from assault by the Indians, Colonel Harmar was directed by Congress to take post between the Muskingum and the Great Miami rivers.[3] Accordingly Fort Harmar was erected at

[1] *St. Clair Papers*, II, 6.

[2] Council of Shawnee, Mingo, Delawares, and Cherokee, May 18, 1785. *Report on Canadian Archives* (1890), p. 153.

[3] *St. Clair Papers*, II, 7.

the mouth of the Muskingum and the militia was called out for three years' service on the frontiers.

At the first opportunity, however, large numbers of those ejected from their lands returned and rebuilt their cabins.[1] The difficulties were exaggerated because of the confusion of titles to land in Kentucky. It was said that scarcely one-tenth of the Kentucky settlers held their land with assured titles. Thousands had gone to the south of the Ohio expecting to secure lands on easy terms, but were disappointed and were finally "obliged to settle on other persons' lands on sufference."[2] Thus Kentucky offered no satisfactory refuge for dispossessed settlers from across the Ohio.

On April 18, 1785, Congress appointed George Rogers Clark, Richard Butler, and Oliver Wolcott special commissioners, with instructions to hold a conference with the northwestern Indians.[3] Six thousand dollars were appropriated for the purchase of goods and for other necessary expenses. October 1 was fixed upon as the time for beginning the conference, and Clark, to whom was intrusted the messages to the tribes, was given power to carry on negotiations providing the other commissioners were not present. Clark reached the falls of the Ohio the middle of September. On October 25, when Clark and Butler fixed on the location for the conference at the mouth of the Miami, there was no positive assurance that any of the tribes would attend.[4] From the reports of messengers, the

[1] Draper MSS, 1 SS 2–11. Craig, *The Olden Time*, II, 437, 438, 440.

[2] Butler, "Journal," in Craig, *The Olden Time*, II, 507.

[3] S. H. Parsons served as third commissioner in the place of Oliver Wolcott.

[4] Butler "Journal," in Craig, *The Olden Time*, II, 456. The spot finally selected was one mile above the mouth of the river. Congress had previously designated that a post for preventing settlers from taking possession of lands should be located on this site.

Delawares, Wyandotte, and Shawnee were not disposed to place themselves under the protection and friendship of the United States.

It was said that Simon Girty, Captain Caldwell, and other agents had shortly before visited the Shawnee and prejudiced them against the Americans.[1] The Indians were assured that peace had not been concluded and that fighting would be resumed in the spring; that they would receive goods at better rates from the British than from the Americans; that the Big Knives were not to be trusted, for it was their intention to collect the Indians and put them to death. While they were among the Miami, the messengers were treated with marked disrespect and their horses were stolen. Chiefs of these tribes in conference at Detroit, September 20, assured McKee that they were determined to follow the advice of the Six Nations and not attend the council called by the Americans. They asserted that they were determined to defend their lands to the last man, and that the British must be strong in their defense.[2]

While awaiting the reply of the Indians, the company of militia consisting of seventy men under Captain Finney which was sent as a guard for the commissioners was engaged in clearing the ground and building block houses.[3] By November 10 this structure, called Fort Finney, near the site of Cincinnati, was completed. Chiefs of the Wyandotte and Delawares, with their followers, with whom the treaty at Fort McIntosh was held, attracted by the presents of flour, rum, and tobacco, soon gathered for the conference. The social usages observed on the occasion were described by an officer as follows: "dancing parties in our council

[1] These men were in the employ of Alexander McKee, British agent at Detroit.

[2] *Report on Canadian Archives* (1890), p. 164.

[3] Craig, *The Olden Time*, II, 457.

house almost every afternoon. . . . . An old fellow has a keg, with a skin drawn over each head—sort of drum on which he beats time . . . . dance in a circle round the fire—can't dance without something to make their hearts warm, and generally break up pretty merry. . . . . Very few went home sober, but those who did were sure to get drunk at night. They would come next day and peremptorily demand a quantity of rum, and on being refused they set homeward very much offended, declaring that the next day should move them off, never to be seen as friends again."[1]

But the Shawnee, for whom the treaty was intended, disregarded the messages. Impatient at the delay, the commissioners issued a final summons in which they declared it necessary for them to decide either upon peace or war, and that fifteen days would be allowed for their answer.[2]

The threat was effective, and on January 13, 150 Shawnee warriors, accompanied by their women and children, arrived at the fort.[3] The day following, the formalities incident to such a conference were observed. Chief Molunthee, beating a drum and singing, accompanied by the other chiefs, marched to the council house, the armed warriors headed by their war chief, followed by the young warriors dancing and by the women and children.[4] Their salute was returned with three volleys by the American troops. During the ensuing three weeks the commissioners endeavored to make clear to the savage mind the terms which would be satisfactory to the American government. The treaty with Great Britain and the boundary line established at

[1] Major E. Denny, "A Military Journal," *Record of Upland and Denny's Journal*, p. 267.

[2] Craig, *The Olden Time*, II, 90.

[3] One hundred sixty-eight women and children were present.

[4] Chief Molunthee was a white man of good character who had lived among the Shawnee for a number of years.

Fort McIntosh were especially emphasized. The Shawnee promised that all American prisoners should be returned, but sullenly refused to give three hostages as pledges for its performance. "We are Shawnee," they declared, "Our words are to be believed. When we say a thing we stand to it." And "as to the lands," they said, "God gave us this country, we do not understand measuring out the lands, it is all ours!"[1] The demands were summarily rejected. With like assurance the commissioners determined not to recede. Clark spurned the black string of wampum presented, and in the ultimatum declared: "It rests now with you; the destruction of your women and children, or their future happiness, depends on your present choice. Peace or war is in your power; make your choice like men and judge for yourselves."[2] The move proved successful, and the Indians resolved to sue for peace. Terms were agreed upon January 31, 1786, the Indians acknowledging the sovereignty of the United States over all the territory ceded by Great Britain. The territory between the Big Miami and the Wabash was to be reserved to the tribes there in conference. Five hostages were given as assurance that all white prisoners were to be released.[3]

To all appearances the Indians were satisfied with the treaty, and the Shawnee sent out messengers to the other tribes urging them also to come to terms with the Americans.[4] The commissioners were confident that all animosities had been wiped out and that it remained only for

---

[1] Butler, "Journal," in Craig, *The Olden Time*, II, 522.

[2] The story was related that Clark brushed the black string of wampum, typifying war, off the table with his cane and stepped on it (Major Denny, *Journal*, p. 277).

[3] *American State Papers*, Vol. V, *Indian Affairs*, I, 11.

[4] Butler and Parsons to the President of Congress, February 1, 1786. Draper MSS, 1 SS 2-11. Such a treaty was proposed by the Commissioners to be held at a place more central to the western Indians.

Congress to survey and sell the lands, and settle upon some form of government.[1]

Scarcely had the Shawnee reached their villages, however, before there were murmurings of discontent, and a few weeks thereafter they were declaring the treaty had been signed only to gain time and prevent the destruction of their villages by the Americans, and that they had no intention of keeping the articles agreed upon.[2] Their wrath was kindled especially against Clark and his associates. It was contended by British officials that no boundary line could be drawn by the Americans, and that no surveys of settlements north of the Ohio would be tolerated.[3] Very clearly the policy inaugurated by Congress of treating either with a few tribes or a single tribe was a failure. The Indians held tenaciously to the idea of confederation which had been inculcated among them by British agents. This was especially marked during the summer of 1786 after the return of Joseph Brant from a visit to London, whither he had gone as special representative of the Iroquois.

Brant could not believe it possible that the Indians had been forgotten in the treaty, and inquired whether the King's support might be counted on to prevent American trespass on their lands.[4] Compensation was demanded for losses of the Indians during the war.[5] His disappointment was evident when he learned from Lord Sydney that of the certified claims only those of the Mohawks, amounting to 15,000 pounds sterling, would be paid, and that similar

[1] Butler, "Journal," Craig, *The Olden Time*, II, 516.

[2] *Report on Canadian Archives* (1890), pp. 174, 175. February 27 and May 29, 1786.

[3] *Ibid.*, p. 175.

[4] *Ibid.*, p. 168. Brant held that the treaty of Fort Stanwix of 1768 was still in force.

[5] *Ibid.*, pp. 171, 172, 177. Brant also claimed half-pay as colonel, which had been promised him. He had received full pay during the war.

claims of the other Indians would likewise receive favorable consideration.[1] No attempt was made to give him a right understanding on the surrender of territory. He was especially advised to prevent hostilities against the Americans and urged to keep the tribes united. In the various councils he strove to fulfil these injunctions.[2]

Efforts at conciliation were neutralized by Cornplanter, a Seneca, who, with other chiefs, accompanied the American commissioners on their return to New York. Upon being presented to Congress, they were informed that all Indian lands had been ceded to the United States, but that they would be protected on their allotments.[3] This statement by Congress was received with derision in a council of the confederates held at Niagara July 25, 1786.[4]

Early in the year 1786 it was evident that the federal government could not gain possession of the Northwest by the methods heretofore pursued. The causes for the failure of this policy were patent to the commissioners at Fort Finney. While advocating the necessity for holding a treaty at a more central point farther west as a step to securing control over the tribes still hostile to the United States, they protested that no peace with the savages, jealous and fickle, could be permanent unless they were first convinced of the strength of the government, and also that there should be a disposition to treat them justly. The influence of British emissaries from Detroit who were paid to reside in the Indian towns, stir up the jealousies of the

[1] *Report on the Canadian Archives* (1906), p. 547.

[2] *Ibid.*, pp. 177, 178, 179.

[3] *Ibid.*, pp. 175, 179.

[4] This council was called together by Sir John Johnson and Joseph Brant, and there were in attendance the sachems and warriors of the Six Nations together with deputies from the Wyandotte, Chippewa, Ottawa, Potawatomi, Shawnee, Cherokee, and Wabash tribes. Brant strove to unite the confederates for a campaign against the Americans, but in this he was not successful.

tribesmen, and prompt them to acts of hostility was cited as a leading cause for the alienation of the Indians from the United States. Exorbitant prices were paid by them for plunder gotten from Americans. Looking to the same end, the western territory was divided into districts for commercial purposes and British traders were established in the Indian towns. Americans traders were closely associated with them, for their trade privileges were greater than any which could be secured from the American government. British agents were also sent to the French villages to report on the attitude of the people, and, unauthorized by their government, urged the French to unite with Great Britain. The Michilimackinac Company established a trading post at Cahokia, and together with British merchants in the other villages practically monopolized the Illinois fur trade.[1]

The tradition of the wealth to be secured in the Illinois country attracted Americans, as we have seen, during the years of the Revolution and those which followed. In spite of the prohibition by Virginia regarding settlement, it is estimated that 150 pioneers found their way to the French villages during these years. Some of them located in the villages, while others settled on farms which had been granted them by local officials.[2] The first permanent settlement of purely English-speaking settlers north of the Ohio River was made in 1779 at Bellefontaine. Others came in 1781, after the abandonment of Fort Jefferson. In response to a petition, the court at Kaskaskia granted this village the privilege of electing a justice of the peace. But Americans were not content to be in any way subordinated to the French, whom they regarded as aliens settled on American soil.

---

[1] *Kaskaskia Records*, pp. 328, 395.

[2] Alvord, *The Illinois Country*, 1673-1818, p. 359.

Among the Americans who came to the French villages were numerous refugees and vagabonds who, disregarding all authority, preyed on these communities. Clark bitterly lamented this influence, and called on the court at Kaskaskia to inflict corporal punishment and even the death penalty upon these disturbers of the peace. Petitions to Congress from both factions to establish some form of stable government were frequent. The French complained of the lawlessness and violence of the American speculators who were coming among them and securing their lands by fraud. Americans, with like bitterness, asserted that the French were in alliance with the Indians, that they opposed the coming of all Americans, and urged that, like the Indians, they should be ruled only with a rod of iron.[1]

The French court, remnant of the legal foundation established by Clark and Todd, was abolished in November, 1782, by Richard Winston, who was serving as acting county lieutenant.[2] Until the re-establishment of the court in June, 1787, Kaskaskia was without any sort of legalized justice. For a time the deputy county lieutenant served as sole judge between the factions. John Dodge, leader of the Americans, seized the old French fort, fortified it with two cannon, and established an absolute rule over the community until the fall of 1786, when Clark returned to Vincennes at the head of an expedition against the Indians of the Northwest.[3]

Anarchy was still more prevalent at Vincennes, a community of some three hundred houses. Sixty American

---

[1] *Kaskaskia Records*, pp. 360, 369, 376.

[2] The county of Illinois as a legal organization came to an end January 5, 1782. The Virginia assembly, because of negotiations with the United States regarding the cession of this territory, declined to renew the act, as had been done each year since 1778.

[3] For the events connected with this period, see *Cahokia Records*, pp. cxxviii ff.

families resided in a quarter of the town where lots had been assigned to them, and there they built a stockaded fort. During the early spring of 1786 they appealed to Clark for advice and besought him to secure, from the government, troops for their defense.[1] An attack by the savages seemed imminent, and this they believed would result in the total destruction of the Americans. They turned out to cultivate their fields only under a guard of armed men, but the French were not molested. The outlying American squatters took refuge within the town. As the days wore on the hostility of the Indians increased. They entered freely the French section of the town, and the Americans were forced to pass their nights within the confines of the stockade. Tales of the barbarous treatment of unprotected Americans were frequent. Early in June, John Filson, an explorer and pioneer trader, the first historian of Kentucky, was attacked by a band of Indians as he was going down the Wabash River. Two of his men were killed, but Filson escaped and finally reached Vincennes, having lost his canoe and all other property except two small trunks. No account was taken by the magistrates of the complaints that his goods were sold within the town.[2]

Shortly after, a party of Americans under Major Daniel Sullivan, who were working in their corn fields, were attacked by savages. Two of the men were wounded; one of them, falling into the hands of the enemy, was scalped, but later recovered. Sullivan and his men rallied and forced the Indians to retreat. Returning to the town, they seized an Indian and put him to death. This act exasperated the French, and the Americans were summoned by Colonel Legras before a council made up of the magistrates and

---

[1] Moses Henry, John Small, and others in a petition to Clark, who was then at Louisville, March 16, 1786. Draper MSS, 53 J 23.

[2] *Ibid.*, 53 J 32.

officers of the militia. A proclamation was drawn up in which it was ordered that any American who was unable to produce a passport from the government under which he last resided should immediately leave the town, "bag and baggage."[1] Clark was solicited to come to their rescue without delay, or to send a guard to accompany them from the country, for which service they would sacrifice all of their property. Crowded into the fort, they prepared to fight for their lives. They were convinced that no assistance in this extremity would be afforded by their French neighbors, who, it was generally believed, were encouraging the Indians to continue hostilities. Indeed, the wavering attitude of the Creole inhabitants is not surprising, for Congress appeared to disregard their petitions for protection against the lawlessness of certain American self-seekers and "vagabonds." No advance had been made toward establishing an orderly government in their midst, and the posts were still in the possession of the British.

Early in July the Wabash tribes determined on a war of extermination against all Americans. On the fifteenth, an army numbering between four and five hundred Indians under their red and white flags, descended the Wabash for this purpose. Approaching Vincennes, they sent messengers to inform the French that they had no desire to attack them, but that their young men were determined upon vengeance against the Americans. All efforts of the French envoys sent to dissuade them from this purpose were unavailing. The chiefs and sachems declared that the red people were united in opposition "to the men wearing hats," who were in league to drive the Indians from their lands. A string of black wampum was presented to a wavering Piankeshaw chief as a warning that any who refused to join them should themselves be destroyed. The

[1] Draper MSS, 53 J 35.

next day they advanced, following their red flags, toward the American fort and completely surrounded it. Seeing the French drawn up prepared for battle, after firing shots at the fort, the Indians hoisted a white flag. In the parley which ensued the chiefs reproached the French for obstructing them. With the exhortation that the Americans, who had occasioned all the evil, should be sent away, they retreated, after shooting large numbers of cattle belonging to the inhabitants.

Fortune again favored the Americans, for scarcely were the Indians well out of the way, when hunters, returning to the village, brought the report of an attack on a party of Indians made up of friendly Piankeshaw and a few Miami who were hostile. This assault was made by a company of 130 Kentuckians who were being sent by Clark to the rescue of the Americans at Vincennes.[1] The expedition was in response to a petition for assistance on the part of a number of Americans and French in that village. "This place," they wrote, "that once trembled at your victorious arms, and these savages over-awed by your Superior power is now entirely anarchial, and We Shuder at the daily expectation of horrid Murthers, and probably total depopulation of the Americans by imperious savages; . . . . it is probable in a few days we shall behold savage hands imbrued in the blood of our brethren. Knowing you to be a friend to the distressed, and possess'd of humanity we therefore earnestly look to you for assistance."[2] After six of the Indians were killed and seven wounded, the survivors fled, leaving all their booty and packs on the field. The Kentuckians, having lost one man who was killed and four wounded, also retired and marched toward Louisville.

[1] *Cal. Va. State Papers,* IV, 156, 157.

[2] March 6, 1786. Draper MSS, 53 J 23.

There was despair during the spring and summer of 1786 in nearly all of the communities west of the mountains, for the havoc wrought by savage bands was general. As on previous occasions, the brunt fell on the Kentucky settlements, where a score of Indian parties from the Wabash committed the customary depredations. The settlers in the vicinity of Louisville suffered most severely. The Limestone and Licking settlements were devastated by warriors of the Chickamauga tribe. A portion of this tribe had settled north of the Ohio. The eastern and southern frontiers were troubled by Indians living on the Tennessee River.[1] The settlements on Beargrass, frequently visited by parties of Indians from across the Ohio, were again raided. Early in April Colonel William Christian, a noted leader on retaliatory expeditions, set out in pursuit of the plunderers at the head of twenty volunteers, and overtook the party after crossing the Ohio. The order to strike all together was disobeyed, and Colonel Christian, with two companions, rode in advance of the others. Three Indians whom they overtook were killed, but in the combat Colonel Christian and Captain Isaac Keller were both mortally wounded.

The sacrifice of other settlers led to the demand for a retaliatory expedition in force.[2] Clark, together with a number of representative men of Jefferson County, besought the citizens of the other three counties of Kentucky to aid in their defense against the incursions of their relentless and common enemies. "You need not surely be reminded," they wrote, "how much you are interested in our

[1] Judge Samuel McDowell to Governor Patrick Henry, April 18, 1786. Draper MSS, 12 S 39–46.

[2] John May to Governor Patrick Henry, April 19, 1786. Draper MSS, 12 S 39–46.

security. Should we, as we have great reason to fear, from the hostile disposition of many of the savage tribes, and their daily incursions, be reduced to the calamitous necessity of abandoning our settlements, your counties must become frontiers, and in that situation will certainly experience all those evils which we now complain of, under which we are suffering."[1]

[1] Draper MSS, 12 S 48–51.

Chapter XVI

Retaliation on Indians and Spaniards

A HUNDRED thousand dollars in specie," said Rufus King, "had been paid in ten years to satisfy the savages, in the hope of pacifying them, but the sacrifice was futile."[1]

Clark appealed to the Governor of Virginia and to the President of Congress for assistance in a retaliatory expedition against the Indians of the Wabash, who were encouraged in their depredations by British traders from Detroit, and who, by combining their forces, were able to summon fifteen hundred warriors. But such support could not be gotten for some time, and with no law by which the militia could be ordered out of the state, he advocated, as a last resort, a volunteer army of sufficient size to penetrate into the heart of the Wabash country. "I doubt great part of these beautiful Settlements will be laid waste," he wrote; "without protected by volunteers penetrating into the Heart of the Enemy's country, nothing else will do, Scouts and Forts on the Frontiers, answer but little purpose and in the end cost more than an Army that would do the Business Effectually at once."[2]

He maintained that if the Indians were defeated in a general action they would sue for peace and agree to any terms by which their country could be saved from destruc-

[1] Justin Winsor, *Westward Movement*, p. 276.
[2] *Ibid.*

347

tion. But loading them with presents and treating them humanely would result in making them think that the Americans feared them, and another attack would only result in more gifts.[1] Similarly, he imparted to Congress his arguments for a policy so vigorous that the tribes would be reduced to obedience. Such a policy, he felt, would cause the tribes with which they had treated to hold to their engagements and would bring the more western Indians to solicit terms of peace. British emissaries encouraging them to war on Americans would be dealt with as enemies, and with the coming of general peace the development of the frontiers would go forward. Once more he urged the necessity for securing possession of Detroit:

If Detroit was in our possession it might in a great measure silence the Indians; but nothing will effectually do it but dissolution, and all humanity shewn them by us is imputed to timidity. Great expenditures, and numbers of lives might be saved by now reducing them to obedience, which they so richly deserve. There is no danger of making them desperate; they are as far from that principle as any people in the world. Before they would suffer their families to perish by the sword or famine, they would become your servile subjects; this I am convinced of from long experience and observation on the disposition of various nations.[2]

The critical conditions in the West were also emphasized in an appeal to Congress by the other commissioners, who reported that British emissaries among the Shawnee and other tribes were stirring up antagonism between the Indians and the Americans. "The Wabash and other Indian nations in that quarter," they wrote, "are more hostilely than peaceably disposed towards the people of the United States and particularly against the settlement of the lower parts of Kentucky. It is to be feared, that unless Congress interfere, mutual and repeated ill-offices will

[1] Clark to Governor Henry, May, 1786. *Cal. Va. State Papers*, IV, 122.

[2] Clark to Richard Henry Lee, president of Congress, June 8, 1786. Draper MSS, 14 S 207-10.

continue between the parties and be the means of spreading war to the nations already at peace with the United States and thereby involve not only these too much distressed settlements, but the whole frontier, in its dreadful effects."[1] Americans residing at Vincennes petitioned Congress for relief against hostile savages whose antipathy to Americans exposed them to daily danger and frequent death. They urged the appointment of "a regular government in this place and territory, under the Conduct of good men, as the Commandant, and Magistracy of this place, have resigned and refused to act on account of disobedience in the people." If these requests were complied with and a strong garrison established for the support of the civil power, the banks of the Wabash, they declared, would soon be inhabited by "numerous valuable subjects."[2]

The Illinois towns were likewise pictured as being without law or government and in greatest confusion. Unless the authority of Congress should be extended to them, Clark held, they were destined to become the victims of savage violence. Meantime he recommended that they should reassume their former customs and appoint temporary officers until the pleasure of Congress should be known.[3] The situation in the villages was set forth in the following letter:

You know neither these regions nor the manners and vices of those who inhabit them. In Canada all is civilized, here all is barbarous. You are in the midst of justice, here injustice dominates. There is no distinction from the greatest to the least except that of force; of the tongue, pernicious, calumniating and slanderous; of crying out very loud, and giving forth all sorts of insults and oaths. Everybody is in poverty, which engenders theft and rapine. Wantoness and drunkenness pass here as elegance and amusements quite in style. Breaking of

[1] Draper MSS, 14 S 211–15.

[2] The names of seventy-one men, evidently none of them French, appear on this petition of June 1, 1786. Draper MSS, 53 J 31.

[3] Clark to Richard Henry Lee, June 8, 1786. Draper MSS, 14 S 207–10.

limbs, murder by means of a dagger, sabre, or sword (for he who wills carries one) are common, and pistols and guns are but toys in these regions. . . . . No commandant, no troops, no prison, no hangman, always as in small places a crowd of relatives or allies who sustain each other; in a word, absolute impunity for these and ill luck for the stranger. I could name a great number of persons assassinated in all the villages of this region, French, English and Spanish without any consequence whatsoever.[1]

But relief seemed distant with a Congress paralyzed through lack of a quorum and with a secretary of war powerless. The treasury board was unable to grant an appeal for a thousand dollars (June, 1786) needed for transporting powder to the western troops, and desertions from their ranks were common because they had received no pay for their services.[2] Finally, alarmed at the reports received from Colonel Harmar that most of the western tribes which had treated with the Americans were, under the influence of British agents and traders, committing depredations and preparing for war, Congress voted, October 20, 1786, to raise a body of 1,340 troops for the term of three years. It was hoped thus to increase the western force to a legionary corps of 2,040 men. But the provision that twelve hundred men should be secured from New England aroused the suspicions of that section that the real purpose of the act was not so much to furnish protection to the Western settlers against the Indians as it was to constitute a force to put down Shays's rebellion. "The country members," wrote Rufus King, November 29, "laugh, and say the Indian War is only a political one to obtain a standing army."[3]

[1] Father Gibault to the Bishop of Quebec, June 6, 1786. *Kaskaskia Records*, pp. 542 ff. Civil authorities agreed with this statement. *Ibid.*, pp. 511, 513, 516.

[2] Winsor, *Westward Movement*, p. 274.

[3] New Hampshire was to furnish 260 men; Massachusetts, 660; Rhode Island, 120; Connecticut, 180, and Virginia and Maryland, 60 cavalry each. Draper MSS, 11 J 64–68.

Meantime the situation of the Americans at Vincennes, numbering some four hundred, was desperate, and despairing of any assistance from Congress, they continued to appeal to Kentucky leaders for relief. A message to Clark ran as follows:

We are dayly alarmed by the Hostile Savages, whose Barbarities I can hardly Express. Our Number is Continually Decreasing and I fear that if Your Excellency Dose not Speedily Assist Us We must Inavitably Perish. Danger And Destruction Stears Every American heer in the face, And Every Night we Look for a general Attack on our Small Garrison. As We are Informed by the Antient Inhabitants that a Large Body of the Enemy is on their Way for that purpose, We have all Crowded into our Small Fort, and have put Ourselves in a posture of Defence.[1] They offered to give all of their property as a reward for their rescue.

The handful of federal troops at Fort Finney were in grave danger of being cut off. In despair, their commanding officer wrote Clark: "the difrent nations on the Miami and Wabash are combining to take this post. . . . . It will be impossible for me to obtain any assistance, except by accident, as their object will be to cut off our boats. Should I have it in my power, I will send the first express to You and hope you will send me the necessary Aid."[2]

Governor Henry, who had lost his good friend, Colonel Christian, at the hands of the Indians, sensed the desperate need of the West for protection.[3] Finally, despairing at the seeming apathy of the federal government, on the advice of the Virginia council, he directed the field officers of the Kentucky counties to "concert measures" for their own defense.[4]

[1] Draper, MSS, 53 J 36. Vincennes was a village of four hundred log houses and contained nine hundred French inhabitants.

[2] *Ibid.*, p. 25.

[3] John May to Patrick Henry, April 19, 1786. Draper MSS, 12 S 39–46.

[4] Letters of Secretarv Henry Knox, No. 150, II, 37, 39, Library of Congress.

Preparations were already under way in Kentucky, under the direction of Clark, for a campaign against the Indians of the Wabash and for the defense of the Americans at Vincennes. Notwithstanding the reports current in Virginia that Clark was but the wreck of his former self —a view usually concurred in by modern writers—to his near associates, he was still the outstanding military leader. One of these, whose good judgment cannot be doubted and who heretofore had opposed his policy, wrote: "I find that it is the unanimous opinion of the inhabitants of this country that General Clarke is the properest person to take command here, and notwithstanding the opinion which prevails below [Virginia] of his not being capable of attending to Business, I am of the same opinion of the Rest of this Country. I have been with him frequently, and I find him as capable of Business as ever, and should an expedition be carried against the Indians I think his name alone would be worth half a regiment of men."[1] This view was concurred in by Colonel Benjamin Logan, recognized leader in Lincoln County, who, sharply criticized for his neglect of duty at the Blue Licks, had tried to shift the responsibility to Clark.[2] Colonel Levi Todd, leader in Fayette County, who had taken part in the battle at the Blue Licks and likewise complained of Clark's policy, now recommended that the general command should be intrusted to Clark.[3] But testimony to the effect that Clark at times "drank to an excess" must be accepted when it came as the expression of James Monroe, a friendly critic; nor was the accusation denied by Clark.[4]

[1] John May to Patrick Henry, July 14, 1786. *Cal. Va. State Papers*, IV, 156.

[2] *Ibid.* "Colonel Logan has authorized me to say that in case a general officer should be appointed he thinks Gen'l Clarke's abilities and experience entitle him to the appointment."

[3] Levi Todd to Patrick Henry, July 12, 1786. Draper MSS, 12 S 67–73.

[4] Monroe to Clark, January 5, 1783. *Clark Papers*, XIX, 178, 179. Monroe wrote: "I shall be glad to hear from you. And after ye communications I have

This was a time, it is to be recalled, "when at gatherings for corn-huskings the green glass quart whiskey bottle was handed to everyone, man or boy, as they arrived, to take a drink. . . . . Either before or after the eating the fighting took place, and by midnight the sober were found assisting the drunken home."[1] "Every man was obliged to keep a kind of grog shop in his home," another contemporary wrote, "for his neighbours, acquaintances, and hangers on, or be esteemed a niggard. . . . . A barrel of rum at that time would in many families last but little longer than a gallon would before the war." Liquor constituted a chief incentive to labor for men engaged in building fortifications against the Indians.[2]

But, as will appear later, the facts do not warrant the pronouncement that Clark, when the Wabash campaign was under way, "had degenerated into an inebriate sloth only occasionally roused for the commission of some lawless act."[3]

---

very candidly made you I think you will readily concur with me that this investigation is very necessary to yr character and interest." *Ibid.*, p. 180. In Monroe's next letter (October 19, 1783) he spoke of having received a reply, but makes no reference to any denial, by Clark, of the accusation. *Ibid.*, pp. 248, 249. That Clark received a consignment of taffia for his personal use is seen from the following letter from Charles Gratiot (May 6, 1780): "I will send you some [taffia] as I hope I have some left of what I reserved for my own use and since I cannot have the pleasure of drinking it with you that I may have that of dividing it between us" (Clark Collection, Missouri Historical Society).

[1] Daniel Drake, *Pioneer Life in Kentucky*, ed. C. D. Drake (Cincinnati, 1870), pp. 163–84.

[2] John Todd to Benjamin Harrison, April 15, 1782. *Clark Papers*, p. 60.

[3] Samuel F. Bemis, *Pinckney's Treaty* (Baltimore, 1926), p. 133. The conclusions are likewise unwarranted as stated by Temple Bodley, *Clark*, pp. 301–4. "Diligent investigation has failed to disclose any contemporary evidence whatever indicating that General Clark was ever once intoxicated, either during, or at any time before, the Wabash expedition." The evidence based on the correspondence of certain men who accompanied Clark cannot be regarded as wholly conclusive. This testimony was secured by Lyman Draper during the years 1833,

For a time Clark declined to lead the expedition, although urging it as a necessity. His attitude was due, in part, to criticisms, by Kentuckians, of the commissioners at the Miami treaty. They were accused of trifling with some of the Indians while others were plundering the frontier hamlets. Moreover, the inhabitants of Lincoln County, chief dependence for troops, were seemingly not in favor of an expedition even if it was for their own protection.[1]

Early in August definite plans for the expedition were adopted by the field officers of the Kentucky district in a meeting at Harrodsburg which was presided over by Colonel Benjamin Logan. One-half of the militia, on foot or on horseback, as they might choose, under their county officers, were to assemble at Clarksville, where Clark was to assume command. A pack horse for every four men and necessary ammunition and provisions for fifty days were impressed. There was opposition to the draft, and supplies were furnished grudgingly, but by the middle of September twelve hundred men, or one-half the number expected, were assembled. Two days later, although the numbers were regarded as too small to carry out the original plan, Clark led them toward Vincennes, a march of eight days.[2]

1845, and 1846. Such statements are not convincing, for they were made at least forty-seven years after the event occurred. One of them, Captain Gaines, wrote: "It has been alleged that the Gen'l was in a state of intoxication during the whole time, which is certainly incorrect or I should have seen it" (Draper MSS, 9 J 238). Mr. Bodley states that "None of the mutineer officers appear to have said Clark was intemperate during the expedition" (Bodley, *Clark*, p. 302). Robard, a quartermaster of the Lincoln County troops, who, as he states, recommended a friend not to join either party, wrote: "I know to my own knowledge that I had business with the General while there and he was drunk chief of the time and not capable of business. I knew him and had great confidence in him" (Draper MSS, 11 J 79).

[1] "Diary of Major Erkuries Beatty," *Magazine of American History*, I, 1, 177.

[2] *Cal. Va. State Papers*, IV, 205.

Colonel Logan, as recommended by Clark in a council of the officers, was ordered to return to the Kentucky settlements for the purpose of marshaling the delinquents and deserters, and one-half of the militia not drafted, and proceed as rapidly as possible to Vincennes.[1]

Notwithstanding the resolution adopted by the officers that they considered themselves engaged in a common cause and bound themselves "to give every aid to each other, without, as well as within, their respective counties, to carry into execution the agreement," the march to Vincennes was scarcely under way when disorder became manifest among certain of the officers and troops. A delay of eight days at Vincennes increased this disaffection, for the supplies which were being brought by boat had been delayed on account of the low water in the Wabash. With assurances from Clark that a further advance of a few days would bring them to the Wabash villages, the march was resumed. At the close of the third day two hundred troops mutinied, the report having been circulated that the supply of provisions would be exhausted before the Indian towns should be reached.[2]

The cause for this unfortunate outcome seems to have been fairly stated in a letter to the President of Congress by an official whose testimony cannot be thought of as prejudiced. "Had the United States last year," Judge John

---

[1] Draper MSS, 12 S 118–20.

[2] This report was based on a statement to that effect made by their quartermaster. This contingent was from Lincoln County. Mr. Bodley asserts that these troops were disaffected from the outset due to the fact that Clark had been made commander of the expedition in preference to Benjamin Logan, senior militia officer in Kentucky who was also a resident of Lincoln County (Bodley, *Clark*, pp. 284 ff.). As previously shown, Colonel Logan was among the officers who advocated the appointment of Clark as commander of the expedition. Judged by his correspondence, Clark bore no ill will toward Logan in later years, and, as will be noted, they were closely associated in a plan of importance to them both.

Cleves Symmes wrote, "countenanced and led an expedition against the present invaders of this country, they had now been as submissive as the Six Nations are. Had Colonel Harmar, agreeable to the request of Governor Henry, been detached with a small body of the Continental troops, it would have given an example of subordination to the detachment of militia under the command of General Clark, the want of which ruined the design. It would have added stability and confidence to the army and the expedition could not have failed of success."[1] Clark had urged that at least a company of federal troops should be sent to cooperate with him, for, as he wrote, "A few regulars is a great advantage among militia." Moreover, in the first stages of recruiting for the expedition Clark had expressed misgivings over the outcome, for he was aware that there was no law which permitted taking militia out of the state against their will.[2] Advised that a campaign might be feasible, providing the law was "kept close," he could not have failed to recognize the hazards incident to an expedition in which the military law might, if invoked at any stage, nullify the authority of a commanding officer and his council of officers.

The expedition of eight hundred men under Colonel Benjamin Logan, early in October, against the Shawnee at the head of the Great Miami proved successful. Most

[1] Draper MSS, 14 S 160-70. Louisville, May 3, 1787. Judge Symmes was one of the three judges associated with General Arthur St. Clair, the first governor of the Northwest Territory, in fashioning a code of laws for the territory. The other two judges were Samuel H. Parsons and J. M. Varnum.

[2] Abraham Chapline to Clark, July 26, 1786. Draper MSS, 53 J 40. Captain Chapline had accompanied Clark on the Illinois expedition and was a lawyer. Clark had appealed to him on this question. As stated by Chapline: "The Sixth Article of Confederation does not prohibit us from Carrying on a Campaign against any Nation of Indians that actually invades our Country or States which is aluded to in the Governors Letter to the Officers of the District."

of the warriors had gone to oppose the advance of Clark. Ten of their villages, containing two hundred houses, together with the winter supply of corn, amounting to 15,000 bushels, were burned. Ten Indians were killed, and thirty-four, including two chiefs, were taken prisoners. Notwithstanding the order that prisoners' lives should be spared, there was one act of barbarism committed which in part neutralized the effect of the victory. Among the prisoners was the old Shawnee chief, Molunthee, who had on many occasions befriended the Americans. Shortly after the surrender Molunthee was killed by McGary, the colonel whose rash act caused the tragedy of the Blue Licks. The demand by the other officers that he should be immediately court-martialed was refused by Colonel Logan, who feared to cause further trouble.[1]

Clark, having returned to Vincennes, established a garrison of 150 men, together with a company of artillery, for one year's service. This force was thought to be sufficient to overawe the Indians, and it was hoped Kentucky would thus be free from further invasion.

Clark then proceeded to pave the way for negotiations with the tribes on the Wabash by a message to their chiefs, similar in content to his messages which had heretofore won favor with the Indians. Whether they chose war or peace was of little moment, but if hostilities were continued, he wrote, "We shall adopt measures without delay to send a great Many Families to take possession of your Lands and make a Conquest of them Forever without showing you any mercy."[2] He invited them, a special favor, to meet in council at Clarksville November 20 for

---

[1] McGary was court-martialed after the expedition returned to Kentucky. Draper MSS, 12 S 131–33.

[2] Draper MSS, 11 J 108.

the consideration of terms of peace and friendship. This appeal was greatly strengthened, as foreseen by Clark, by a communication accompanying it which had been prepared by Colonel J. M. P. Le Gras, French leader at Vincennes. The Americans had returned from their expedition, he stated, only on the entreaties of the French, who had given a pledge to Clark that the Indians would agree to "remain quiet" on their lands. The move proved successful, and the confederated chiefs, one after another, returned replies in which they expressed a willingness to meet in council. Their appeal for the postponement of the meeting until the following spring was readily approved by Clark. Vincennes and Kentucky would be protected during the truce, and the period of delay could be used to advantage by Congress in preparing conditions for a more lasting peace.

Meantime, the problem of providing food, clothing, and other necessities for the garrison was a serious one, and Clark appealed to the inhabitants of the Illinois villages for provisions. His agent, John Rice Jones, was well received by the villagers, for the name of Clark was still greatly honored by them. An American merchant, John Edgar, who had recently arrived at Kaskaskia and established friendly relations with the French, guaranteed payment for the supplies purchased. Their delivery was prevented by John Dodge until troops brought from Vincennes by Jones forced him to submit. The outcome was thus quaintly described in a French letter: "Mr. Jones seemed a fine gentleman who caused no hurt to anybody, but he entered in the above said fort on the hill occupied by John Dodge, he threatened him to cast him out from it if he continued to be contrary to America as he was before. He remained there some days with his troops, during which time the wheat has been delivered peaceably and nobody has been hurted."[1]

The immediate needs of the garrison for clothing and other supplies were met through the seizure of the property belonging to three Spanish merchants who had come to Vincennes for trade. The order for confiscation followed the findings of a court made up of officers appointed by Clark. The testimony showed that the goods were brought from New Orleans, that none of the traders possessed a pass, as required by Spanish officials, and that American products taken to New Orleans without permission were seized and sold.[2]

A recent illustration of the attitude of the Spaniards was known to Clark. A flatboat, the property of an American, loaded with flour and other supplies was seized after it had passed Natchez, the cargo was confiscated, and 100 barrels of the flour were sent to New Orleans, where it was sold at auction.

While preparing for his expedition against the Wabash confederacy, Clark probably knew of the conditions which were set forth in the following letter:

Poor Calvit brought only 40 barrels [flour] for his own use and it was confiscated and so will everything that comes directly from there unless the Kentucky lads put a stop to it, indeed I wonder how they have born it so long, they must have degenerated since I saw that country. . . . . Is it possible that our countrymen will forever suffer themselves to be bound up in this manner. What can they mean? . . . . What I have seen lately is torment to bear, the Creeks have murdered a number of our friends in Georgia and immediately after the stroke their King came here, 5 thousand Pounds of Ball and near as much powder and I believe some arms to enable them to stand against our country, this was done underhand but I found it out and am of oppinion

[1] *Kaskaskia Records*, p. 426. Dodge, seeing that his arbitrary rule was at an end, made his escape to the Spanish side of the Mississippi.

[2] Draper, MSS, 53 J 53.

these people will do their utmost to encourage all the savages against us—this moment my very Blood calls for Vengeance—I give you this hint that you may know what kind of neighbours we have and that you may make it known to our brethren. They have a store fixed at Mobile where our enemy Indians are furnished with anything they want.[1]

During the preceding two years similar acts on the part of Spanish officers had left no doubt in the minds of the men of the western waters regarding a determination by Spain to convert the Gulf of Mexico into a Spanish lake and to close the Mississippi River to all foreign commerce.

By royal order (March 12, 1784) no American vessels were to be admitted to any of the Spanish posts for trade. This decree was aimed especially at the communities bordering on the Ohio, from which flatboats loaded with flour and other produce were being brought to Spanish forts on the Mississippi. To prevent such traffic, the commandant at Natchez was directed to detain these boats until orders for their disposal were received from the governor at New Orleans.[2] An order published in July, 1784, forbade the admittance of any American vessel to the Mississippi upon any pretense whatsoever.[3]

Reports were prevalent that a schooner from Philadelphia, ordered out of the river, had not even been granted permission to secure necessary provisions for her crew. Boats from Pittsburgh were held at Natchez for the space of fifty days, some members of the crews dying of starvation.[4] Spanish customs officers boarded every American

[1] Draper MSS, William Clark Papers ., 136. The letter was dated New Orleans, July 13, 1786. During July, 1784, Spanish agents completed a treaty with the Creek. The Indians returned to their villages with great quantities of presents, having been assured that war with the Americans was shortly expected. Draper MSS, *Trip* IV, 20, 21.

[2] Miró to Galvez, March 12, 1784. Ayer Collection.

[3] Draper MSS, William Clark Papers, I, 98.

[4] *Ibid.*, I, 114.

boat which attempted to pass Natchez, compelled the traders to pay heavy tolls, subjected them needlessly to delay, and in other ways subjected them to petty annoyances.

By this time the population of the Cumberland settlements had reached 3,500, while Kentucky numbered over 30,000. Washington, who made a tour of 680 miles, on horseback, through the western country (September, 1784), wrote of the critical conditions in that section as follows:

The western states (I speak now from my own observation) stand as it were upon a pivot. The touch of a feather would turn them any way. They have looked down the Mississippi, until the Spaniards, very impolitically I think for themselves, threw difficulties in their way; and they looked that way for no other reason than because they could glide gently down the stream, without considering, perhaps, the difficulties of the voyage back again, and the time necessary to perform it in, and because they have no other means of coming to us but by long land transportations and unimproved roads. These causes have hitherto checked the industry of the present settlers; for except the demand for provisions, occasioned by the increase of population, and a little flour, which the necessities of the Spaniards compel them to buy, they have no incitements to labor.[1]

Americans at Natchez and New Orleans spoke in other terms of the hardships to which they were subjected. One of them wrote to his friend in Kentucky:

It is impossible to imagine the injustice and injuries commited upon our poor fellow subjects here for God's sake send me something as soon as possible that I may clear myself and put myself in a state to hop the twigg and go and enjoy peace and quietness with you all upon our fruitfull Banks of Ohio then will I be ready to drop down when the hour of retaliation will come. . . . . Pray let me know if you can explain a quible they make here about the line being at the northernmost part of 31° for my part I am not Geographer enough to do it, if they meant anything why did not they write it 32 at once or 31 or

[1] *Writings of Washington*, ed. Sparks, IX, 63.

whatever number of miles they lik'd, then a body would know what to be at.[1]

A month later, sending his compliments to Clark "for his goodnesses to me," he wrote: "What in the name of God are Congress about that they let their subjects be so vilainously treated in this place and suffer the treaty to be so notoriously violated?"[2]

[1] July 22, 1784. Draper MSS, William Clark Papers, I, 89.
[2] Ibid., p. 95.

Chapter XVII

Frontier Expansion and Spanish Conspiracy

WE HAVE seen that John Jay, in his more than two years at Madrid, had accomplished nothing through attempted negotiations over the navigation of the Mississippi River and the Florida boundary line. Arriving in Paris, he attempted to negotiate on these points with Count d'Aranda, the Spanish ambassador, but made no headway. By the definitive treaty of peace between Great Britain and the United States (1783) it was provided that the navigation of the Mississippi from its source to the ocean should remain forever free and open to the subjects of Great Britain and the subjects of the United States. The southern boundary of the new nation was fixed at the thirty-first parallel east from the Mississippi. By a secret article in the treaty, however, provision was made that in the event that Great Britain continued in the possession of the Floridas, the boundary should be 32° 30′, or a line east from the mouth of the Yazoo River. But Spain was not a party to this agreement, and moreover, through the conquests of Galvez and the cession by Great Britain, the Floridas had become her possessions.

A month after the conclusion of peace Spain consented, grudgingly, to acknowledge the independence of the United States. This concession was gained through the friend-

ly offices of La Fayette on a visit to Madrid. He went to
the assistance of Carmichael, appointed American chargé
d'affaires, who, after a further period of six months waiting, marked with the usual promises, excuses, and formalities, was presented at court.[1] While professing the desire
to form an "everlasting friendship" with America, La
Fayette gathered, through his conversation with Florida
Blanca, that Spain, fearing the loss of her own colonies,
was full of resentment over the independence of America.
Josef de Galvez, Minister of the Indies, expressed the wish
that the whole continent of America might be sunk to the
bottom of the ocean, and Florida Blanca refused even to
discuss the navigation of the Mississippi.[2]

Spanish officials maintained that West Florida extended north to 32°30', or the line which England had established in 1763. When they learned of the secret agreement
in the treaty of 1783 their indignation was without measure. Unless, they demanded, the United States agreed to
the unconditional surrender of the strip of territory between the 31° and 32°30', no treaty on commercial subjects
between the two nations could be considered, and the Mississippi River below Natchez was absolutely to be closed to
all American trade. This threat, as already noted, soon became a reality after the re-establishment of Spanish authority in Florida.

Shortly after the return of John Jay from Paris, in the
spring of 1784, Congress chose him secretary of foreign
affairs. A few days earlier the committee on Foreign Affairs passed a resolution declaring that they would not in
any way cede the rights of the Americans to freely navigate the Mississippi.[3] Madison expressed the sentiment

---

[1] August 23, 1783. Wharton, *Diplomatic Correspondence*, VI, 667.
[2] *Ibid.*, 239, 268, 269, 571.
[3] *Secret Journals of Congress*, V, 126.

general throughout the South when he referred in a letter to Jefferson "to the impolitic and perverse attempt in Spain to shut the mouth of the Mississippi against the inhabitants above . . . . because she can no more finally stop the current of trade down the river than she can that of the river itself."[1]

That the situation was serious may be gathered from the language of Jay, who was to negotiate on the points at issue with Don Diego de Gardoqui, the first Spanish envoy appointed to the United States. "Don Diego Gardoqui is arrived," Jay wrote, "and has been received so much in the spirit of friendship, that I hope his master and himself will be well pleased. Our negotiations with him will soon commence, and I sincerely wish that the issue of them may be satisfactory to both countries. To prepare for war, and yet be tenacious of peace with all the world, is, I think, our true interest."[2]

As defined in his credentials, Gardoqui, with the rank of chargé d'affaires, was given full powers to confirm the friendship between the crown of Spain and the United States, to regulate their mutual commerce, and establish the boundaries of their frontier possessions.[3] But by his secret orders he well understood that the regulation of the boundaries and the exclusive navigation of the Mississippi, through territory held by Spain, were the most important subjects upon which he would have to treat.[4] Jay was specifically directed to secure a treaty which should stipulate the free navigation of the Mississippi from its source to the ocean, as established in the treaties with Great Britain.[5]

[1] Writings of Madison, ed. Hunt, II, 68.

[2] Writings of John Jay (ed. Johnston), III, 160.

[3] Wharton, Diplomatic Correspondence, VI, 827.   [4] Ibid., VI, 826.

[5] August 25, 1785, Secret Journals of Congress, III, 586.

The coming of Gardoqui renewed the hopes of Americans for a satisfactory settlement of all questions in dispute, and the sale of western lands was greatly enhanced.[1] Recalling his futile efforts at treaty-making with Gardoqui five years earlier, Jay could not have partaken of this enthusiasm. "I am not sanguine," he wrote, "that a satisfactory termination of this negotiation is practicable, in whatever way it may be managed."

Moreover, Jay had in his possession a letter from Oliver Pollock, then American agent at Havana, in which it was asserted as a result of interviews with Bernardo de Galvez and Gardoqui, Pollock having the confidence of both men, that Spain was determined, notwithstanding the English cession to the United States, to maintain her claims to territory beyond the Natchez settlements and to assert supremacy over the navigation of the Mississippi within the bounds of her territory.[2]

When negotiations were opened, July 26, the three fundamental matters which received attention were a treaty of commerce, the reopening of the Mississippi to American trade, and the boundaries. Gardoqui was firm in his contention that a satisfactory treaty of commerce could be obtained only on the one condition: that the United States should definitely abandon all claims to the right of navigating the Mississippi below Natchez.[3]

A treaty of commerce would satisfy the New England demand for the protection of their commerce, and a period

[1] *Writings of Madison*, ed. Hunt, III, 149.

[2] Draper MSS, 43 J 160.

[3] Gardoqui knew how to frame his appeal for support from the commercial states. "No one is ignorant of the great advantages," he said to Jay, "which the United States derive from their trade with Spain from whence they yearly extract millions as well by their productions as by their navigation which so much promotes the growth and maintenance of their marine" (Papers of James Monroe, New York Public Library).

of business prosperity would result. But in general representatives of the South in Congress were equally insistent on protecting the commercial interests of the West. Washington was not in sympathy with the prevailing opinion in Virginia. "I do not think the navigation of the Mississippi," he wrote, "is an object of great importance to us at present." But he added, "When the banks of the Ohio and the fertile plains of the western country get thickly inhabited, the people will embrace the advantages which nature offers them in spite of all opposition.[1]

During a year of fruitless negotiation it became clear to Jay that Spain was inflexible in her determination to maintain control over the Mississippi navigation and in the assertion of her claim to the disputed territory. Finally, on August 3, 1786, in the hope that a satisfactory treaty of commerce might be obtained, he advised Congress to consent to the closing of the Mississippi during a period of twenty-five or thirty years. Jay made it clear that he had no thought of relinquishing the right to the free navigation of that river. He enumerated a number of reasons for this adjustment, even though it might be unpalatable to a large number of Americans. Great commercial advantages, he affirmed, were to be gotten from Spain, a nation which was buying produce and paying for it in gold much more than they were selling. France was the ally of the United States, but her friendship for Spain was prob-

[1] Rufus King expressed one phase of the commercial question as follows: "Our Fish and every article we sell in Spain is sold upon the Footing of the most Favored Nation in that country. This is favor and not right: Should we embarrass ourselves in the attempts of imprudent men to navigate the Mississippi below the northern boundary of Florida we can expect no favors from the Spanish Government. England is our rival in the fisheries, France does not wish us prosperity in this branch of commerce. If we embroil ourselves with Spain what have we to expect on this subject? The answer is too obvious or important to leave a doubt of the policy of forming a treaty of commerce between the United States and Spain" (Letters of Rufus King, New York Historical Society).

ably stronger. England, desirous of profiting by Spanish trade, would welcome a struggle between her former colonies and Spain. He pointed out that Spain would never willingly yield the navigation of the Mississippi, that force alone could bring it about, and that the United States was in no way prepared for war. "Why should we not," he urged, "consent to forbear to use what we know is not in our power to use?" The advantages to be derived from favorable commercial relations, Jay argued, were immediate, whereas the West would not need the much-desired navigation for another half-century. Moreover, the boundary questions would be more easily adjusted, he thought, should Spain be awarded her position on the Mississippi question.[1]

In his advocacy of what he believed at the time expedient, Jay was unable to state whether it would be acceptable to Gardoqui. The privilege of advancing such a proposition must first come from Congress, and a heated controversy, largely sectional, modifying Jay's instructions, was precipitated and continued during a period of three weeks. New England members, alarmed at the spread of population to the West and jealous of the development of that section, demanded immediate conclusion of the treaty on the terms suggested by Jay. Rufus King, of New York, declared: "Should there be an uninterrupted use of the Mississippi at this time by the citizens of the United States, I should consider every emigrant to that country from the Atlantic states as forever lost to the confederacy."[2] Members from the South were insistent in their demand that the resolution of August 25, 1785, should be rescinded and that Jay should break off all

---

[1] Secret Journals of Congress, Foreign Affairs, IV, 81–84.

[2] August 13, 1786. Rufus King to Robert C. Winthrop (Papers of Rufus King, New York Historical Society).

further negotiations with Gardoqui. In their contention they were unknowingly pointing the way to the future expansion of the United States.

Madison characterized such an act, if passed, as an indication to the people of the western waters that they had been sold by the men of the coast. Might they not, therefore, be justified in considering "themselves absolved from every federal tie and court some protection for their betrayed rights."[1] Such an occasion, he surmised, would be quite agreeable to Great Britain "to seize an opportunity of embroiling our affairs."[2] Monroe interpreted the attitude of the eastern states as "an attempt to break up the settlements on the western waters and prevent any in the future. . . . . To throw the might of population eastward and keep it there, to appreciate the vacant lands of New York and Massachusetts."[3] Rather than fail in their purpose, Monroe predicted that the eastern states would even attempt a dismemberment of the Confederation with the aim of forming a union of the states north of the Potomac.

Disregarding the opposition of the southern members, a report was adopted by a strictly sectional vote of seven states to five rescinding Jay's instructions regarding the Mississippi and the southern boundary. But under the Articles of Confederation the vote of nine states was required to give validity to any treaty. It became increasingly evident, therefore, that the South, voting as a unit,

[1] Letter to Jefferson, August 12, 1786. *Writings of Madison*, ed. Hunt, I, 263.

[2] No conclusive evidence has yet been found to prove that it was an object of English diplomacy, in making the treaty of 1783, to embroil Spain and the United States, but there seems some justification for Madison's suggestion. See *Writings of Jefferson*, ed. Ford, V, 228.

[3] To Governor Patrick Henry, August 12, 1786. *Writings of James Monroe*, ed. S. M. Hamilton (New York, 1898–1903), I, 150.

would reject any agreement to yield the navigation of the Mississippi even for a limited number of years. Madison expressed the fear that the sectional antagonism which was aroused would frustrate the hopes of carrying Virginia into the federal system.[1]

In another comprehensive statement to Congress, April 11, 1787, Jay reported frequent conversations with Gardoqui "which produced nothing but debate, and in the course of which we did not advance one single step nearer to each other. He continued and still continues, decided in refusing to admit us to navigate the river below our limits on any terms or conditions, nor will he consent to any article declaring our rights in express terms, and stipulating to forbear the use of it for a given time."[2]

Hatred for Spain in the West aroused over the acts of Spanish officials became more intense toward the close of the year 1786, when it was rumored that Congress had agreed to a treaty with Spain on the terms suggested by Jay. A letter addressed to the Governor and council of Georgia declared this treaty to be cruel, oppressive, and unjust. "The prohibition of the navigation of the Mississippi has astonished the whole Western Country. To sell us and make us Vassals to the Merciless Spaniards is a Grievance not to be borne, Should we tamely submit to such menaces we shou'd be unworthy the name of Americans and a Scandal to the Annals of History. . . . . We may as well be sold for Bondmen as to have the Spaniards share all the benefits of our Toils. . . . . The minds of the People here are very exasperated against both the Spaniards and Congress."[3]

---

[1] *Writings of Madison*, ed. Hunt, V, 296.

[2] *Writings of John Jay*, ed. Johnston, III, 240.

[3] December 3, 1786. Draper MSS, 53 J 58.

Another letter from a "gentleman" at Louisville to his friend in New England likewise expressed, in striking language, western sentiment of the time:

The late commercial treaty with Spain, in shutting up, as it is said, the navigation of the Mississippi for the term of twenty-five years, has given this western country a universal shock, and struck its inhabitants with an amazement. Our foundation is affected; it is therefore necessary that every individual exert himself to apply a remedy. . . . . To give us the liberty of transporting our effects down the river to New Orleans, and then be subject to the Spanish laws and impositions, is an insult upon our understanding. . . . . Flour and pork are now selling here at twelve shillings the hundred; beef in proportion; any quantities of Indian corn can be had at nine pence per bushel. Three times the quantity of tobacco and corn can be raised on an acre here that can be within the settlement on the east side of the mountains, and with less cultivation. . . . . Do you think to prevent the emigration from a barren country loaded with taxes and impoverished with debts, to the most luxurious and fertile soil in the world? . . . . Shall all this country now be cultivated entirely for the use of the Spaniards? Shall we be their bondsmen as the children of Israel were to the Egyptians? Shall one part of the United States be slaves, while the other is free? In case we are not countenanced and succured by the United States (if we need it) our allegiance will be thrown off, and some other power applied to.[1]

These letters, written within a day of each other, not only state the views of the men of the West with regard to Jay's proposal on the navigation of the Mississippi but assert the determination to defend their rights. It is not surprising, therefore, that the seizure of Spanish property at Vincennes by order of Clark was, in general, applauded by them. "We have taken all the goods belonging to the Spanish merchants of post Vincennes in the Illinois," one of them stated, "and are determined they shall not trade up the river, provided they will not let us trade down it." Another declared that General Clark, "who fought so glo-

[1] Draper MSS, *Trip* VI, 139-45.

riously for his Country and whose name strikes all the Western savages with terror," seized Spanish property "in retaliation for their many offences."[1]

Permission was sought from the Georgia authorities for an expedition to be led by Clark to take possession of the territory in dispute at Natchez. Thomas Green, the writer of the second of these letters, had resided at Natchez since 1782. He proposed to found a county at the mouth of the Yazoo River under the authority of Georgia. The legislature granted the request of certain persons in Natchez and erected the district into a county under the name of Bourbon. It can scarcely be doubted that Clark knew of Green's plans, for he was one of the two largest subscribers to a fund to cover the expenses of the messenger who bore the letter to Augusta. His statement, however, that there was no purpose to molest the Spaniards at Natchez would not have sufficed to remove the apprehensions of Spanish officials.[2]

American frontiersmen were to them "an ambitious class of people whose desires knew no bounds, who were not limited by a Sense of justice and who would dare to commit any excesses against the Spaniards on the pretense of their right to secure the free navigation of the Mississippi.[3] Moreover, since the early summer of 1785, rumors were prevalent at the Spanish posts that expeditions were being organized for the purpose of capturing Natchez and surrounding territory.[4] It was reported that 2,500 men, with artillery, were assembled at the mouth of the Ohio and were shortly, under the leadership of Clark and Montgomery, to descend the river; that Clark had recruited twenty-four companies of sixty men each in the Kentucky,

---

[1] *Ibid.*, 53 J 58.

[2] December 20, 1786.

[3] *Gardoqui Papers*, I, 65.   [4] *Ibid.*, III, 262–67.

Cumberland, and other settlements with the design of setting out in the spring for Natchez.[1]

Spanish officials were perceptibly alarmed over these
repeated rumors. All of their posts were poorly garrisoned,
and a force of only 695 officers and soldiers, two-thirds of
them recruits, were available, at New Orleans, to be sent
to the defense of Natchez, the only post in the district
capable of making any resistance. They were poorly supplied with necessary artillery and their ammunition was
almost exhausted.[2] Inhabitants of the Natchez district
were called upon to unite against the invaders, who were
shortly to appear, as rumored, under the leadership of
Clark. Spies were constantly on the lookout for the coming of the Americans.[3]

Spanish fears were in part quieted when the Governor
at New Orleans learned of the disavowal of Clark's acts
at Vincennes by an "assembly of Kentucky notables," and
of the inquiry thereon which was instituted by the state
of Virginia.[4]

This Kentucky committee of six men were among those
who had been selected to attend a convention called to
meet in September, 1786, to take action on the independence of Kentucky. Because of the expedition of Clark and
Logan a quorum was not present until the following January.

For two years the question of separation from Virginia

[1] McGillivray to Miró, May 16, 1785, *American Historical Review*, XV, 73.
June 3, 1785, Peter Favrot to Miró, Ayer Collection. June 14, 1785, Miró to
Galvez, *ibid.*, July 24, 1785, Bouligny to Miró, *ibid.*

[2] Miró to Galvez, June 14, 1785, Ayer Collection.

[3] June 16, 1786, *ibid.*

[4] Miró to Sonora, June 1, 1787, Ayer Collection. Four commissioners, Green
being one of them, sent by the legislature of Georgia to Natchez for the purpose
of organizing Bourbon County violated their instructions and were finally expelled by order of Governor Miró.

had been hotly agitated in Kentucky and a number of conventions had been called for its discussion. In a convention held at Danville, December, 1784, resolutions were agreed upon looking toward the separation of Kentucky from Virginia. This action was referred to a third convention which met the following May, where it was determined that only constitutional methods should be employed. A petition to the Virginia Assembly was prepared which declared in favor of a separation from Virginia and admission to the Confederation as a separate and equal state. An address to the people favoring this procedure was prepared, and, confirmed in the convention habit, another was called to meet in August for decision on this action.

In the new convention the radical element was in the saddle under the leadership of James Wilkinson, a man who for years was to be a dominant factor in western affairs. As an officer in charge of clothing for the army of the Revolution, he was given the rank of brigadier general. Having lost his family estate in Maryland, he saw in the West an opportunity to improve his fortune, and came to Lexington, Kentucky (1784), where he became a trader in skins and salt. Then thirty-one years of age, he was a marked man because of his handsome face, his gracious manners, and his ready command of language. Moreover, he was possessed of a cunning mind, proficiency in corruption and intrigue, daring and selfish ambition—a combination of qualities which fitted him to become the outstanding political demagogue of the time. His correspondence reveals him as one of the most despicable characters in our history, and likewise "the most consummate artist in treason that the nation ever possessed."[1]

Kentucky offered him a fruitful field for his machina-

[1] Frederick J. Turner, "Genet's Attack on Louisiana and the Floridas," *American Historical Review*, III, 652.

tions. Because of illness he was not in attendance upon the May convention. It was his boast that final action on separation was delayed until the August convention in order that the members might be guided by his views. This convention adopted the petition calling upon the Virginia assembly to sanction the separation of Kentucky. An inflammatory address to Kentuckians stated the necessity therefor.

Impressed by the tone of the appeal, the Virginia Assembly (January, 1786) passed an act for separation providing a convention to be called at Danville the next September should accept the terms. As a condition, Congress was to consent, before June 1, 1787, to the admission of the new state into the federal Union.

Through trickery in a district election, Wilkinson was returned victor over his opponent, Humphrey Marshall.[1] As already noted, because of the expeditions of Clark and Logan a quorum was not present in the convention until January, 1787. Certain of the members who came to Danville for the convention met from day to day. Assuming authority, they proceeded to inquire into the cause of "certain commotions" within the district of Kentucky. It quickly became evident that the leading questions for consideration concerned the conduct of Clark at Vincennes and his relation to the project of Thomas Green.

[1] From the personal enmities aroused over this election there was to develop the controversy which has been set forth in the well-known volume, *Spanish Conspiracy*, by Thomas M. Green. For a restatement of the issues, consult Temple Bodley, Littell's "Political Transactions," pp. xi ff., and S. F. Bemis, *Pinckney's Treaty*, pp. 128 ff. The original statement was made by Humphrey Marshall, *History of Kentucky* (1824 ed.), I, 279 ff. (1st ed., 1812). This was replied to by John Mason Brown, "The Political Beginnings of Kentucky," *Filson Club Publications* (1889). This was followed by Green's *Spanish Conspiracy*. John Mason Brown was the grandson of Senator John Brown, of Kentucky, and Thomas Marshall Green was the grandson of Humphrey Marshall. The two volumes are replete with extreme partisan statements.

In fact, Clark had not been unmindful of the criticisms which followed the Vincennes episode. In December he prepared a statement which was dispatched to the Governor by Colonel Logan. "Various Reports," he wrote, "no doubt, hath spread Respecting this affair, but, Sir, that the truth may appear, you will pardon me in Recommending a Court of inquiry as soon as possible. Without something of this nature takes place, it will be in vain to attempt anything for the future."[1]

Of the committee of six members appointed to wait on Clark, Wilkinson was chairman. While the evidence is not wholly convincing, there seems some warrant for the statement that the plot was germinating in his mind to acquire leadership in Kentucky and thus promote the selfish ambitious project which was to be launched the following year. Clark blocked his way.

Some ten days before the appointment of the special committee of inquiry, a letter attacking Clark was written by a "gentleman in Kentucky to his friend in Philadelphia."[2] Internal evidence seems to point to Wilkinson as the writer, and it has been attributed to him. "Clarke," it reads, "is playing Hell. He is raising a regiment of his own and has 140 men stationed at Opost, already now under command of Dalton. Seized on a Spanish Boat with 20,000 Dollars, or rather seized three stores at Opost worth this sum and the Boat which brought them up. . . . . Clarke is eternally drunk, and yet full of design. I told him he would be hanged. He laughed and said he could take refuge among the Indians. A stroke is meditated against St. Louis and the Natchez."

The report of the committee, made by Wilkinson, was ordered to be submitted to Governor Edmund Randolph.[3] Clark, without authority, it was asserted, was engaged in

[1] *Cal. Va. State Papers*, IV, 213.

[2] *Ibid.*, p. 202.　　　　　[3] Draper MSS, 53 J 59–61.

raising a body of troops which he was himself to command. As we have seen, Clark had declared, when interviewed, that his object in seizing Spanish property at Vincennes was for the sole purpose of clothing and subsisting his troops. In answer to the charge of complicity, Clark said that he had never seen Green's letter; that he understood the object was to establish a settlement at the mouth of the Yazoo River; that he had no thought of molesting the Spaniards or of going with the expedition. He hoped, by encouraging the settlement, to obtain a small grant of land. As recommended by the committee, the mode adopted for the establishment of the garrison at Vincennes was disavowed, and the seizure of Spanish property was reprobated. They solicited the interference of the Governor, urged the necessity of carrying into effect the treaty proposed by Clark, and recommended the establishment of military posts at Vincennes and at the mouth of Eagle Creek.

The special report of the committee which was prepared by Wilkinson and fifteen associates, accompanied the communication to Governor Randolph. In it they wrote "of the outrage which has been committed at Post St. Vincennes," and of the illicit views of Green and his accomplices. "We are fearful," they wrote, "that Green will find no difficulty in levying auxilliaries in the titular State of Frankland and the settlements on Cumberland; in the meantime, attempts are daily practiced to augment the banditti at St. Vincennes, by delusive promises of lands, bounty, and clothing from the officers appointed by Clark." Colonel Logan, who maintained close relations with Clark after the Wabash expedition, in a communication to the Governor, approved the manning of the garrison at Vincennes.[1] It was a wise and prudent plan, he asserted, to keep the Indians in terror until a treaty. No ref-

[1] *Ibid.*, 12 S 125, December 13, 1786.

erence is made by him to the disability of Clark which was stressed by the Kentucky committee.

While advocating the carrying out of Clark's plan for a treaty with the Wabash Indians in April, it is evident Wilkinson was the manipulator of a committee of nine men which sought to determine the choice of commissioners. In a letter addressed to Governor Randolph on the same day as the communication criticizing the conduct of Clark at Vincennes the following statement appeared: "In the progress of the American Republic, it is but too frequent, that we have beheld men wriggled into office by their own act or the influence of their friends, without regard to public interest; from this cause it has frequently happened that we have seen characters appointed to remote quarters of the States to transact business on ground adjacent to which men better qualified could be found."[1] They declared that the treaty at the mouth of the Miami had cost the government many thousands of dollars without effecting one solitary purpose. The failure was attributed to Generals Butler and Parsons, two of the commissioners, one of them from a distant northern state and the other embittered by "ancient prejudices against the frontier citizens of Virginia." Specific charge was also made that thousands of dollars appropriated for treaty purposes had been pocketed by these commissioners.

Clark, who was the third commissioner, was likewise not to be considered for appointment. Deeming his reputation not already sufficiently blasted, they declared: "We lament that the unfortunate habit to which General Clark is addicted, obliges us to observe, that we consider him utterly unqualified for business of any kind." They besought the Governor to use his influence to appoint a commission from Kentucky and recommended General

[1] *Ibid.*, 14 S 80–99.

James Wilkinson, Colonel Richard Clough Anderson, and Isaac Shelby as men well qualified for the purpose and "against whom no exception can be taken."

The Virginia Council proceeded to the consideration of these reports. In urging the necessity for a treaty with the Wabash Indians on the part of the federal government, they proposed the appointment of Wilkinson and the other two mentioned as suitable commissioners. The correspondence was to be transmitted to the Virginia delegates in Congress with the request that it be communicated, as a whole or in part, to that body. Clark was to be notified of the disavowal of his acts and authority in raising recruits, appointing officers, or impressing provisions. They recommended further that the executive "declare their displeasure" at the conduct of Clark in seizing Spanish property. This offense against the law of nations was to be disclaimed by a special proclamation which was to be sent to the Virginia delegates in Congress, who, in turn, were to acquaint the Spanish minister with these sentiments. The Attorney-General was to be requested to bring to punishment all persons who were "guilty in the premises."[1]

In his proclamation, February 28, 1787, Governor Randolph followed these instructions.[2] Madison submitted this action to Congress, and the Virginia delegation imparted its contents to Gardoqui. The attempt was made to convince him that this act was a symptom of the unfriendly temper of the western people growing out of the closing of the Mississippi. Spain, he replied, would never accede to the claim of the United States to navigate that river. On April 24 Congress directed General Henry Knox, the secretary of war, to provide means "for dispossessing a body of men who had, in a lawless and unauthorized man-

---

[1] *Ibid.*, 53 J 63.   [2] *Ibid.*, 64, 65.

ner, taken possession of Post Vincennes in defiance of the proclamation and authority of the United States."

In due time Governor Randolph forwarded the proclamation of the Council to Clark which embodied the complaints brought against him. "I do hereby declare," it stated, "with the advice of the Council of State, that the said violence was unknown to the Executive until a few days past, and is now solemnly disavowed; and that the Attorney General has been instructed to take every step allowed by law, for bringing to punishment all persons who may be culpable in the premises."[1]

In his reply Clark made no effort to justify his conduct. If he knew of the plottings against him, he made no counterattack upon the instigators by name. There is a striking note of confidence in his language, such as may be found in his words of command flung out on the dreadful march for the capture of Vincennes. "I respect the State of Virginia," he wrote. "The information you have received hath already been stained with the blood of your country. Things will prove themselves."

Meantime, the Kentucky convention, having passed favorably on the terms of separation as defined by the Virginia Assembly, learned that the act had been superseded and that another convention had been called for September, 1787. The purpose of the Assembly, it appears, was merely to extend the time wherein Kentucky might declare in favor of separation and gain the permission of Congress for her entrance into the Union. Unfortunately at that time rumors became current that Jay's plan to close the Mississippi for twenty-five years had become a law.

It is not surprising that western leaders were deeply aroused over the suggestion of bartering with what they esteemed their rights. As reported, a member of Con-

[1] *Ibid.*, 53 J 64, 65. This is a printed broadside.

gress of high rank declared in the course of debate "that it would give him real pleasure to see the ocean wash the western foot of the Alleghany hills.[1]

Moreover, a number of raids by Indian bands occurred during the winter, and it was feared the whole country would be overrun with the return of spring. Congress, as Kentuckians believed, was oblivious to their petitions for protection, and Clark had been severely censured by the governor of Virginia.[2] The spirit of revolt was rife.

On March 29 (1787), John Brown, Benjamin Sebastian, Harry Innes, and George Muter, associates of Wilkinson, at "the request of a respectable number of inhabitants," prepared an address to the people which was virtually a remonstrance against Jay's proposal. They recommended the selection of delegates to a convention at Danville to be called on the first Monday of May for the consideration of this measure, "which tends to almost a total destruction of the western country." Similar conventions in the other districts were suggested to the end that Congress may be convinced "that the inhabitants of the western country are united in their opposition and consider themselves entitled to all the privileges of freemen, and those blessings procured by the revolution; and will not tamely submit to an act of oppression, which would tend to a deprivation of our just rights and privileges."

By the time of the May convention it was known that the southern states were a unit in opposition to Jay's proposal, and no action was taken. Much was anticipated from the September convention. Wilkinson was then in New Orleans, endeavoring, as will shortly be shown, to

[1] William Littell, "Political Transactions," *Filson Club Publications*, XXXI, 18.

[2] Retaliatory expeditions were organized by Colonel John Logan against the Indians of the Cherokee country and by Colonel Robert Todd against those on the Scioto. Draper MSS, 13 S 152–54.

pave the way for the next step in his plot. With unanimity the convention accepted the terms of separate statehood, as proposed by Virginia, and applied to Congress for admission into the Union. December 31, 1788, was fixed as the date for the termination of Virginia's authority.

But could a majority in Congress be counted upon to grant their petition, and thus relieve, as was hoped, the distress due to the closing of the Mississippi and the raids of Indian banditti? The query was a natural one. Nor is it surprising that advocates arose who demanded immediate independence for Kentucky and the setting up of a new state government as a step which would hasten their admission into the Union. How imminent the danger appeared was expressed in a communication to Governor Randolph. It stated:

> The Indians have been very troublesome on our frontiers and still continue to molest us, from which circumstance I am decidedly of opinion that this Western Country will in a few years revolt from the Union, and endeavor to erect an independent government for under the present system we cannot exert our strength, neither does Congress seem disposed to protect us, for we are informed that those very troops which Congress directed the several States to raise for the defence of the Western Country are disbanded. I have just dropped this hint to your Excellency for matter of reflection—if some step is not taken for our protection, a little time will prove the truth of the opinion.[1]

Notwithstanding the disapproval by Congress of the plan engineered by Thomas Green whereby Clark was to seize Natchez, Esteban Miró, Spanish governor at New Orleans, and Don Martin de Navarro, intendant of Louisiana, were, as related, apprehensive over possible encroachments by Americans upon Spanish domain. In spite of drastic measures against unlicensed trade on the Mississippi, smuggling went on apace and at times was con-

---

[1] July 21, 1787. Harry Innes to Governor Randolph. Draper MSS, 12 S 147.

doned by Spanish officials. Permission was granted also to bring selected products to the Spanish posts. Thus, in May, 1786, 1,500 barrels of flour from the Monongahela country were taken to Natchez and New Orleans and disposed of by a Colonel Perrie.[1] The unusual profits connected with such a venture appealed to the cupidity in Wilkinson, who, after failing to secure the required passport, loaded some flatboats with flour, tobacco, and bacon, and floated down to New Orleans. That he had other objects in mind will shortly appear.

Aware of the military and political reputation of the owner, Governor Miró did not seize the cargo as contraband. In his interview with Miró and Navarro, Wilkinson made a favorable impression, for he was permitted to dispose of his goods free of duty. They became much interested in the project which he unfolded. This he elaborated into a "memorial" and presented it to them on the fifth of September. As a token of his good faith, he renounced his allegiance to the United States and as readily took an oath as subject of Spain.[2]

In the memorial he began with a discussion of the increase of population in the West at the close of the Revolution due to dissatisfaction with the central government. The willingness of seven of the states to barter away the navigation of the Mississippi for commercial concessions which favored the Atlantic states was regarded by the westerners as an infraction of the federal compact. This, together with the failure to protect them against the savages, led them to believe that they had nothing to hope for

[1] Major Erkuries Beatty, "Diary," *Magazine of American History*, I, 177. *Gardoqui Papers*, IV, 151.

[2] This pledge was given August 22, 1787. W. R. Shepherd, "Wilkinson and the Spanish Conspiracy," *American Historical Review*, IX, 496, 497. Copies of the documents have been consulted in the Ayer Collection, Newberry Library.

from the friendship and justice of Congress. As a consequence of the incompetence of Congress, he predicted the formation of "a distinct federation of the Western States for their common well being." Independence once achieved, he assured the Spanish officials, they would resort to any means to secure the free navigation of the Mississippi, "an object in which center all their hopes of temporal prosperity and without which only poverty and misery will be their lot." This, their supreme desire, was, he declared, to be obtained with the assistance of Great Britain, provided negotiation with Spain should fail. The reward of Great Britain was to be ultimately Mexico. He then outlined what he deemed the proper policy of Spain, namely, "to attract settlements by means of some favor, making them serve the interests of Spain."

Gardoqui, he counseled, should persist in his refusal to grant the navigation of the Mississippi, and the prohibition should still be rigorously supported, but concessions should be made to certain men of real influence. Spanish officials were to await the coming of agents who should be sent to treat with them after the independence of Kentucky had been secured. Overtures having once been made by the Kentuckians, Spain, he argued, "will have the Game in her own hands."

As a second recommendation he proposed the erection of a fortified post at L'Ance à la Grace (New Madrid), where Kentuckians and other men of the West might be permitted to settle, thus inaugurating a migration to Louisiana as rapid as it ever was from the Atlantic States to the western country.[1]

As a reward for his influence as go-between in the plan,

---

[1] W. R. Shepherd, "Wilkinson and The Spanish Conspiracy," *American Historical Review*, IX, 496 ff. Copies of the documents in the Ayer Collection have also been used.

he asked permission to transmit to his New Orleans agent a cargo, amounting to fifty or sixty thousand dollars, which should consist of Negroes, live stock, tobacco, flour, bacon, lard, butter, cheese, tallow, and apples. The proceeds of the sale were to be held by the Governor as a pledge for his good conduct "until the issue of our plans is known, or I have fixed my residence in Louisiana."[1]

The Spanish officials, duly impressed with the proposal, on the following day made their reply wherein they granted him permission to send down goods amounting to one-half the amount he had suggested. The proceeds were to be deposited in the provincial treasury until the King's pleasure should be known.[2] With assurance of success from the Governor and Intendant, Wilkinson, elated over his promise of good fortune, set out for Kentucky, going by the way of Philadelphia.

In a joint report forwarded to the King the arguments in the memorial were unquestioned, and Miró and Navarro asked for instructions permitting them to deal with any representatives who might come from the Ohio country.[3] The annexation of Kentucky was thought of by them as a remote possibility.

But Gardoqui, who was not in sympathy with New Orleans officials, proceeded to foster his own plans for the dismemberment of western communities and for inducing immigration to Louisiana. On one occasion he surprised James Madison with the suggestion that the Kentuckians would make good Spanish subjects. In fact, James White, superintendent of Indian affairs for the southern depart-

---

[1] *American Historical Review*, IX, 502.

[2] The reply from the Spanish court was not received until March, 1789. This delay was due, in part, to the conflicting plans of Gardoqui.

[3] *Archives Generales de les Indies*, LXXXVI, 6, 16 (Audiencia de San Domingo), No. 13, Reservada. September 25, 1787. Copy in Ayer Collection.

ment under the Confederation, and later delegate in Congress from North Carolina, in an interview with Gardoqui asserted his belief that the "New States," when formed, would withdraw from the Union and ally themselves with Spain or with England.[1] So significant was the proposal that Florida Blanca assured Gardoqui there would be no difficulty in opening New Orleans to their commerce once they placed themselves under the protection of Spain.[2]

The dilatory policy so marked in the attempts of Jay to come to an understanding with Gardoqui was accentuated by this incident. Gardoqui was forbidden to make any terms whatever until he should learn of the outcome of the movement for the new constitution, of the success of the plan of White, and of the scheme for colonization to be promoted by one Pierre Wouves d'Argès.[3]

During May, 1788, White was on his way west to determine the attitude of the Watauga and the Holston settlements and the Cumberland communities toward this phase of Spanish intrigue.

The founding of the Watauga government must here be recalled. By 1784, when this territory was ceded to the Confederation by North Carolina, its population had grown to about ten thousand. Over and again they had petitioned North Carolina for protection against the inroads of Cherokee bands. There was little prospect of relief from the federal government, and it was not unnatural that these men of the backwoods should have proceeded to set up an independent government.

In due time (August 23, 1784) delegates from Washington, Greene, and Sullivan counties met in convention at

---

[1] *Gardoqui Papers*, IV, 155-59.   [2] *Ibid.*, pp. 242-46.

[3] Wouves d'Argès received instructions authorizing him to promote settlements in Louisiana with emigrants from the United States. This plan interfered with that of Wilkinson, and he was detained at New Orleans. His project failed.

Jonesboro and decided to secede from North Carolina. Improvements in agriculture, manufactures, and literature, they declared, would result from their independence. The new state, it was hoped, would embrace the whole of the upper Tennessee Valley, and a portion of Virginia.[1] John Sevier, the hero of King's Mountain, was made president of the convention. The provisional government, within a year, was organized as the state of Franklin, with a constitution modeled after that of North Carolina, and Sevier was chosen governor. In their reply to a letter from Governor Martin they protested against the epithets applied to them by certain members of the North Carolina assembly, such as off-scourings of the earth and fugitives from justice, and declared that the people of the western country found themselves taxed to support government while they were deprived of all the blessings of it.[2]

Appeals were made to Congress for the admission of Franklin into the Union as the fourteenth state, but these overtures were refused. North Carolina proposed liberal concessions and ordered a reorganization of the courts. Two factions resulted, one in favor of yielding to North Carolina, the other supporting the plan for the new state. In the battle which ensued "the Franklinites" were defeated and Sevier, with a remnant of his followers, escaped to the frontier.

When White, as agent of Gardoqui, appeared in May, 1788, Sevier was engaged in fighting the Cherokee, hoping thus to regain his prestige. Sevier proved to be a ready listener, and the effect of the interview is indicated in two

---

[1] There were a number of persons in Washington County, Virginia, under the leadership of Colonel Arthur Campbell, who were ready to join the movement. G. H. Alden, "The State of Franklin," *American Historical Review*, VIII, 281.

[2] *Ibid.*, pp. 271 ff.

letters which Sevier wrote Gardoqui in September. In one he asserted that the inhabitants of Franklin were unanimous in their desire to form an alliance and treaty of commerce with Spain and to put themselves under her protection. Referring in the second letter to the war he had been waging against the Indians and to a settlement which he proposed to found at Muscle Shoals, the latter probably his real objective, he asked for assistance in both.[1] These appeals had barely reached Gardoqui when Sevier was under arrest, for debt, by a North Carolina sheriff.

In an impassioned letter addressed to the North Carolina assembly he complained of the persecutions to which he had been subjected, which he attributed to private malice.[2] The appeal evidently had no effect upon the authorities, and neither Gardoqui nor Miró were disposed to make concessions which would in any respect neutralize Spanish control of the southern tribes. Sevier, regaining his freedom through the aid of a group of his Holston friends, was soon restored to office as brigadier general of militia. In 1790 he was elected representative in Congress from the western district of North Carolina, and "became a man of property and family, church-goer and capitalist."[3]

White also visited the fringe of settlements on the Cumberland River, where he had previously taken up a military

---

[1] For a discussion of the significance of these letters, and Sevier as a land speculator, see A. P. Whitaker, "Spanish Intrigue in the Old Southwest," *Miss. Valley Hist. Rev.*, XII, 159, 160.

[2] *State Records of North Carolina*, XXII, 697-99.

[3] Whitaker, "Spanish Intrigue," *Miss. Valley Hist. Rev.*, XII, 162. The contention of Dr. Whitaker seems well established that the chief purpose of Sevier, in his Spanish intrigue, was to gain better terms from North Carolina "for his faction." William Blount and Wade Hampton were associates of Sevier in this speculation. Dr. Whitaker has continued his suggestive studies in this field and it was my pleasure to read the manuscript of his volume, "The Spanish-American Frontier, 1783-1795." It was not off the press in time to give page citations in this chapter.

grant. This colony, still an extreme outpost on the western frontier, contained (1785) some four thousand inhabitants. From time to time the settlers were harassed by attacks of warriors from both the Creek and the Cherokee tribes, and there was retaliation in kind by the frontiersmen under the leadership of James Robertson, the founder of Tennessee. North Carolina responded to their appeals by sending a few troops, but finally, in a note of despair, Robertson asserted that "immigration and commerce seem to be finally stopped."[1]

At the time, no aid was to be expected from Congress. The course which seemed to promise relief was to secure from the Creek nation, or through the influence of Spanish officials, a cessation of hostilities, and at the same time to force North Carolina to cede this territory to Congress.

The approaches made to Alexander McGillivray, Creek leader, and to Gardoqui were barren of results, and Robertson and his associates turned their attention to New Orleans.[2] In letters to Miró they express the desire of cultivating friendly relations with the Spaniards and of the better prospect for trade. Special emphasis is placed upon the petition that he should use his influence in securing for them relief from Indian attacks.[3] As a partial reflection of their attitude they applied the name Miró to the district, and in a convention the following September determined upon separation from North Carolina. "Unprotected," Robertson declared in a letter to Miró, "we are to be

---

[1] January 4, 1788, *State Records of North Carolina*, XXI, 437–38.

[2] The nature of these advances, as well as an excellent presentation of the evidence on this phase of "Spanish intrigue," is to be found in an article by A. P. Whitaker, "Spanish Intrigue in the Old South West," *Miss. Valley Hist. Rev.*, XII, 165 ff.

[3] These items are included in the letters of James Robertson (January 29, 1789) and Daniel Smith (March 11, 1789), edited by A. P. Whitaker, *Miss. Valley Hist. Rev.*, XII, 410–12.

obedient to the new Congress of the United States but we cannot but wish for a more interesting connection. The United States afford us no protection, ... For my own part, I conceive highly of the advantages of your immediate Government."[1] On the same day he wrote Governor Johnston of North Carolina that distress was driving many of the Cumberland people to seek refuge under a foreign government which offered them encouragement. He concluded with the significant expression: "The people are in a dangerous mood, but a cession of this country to Congress would probably quiet their minds."[2]

No definite estimate can be made of the results of this phase of western intrigue. The conclusion seems warranted that the letters "were designed to serve as a threat and a promise. As a threat to reluctant North Carolina, it would secure a cession of that state's western territory to Congress. As a promise to Spain, it would obtain from the Spanish governor of Louisiana commercial concessions, and, above all, relief from Indian attacks."[3] Upon the organization of the Southwestern Territory by Congress (1790), William Blount was appointed governor. In keeping with his recommendation, Sevier became brigadier general for Washington, the eastern district, and Robertson was accorded the same office for Miró, the western district.

Spanish officials at New Orleans were, as we have noted, in favor of waiting for a more opportune occasion in which to work out the more radical part of Wilkinson's project. The suggestion that emigration from the Ohio settlements to Spanish territory might be fostered appealed to them as immediately practicable. The very ar-

[1] A. P. Whitaker, "Spanish Intrigue," *Miss. Valley Hist. Rev.*, XII, 170, 171; Archibald Henderson, *The Spanish Conspiracy in Tennessee*, pp. 242, 243.

[2] *State Records of North Carolina*, XXII, 792.

[3] Whitaker, "Spanish Intrigue," *Miss. Valley Hist. Rev.*, XII, 172.

guments which Wilkinson used were already familiar. We have seen the Spanish government striving to establish a barrier to English expansion prior to the Revolution by inducing Canadians and other immigrants to settle as communities in Louisiana.[1] "There is no time to be lost," Navarro wrote his government (February 12, 1787). "Mexico is on the other side of the Mississippi, in the vicinity of the already formidable establishments of Americans. The only way to check them is with a proportionate population, and it is not by imposing commercial restrictions that this population is to be acquired, but by granting a prudent extension and freedom of trade."[2] This suggestion was embodied in a royal order the following year.

El Dorado, to the discontented elements in Kentucky and Tennessee and in the Northwest, where settlers were not able to pay even the one dollar an acre required for government lands, lay in Louisiana or at Natchez, where an individual might become possessed of a 1,000-acre grant of rich land. It was reported that 6,000 acres were presented to one person.[3] Slaves, stock, provisions for two years, and farming utensils and implements might be introduced free of duty. There was the promise, also, of freedom of religion, a concession which indicates the importance attached by Spain to the development of these provinces. Ten silver dollars a hundred pounds was the price for tobacco which should be delivered at the King's treasury in New Orleans.[4] This gesture toward a policy of liberalization was later commended by Thomas Jefferson as a possible boon to the United States. "Our citizens have a right to go where they please," he wrote. "I wish a hun-

---

[1] The number of Acadians who had settled in Louisiana by 1787 amounted to 1,587. Gayarré, *History of Louisiana*, III, 185.

[2] Gayarré, III, 183.

[3] Draper MSS, 14 S 170.   [4] *Ibid.*, October 2, 1787.

dred thousand of our inhabitants would accept the invitation. It will be the means of delivering to us peaceably, what may otherwise cost us a war." He then suggested that the United States should protest, "just enough to make them believe we think it a very wise policy and confirm them in it."[1]

That a number of men already well known, such as George Rogers Clark, George Morgan, and Thomas Hutchins, were ready to make terms with the Spaniards and even to become expatriate in order thus to secure liberal land grants for the founding of colonies is not altogether surprising. The federal government was at best but a weak form of union, and had as yet failed to arouse a spirit of loyalty on the part of the masses of the people. The West did not trust the policy of the seaboard states. As has been well stated: "their patriotism was dormant, not dead."[2] Moreover, they had repeatedly petitioned Congress and the state assemblies for a redress of their grievances, but to no effect. The Indian policy of the general government did not afford them security against attack, and retaliation was forbidden.

Clark was among the first to propose founding a colony within Spanish territory. In his application to Gardoqui (March 15, 1788) on behalf of his associates, whose names are not divulged, save that of John Rogers, bearer of the letter, Clark stated the motives which impelled him to make the proposal. Governor Randolph's criticism of his seizure of Spanish goods at Vincennes was, he declared, due to the influence of a group of men who were themselves striving to promote their own selfish interests by securing the right to trade at New Orleans. These same persons had already conferred with him, he said, on the subject

[1] *Writings of Jefferson*, ed. Ford, V, 316.

[2] Roosevelt, *The Winning of the West*, III, 138.

of reducing the Spanish posts on the Mississippi. "This," he continued, "and other circumstances of like nature convince me that no property or person is safe under a government so weak and infirm as that of the United States, and as a result I have been induced to put into practice what I have for so long a time contemplated, of offering myself to the King of Spain with a numerous colony of desirable subjects."[1]

Shortly before, in reply to a letter from the Governor requesting him to assist in the collection of books and papers dealing with western accounts, he wrote:

When I reflect on those accounts, and the great expense that hath already and is likely to attend the settlement of them, and the various circumstances attending the reduction and defence of those countries and all their great consequences, it then appears more obvious to me what mischief false informers, envious and malicious persons have in their power to do in a country, when listened to at a great distance from the seat of government. . . . . We were obliged to lay aside all attention to instructions, and act discretionary, which answered the salutory purpose. We dared to do this as the salvation of the country was of more importance to us than the commissions we bore. . . . . After suffering the fatigues that I have undergone, bearing so many malignant pens, paying and yet having to pay large sums of money for supplies that the State could not get credit for, it might reasonably be supposed that I, of course, must be unhappy. The reverse is true. I am conscious of having done everything in the power of a person under my circumstances not only for the defense of the country, but to save every expense possible.[2]

Virginia, moreover, was indebted to him $11,599, an amount which had been approved by the Assembly but upon which no payments had been made. Like many persons in Kentucky, he was the owner of large tracts of land for which there was no market. He was opposed to the congressional policy of treaties and presents in dealing with

[1] *Gardoqui Papers*, I, 269–72.
[2] Draper MSS, 12 S 161–63. October 8, 1787.

the Indians, for that was to them a sign that "we are affraid of them and whenever they want presents they will make war."[1] But greater than any other cause for his discontent, it must be believed, was the thought that there had been filched from him his place of leadership.

The site favored by Clark for his Spanish settlement was to be opposite the mouth of the Ohio, for the climate was good and the soil was well suited for the cultivation of wheat and of corn.[2] The terms he submitted for establishing a colony on this tract of some 100 miles square provided that each head of a family who should become resident within the territory should receive 1,000 acres of land, and every member of the family, 100 acres; that they should be guaranteed freedom in matters of religion; that the governor, whose term of office was to continue during good behavior, was to be appointed by the King; that after three years there should be elected by the people six "councillors or assistants to the Governor" who should hold office during a term of three years; and that a body of troops, adequate to prevent surprise, should be maintained in garrison.[3] The Spanish government was prepared to make the grant of land providing some of the privileges sought were modified, but this Clark refused to concede, and there the project ended.[4]

Another of the numerous plans of the period for founding a colony on Spanish territory originated with Colonel George Morgan, sane adviser on western affairs during the early days of the Revolution. His associate was Thomas Hutchins, geographer of the United States, whom Gardo-

---

[1] Letter to Jonathan Clark, April 20, 1788. Draper MSS, 2 L 26.

[2] *Gardoqui Papers*, I, 267.

[3] *Ibid.*, pp. 269–72. It extended from 36° to 38°, and two degrees east and west.

[4] Draper MSS, 33 J 134.

qui referred to as a confidant and a man who served him with honor. Morgan was likewise on terms of intimacy with Gardoqui and carried on the project after the death of Hutchins.[1]

A tract of 2,000,000 acres across the Mississippi and nearly opposite the mouth of the Ohio was to be assigned to him, where, as he prophesied, several thousand families would be living within a few years. Gardoqui entered enthusiastically into the plan, and on his own responsibility granted Morgan authority to go forward, even advancing funds for carrying on the enterprise.[2] On January 3, 1789, Morgan, together with seventy "respectable" farmers, artisans, and sons of German farmers, embarked on four boats at Pittsburgh for New Madrid, a town which it was thought would become the metropolis of the colony and of the West. Nor was their optimism exhausted with this colorful picture, for New Orleans was within twenty years "to be the greatest city of America."[3]

On account of numerous obstacles the enterprise collapsed after the founding of the village of New Madrid.[4] The real cause for failure, however, is readily seen when it is known that Wilkinson, who had returned to Kentucky early in 1788, was familiar, through the activity of one of his spies, with Morgan's plan, and deliberately set about destroying it.[5] In his dispatch to Miró he declared Morgan to be a man governed entirely by the "vilest self-interest,"

[1] *Gardoqui Papers*, V, 42–45.

[2] Gardoqui to Morgan, October 4, 1788, Gayarré, III, 221.

[3] Thomas Hutchins to Gardoqui, January 25, 1789. *Gardoqui Papers*, IV, 407–15.

[4] Baron Steuben, among others, applied to Gardoqui for a large tract of land in Louisiana upon which he proposed to establish a colony of 4,200 German farmers. *Gardoqui Papers*, I, 143, 156, 189. For other proposals, see *ibid.*, pp. 113, 117, 119, 120, 121, 307.

[5] Gayarré, III, 244.

and that his project, if successful, could have only pernicious consequences.[1]

In the meantime, Wilkinson had taken advantage of
his trading pact by sending flatboats with a cargo, chiefly
of tobacco, tallow, butter, and hams, to New Orleans.[2] On
the return trip his agent loaded a boat with eatables and
dry goods to the amount of $18,000, which should be sold,
Miró urged, at cost, in order that Kentuckians might thus
have their hopes raised for future successful commercial
relations.[3] Their produce was to be admitted to the New
Orleans market with a duty of only 15 per cent, instead
of the 25 per cent heretofore charged.

Wilkinson, early in 1789, started his second fleet for
New Orleans consisting of twenty-five flatboats, some of
them armed.[4] For some time his agents had been engaged
in buying the cargo consisting of tobacco, flour, and all
sorts of provisions. His popularity was at its peak. He
was received by his friends as an ambassador who had won
great concessions from a foreign sovereign.[5] He had made a
market for goods which in some instances had been stored
in warehouses three or four years. Through his influence
large numbers of Kentucky exporters were likewise enabled
to obtain passports. Prices advanced, tobacco selling for
$9.50 instead of $2.00 a hundred. As many as 15,000 barrels of flour were sent down the river within a year, and

---

[1] In January, 1790, however, Wilkinson wrote of Morgan as a friend of
Spain. Gayarré, III, 279. Wilkinson, on behalf of himself, Harry Innes, Benjamin Sebastian, and Isaac Dunn, petitioned Gardoqui for a grant of 600,000
acres between the Yazoo and the Big Black River, where he proposed to establish
a colony under the jurisdiction of Spain. *Gardoqui Papers*, V, 59-66.

[2] These boats arrived at New Orleans early in June, 1788.

[3] *American Historical Review*, IX, 503.

[4] *Gardoqui Papers*, IV, 415-17.

[5] N. S. Shaler, *Kentucky*, p. 101.

land values increased appreciably.[1] The duty at New Orleans was later reduced to 6 per cent, and river trade for a time continued to flourish, although Wilkinson protested that he had gained but little profit in the venture, due to the destruction of some of the boats and the rejection of the damaged tobacco.[2]

The facts relating to the collapse of the so-called "Spanish Conspiracy" are well known, but a brief summary may contribute to an understanding of the period. The petition from the convention held in September, 1787, asking that Kentucky should be admitted into the Union as a separate state was presented to Congress by delegate John Brown of Danville. Scarcely had he arrived in New York before he sought an interview with Gardoqui, who later referred to Brown as one of the leading citizens of Kentucky and a man upon whom he could depend.[3]

Gardoqui informed him that as long as Kentucky remained a part of the Union the free navigation of the Mississippi would never be granted, but that should the people agree upon separation from the United States, commercial concessions would follow.

Because of the adoption of the Constitution by the requisite number of states, the petition from Kentucky was referred to the new Congress. As represented to Kentuckians by Brown, the cause for postponement was due to jealousy of the West on the part of eastern members.

[1] Louis Pelzer, "Economic Factors in the Acquisition of Louisiana," *Miss. Valley Hist. Assoc. Proc.*, VI, 117.

[2] September 17, 1789. "Wilkinson's Second Memorial," *American Historical Review*, IX, 756.

[3] July 25, 1788. *Gardoqui Papers*, IV, 315–26; 363–83. That he was ready stuff for molding is clear from Wilkinson's statement that Brown was a young man of fair ability, without political experience, timid, and with very little knowledge of the world. Gayarré, III, 241.

He made known to them also the proposal submitted by Gardoqui.

Wilkinson declared in a communication to Miró and Navarro that by January (1789) Kentucky would cease to be a part of Virginia, and that it was his purpose in the July convention following to secure absolute independence for the district.[1] As a member of this convention he strove to secure a vote in favor of immediate independence. In this he failed, but his followers succeeded in getting another convention ordered for November. It was evident when the convention assembled that the conservatives were in the saddle and that they would reject any suggestion which pointed toward a plot with Spain. A temperate address to Congress was adopted, urging their claim to the navigation of the Mississippi, and a motion was carried respectfully urging upon the Virginia Assembly independence for Kentucky.[2]

By the close of the year (1788) Wilkinson, through a warning to one of his confederates, must have sensed the fact that failure was inevitable.[3] Somewhat later the relation of John Brown to the project was published. President Washington learned with alarm of these disclosures of an intrigue which was "pregnant with much mischief."[4]

Even then Wilkinson was not prepared to surrender

---

[1] Gayarré, III, 209. Navarro returned to Spain and became the adviser of Florida Blanca on Louisiana affairs upon the death of José de Galvez and of his nephew Bernardo (1788).

[2] Green, *Spanish Conspiracy*, p. 227.

[3] Gayarré, III, 240. December 5, 1788, General Arthur St. Clair wrote Major Dunn: "I am much grieved to hear that there are strong dispositions on the part of the people of Kentucky to break off their connection with the United States and that our friend Wilkinson is at the head of this affair."

[4] *Gardoqui Papers*, IV, 401-2. The evidence is given in full in Green, *Spanish Conspiracy*, pp. 238, 239, 240.

the main feature of his project. In his second memorial to Miró he urged that emigration to Louisiana should be promoted and that the designs of Great Britain for establishing her supremacy in the West should be overthrown.[1] But the one aim beyond all others to be fostered was separation and independence from the United States. Ultimate success would crown their efforts, he asserted in his final appeal, providing Spain should win the support of two or three prominent men of the most select kind in every district.[2] Modern corrupt politician to the core, he asserted that while throughout his life he had "abhorred Venality," $7,000 rightly placed would accomplish the purpose.[3]

The northern states, appreciating the effect of opposition in the West on the adoption of the Constitution, were more disposed to yield their ground on the free navigation of the Mississippi. With this knowledge Jay recommended that the problem should be passed on to the new government, "who will undoubtedly be tenacious of the publick rights, and may be enabled, by circumstances not yet developed to terminate these negotiations with Spain in a manner perfectly consistent with the rights in question and with interests and wishes of their constituents."

In keeping with the spirit of this recommendation, one of the last acts of the Continental Congress provided "that the free navigation of the River Mississippi is a clear and

[1] He refers to a plan of Lord Dorchester which was being promoted by his agent, Colonel John Connolly. *Gardoqui Papers*, IV, 245–55. *Ibid.*, V, 4, 5, 15.

[2] This grand scheme comprehended settlements west of the Alleghanies under Spanish control.

[3] September 18, 1789. *American Historical Review*, IX, 764–66. He claimed to have expended in this cause $12,000 as loans. He suggested also the annual distribution of from $20,000 to $30,000 among Americans, twenty-two names being mentioned.

essential right of the United States, and that the same ought to be considered and supported as such."[1]

Notwithstanding his position was becoming delicate because of the publicity given his relations with Brown, Gardoqui remained in the United States until October (1789). His time was devoted to observing the effects of the inauguration of the new government upon western affairs and to conferences with Brown, Isaac Dunn, and other Wilkinson satellites.[2] On the eve of leaving New York he was persuaded, through assurances oft repeated, of the favorable attitude of the West toward Spanish objectives and of their ultimate success.[3]

Early in 1790 Wilkinson declared that all the politicians of Kentucky had seemingly fallen asleep due to the effects of trade privileges accorded them by the Spanish government and to the conciliatory policy toward the rebellious West inaugurated by the federal government. During the days of organization, so vividly described in the diary of Washington, no topics excited a livelier interest than those pertaining to the West. This is manifest through his letters "to characters in the Western Country, relative chiefly to Indian affairs"; on "the real views of Mr. McGillivray";[4] on advantages held out "to emigrants from the United States to settle in the Spanish Territory"; and "the obnoxious influence of land jobbers."[5] Appointment of leaders to office was a method used by

---

[1] September 16, 1788. *Secret Journals of Congress, Foreign Affairs,* IV, 448-54.

[2] *Gardoqui Papers,* IV, 383.   [3] *Ibid.,* III, 36-39; IV, 363.

[4] McGillivray was a half-breed chief of the Creek nation. He was induced, together with other Creek chiefs, to visit New York, and because of his pleasing reception at the hands of Washington and other officials, he concluded a treaty and signed an oath of allegiance to the United States (August, 1790).

[5] John C. Fitzpatrick, *The Diaries of George Washington,* IV, 54, 58, 75, 95, 196.

Washington to win the support of those who were account-
ed friendly to Spanish interests. Harry Innes was appointed federal judge of the Kentucky district, although he was
still referred to secretly, by Wilkinson, as "our friend."[1]
Clark was not unmindful of the fact that he had no
share in the President's confidence, and in one of the few
outbursts of passion to be found in his letters thus expresses himself to his brother: "The United States had to
fill all the posts of honor or profit in this western territory.
Kentucky was to be a new government; her posts were
also to be filled. Every little body was looking forward,
and supposed himself capable of filling those of the first
magnitude, either under Congress or Kentucky. I stood
in the way of the whole of them. Of course, their object
was to destroy me by ten thousand lies and circular letters; and the public paying attention to this class of
bodies, whom I call big little men, hath cost the continent
millions of money and rivers of blood. Foreseeing all this,
I fixed myself a colossus to shoot their darts at; but I
believe that they begin to discover that they have no effect.
I despise them and pity the public."[2]

In the attitude of the July convention Wilkinson must
have sensed the fact that his separatist movement was on
the wane. In this vein he wrote Miró: "I have given my
time, my property, and every exertion of my faculties to
promote the interests of the Spanish monarchy. By this
conduct I have hazarded the indignation of the American
Union."[3]

[1] William Blount was appointed governor of the Southwest Territory and
superintendent of Indian affairs in the South, although his questionable acts as a
land speculator were well known. John Sevier and James Robertson were made
brigadier generals under him.

[2] September 2, 1791. Draper MSS, 34 J 7.

[3] September 17, 1789. Gayarré, III, 28c.

Despite his reiteration that he was prepared to defend the Spanish interests with tongue, with pen, and with sword, Miró was not deceived with the tinsel of this actor and advised that the time was not yet ripe for Wilkinson to become a Spaniard.[1] Two thousand dollars as an annual pension for Wilkinson was thought by Miró to be a good investment in an agent who was so capable of neutralizing any effort on the part of men of the West to overcome Spanish authority. With naïveté he also recommended that $1,000 should be paid Sebastian, who, in turn, was to shadow Wilkinson.[2] Meantime Wilkinson (October, 1791) was commissioned a lieutenant colonel in the United States Army, and shortly after was promoted to the rank of brigadier general.

At the time, Miró was gravely alarmed over a colonization project which in its proportions dwarfed any of those heretofore described. While the evidence is voluminous and the names of Clark, Sevier, and a number of other western leaders are prominent, the main features only of the plan will be stated.[3]

The year 1789 seemed promising for land speculation in the Southwest through the organization of three companies which obtained from Georgia large tracts of land in the Yazoo country. The Muscle Shoals region was secured by the Tennessee Company. South of this grant was that of the Virginia Company, of which Patrick Henry was a prominent member, comprising a portion of the hunting grounds of the Chickasaw. The third, the South Carolina

[1] Gayarré, III, 284.

[2] *Ibid.*, p. 286. Wilkinson was pensioned by the Spanish government for the sum named, in 1792, and continued to receive that amount for a number of years. Sebastian also received $1,000 a year.

[3] For a full discussion, see, C. H. Haskins, "The Yazoo Land Companies," *American Historical Assoc. Papers*, V, 395 ff.

Yazoo Company, which was the most active, was formed
at Charleston and contained in the list of twenty members
the names of a number of distinguished Carolina Whigs.[1]
Alexander Moultrie, but recently governor, was one of
these. Their grant extended from the mouth of the Yazoo
River along the Mississippi almost to Natchez, and included the important site of Walnut Hills. Any colonies which
might be founded would be in an anomalous situation, for
Georgia refused to guarantee the title to the cessions and
also to exercise jurisdiction over any settlements. Nor had
the offer made by Georgia to cede the territory to the federal government been accepted. Over all the area comprised within these grants, some 25,000,000 acres, the
Spaniards claimed jurisdiction, and Indian rights were likewise disregarded.

Plans were formed by the South Carolina Company to
begin a settlement, and as a first step thereto they hoped
to win the acquiescence of Spanish officers. Early in January, 1790, the project was submitted to Wilkinson, who
glimpsed the opportunity for gain which would enable him
to meet the pressing demands of his Kentucky associates.[2]
His proposal to become chief agent for the company was
rejected, since to one Dr. James O'Fallon had already been
assigned that task.

O'Fallon was born in Ireland of a family claiming descent from the kings of Ireland. After receiving a liberal
education he studied medicine at Edinburgh and came to
America at the close of the Revolution. He served for a
time in the army and in military hospitals, and then returned to Charleston, where he was favorably received by
some of the good families. His spirit for adventure found
an outlet in the mania for land speculation then prevalent

[1] Gayarré, III, 272.   [2] Ibid., pp. 275, 276.

and he became chief promoter of the South Carolina Yazoo Company. With instructions to provide for the establishment of an independent state which was to serve as a buffer between the Spanish possessions and the United States, O'Fallon set out for Kentucky. He was to cultivate friendly relations with Spanish officials and with the Choctaw and Chickasaw nations. Walnut Hills was to constitute the center for Indian trade, the slave trade, and land speculation.

Evidently O'Fallon found willing listeners in the West, for in a lengthy communication to Miró (January 15, 1791) he referred to Clark as his deputy agent for Kentucky, and to Sevier in the same capacity for Franklin.[1] With a gesture of the braggart he outlined the project which, as he asserted, was to be carried out through a descent to the Yazoo by at least 1,000 regular troops, well armed, infantry, cavalry, and artillery.[2] They were to be accompanied by 2,000 families as a nucleus for the colony. Very blandly he referred to organizing a western confederation independent of the United States. There was then to be formed an alliance, offensive and defensive, with Spain. Failing in this, one was to be formed with Great Britain in keeping with the invitation already tendered by Lord Dorchester. Any attack by the Indians was to be construed as an act of aggression by Spain and would result in a general war which would lead to the capture of Natchez and New Orleans.

[1] *Archives of the Indies*, Ayer Collection. He had previously written Miró from Clark's home. The following year he was married to Frances Clark, the youngest sister of George Rogers Clark. Dr. John C. Parish has been making an extended study of the career of O'Fallon. Some of his conclusions were presented at the meeting of the Mississippi Valley Historical Association, 1928.

[2] As he wrote he became increasingly voluble and stated that by the end of the next summer he would have a force of at least 10,000 regulars and militia.

At the time he was boasting to Miró of winning the consent of the Company to becoming the slaves of Spain, under the appearance of a free and independent state, he was writing President Washington denouncing the Spanish governor and urging that permission be granted him to send an army for the conquest of New Orleans.[1]

Miró, in keeping with the advice of Wilkinson, proceeded to excite the hostility of the Indians toward the establishment of any colony. As an alternative he urged his government to foster immigration to the region, to declare New Orleans a free port for all European nations and even the United States, but to grant him authority to prohibit all commerce with Kentucky and the Ohio country.[2]

Spanish officers at Natchez and New Orleans were fully persuaded, through reports from secret agents, that Clark as commander-in-chief of an army numbering at least 750 would arrive not later than May (1791).[3] Their dispatches show evidence of great fear, and various plans were suggested in the emergency. Walnut Hills was to be fortified and held by Spanish troops and an armed force on two flatboats, a galley, and a felucca, the last carrying eight swivel guns, were to be sent against the enemy.[4]

Any effort to reach an agreement through diplomacy would of course be nullified in such a crisis. Moreover, the success of such a colony would precipitate a clash with the Indians, whose lands had been confirmed to them by the federal government at the treaty of Hopewell (1786).

[1] Gayarré, III, 289.

[2] *Ibid.*, p. 297. This was in keeping with Wilkinson's views.

[3] Captain Simon Kenton was designated as one of Clark's recruiting officers. To each man enlisting was to be assigned 300 acres of land and necessities for eighteen months. Transcript from *Archives of the Indies*, Ayer Collection. John Williams to Gayoso de Lemos, Governor at Natchez, January 16, 1791.

[4] Gayoso de Lemos to Miró, April 8, 1791. Ayer Collection.

A telling blow was administered to the movement by Washington when he issued a proclamation against the lawless projects of the companies.[1] O'Fallon dropped from sight, but, as will be seen, within two years he had, in conjunction with Clark, evolved a new plan which appeared even more dangerous to Spanish interests.

Thomas Jefferson had shown an understanding of western problems, and his aggressive policy as secretary of state was well calculated to win the allegiance of frontiersmen. In his instructions to Carmichael at Madrid he urged bringing matters to a crisis. "It is *necessary* to us," he wrote. "More than half the territory of the United States is on that river. Two hundred thousand of our citizens are settled on them, of whom forty thousand bear arms. These have no other outlet for their tobacco, rice, corn, hemp, lumber, house timber, ship timber."[2] He even suggested the necessity of joining the West in a war against Spain in order to "preserve them in our Union."

Jefferson concluded that since it was "not our interest to cross the Mississippi for ages," Spain should concede the free navigation of that river and a port at its mouth and grant to the United States the Floridas. In return we were to help protect Louisiana and her other territory to the west.[3] Jefferson's pledge to Kentuckians was received with favor. He wrote: "We are not inattentive in the interests of your navigation. . . . . I can assure you of the determined zeal of our chief magistrate in this business, and I trust mine will not be doubted as far as it can be of any avail. The nail will be driven as far as it will go peace-

[1] *American State Papers, Indian Affairs*, I, 112.

[2] *Writings of Jefferson*, ed. Ford, V, 225.

[3] Jefferson was led to suggest this solution on account of the possibility of war between Great Britain and Spain growing out of the Nootka Sound affair. Should this occur, he feared lest Great Britain should get possession of the Floridas and Louisiana.

ably, and farther the moment circumstances become favorable."[1] In the meantime the spirit of national pride was developing in Kentucky. Details of separation from Virginia having been agreed upon, an enabling act was passed by Congress, a constitution was adopted, and Kentucky was admitted into the Union as the fifteenth State (June 1, 1792).

[1] May 7, 1791. *Writings of Jefferson*, ed. Ford, V, 295.

Chapter XVIII

Clark and the Growth of French Empire

SOME of the problems of the West with which Washington and his advisers were confronted have already been outlined. It became clearly evident that colonization under whatever form it might be proposed, by Spain or by western leaders, would never quite satisfy the discontented backwoodsmen. Diplomacy, dominated by the spirit of procrastination, offered little as a solution for their difficulties. Relief, then, from an intolerable situation could be achieved, as they came to believe, only by the use of armed force.

The period, therefore, from the inauguration of the new government until Louisiana came under the control of the United States was a critical one from the viewpoint of the ultimate development of the new nation. French leaders gazed longingly upon lands which had once belonged to France, and sought to break the strangle hold of Spain upon them. Their thought recurred to the imperialistic policy of French statesmen who, at the close of the American Revolution, strove to delimit the United States by the Alleghanies. Great Britain also had not forgotten the sacrifice of an empire by her representative in the treaty of 1783.[1]

A keen French observer (1785) foresaw that the United

[1] See *American Historical Review*, VIII, 84.

States, grateful to France but fearful of allowing her to gain too much power, hating England and irritated by the trade restrictions placed upon them, anxious to play a leading part in the world, but hampered by the mediocrity of their means to do so, was a nation which would never be satisfied with the free navigation of the Mississippi, but in time would demand possession of New Orleans.[1] Numerous memoirs and letters from the United States written by French officers and travelers toward the close of the confederation and during the first years of the new government stressed the desirability of recovering Louisiana for France.[2]

An unsigned memoir written early in 1789 gave an account of the discontent of the Spanish colonists and of Spanish fear of aggression by Americans who were not to be satisfied with lands for colonies, but were already talking of reaching the Pacific Ocean and opening trade with China. The two powerful forces putting pressure on Congress for the opening of the Mississippi were the western settlers who threatened independence and the speculators who held large tracts of land in the West. It is impossible, the unknown writer urged, for Spain to hold Louisiana for any length of time, and England would neglect nothing in their efforts to divide it with the Americans at the first opportunity. "Louisiana at the time of the cession to Spain was

[1] Memoir of Louis-Guillaume Otto. *Affaires Étrangeres, États Unis*, III, 78. William Smith Mason Library, Evanston, Illinois. Otto had been French chargé d'affaires in the United States since 1779.

[2] Frederick J. Turner made a number of these documents accessible in a "Report of the Historical Manuscripts Commission," *Report of the American Historical Association* (1896), pp. 947 ff. This thought was stressed in a memoir attributed to Vergennes, which was written prior to 1778. Turner, "The Policy of France toward the Mississippi Valley in the Period of Washington and Adams"; see also Turner, "Origin of Genet's Projected Attack on Louisiana and the Floridas," *American Historical Review*, X, No. 2, 251 ff.

insignificant," he continued, "but the English settlements in the West have changed the entire situation. . . . . The military position of Louisiana would be invaluable as a support to the French colonies. In case of a rupture with the United States the masters of Louisiana could easily win the western settlements from the Union. France could win the good will of Spain by guaranteeing to her the possessions of New Mexico and her lands farther west. The United States recognizes that she must either have France or England in Louisiana, and would prefer France."[1]

With the French Revolution flaming into a European conflagration and with a declaration of war imminent against both Great Britain and Spain, Lebrun, French minister of foreign relations, proposed (November 6, 1792) sending Citizen Edmund Genet as minister to the United States, secretly instructed to foment a revolution in the Spanish colonies.[2] According to his instructions, prepared, it has been stated, by himself, he was to endeavor to secure a treaty with the United States.[3] Such a compact, it was urged, would conduce rapidly to the freeing of Spanish America, to opening the navigation of the Mississippi to the inhabitants of Kentucky, to delivering our ancient brothers of Louisiana from the tyrannical yoke of Spain, and to reunite, perhaps, the fair star of Canada to the American constellation. Should there be timidity in cooperation on the part of the American government, he was

---

[1] "Memoir on the Retrocession of Louisiana" (1789), *États Unis*, Vol. III, Cahier 2 (Mason Library). See also Turner, "Genet's Attack on Louisiana," *American Historical Review*, III, 652, note 1. Professor Turner wrote of Jefferson's attitude toward this question, which was projected by the *Nootka Sound Affair* (1790), "Our representative in France was directed to attempt to secure the assistance of France in an effort to induce Spain to yield the Island of New Orleans to the United States." *American Historical Review*, X, No. 2, 258.

[2] War was declared against Great Britain February 1, 1793, and against Spain March 9, 1793.

[3] *Affaires Étrangeres, États-Unis*, XLVII, fol. 401 ff.

to take all measures which comported with his position to develop in Louisiana and in the other provinces of America adjacent to the United States the principles of liberty and of independence. Kentuckians who had "long burned" with the desire for the free navigation of the Mississippi, it was pointed out, would doubtless assist him without compromising Congress, and he was authorized to support agents in Kentucky and in Louisiana for carrying out the project.[1] How far the suggestion for an attack on Louisiana, which emanated from Clark, led to these definite proposals by the French government cannot be positively stated. There can be no doubt that he forwarded such a plan to that government before the close of 1792 and offered his services for its accomplishment. That it was received with favor by the French Executive Council is likewise certain.[2]

The bursting of the South Carolina Yazoo Company bubble, promoted by O'Fallon, of which Clark was to be chief military officer, has been previously discussed. In retirement at Mulberry Hill, the home of his father, Clark devoted his time, as he wrote, to reading, hunting, fishing, fowling, and corresponding with a few chosen friends.[3] While his family, as he expressed it, was "by far the best settled of any persons in this part of the country," he was himself, like many others, burdened with lands for

[1] December, 1792. "Genet's instructions," Turner, "Correspondence of Clark and Genet," *Report Amer. Hist. Assoc.* (1896), I, 1, 960–62.

[2] This is established by a letter of Tom Paine, then a naturalized French citizen, to Dr. James O'Fallon, February 17, 1793. The letter was discovered in the Draper Collection by Dr. Louise Phelps Kellogg. *American Historical Review*, XXIX, 504, 505. About the same time other plans were submitted to the French government for the reduction of Louisiana by the aid of Kentucky riflemen. Turner, "Genet's Attack on Louisiana and the Floridas," *American Historical Review*, III, 658.

[3] September 2, 1791. Draper MSS, 34 J 7. Letter to his brother Edmund. Mulberry Hill is now the "George Rogers Clark Park" of Louisville.

which there was no market.[1] He had lost interest in public affairs. "As for the Politicks of this country," he writes, "first suppose a swarm of Hungary persons gaping for bread you may conclude that their' ideas are not Genly Virtuous but as I dont meddle in their affairs I know but little about them."[2] Toward the close of the year 1788 he resigned his appointment as surveyor for the state line. Very little of his correspondence during the ensuing four years has been preserved. He had, it was said, "grown temperate."[3] At any rate this was the period when he took up with enthusiasm the writing of his memoir, a document so essential to the complete understanding of the conquest of the Northwest.[4]

At that time [1789] descriptions by travelers of the mounds in the Ohio and Mississippi valleys prompted inquiry as to their origin. Noah Webster, in response to a question submitted to him on this subject by Ezra Stiles, president of Yale College, advanced views which furnished the basis for extended discussion. President Stiles had himself ventured the opinion that the mounds were constructed by the followers of Madoc, a Welsh prince of the twelfth century. This theory was not wholly rejected by Webster, for, as he wrote: "There is such a surprising affinity between the Indian mounds and the barrows or cemeteries which remain in England but particularly in Wales and Anglesey the last retreats of the original Britons."[5] His preference was for the theory that the mounds were constructed by the followers of Ferdinand De Soto—a view also advanced by Benjamin Franklin. Two years later, Sep-

---

[1] April 20, 1788. Draper MSS, 2 L 26.   [2] *Ibid.*

[3] May 30, 1790. Jonathan Clark Papers, Draper MSS, 2 L 28.

[4] For the writing of the memoir and its significance, see Appendix I, pp., 474–94.

[5] *American Museum,* VII, 323–28.

tember 3, 1789, Webster acknowledged his error in this conclusion and developed the theory which was generally accepted for many years. The Indians of Mexico and Peru, he stated, whose ancestors had lived in the territory beyond the Alleghany Mountains were descendants of the Carthaginians or other Mediterranean nations. At an unknown date, possibly in the thirteenth century, the Siberian Tartars, "Goths and Vandals" of North America, found their way to the northwest parts of this continent and pushed on until they met the southern and more ancient settlers. In the warfare which ensued the more civilized tribes were driven into Mexico, but in the conflict "between these different tribes or races of men were constituted the numerous fortifications discovered on the Ohio and in all parts of the western territory."[1]

On this question, Clark, with good reason, thought himself an authority. As he wrote to the editor of the *American Museum:* "I think the world ought to be undeceived in this point, so great a stranger to the western cuntrey as Mr. Webster appears to be ought to have informed himself better before he ventured to have pamed (palmed) his conjectures on the world. I don't suppose there is a person living that knows the Geography and Natural History of the back cuntrey better if so well as I do myself, it hath been my study for many years." He then developed a theory which, unknown for three-fourths of a century, is now universally accepted by archaeologists, namely, that the builders of the mounds were the ancestors of the Indian tribes occupying that region.[2]

Again, his versatility is evident in an application for a patent right which would serve to protect his interest in an invention intended to facilitate river navigation by means

---

[1] *Ibid.*, VIII, 11, 12.

[2] For the letter, which was not published before 1860, see Appendix II, pp. 495–99.

of boats.[1] While a number of similar proposals had been made, no patent for the purpose had yet been issued.[2] So confident was Clark of success that in his presentation he asked for a resolution by Congress granting him a monopoly in the use of his machine throughout the continent for a period of fourteen years. He writes:

I doubt Sir, you smile at the contents of this letter, as it may appear to border a little on the marvelous, when I inform you of an invention that will give a new turn to the face of things throughout the Western country.

Frequently navigating those rivers in the course of the War, with various kinds of vessels, I was led to believe that great improvement might be made, which I was determined to study, when I should have leisure to apply myself. But at that period, Mr. Rumsey and others amused us with vessels so constructed as to answer every desirable purpose. This I believed they would have done, having a similar idea myself. They failing, I again resumed the study, and soon found that it was necessary to make myself master of the mechanical powers, which I did, and to my astonishment, found that by a combination of those powers properly applied, that a boat of any size, with a small given force (either by men or horses on board) would be forced against a stream that no number of oars applied in the common way, could move her. . . . . Not being able to discover any defect, and further to satisfy myself, I had the machine actually made on a small scale and proved every conjecture beyond a doubt. It moves any number of oars you choose to apply, with more regularity and despatch than men can possibly do.

Shortly after, a well-known traveler gave an account of his interview with Clark as follows: "Arrived at his house under an apprehension that he had forgotten me. He immediately recognized me and without ceremony entered into familiar though desultory conversation, in which I was highly pleased with the Atticism of his wit, the genuine

[1] For this application, see Appendix III, pp. 500–501.

[2] Reply of John Brown, representative in Congress from Kentucky, April 27, 1790. Draper MSS, 53 J 88.

FROM A PORTRAIT PAINTED BY JOHN WESLEY JARVIS

offspring of native genius. On serious and important occasions he displays a profundity of judgment aided by reflection and matured by experience."[1]

Clark was not unmindful of the terror which was then sweeping over the frontier communities following the surprise and disorderly retreat of General Josiah Harmar's army from the Maumee Indian villages, and after the dreadful blow to the force led by General Arthur St. Clair at the hands of Little Turtle and his Indian braves. Like Washington, Clark cried out for a leader who might be able "to put an end to this horrid Indian war that rages, and will more universally rage, on the frontier."[2] He once more defined his policy for the settlement of the Indian problem:

It is a pity that the blood and treasure of the people should be so lavished, when one campaign properly directed, would put an end to the war; and a well directed line of conduct, after such event should take place, might establish harmony between us and the Indians that might exist for many years. Two armies hath already been defeated, and I doubt [not] the third will share the same fate, if the greatest precaution is not made use of. We are suing the Indians for peace. This convinces them that we are beat and cowed, and of course will cause nations not yet at war to join the confederacy, and if they treat at all, their demands will be so great that it will be as dishonorable for the states to grant as it is for them.[3]

He confessed to his brother the secret hope that he might be called upon to put this policy to the test.

Such expression of confidence in himself was awakened, doubtless, through a friendly message from Jefferson but recently imparted to him. "Will it not be possible," it reads,

---

[1] December 15, 1790. John Pope, *A Tour through the Southern and Western Territories of the United States of North America*, p. 19.

[2] September 2, 1791. Letter to his brother Edmund. Draper MSS, 34 J 7.

[3] To Jonathan Clark, May 11, 1792. W. H. English, *Conquest of the Northwest*, II, 788.

"for you to bring Gen'l Clark forward? I know the greatness of his mind, and am more mortified at the cause which
obscured it. Had this not unhappily taken place there was
nothing he might not have hoped; could it be Surmounted
his lost ground might yet be recovered. No man alive rated
him higher than I did, and would again were he to become
again what I knew him."[1]

In expressing gratitude to Jefferson, Clark wished it
understood that his acknowledgment of such appreciation
came "untainted with the sordid desire of cultivating your
patronage from selfish views. I am above that design but
when duly called on I shall never be above the service of
my Country at the risque of life and reputation, blood and
treasure might have been and may yet be saved. . . . . On
no public occasion shall my exertions be wanting, My
country and yourself may at all times, command me."[2]

Alike cheering words came from Virginia, in letters from
his brother Jonathan who had been spending some time in
Richmond:

I am told your Kentucky enemies are done yelping. Some of them
I understand begin to fondle,—sorry Dogs. as to your enemies here, I
knew them not—that you had some I was certain—but I was the last
person to be informed of them—but I believe they likewise are at present still—your friends begin to talk very bold and loud—some begin
to [in] quire how you came to be left in the manner you were on your
last expedition, and whether some of those who were at the head of
those who came off, were not afraid you would actually and in earnest
carry them where there were Indians—and others think you are not an
improper person to be sent on the present expedition and I have lately

---

[1] March 7, 1791. *Writings of Jefferson*, ed. Washington, III, 217, 218. Judge
Innes, to whom the letter was addressed, wrote Jefferson: "I took the liberty of
showing him your letter from a hope that it might cause him to reflect upon his
present folly. He was perfectly sober, was greatly agitated by the contents,
observed it was friendly and shed tears" (Innes Papers, May 30, 1791, Library of
Congress).

[2] June 29, 1791. Draper MSS, 16 S 78–80.

heard that there are those who have become bold enough to say you ought to command it; these things must give you some pleasure, after the evils that have been attempted to be done you.[1]

In reply, Clark declared that he was more capable of negotiations and military life than ever, for his whole life had been devoted to its study.

Whatever assurance he may have gotten from these hopeful messages of the possible opportunity for regaining military prestige, it was but short lived. The honor of retrieving the situation by bringing the Indians of the Northwest into subjection was to be the achievement of General Anthony Wayne, who, in the spring of 1792, was commissioned to raise an army for that purpose.[2]

The year 1792 was in other respects a critical one in Clark's life. His claims against Virginia, including his pay as an officer and the purchase of flour and other necessities for his army in the Revolution, amounting to $20,500, had again been rejected by the Assembly.[3] The arguments against their assumption were: that there was doubt whether the bills had been paid in specie, and that they should have been presented earlier. The main reason, as stated by his brother, was the spirit of parsimony which controlled the majority. The court of appeals also, in June, decided adversely against the granting of half-pay to troops serving in the state line.[4] A month earlier, Clark declared, while preparing another petition to the Virginia legislature, "I have given the United States half the territory they possess, and for them to suffer me to remain in poverty, in

[1] April 8, 1792. Draper MSS, 53 J 92.

[2] August 20, 1794, Wayne's army totally defeated Little Turtle and his followers at the Battle of Fallen Timbers. The Treaty of Greenville, concluded August 3, 1795, brought peace to the Old Northwest lasting many years.

[3] Letter of Jonathan Clark, December 17, 1791. Draper MSS, 53 J 91.

[4] Letter of Jonathan Clark, June 28, 1792. Draper MSS, 53 J 93.

consequence of it, will not redound much to their honor hereafter. If I meet with another rebuff I must rest contented with it, be industrious, and look out further for my future bread."[1] Then it was, no doubt, that he recalled the prophecy of his friends, Jefferson and Mason, when he was setting out for the conquest of the Northwest: "We think you may safely confide in the Justice and Generosity of the Virginia Assembly."[2] His last hope for relief was evidently shattered through the report on his memorial (November 1, 1792) containing the following statements: "Have not been able to bring on your memorial, and begin to fear I shall not have it in my power to do anything for you this Assembly. . . . . As to the flour I am certain from all I can discover you will get nothing . . . . as to commutation [compensation] I shall bring that on—I have your discharge from the Governor, and hope to succeed. I understand you intend in—therefore do not expect you will get this. . . . ."[3]

Then scarcely forty years of age, proud, ambitious, with his services seemingly unappreciated by his country, with prospects blighted, without employment, dependent on the generosity of his family, there was left to Clark, as he thought, only a life of obscurity.

It was but a short time after that his proposal was sent to the French government. The letter of Paine heretofore mentioned gives a possible clew to Clark's motives at this time.[4] "In my private opinion," he wrote, "a Spanish war

[1] Letter to Jonathan Clark, May 11, 1792. English, *Conquest of the Northwest*, II, 788–90.

[2] *Clark Papers*, 38.

[3] Letter of Jonathan Clark, November 1, 1792. Draper MSS, 53 J 94.

[4] *Archives des Affaires Étrangers*, XLVI, fol. 181–84. Mangourit, French consul at Charleston, assisted Genet in promoting this phase of his plan. Documentary material is to be found in "The Mangourit Correspondence in Respect to Genet's Projected Attack upon the Floridas," 1793–94, ed. F. J. Turner, *Report. Amer. Hist. Assoc.* (1897), pp. 569–79.

is inevitable. You may, therefore, in all human probability, expect very soon to hear of the General's nomination to the post and command solicited by him." He further stated that Jefferson's private opinion of Clark had been presented to the Executive Council and that it was feared "the intrigues of certain personages in the American cabinet, who are the friends of Britain, and the votaries of Kings may obstruct the General, in his plans of raising men and procuring officers." The expedition successful, the confirmation of the grant originally made to the South Carolina Yazoo Company was suggested. Full confidence was to be placed in Genet, who was speedily setting out for America.

On April 8, 1793, Genet arrived at Charleston, where he was enthusiastically received by the Jeffersonian faction. Misinformed regarding the real attitude of America toward the European conflict, and carried away by his reception, he proceeded to fit out privateers which were sent out to prey on British commerce. He provided also for an armed expedition, made up of 1,500 Georgia frontiersmen under Samuel Hammond, which was to proceed against the Spanish in East Florida. Another American adventurer, William Tate, was to be commander-in-chief of an expedition consisting of 2,000 frontiersmen which was to proceed along the Tennessee and the Mississippi for an attack on New Orleans. This accomplished, he was to make a treaty with the Creek nation whereby the Indians were to be guaranteed the free and peaceable possession of their lands.

Genet's reception also by the democratic admirers of France as he traveled overland to Philadelphia convinced him that the American people were in sympathy with the French cause. In this he was soon disillusioned, for Washington received him with that icy reserve so effective on various occasions, and he learned of the proclamation of neutrality which was published by order of the President

(April 22, 1793). Neutrality was declared to be the duty of the United States, and no aid from the government was to be expected by Americans who should assist either of the belligerents. This policy was bitterly opposed by Jefferson and the members of the Republican party, who hoped for friendly relations, if not a positive alliance, with France. Genet was convinced that it would be possible to nullify the executive policy by securing a majority in Congress favorable to his plans.

Upon arriving in Philadelphia Genet received a letter from Clark written at Louisville February 2, 1793. In this message Clark wrote of his services during the Revolution, of his investigation of Spanish defenses in Louisiana and Mexico, and of his friends in various centers of those provinces. With four hundred men, he declared, the Spaniards could be driven from upper Louisiana, and with eight hundred, from New Orleans. While he was ready to raise such a force, he asked for 3,000 pounds sterling to promote the project and for naval assistance consisting of two or three frigates.[1] Genet decided to accept this plan for an attack on New Orleans and appointed Clark "major general of the Independent and Revolutionary Legion of the Mississippi."[2]

From the reports on conditions in the West received from André Michaux, a French botanist, and other agents, Genet was satisfied that the plan was working satisfac-

[1] *Report Amer. Hist. Assoc.* (1896), I, 971-72.

[2] His title became later "Major General in the Armies of France and Commander-in-chief of the French Revolutionary Legion on the Mississippi River," Draper MSS, 11 J 242. The achievements of Clark were well known to French authorities. Lyonnet, a former resident of New Orleans, sent a plan to them early in 1793 in which he wrote: "At the head of these filibusters of the woods must be placed General (Clark), who in the late war took Vincennes among other posts. His name alone is worth hosts and there is no American who has not confidence in him." *American Historical Review*, III, 501.

torily. The project comprised a combined attack by the frontiersmen and the "independent" Indians of the Southwest against the Floridas, the advance of Clark's force upon New Orleans, the blocking of the mouth of the Mississippi by a French naval force, and the sending of a fleet against Canada.[1] He then unfolded his plan to Jefferson, "not as Secretary of State, but as Mr. Jefferson."[2] As interpreted by Jefferson, the expedition was to rendezvous outside the United States—he supposed in Louisiana—and after the capture of New Orleans, Louisiana was to be constituted an "independent State connected in commerce with France and the U.S." "I told him," Jefferson said, "that his enticing officers and souldiers from Kentucky to go against Spain, was really putting a halter about their necks, for they would assuredly be hung, if they commd. [commenced] Hostilities agt. a nation at peace with the U.S. that leaving out that article I did not care what insurrection should be excited in Louisiana."[3] This merely formal protest on the part of the Secretary of State, who shortly before had declared that a French alliance was his "polar star," was due to the fact that Great Britain and Spain, because of their relations to the Indians and their known attitude toward the United States, were dangerous neighbors.[4]

By the middle of July (1793) Michaux, presumably with the desire of examining plants and other objects of nature,

[1] Turner, "Policy of France toward the Mississippi Valley," *American Historical Review*, X, 263. On Michaux, see Turner, "Genet's Attack on Louisiana and the Floridas," *American Historical Review*, III, 666. His commission is given in *Report Amer. Hist. Assoc.* (1896), I, 995.

[2] *Ibid.*, I, 984, 985.

[3] Jefferson's "Conversation with Genet," July, 1793, *Report Amer. Hist. Assoc.* (1896), I, 984, 985.

[4] *Writings of Jefferson*, ed. Ford, I, 212. Washington had raised the question of a closer relationship with France.

was again on his way to the West bearing letters of introduction to Clark and Governor Shelby from John Brown,
congressman from Kentucky, who had been in conference
with Genet.[1] As interpreted by Genet, optimistic for the
success of the venture, his purpose in sending Michaux was
to inform "the celebrated General Clark," who was devoted
to the desire to free Louisiana from the Spanish yoke, of his
arrival. Accompanied by two artillery officers, who would
be serviceable to Clark in raising his revolutionary contingent, the "Botanist" was authorized to conclude alliances with Indian nations and with the French of New
Orleans reported as zealous to secure their freedom from
Spain.[2]

Governor Carondelet, at New Orleans, appealed to
Spain for additional troops, urging that "if some four frigates were to present themselves here with 1,200 French
troops there would arise a faction in this city in favor of
the Convention which would cause great havoc and perhaps the loss of the province. . . . . To these important
reasons must be added the fears inspired in us by the very
disquieting movements of the Americans settled in the
West, against whom I cannot oppose sufficient forces in
case of any hostility from them."[3] The Spanish representatives in Philadelphia, likewise, communicated to Jefferson
their apprehension regarding this invasion.[4] They were assured that President Washington would employ all means

[1] *Report Amer. Hist. Assoc.* (1896), pp. 982, 983. Jefferson also sent a letter
by Michaux introducing him to Governor Shelby, *ibid.*, pp. 984, 987.

[2] At a French dinner party, April, 1793, plans were said to have been made
for the capture of New Orleans by a force from Kentucky. *Report. Amer. Hist.
Assoc.* (1896), p. 1103. Governor Carondelet was apprehensive of the outbreak
of the insurrection (*ibid.*, pp. 975–77).

[3] July 31, 1793. *Report Amer. Hist. Assoc.* (1896), pp. 998, 999.

[4] August 27, 1793. These officers were Josef de Jaudenes and Josef de Viar
(*ibid.*, p. 1000).

within his power to restrain the citizens of the United States "from sharing in any hostility by land or sea against the subjects of Spain or its dominions."[1]

Such a promise was not wholly satisfying to Carondelet, who was feverishly engaged in strengthening his defenses.[2] He hoped for the early arrival, as promised, of Wilkinson and two or three "men of the highest consideration" in order to negotiate a treaty which looked toward the separation of the West from the Atlantic states. This accomplished, the safety of Louisiana and even Mexico would be assured.[3]

In the meantime, Clark was engaged in setting the machinery in motion for an attack on Louisiana. Boats were under construction, provisions and stores were collected, Benjamin Logan, John Montgomery, and others of his associates of Revolutionary days proffered their assistance, and his agents were sent in all directions throughout the Spanish territory. A few troops only were actually assembled at the mouth of the Cumberland, for, as stated by Clark, men can be gotten at any time. "I must be very circumspect," he adds, "while in this country and guard against doing anything that would injure the United States or giving offence to their Govt but in a few days after seting sail we shall be out of their Government I shall then be at liberty to give full scope to the authority of the Commission you did me the Honour to send."[4] His plan comprehended advancing with a small force against New Madrid, a post supported only by from twenty to forty men with ten cannon. Next to be reduced was St. Louis, which was to constitute the "principal place of Independence in the

---

[1] *Report Amer. Hist. Assoc.* (1896), p. 1005.   [2] *Ibid.*, p. 1019.

[3] *Ibid.*, p. 1069. $12,000 was the tidy sum exacted by Wilkinson for carrying on this project. *Ibid.*, pp. 1079, 1081.

[4] Clark to Genet, October 25, 1793. *Ibid.*, p. 1016.

upper country." With an augmented force, Natchez was counted on as easy prey because of the assistance from the French and American settlers there resident. New Orleans was then to be invested. Here, likewise, French insurgents would add strength to the invaders, and it was anticipated that a French fleet would block the mouth of the river. Simultaneously, St. Augustine was to be attacked by the force under Hammond. The backwoodsmen from the Carolinas, under Tate, were to descend the Tennessee and unite with Clark for the reduction of New Orleans.

The success of the enterprise was more promising because of the attitude of the democratic societies of the West, and especially those of Kentucky. Organized after the model of the Philadelphia Society, with the same objective, namely, to promote the rising tide of opposition to the federalist program, the Kentucky societies spoke as one man for using any possible method for opening the Mississippi to navigation.[1] Resolutions, thirteen in number, adopted by a convention "of respectable citizens" assembled at Lexington from various parts of Kentucky, were virtually a western bill of rights. "That we have a right to expect and demand," they wrote, "that Spain should be compelled immediately to acknowledge our right or that an end be put to all negotiations on that subject."[2] A "Remonstrance" addressed to Washington and Congress was a similar explosive:

Eight years are surely sufficient for the discussion of the most doubtful and disputable claim; the right to the navigation of the Mississippi admits neither of doubt or dispute. Your remonstrants, therefore, ... expect, that it be demanded, categorically of the Spanish King whether he will acknowledge the right of the citizens of the United States, to the free and uninterrupted navigation of the river Mississippi,

[1] The first Democratic Society in Kentucky was organized August 29, 1793.

[2] May 24, 1794. Resolution 6. *Report Amer. Hist. Assoc.* (1896), pp. 1056–58.

and cause all obstructions, to the exercise of that right in future to be withdrawn and avoided, that an immediate answer thereto be required; and that such answer be the final period of all negotiations upon this subject.

Your remonstrants further represent, that the encroachments upon the territory of the United States is a striking and melancholy proof of the situation to which our country will be reduced, if a tame spirit should still continue to direct our councils.[1]

Clark hoped to have everything in readiness for an advance by the middle of February, providing Genet could procure the necessary funds. The democratic societies made contributions for the army in provisions and ammunition. Individual members, men prominent "in Kentucky society," subscribed money, and Clark himself advanced $4,680 in preparation for the expedition.[2]

Genet, opposed by Alexander Hamilton, had failed to procure advance payments on the indebtedness due to France by the United States, and thus, without financial resources, Clark's preparations were delayed, and in fact were doomed to failure. Moreover, Genet had lost favor with Jefferson, who was convinced that it was his design to force the United States into a war as an ally of France. His policy was also sharply criticized by Defourges, Jacobin minister of foreign relations, who charged him, in words which could not be misinterpreted, that his duty was to treat with the government, and not with a portion of the people, and that he was to gain the confidence of the President and of Congress.[3]

Finally, in spite of all protests and under the hallucination that the majority of the Americans were friendly to

[1] *Report Amer. Hist. Assoc.* (1896), p. 1059.

[2] *Ibid.*, p. 1071.

[3] Turner, "Genet's Attack on Louisiana and the Floridas," *American Historical Review*, III, 670, 671. The Jacobins were then in power, having displaced the Girondists, June, 1793. It was the period of the "terror" and of military reverses.

French principles, he determined, December, 1793, to appeal to the representatives of the people. This was the last stroke. By order of the President, Genet was given a pointed rebuke by Jefferson.

Some months earlier (August, 1793), because of continuous refusals to heed the demands made upon him by the American government, Washington and his cabinet decided to ask for Genet's recall.[1] This was immediately complied with by the Jacobin government, but his letters of recall and repudiation did not reach the United States until the following February.[2]

Toward the close of January, Clark had made an appeal through the press, as major general in the armies of France, which it was hoped would prove sufficiently attractive to induce volunteers to enlist for the reduction of the Spanish posts on the Mississippi, for opening the trade of that river, and giving freedom to its inhabitants.[3] All persons serving in the expedition were to be entitled to pay at one dollar a day or to 1,000 acres of unappropriated land which might be conquered. Two thousand acres were to be the reward for those who should serve for one year, and for those serving two years, during the present war with France, 3,000 acres. Officers were to receive the same pay as those in the French armies, and all "lawful Plunder to be equally divided agreeable to the custom of War."

[1] Washington's wrath was aroused especially over Genet's act of defiance in sending the "Little Sarah," a prize ship mounting eighteen guns, to sea. By this act he had also violated his own promise.

[2] Gouverneur Morris, American minister to France, on the request of the French government was also recalled. The new French embassy, consisting of four members, was instructed to arrest Genet and send him home for trial, but Washington refused to allow his extradition. He remained in America during the rest of his life.

[3] Draper MSS, 11 J 242. Printed in the *Centinel of the Northwestern Territory*, January 25, 1794; also in the *Kentucky Gazette*, February 8, 1794, and the *Maryland Journal*, March 10, 1794.

In accordance with their instructions, the new French embassy disavowed the conduct of Genet. With some regret, Fauchet, minister plenipotentiary, issued a proclamation March 6, 1794, forbidding the violation of the neutrality of the United States and revoking the commissions of the filibusters.[1]

A proclamation by Washington within a few days was the last stroke in the defeat of the project. All American citizens were forbidden to enlist or assemble themselves for such unlawful purposes. Officers of the federal government were charged to enforce the laws and bring to condign punishment all guilty of violating them.[2]

But to a man overcome with fear as was Governor Carondelet, a proclamation was but little more than a scrap of paper. A fortified camp established by Clark 400 miles beyond Louisville and within 50 miles of the Spanish lines, and the assemblage of troops along the Georgia frontier for an attack on St. Augustine, were to him very real danger signals. An order by the President of the United States for the construction of a fort on the site of old Fort Massac prompted new Spanish alarms. New Madrid was hurriedly reinforced by a garrison of 150 regulars and five galleys each with a force of sixty men. All available militia were put under arms, and a large body of Indians were concentrated at that post for the purpose of opposing the expedition under Clark.[3]

It is conceivable that Carondelet shared the thought of Luis de las Casas, his well-known brother-in-law, who, in a summary of the situation, took on the prophet's rôle.

[1] *Report Amer. Hist. Assoc.* (1897), p. 629.

[2] James P. Richardson, *Messages and Papers of the Presidents*, I, 157, 158.

[3] William Clark to Jonathan Clark, May 25, 1794. Draper MSS, 34 J 6. Toward the close of 1795 Carondelet stated that $294,562 had been spent since 1791 in putting the provinces on a defensive basis.

The real instigators of the attack were, he declared, the Americans, who, under the guise of the French name, were pursuing their favorite objective of an opening to the sea by the way of the Mississippi.[1]

This is an object of greatest importance for them, which they will not give up, nor can they desist but I do not believe it convenient to yield to them. With time it will be a matter which will inevitably be consented to, which it will be useless to deny, for at last a great people must break the dikes which oppose their interests; interests of the first magnitude without whose possession their existence would remain languid. . . . . I do not doubt that the movement can still be banished without the hurricane breaking which is menacing Louisiana, but not in a permanent way; the people of the Western Settlements must overcome in time whatever obstacles oppose their departure to the sea and they will absorb Louisiana.

A month earlier Las Casas declared that strenuous action on the part of the American government would have contributed more toward the tranquillity of Louisiana than the tardy advice of the Secretary of State to Spanish representatives that hostile preparations were being made, "in his territory," under the influence and authority of a foreign power. He added that although these preparations and movements had been public for some time, that complaints on the part of Spanish officials had been met through protests of American friendship instead of by a real effort to remedy the situation.[2]

French designs on Louisiana were by no means ended with the collapse of Genet's project, and Clark was again to be called upon to further their promotion. His immediate attention was given to securing repayment of the money he had already advanced, which, as he wrote,

[1] Havana, May 19, 1794. Luis de las Casas to del Campo de Alange (minister of war). *Archives of the Indies*, Ayer Collection. Las Casas was the governor of Havana and captain general of Louisiana and the Floridas.

[2] April 5, 1794. Las Casas to Jaudenes and Viar. Ayer Collection.

though not considerable, "it is sufficient to ruin me."[1] His agent, Samuel Fulton, an adventurer who had joined Clark, receiving the rank of major of cavalry, found Fauchet lacking in authority to meet such obligations. With assurances from the minister that if the accounts were properly presented before the national convention they would be paid, and with the suggestion of the probability of a renewal of the expedition against Louisiana, Fulton set out for Paris.

After a delay of some weeks Fulton was informed by the Committee of Public Safety that payment of the claims of Clark and himself could be made only after they had been properly certified by the French minister in America.

Disappointment over the fruitless mission was rendered less bitter to Clark, for the Committee had formally ratified his relations with Genet. Expressing his gratification for this mark of confidence, he wrote:

> The interest of the Republic in this detached Country was always considerable but the Invitation in America and the arrival of Citizen Fulton with the information of the favorable point of view our late attempts met with hath invited the affections of the body of the people to the interest of France and no oposition that would be made in this quarter could stop their career were they again to be put in motion.
>
> The peculiar situation of Kentucky is such that their only natural door to Foreign Commerce is the Mississippi. They despair of ever geting it opened through the mediation of the present American Ministry. This is not the only reason for their desire to assist France but a more powerful one that of gratitude towards you and the Idea they possess of the rights of man.[2]

An official statement, of like intent, was prepared by Clark, Benjamin Logan, Fulton, and others of their asso-

[1] To Genet, April 28, 1794. *American Historical Review*, XVIII, 781, 782.

[2] Clark to the Committee of Public Safety, November 2, 1795. *Affaires Étrangeres, États-Unis*, XLVIII, 301. *Report of Amer. Hist. Assoc.* (1896), p. 1095.

ciates in which they asserted that throughout the West there was not an individual who could be induced to change his love for France for the gold of England.[1] "More than 200,000 persons living in this territory, deprived of the use of a river which nature has given them," they continue, "are forced to see the most beautiful country in the universe become as barren as Tartary. They despair of obtaining this privilege through the American government. Should France turn her attention toward Louisiana and the Floridas, the West may then expect to secure this right."

In their declaration of loyalty to French principles Clark and his associates were moved, no doubt, by the spirit of antagonism toward Jay's treaty which found expression in Congress as well as in all sections of the country. Moreover, they were not aware that Thomas Pinckney, at San Lorenzo (October 25, 1795), had succeeded in inducing Spain to concede the free navigation of the Mississippi and the boundary line of 31°. For three years citizens of the United States were granted the right of deposit for merchandise at New Orleans. This permission was to be continued unless another establishment on the Mississippi was assigned to them.[2]

In this manner Manuel de Godoy, Spanish minister of

[1] *Affaires Étrangeres, États-Unis*, Vol. XLVIII, fol. 302.

[2] An excellent account of the effect of Jay's treaty in inducing Godoy to reopen negotiations with the United States is to be found in S. F. Bemis, *Pinckney's Treaty*, pp. 249–79. A. P. Whitaker, in a paper read before the Mississippi Valley Historical Association (1928), declared that the terms of Jay's Treaty were known to Godoy a month before he agreed to the treaty of San Lorenzo. In *Pinckney's Treaty* is to be found also the evidence regarding "Our Brigadier Wilkinson's renewed proposal (1794) for the secession of Kentucky from the United States and union with Spain." Various sums of money were sent to Wilkinson, who, on the death of Wayne (1796), was to be appointed major general to aid in this intrigue. Ten thousand dollars, concealed in barrels of sugar and bags of coffee, were forwarded to him by one messenger even after the terms of the treaty at San Lorenzo were known at New Orleans. Carondelet stated (June, 1795) that $100,000 would be at the disposal of Sebastian,

foreign affairs, hoped to secure the friendship of the United States at a time when he feared, as a result of the Jay treaty, that a joint attack by England and the United States would lead to the loss of Louisiana. He was in better position also to resist the efforts of France to repossess herself of that province. On this significant phase of the diplomacy of the period the main features alone will be presented.

Fauchet was keenly alert to the influence of Jay's treaty on French interests, since it nullified the terms of the treaty of 1778 between France and the United States and likewise granted concessions to Great Britain in the matter of neutral rights. As a step toward regaining French ascendancy in America he recommended the acquisition of Louisiana. This province, in his opinion, would "furnish France the best entrepôt in North America, raw material and a market for her manufactures, a monopoly of the products of the American states on the Mississippi, and a means of pressure upon the United States."[1] But at Basel (July, 1795), where terms of peace were agreed upon between France and Spain, Godoy remained obdurate in his refusal to cede Louisiana. It was at this juncture that he determined to yield to the demands of the United States, fearing the loss of the Spanish colonies through a joint attack by an American and English force.

French diplomats redoubled their efforts to gain Louisiana as a base for the support of their West Indian possessions. A memoir submitted to Delacroix, minister of foreign relations, declared:

If the Anglo-Americans possess these rich countries they would become masters of the Gulf of Mexico. They would have everything in their hands to create a formidable marine power which, in their service,

---

Nicholas, and Innes to be used in the formation of a confederation of the western country which should be independent of the Atlantic states. Gayarré, p. 360.

[1] *American Historical Review*, X, No. 2, 265, 266.

would make all the commerce of America and of our colonies dependent upon them. It is not necessary, then, to demonstrate that the Anglo-Americans would become strong at our expense and would seize upon the richest provinces. On the other hand, it is desirable for us to rival them in negotiating for Louisiana. . . . . By the acquisition of this country we should have, in abundance, timber for building, pasturage for animals, rice, indigo, cotton, peltries, and a thousand other valuable products which would be at the ports of our colonies. We would then be more powerful in the New World than in Europe; we would attach the Americans to our political existence; they would be forced to observe strictly the treaties with France.[1]

In these words we see clearly set forth the motives underlying the future plans of Talleyrand and of Napoleon.

Throughout the year 1796 France strove to induce Spain to agree to the cession of Louisiana, but to this suggestion the "Prince of Peace" turned a deaf ear, although consenting to a treaty of alliance. The French policy which gradually took shape included a continuation of these negotiations, an attempt to break the friendly relations between Great Britain and the United States, and the suspension of diplomatic relations with the United States.

As a first move, during the winter of 1795, Colonel Fulton, the associate of Clark, was sent by Adet, the new French minister to America, to consult with Clark and intrigue with the Indians of the Southwest. In March he authorized General Victor Collot, a French military observer, to make a survey of the defenses and lines of communication west of the Alleghanies. On his trip down the Ohio and the Mississippi Collot pointed out to certain men in whom he had confidence the advantages of a French alliance. He referred to the Alleghanies as destined at some time in the future to become the limits of the Atlantic states.[2] He visited the Illinois villages and gave a somber picture

[1] September, 1796. *Affaires Étrangeres, États-Unis*, XLVII, 180.
[2] Victor Collot, *Voyage dans L'Amerique Septentrionale*, I, 40.

of the French inhabitants who "were indolent, lazy and addicted to drunkenness, cultivating the earth but little or not at all. . . . . Should it be suggested to them to change anything for the better, ... their only answer is: it is the custom; so it was with our fathers. I get along with it —so of course will my children."[1] In his report, which was to constitute the basis for French thought until Louisiana finally passed under jurisdiction of the United States, Collot referred to the posts on the left bank of the Mississippi as wholly inadequate for the defense of Louisiana without the alliance of the western states. New Orleans, with its five miniature forts more like playthings intended for babies than military defenses, would fall before a vigorous assault.[2] "I conclude," he wrote, "that the Western states of the North American republic must unite themselves with Louisiana and form in the future one single compact nation; else that colony to whatever power it shall belong will be conquered or devoured."

It is significant that while Collot was marking out the lines for a French invasion of the Mississippi Valley, Washington, in his farewell address, was warning the West that their future prosperity was dependent upon the protection of the general government. "Will they not henceforth be deaf to those advisers, if such there are, who would sever them from their brethren and connect them with aliens?"[3]

Relations between Great Britain and Spain becoming more strained, rumors were current that in the event of war an expedition was to be sent from Canada against Louisiana. With the declaration of war by Spain, in the fall of 1796, English agents became more aggressive in their efforts to gain recruits among American frontiersmen for an expedition against Spanish possessions. Clark informed

[1] Collot, *Voyage*, I, 319.   [2] *Ibid.*, II, 129.
[3] Richardson, *Messages of the Presidents*, I, 217.

Fulton, who was then in Paris, that a representative of the governor of Canada had proposed that he should "march at the head of two thousand men against Spanish New Mexico." Another wing of the army was to descend the Mississippi from St. Louis. Clark refused to consider the proposal.[1]

Panic seized Carondelet and Gayoso, governor at Natchez, when they learned of the affair, and they set to work with feverish haste at strengthening their defenses. An effort to gain the assistance of Wilkinson seemingly failed, although a Spanish agent during the summer of 1797, bearing "letters on business from New Orleans" to the then Major-General, visited him at Detroit.[2] No hope was to be gotten by Spanish officials out of the reply, by other supposed friends, to the approaches of this emissary. "We have seen the communication made by you to Mr. Sebastian," they wrote. "We will not be concerned either directly or indirectly in any attempt that may be made to separate the Western country from the United States. That whatever part we may at any time be induced to take in the politics of our country, that her welfare will be our only inducement and that we will never receive any pecuniary or other reward for any personal exertion made by us to promote that welfare."[3]

[1] This proposal was probably not connected with the plan of William Blount, United States senator from Tennessee, in which an attack on New Orleans was contemplated by a force to be made up of Canadians, frontiersmen, and Indians, in concert with the English fleet. During the summer of 1797 the plot was exposed and Blount was expelled from the Senate, the vote lacking one of being unanimous.

[2] It was generally understood that this agent, Dr. Thomas Power, an Irishman naturalized in Spain, brought money from Carondelet to Wilkinson and Sebastian. Wilkinson went through the form of having Power arrested, but he soon made his escape. *Harry Innes Papers*, September 14, 1797 (Library of Congress), XIX, 74.

[3] George Nicholas and Harry Innes to Thomas Power. *Harry Innes Papers*, XIX, 74. All of those whose names had been associated with the Spanish intrigue

Explicit denial was made by Robert Liston, English minister to the United States, of any plan for an expedition from Canada against the Spanish possessions. Such designs, he declared, were fashioned in the imagination of the Marques de Casa Yrujo, Spanish minister to the United States, who made the charge.[1] In spite of his professed ignorance, Liston was familiar with the main features of the plan, even though he refused to give it official countenance. The British government asserted that no such plan had been formed.

But this incident served as pretext for further delay in carrying out the terms of the treaty of San Lorenzo. It was not before March 21, 1798, upon the order of Godoy and the telling effect of the appearance of an additional detachment of United States troops, that the Spanish, shortly after, retired under cover of the night.[2] The next morning

---

were now weaned of that connection save Wilkinson and Sebastian, the chief conspirators.

[1] His explanation is presented in an article which I wrote, "Louisiana as a Factor in American Diplomacy," *Miss. Valley Hist. Rev.*, I, 44-56. See also Turner, "The Policy of France toward the Mississippi Valley in the Period of Washington and Adams," *American Historical Review*, X, No. 2, 274. Timothy Pickering, secretary of state, was convinced that "no such expedition is or has been contemplated by the British," and that it was a creature of the imagination of the Spanish minister. Pickering MSS, Department of State, August 30, 1797. It is interesting to note, however, that Liston gave an audience to Captain Chisolm, one of Blount's associates, and paid his passage to England. This was done, according to Liston, because of "the probability of the cession of Louisiana to the French by the Spaniards and the serious consequences that must attend it together with the advantages which might accrue to his majesty's interests from even a temporary possession of that country are considerations that struck me as being of such importance as to render it improper for me to discourage the idea of his voyage." March 16, 1797. Public Record Office, F. O. R., *America*, Vol. XVIII.

[2] A good account of the effort to gain possession of the posts by Andrew Ellicott, United States commissioner, is to be found in Franklin L. Riley's "Spanish Policy in Mississippi after the Treaty of San Lorenzo," *Report Amer. Hist. Assoc.* (1897), pp. 183-92. Also Winsor, *The Westward Movement*, pp. 565 ff.

the American flag was run up. This event marks the beginning of the rapid decay of Spanish continental power in the New World.

Meantime, by the close of the year 1796, Fulton, with renewed hope for success in the collection of debts due Clark, again appeared before the Directory. While giving information as to the best time to occupy Louisiana, he assured them that Clark and his old soldiers were still loyal to France. If they were provided with the necessary arms, ammunition, and uniforms, he declared, "France will find itself in the vast regions which the Republic will possess."[1]

At that time Clark was suffering severely, we are told, from periodic attacks of rheumatism.[2] Unfavorable reports, by his brothers, on the lawsuits brought against him and of their inability to secure an adjustment of his claims against Virginia tended still further to depress his spirits.[3] Among the suits in which he was defendant, during the summer of 1797, was one brought by Humphrey Marshall for the first payment on land "at Tennessee"; one for 3,000 pounds with the heirs of Captain William Shannon, who had served as commissary for the western department, and another "for 24,000 dollars against him, in Illinois, by Bazadone, the Spaniard, for the seizure of his goods at Vincennes (1786).[4] William Clark declared that within twelve months he had been forced to ride 3,000 miles on horseback in attempting to protect the interests of his brother. After the dismissal of the Spanish suit and the securing of his brother's property north of the Ohio, William

---

[1] Turner, "Policy of France towards the Mississippi Valley," *American Historical Review*, X, No. 2, 271.

[2] Draper MSS, Jonathan Clark Papers, II, 45.

[3] Jonathan Clark continued to appeal to the assembly of Virginia. William Clark was giving his attention to the cases before the courts.

[4] William Clark to Edmund Clark, August 18, 1797. Draper MSS, 2 L 45.

was himself forced to forego any further effort on account of the depletion of his own funds.

Fulton's appeal to the Directory for money was once more futile, but the commission "brigadier general, without activity," was bestowed on Clark, on the theory that it was to French interests to foster among the westerners a favorable attitude toward France. "In case we shall be put in possession of Louisiana," Delacroix states, "the affections of those regions will serve us in our political plans toward the United States."[1]

While the title was to prove an empty one for Clark, and one which was, as we shall see, to bring additional reproaches upon him, the fact of its bestowal constitutes a key to the objective of French leaders. What this goal was, the methods to be used in its accomplishment, and their relation to the future welfare of the United States needs here to be related, at least in outline.

[1] May 26, 1797. Report of Delacroix to the Directory. *Affaires Étrangeres États-Unis*, XLVII, 305–8.

CHAPTER XIX

Louisiana Continues To Be the Chief Factor in International Affairs

VICTORIOUS in Europe, France had determined to overcome any advantage gained by Great Britain through the Jay treaty, which, as interpreted, was but a step toward a treaty of alliance between Great Britain and the United States. Her acts seemed to indicate the desire to bring about a revolution in the United States which would eventually produce the dissolution of the Union.[1] This accomplished, the setting up of a French protectorate would be the next step.[2] For the foundation of such an American colonial empire the Directory, toward the close of the year 1796, considered the following proposals: to secure Canada by conquest, to acquire Louisiana by cession or through the retransfer of French Santo Domingo to Spain,[3] to send a powerful armament to New Orleans.[4]

---

[1] Bernard C. Steiner, *The Life and Correspondence of James McHenry* (Cleveland, 1907), pp. 228, 246, 256. John Quincy Adams, American minister at the Hague, wrote, March 3, 1794: "They have vowed the destruction of the American government and are desirous to ascertain whether the American people will assist them in the laudable work. If not, the people will share their animosity with the government, and both will be forced into a war. . . . . But my concern is for my country, and for the interests of humanity." *Writings of John Quincy Adams*, ed. W. C. Ford, II, 68, 82.

[2] *Writings of Adams*, II, 111.

[3] The eastern portion had been acquired by France by the treaty of Basel, July 22, 1795.

[4] *Writings of Adams*, II, 20, 31, 128, note.

Scarcely were the ceremonies connected with the inauguration of President John Adams, who, as Hamilton said, "had been elected by a miracle," over, when it was learned that France had severed diplomatic relations with the United States by summarily refusing to receive Charles Cotesworth Pinckney as minister. A special session of Congress was called (May 15, 1797). Laws were passed providing for the raising and equipping of an army and a fleet and for the loans and additional taxes necessary in preparation for war with France. Nevertheless, the President was still ready to continue negotiations, and sent a commission to Paris for that purpose composed of C. C. Pinckney, John Marshall, and Elbridge Gerry. Upon arrival, they found Charles Maurice de Talleyrand, formerly bishop of Autun, master of the French foreign policy.

His travels in America, whither he had come, in order to save his head, during the Jacobin régime, had convinced him of the future importance of Louisiana. Three months before taking up the duties of his office he pointed out the advantages which would accrue to France through the acquisition of that territory as a colony.[1]

These arguments were made familiar to the Directors through proposals, many times repeated, by their representatives in the United States. Létombe, claiming confidential relations with Vice-President Jefferson, declared that the Directory should carry out a policy of temporization in dealing with the representatives of the United States, for Adams will be president for only four years and the seductions around the people will soon end.[2] "By negotiation and delay," he says, "France and Spain will have time to arrange for Louisiana and Canada and put up a dam which without them would submerge Mexico, Peru,

[1] *American Historical Review*, X, 275.

[2] *Affaires Étrangeres, États-Unis*, XLVIII, 420.

and all their islands. A double barrier to the ambition of the United States and England must be established at once, for in a few years it will be too late."[1] "I have said to you as well as to others," another official writes, "that Louisiana and Florida are indispensable to the establishment of our colonies, for the building up of our commerce, our manufactures, and our marine; . . . . that upper Louisiana, once well peopled, will be a check against the Americans—a people active, ambitious, and enterprising."[2] In the event of war he declared that Kentucky and Tennessee, devoted to Thomas Jefferson, would observe strict neutrality.[3]

Day after day the American commissioners waited for some indication from the French government regarding the opening of negotiations. No official recognition of their presence had been given, but it was intimated through mysterious agents that the way might be paved if a sum of money ($250,000) were paid to the Directors and to Talleyrand and a loan should be made by the United States to the French government. "No, no, not a sixpence," was the indignant reply.[4]

Early in March the first dispatches announcing the failure of the commissioners to secure recognition from France arrived in America. In a communication to Congress the President declared that he would "never send

[1] *Ibid.*, XLVIII, 389.

[2] A. Sachouse, special agent in the United States on behalf of Santo Domingo to Delacroix, March 9, 1797. *Affaires Étrangeres, États-Unis*, XLVII, 151.

[3] *Ibid.*, p. 152.

[4] It is stated by Whitelaw Reid in his Introduction to the *Memoirs of Talleyrand* that "his venality was so notorious and so monstrous that Napoleon denounced him for it again and again." He continues: "In the life of Talleyrand by Louis Bastide, published in 1838, a few months after Talleyrand's death, a table is given of his receipts for three years, amounting in all to 14,650,000 francs." Whitelaw Reid, *Memoirs of Talleyrand*, I, xviii.

another minister to France without assurances that he will be received, respected, and honored as the representative of a great free, powerful, and independent nation." Publication of the dispatches in which the letters X, Y, Z, were substituted for the names of the French emissaries aroused intense excitement throughout the country. War fever ran high. "Millions for defense, but not one cent for tribute," uttered as a toast, became a slogan.[1]

War addresses poured in from the trading centers, that from Philadelphia having five thousand signatures. Young men of New York, Boston, and other cities, and students of the colleges formed "associations" and prepared addresses in which they offered their lives in the service of their country. Twelve hundred young men of Philadelphia, each wearing the black cockade in his hat, the symbol of Americanism, marched to the President's house with their addresses. They were received by President Adams in person, who also wore the black cockade. But the Republicans were by no means silenced. They set up liberty poles, wore the tricolored cockade, and burned the President in effigy.[2]

New regiments were added to the army. Supervision of the navy was taken from the War Department and the Department of the Navy was created under the direction of a secretary. Washington was appointed commander of the army, but Hamilton, as major general, was to be in actual command. "Our Naval War with France" went on although there was no declaration of war on either side.[3] Eighty-five vessels were captured by our navy.

[1] This was toast number thirteen offered at a banquet which was tendered John Marshall in Philadelphia on his return from France. *Philadelphia Gazette*, June 25, 1798.

[2] *Life and Correspondence of Rufus King*, ed. Charles Rufus King (New York, 1894).

[3] Gardner W. Allen, *Our Naval War with France* (Boston, 1909). This volume gives a good account of the influence of our navy at this time.

The excitement became more pervasive during the summer of 1798 because of the belief that the French were preparing to invade America. Such an attack, if it should be made, would be directed, Washington thought, toward the South, for the reason that the greater number of their friends were in that section of America, and "because they will be more contiguous to their islands and to Louisiana, if they should be possessed thereof; which they will be if they can."[1]

Early in May plans for an alliance between Great Britain and the United States seemed promising. Munitions of war were tendered and it was proposed that a portion of her fleet, manned by American seamen, with British officers, should be used for the protection of American commerce.[2] Liston was instructed to state that any proposals for concert and co-operation would be cordially received by Great Britain, that guns were to be loaned or sold to the United States, that engagements entered into would be scrupulously fulfilled even though Great Britain and France should come to terms, and that on all occasions the minister was to disclaim any desire, on the part of his government, to bind the United States to any permanent system of alliance for general purposes.[3] To what extent these favorable proposals by the British government were linked with the project of Francisco de Miranda, in which Hamilton was much interested, for the revolutionizing of Spanish

[1] Washington to Pickering. Alexander Hamilton, *Works*, ed. H. C. Lodge (New York, 1886), VI, 319. *Life and Correspondence of Rufus King*, ed. Charles Rufus King (New York, 1894), II, 294, 295, 301, 302, 308.

[2] British Public Record Office, F. O. R., *America*, XVIII, 2. "His majesty has been graciously pleased to consent to this request of the American government on condition that the cannon shall be returned into his majesty's stores at Halifax whenever his Majesty shall think proper to require them" (*ibid.*, p. 22).

[3] *Ibid.*, Vol. XXII, October, 1798; December, 1798.

America can only be conjectured.[1] By the close of September, however, it was clear that for the time being there was to be no alliance with Great Britain.[2] Should Spain be permitted by France to maintain absolute neutrality in relation to the United States, the project for the seizure of Louisiana and the Floridas was to be suspended.[3]

By the middle of June (1798), Timothy Pickering, secretary of state, took satisfaction in declaring: "The Rubicon is passed, war is inevitable, negotiation is at an end."[4] "Hail, Columbia," a song composed at the time, was the favorite on public occasions. The Federalists, in Congress, assisted by many Republican votes, were able to secure the adoption of a thorough program of war legislation, but this served to arouse fierce denunciation of the government on the part of the minority. The campaign of abuse by public speech and through the press was enhanced through the utterances of many radical foreigners, French fugitives, the total number in the United States being estimated at 30,000, English refugees, and Irish exiles.[5] To conservatives such expressions of democratic frenzy were inter-

---

[1] W. S. Robertson, "Francisco de Miranda," *Report Amer. Hist. Assoc.* (1907), I, 317–25. Turner, "Policy of France," *American Historical Review*, X, 276, 277.

[2] Public Record Office, *America*, Vol. XXII, September 27, 1798.

[3] "Ought not Mr. King to inform the British cabinet without loss of time, that the United States can in no event permit New Orleans to pass from the hands of Spain, unless to become a possession and part of the United States." McHenry to Pickering, July 22, 1798. Bernard C. Steiner, *Life and Correspondence of McHenry*, p. 315.

[4] Pickering MSS, *Mass. Hist. Soc. Colls.*, VIII, 580. Finding negotiation impossible, Marshall and Pinckney left Paris. Against the remonstrances of his colleagues, Gerry remained, on invitation from Talleyrand, under the mistaken notion that he would be able to preserve peace between the two nations. President Adams ordered him to return.

[5] George Gibbs, *Memoirs of the Administrations of Washington and Adams* (New York, 1846), II, 77.

preted as germs of anarchy. The Federalists sought to meet this situation through repressive legislation. Two alien acts were passed. The first of these, limited to two years, authorized the President to order any alien whom he deemed dangerous to the peace and safety of the United States to depart within a given time or be liable to imprisonment for a term not exceeding three years. The second, or Alien Enemies Act, gave the President authority to deport all subjects of governments at war with the United States or to prescribe the conditions under which they were to be allowed to remain. The Sedition Act, after the passage of which the Federalist party went gradually toward its downfall, provided especially for the punishment of any persons by fine and imprisonment who should conspire to oppose any measures of the government, or who should, by writing, printing, or uttering anything "false scandalous and malicious" against the government, Congress, or President of the United States, bring them into disrepute.

The alien bill pending before Congress was referred to by Jefferson as legislation worthy of the eighth or ninth century.[1] As a candidate for election to the House of Representatives, John Marshall stated that the alien and sedition bills were "calculated to create unnecessarily, discontents and jealousies at a time when our very existence, as a nation, may depend on our union."[2] The statement has gone unchallenged that while President Adams did not veto the alien acts, he was only slightly interested in them; that they were never enforced; but that a number of French refugees fled while the Alien Enemies Act was pending.[3]

[1] Jefferson Papers, Library of Congress, Vol. CIV.

[2] Beveridge, *The Life of John Marshall*, II, 389.

[3] See Edward Channing, *History of the United States*, IV, 223. There were ten convictions under the Sedition Act.

Judged by the following testimony of Clark, there was one case under these acts with which he was unfortunately familiar. Early in June, 1798, he visited Philadelphia, under the conviction, as he states, that the United States was about to be plunged into a perilous position by an English faction which dominated the government, and that war with France—"the generous nation to which every American owes his liberty"—was inevitable. No sooner had he reached the capital than he was threatened with imprisonment. Later on he was informed that he must either resign his commission in the French army or quit the United States. Having refused to comply with the first part of the request, and meeting with no satisfactory reply from the French consul regarding his suggestion of taking up residence in France, Clark turned to the minister of Spain, who as he wrote, "immediately offered me all the protection which a friend and ally of France could to one of her officers." Returning to Kentucky he was confronted with an order for his arrest, purporting to come from the President of the United States. Volunteers from among his former followers, collected for his defense, disarmed the officers attempting to serve the writ, while Clark made good his escape to St. Louis.[1]

[1] These statements are to be found in two letters of June 3 and September 9, 1798. Samuel Fulton, then in Paris, sent them to the Directors. *Affaires Étrangeres, États-Unis,* Vol. XLVIII, fol. 130. *Ibid.,* Vol. L, fol. 221; *ibid.,* fol. 376. See Appendix V, pp. 511–15. It is difficult to reconcile this incident with the interpretation of Pickering given shortly before. On August 28 he wrote the attorney of the district of Pennsylvania: "Judge Peters thinks there are some dangerous aliens in the neighborhood of Philadelphia who require his and your attention. I shall be happy to do anything to Aid the measures you shall think proper respecting them." *Domestic Letters,* Department of State, XI, 64. On the same day he replied to communications from President Adams received August 16, 17, and 18: "The idea which then occurred to me was that the person referred to and all Similar characters were objects of the Alien Law and ought to be sent out of the country, but an embarrassment will arise, I have been apprehensive,

Evidence is abundant that Clark, when he wrote of the control of the American government by an English faction, that the detractors of France had been won by English gold, and that there was grave danger to American liberty in an Anglo-American alliance, was expressing the views of large numbers of Republicans throughout the country, and especially of his friends and other men prominent in Kentucky. Attention was frequently called to the rapid propagation of Anglo-monarchical-aristocratical principles, and the demand was insistent for a united effort in the frustration of the wicked designs of the enemies of the doctrine of equality and the rights of man.[1] A year earlier Jefferson wrote of the endeavors of the Republican party to unite our destinies with those of Great Britain and to assimilate our government to theirs: "Our lenity in permitting the return of the old tories gave the first body to this party; they have been increased by large importations of British merchants and factors, by American merchants dealing on British capital, and by stock dealers and banking companies who, by the aid of a paper system, are enriching themselves to the ruin of our country, and swaying the government by their possession of the printing presses."[2]

"We were in hopes a greater degree of unanimity had prevailed in your country in support of government," a letter from Philadelphia states, "and cannot account for the backwardness of your citizens relinquishing their attachment to the French and their measures, except from the circumstance of their being kept very much in igno-

---

out of the law itself, in its not authorizing the Executive to apprehend and confine or require sureties for their going until they can be sent off, or that they depart from the United States" (*ibid.*).

[1] John Page to Thomas Jefferson, Jefferson Papers, Library of Congress, p. 104.

[2] *Writings of Jefferson*, VII, 169, 170.

rance of what has passed. We are told all your printers publish only what is in favor of the French faction."[1]

During the summer many memorials appeared, the fruit of county mass meetings throughout the state. In general there was unanimity in the condemnation of the alien law, "inhuman, unjust, unconstitutional and degrading to the American character," and of the measures of the national government looking toward war with France.[2] Such a war, impolitic and unjust, would, they declared, bring America into the political entanglements of Europe and thus endanger our liberties and independence.[3] No lasting happiness was to be anticipated so long as the administration of government was dominated by the commercial class to the manifest disadvantage of those engaged in agricultural pursuits. The climax seems to have been reached with expressions such as: "that under the full influence of the principles which actuated the Americans of 1776, we solemnly declare before God and man,

[1] *Kentucky Palladium* (Lexington), August 3, 1798. The statement was denied by the editor, who gave a list of the documents which had been published.

[2] "Republicans ought not to despair," one of Kentucky's most representative men declared; "the Irish are fighting for us. The French can never be conquered and woe be to those who foolishly mistake the convulsive struggles of expiring Despotism, in England, for a renovation of healthful spirits and nationa vigor." Doctor Samuel Brown to Jefferson, *Jefferson Papers*, Library of Congress, p. 104.

[3] Lexington, August 29, 1798. From the resolutions of Bourbon County citizens, *Kentucky Palladium*. That these expressions were not materially different from those of the opposition elsewhere may be gathered from an expression in one of the representative newspapers. "Who favor war with France?" is the query propounded in the *Boston Independent Chronicle* for July 16, 1798. "Are not some of them bankrupt Speculators, a few of whom have been negotiating Georgia lands and expect to relieve themselves by throwing all into confusion? Among the number, are there not men who are seeking lucrative appointments? Who enjoy and anticipate agencies, contracts, building ships, Commissions in the Army and navy? Are they not the remnants of the enemies to our Revolution; the English agents who in multitudes reside in every seaport of the United States?"

that we will despise the man and oppose the measure that
leads to an embrace with the corrupt government of Great
Britain."[1] Here, then, was fallow ground for the seed of
opposition sown by Jefferson through his Kentucky resolutions.[2]

That these men were not hostile to the Union and were
opposed to insurrection and revolt is manifest from the
letter of one with whom the charge of conspiracy has heretofore been associated. There could be no reason why the
Vice-President should not be a sharer in the inmost thought
of John Brown, expressed as follows: "The [people of Ken-
tucky] are warmly attached to the Union & to the Constitution of the States but they are equally determined to defend their Rights & to resist every attempt to violate the
fundamental principles of their freedom."[3]

During the summer of 1798, while still at Louisville,
Clark prepared a lengthy statement on the celebrated
speech of Chief Logan. This was in response to criticisms
which had been made on the accuracy of certain portions
of *The Notes on Virginia*, written by Jefferson. Clark's
letter served not only as a defense of Jefferson but has al-

[1] From the *Kentucky Mirror*, August 27, 1798.

[2] Under the influence of Jefferson the legislatures of Kentucky and Virginia
(1798) each passed a series of resolutions condemning the Alien and Sedition
acts as "unconstitutional, void, and of no force," and asserting the right and
duty of the states to interpose and "arrest the progress of the evil." The more
moderate Virginia resolutions were prepared by Madison. Jefferson was the
author of the Kentucky resolutions. The legislatures of the other states refused
to sanction these resolutions. The legislature of Kentucky (1799) passed a still
stronger set of resolutions declaring the states to be sovereign and independent,
and "that a nullification by those sovereignties, of all unauthorized acts done
under color of that instrument [the Constitution] is the rightful remedy." It is
notable that *nullification* by a single state is not sanctioned. Madison denied this
doctrine. But the sectionalists of New England (1814), South Carolina (1832),
and those who favored secession (1861) claimed support in these resolutions.

[3] September 15, 1798. Jefferson Papers, Library of Congress, Vol. CIV.

ways been cited as proof that Logan actually delivered the speech.[1]

He was still hopeful that the Directory, even after the lapse of five years, would compensate him in part for services for which he had not as yet received "a single sou." For he was fully persuaded, as he wrote, that a person who had given so much evidence of attachment to a cause would not be forgotten or neglected at a time so important.[2]

Moreover, the statement seems warranted that Clark was aware of the attitude of French leaders toward the possession of Louisiana. As we shall see, this continued to be the dominating interest in their kaleidoscopic diplomatic dealings with America. This objective accomplished, could he have hoped to re-establish his economic independence, and on a new frontier regain that military preferment which had once been his—for he was then only forty-six years of age?

While residing in St. Louis he was interested in observing the means for defense, the number of troops, some two thousand, in upper Louisiana wholly inadequate for resisting invasion. Neither the inhabitants nor the army were, he thought, attached to Spain, and in the event of a war with the United States, Louisiana could be taken with ease. "If the Executive Directory desires to possess Louisiana, there is no time to lose," he writes. "In nine months, at most, it will be too late, this country will be conquered by America or England."[3] Here was a suggestion in keeping with the significant "negotiation and delay" message of Létombe.[4]

Turning to France, we find Talleyrand continuing to play at negotiation with Gerry. "It would be only with

---

[1] See Appendix IV, pp. 502–10.   [2] Letter, June 3, 1798.

[3] Letter of September 9, 1798. *Affaires Étrangeres, États Unis,* Vol. L, fol. 221.

[4] Létombe to Delacroix, June 18, 1797. *Ibid.,* Vol. XLVII, fol. 389.

serious inconveniences," he said, "to break at once with the United States, while our present situation, half friendly, half hostile is profitable to us, in that our colonies continue to be provisioned by the Americans and our cruisers are enriched by captures made from them."[1]

Moreover, he was gaining time for furthering his negotiations for Louisiana, and to that end his agent, Guillemardet, was attempting to carry out his instructions at Madrid. Spain was to be made to realize her error in surrendering the forts on the Mississippi, thereby sacrificing her defense against the encroachment of the Americans upon her colonies.[2] The United States were to be shut up "within the limits which nature seems to have traced for them." Spain is not in condition to do this great work alone, but Louisiana and the Floridas, as French possessions, "would be a wall of brass forever impenetrable to the combined efforts of England and America."[3] By July 10, 1798, Talleyrand was able to report a yielding on the part of Spain and her increasing favor toward the plan of having French troops, rather than Spanish, meet the expected invasion of Louisiana by England and the United States.[4] There were other significant influences which tended to bring about peaceful relations between France and the United States.

A month before Talleyrand's induction into office, Louis-Guillaume Otto, who for a dozen years had resided in the United States as secretary to Luzerne, French minister, and as chargé des affaires, presented for the consideration of

---

[1] G. Pollain, *Le Ministere de Talleyrand sous le Directoire* (Paris, 1891), p. 309.

[2] Henry Adams, *History of the United States*, I, 355.

[3] Compare with the language of Létombe, June, 1797.

[4] Turner, "Policy of France," *American Historical Review*, X, 276.

the minister of foreign affairs an extended report which must have contributed materially toward bringing about a better understanding between the two nations.[1]

During the month of May, Victor du Pont, formerly French consul at Charleston, was sent as consul-general to the United States. President Adams refused his exequatur, and after an interview with Jefferson he returned to France. In his report to Talleyrand he demonstrated that it would be to the interest of France, by all means within her power, to avoid war with the United States.[2] Talleyrand asked for facts, and Du Pont replied that there were so many it was difficult to make a choice, since the acts of violence, brigandage, and piracy committed by French cruisers or under the French flag in American seas would fill many volumes. The report showed unmistakable evidence that Talleyrand's whole plan for American colonial power was in

[1] Delacroix was then minister of foreign relations. The report was entitled, "Considerations on the Conduct of the Government of the United States toward France, 1789–1797," *Affaires Étrangeres, États-Unis*, Vol. XLVII, fols. 401–18. For years after his return to France Otto received marked governmental favor. He accompanied Sieyés to Berlin as secretary of legation (1798), and it was chiefly through his efforts that the preliminaries for the peace of Amiens (1801) were brought to a successful issue. Continuing to serve as counselor extraordinary in the Department of Foreign Affairs, he represented France as minister at Munich and as ambassador at Vienna. He negotiated the marriage between Marie Louise and Napoleon, and was named minister of state and made Compte de Mosloy by Napoleon. I called attention to the influence of Otto and a number of other French leaders in bringing about peace between France and the United States in a paper read before the American Historical Association (1924), "French Opinion as a Factor in Preventing War between France and the United States, 1795–1800," *American Historical Review*, Vol. XX.

[2] Du Pont's first dispatch to Talleyrand was from Bordeaux, July 6, 1798. *Affaires Étrangeres, États-Unis*, Vol. L, fol. 8. I first called attention to the influence of Du Pont in an article, "Louisiana and American Diplomacy," *Miss. Valley Hist. Rev.*, I (June, 1914), 44–56. The *Memoire* and correspondence were published (November, 1915) in *Mass. Hist. Soc. Proc.* (ed. S. G. Morison), XLIV, 63.

danger. Basing his opinion on "confidential conversations" with Jefferson, Du Pont argued that it would not be prudent to throw the power of America into the balance with England, for that would mean the loss of American commerce to France; that a war between the two republics would cause the United States to sacrifice their liberty through an alliance with Great Britain and would enhance the maritime strength of the latter power. France and Spain would be forced to sacrifice their colonies; Mexico would be exposed; and England would become doubly powerful. He argued that a policy of justice and moderation should be adopted in treating with America. To this end the acts of French privateers were to be disavowed and their commissions retired; the laws against neutrals were to be revised; and the American government was to be informed that a new commission sent to Paris, Holland, or Spain would be received. These were likewise the opinions, he declared, of other leaders, associates of Jefferson, and if this policy were adopted the Republican party would be victorious in the approaching presidential elections.[1]

These arguments and the further influence of Du Pont on French public opinion have been stated to be the cause for the steps leading to a friendly disposition toward the United States.[2] While it is evident that Talleyrand was possessed of the facts in the controversy and had reached conclusions similar to those of Du Pont, he hastened to take advantage of this *Memoire*.[3]

---

[1] July 21, 1798. *Affaires Étrangeres, États-Unis,* Vol. L, fol. 99.

[2] *Writings of John Quincy Adams,* ed. Ford, II, 361, 362.

[3] On June 1 he prepared a report to the Directory in which he urged the policy of temporizing in order to produce a Republican victory in the coming elections. Morison, *Mass. Hist. Soc. Proc.* (November, 1915), Vol. LXXVI, notes.

On July 21 Talleyrand used it as the foundation of an appeal to the Directory to remove all causes for fermentation, and ten days later a decree was passed restraining French privateers in the West Indies within the limits of the laws.[1] This decree was received by Gerry on the eve of his embarkation for America. It was accompanied by a personal note from Talleyrand stating that it was within the power of the United States to cause all misunderstandings between the two nations to disappear.[2] A dispatch sent by Létombe was not without weight at this time. In it he discussed the great activity in preparing for war and the evidence that an alliance was developing between the United States and Great Britain which, accomplished, would inevitably lead to the invasion of the Floridas and Louisiana and the independence of the French colonies.[3]

Some days earlier, William Vans Murray, American minister at The Hague, was visited by Pichon, French secretary of legation, and informed that the French were solicitous for an accommodation with America.[4] This interview, interpreted by Murray as a ruse to get him into informal negotiation, was followed by others. Finally, a communication from Talleyrand on September 28, which

[1] In a letter to his mother, John Quincy Adams wrote: "Dupont gave it as his opinion that rupture would only strengthen the English party and English influence in America, and that the true patriots, French and American, wished rather for conciliatory measures on the part of France. From that moment the French government have affected a friendly disposition toward the United States." *Writings of Adams*, ed. Ford, II, 361, 362.

[2] August 8, 1798. *Affaires Étrangeres, États-Unis*, Vol. L, fol. 147.

[3] June 19, 1798. *Ibid.*, XLIX, fol. 462.

[4] Murray to President Adams, July 17, 1798. J. Adams, *Works*, VIII, 679, 687. Pichon declared that an American war would be highly unpopular in France, and that her colonies would be in danger should it occur. Pichon, as secretary to Genet and Fauchet, had become acquainted with Murray in Philadelphia.

was sent to Murray, declared that any minister sent by the United States to France would be "received with the respect due to a representative of a free, independent, and powerful nation."[1] The appointment of a second commission consisting of William Vans Murray, Oliver Ellsworth, chief justice, and William R. Davie, governor of North Carolina, and the results of their labor in bringing about the Convention of 1800 will be discussed at another time.[2] The arguments by Talleyrand in favor of a friendly reception to this commission by the French government were stated as follows: that the power of the Republican party will thereby be increased; that the alliance, both offensive and defensive, between Great Britain and the United States will be made impossible; and that the Americans will be prevented from carrying out their plan for war against Spain, whereby they will be enabled to seize Louisiana.[3] Among the other objects urged in his report to Napoleon on the need for reconciliation were: security for the French and Spanish insular possessions; the desirability of developing trade relations with the Americans, thereby depriving the English of this source of gain, since the ship-

---

[1] *Affaires Étrangeres États–Unis*, Vol. L, fol. 233; *American State Papers, Foreign Relations*, II, 242. This language is identical with that used by President Adams in his message to Congress, June 21. Richardson, *Messages and Papers of the Presidents*, I, 266.

[2] It was my privilege, some years ago, to give the Albert Shaw Lectures at Johns Hopkins University. I selected the subject, "French-American Diplomacy during the Administrations of Presidents Washington and Adams." Publication has been delayed because of the necessity of securing supplementary material from the French archives and also on account of the intimate relation of that material with the contents of the present volume. The volume on "French-American Diplomacy, 1793–1800," will be published at an early date by the Johns Hopkins Press.

[3] Talleyrand, November 18, 1798. *Affaires Étrangeres, États-Unis*, Vol. L, fol. 127.

ping of the United States would soon be the equal of that of England. Moreover, they would aid in the creation of a rival to Great Britain, since the United States, with its rapidly growing population, great territorial possessions capable of cultivation, will ultimately be inhabited by a people greater in number than that of any European state.[1]

It is noteworthy that the day following the signing of the treaty (October 1, 1800), preliminary articles were drawn at San Ildefonso which ultimately led to the retrocession of Louisiana to France. Two years later Napoleon, sending his representative to New Orleans, referred to the fact that as the master of both banks of the Mississippi, at its mouth, France held the key to its navigation—a matter of highest importance for the western states.[2] "The inhabitants of Kentucky especially should fix the attention of the Captain General. . . . . He must also fortify himself against them by alliance with the Indian nations scattered to the east of the river."

But President Jefferson, friend of France, that he was, was not unmindful of the possibility of carrying out this policy and of its danger to the future of the United States. His interest in the West had not relaxed from that day, early in 1778, when he wished success to the young Virginia major who was setting out for the conquest of the Illinois country.[3] Now, thoroughly alarmed, he was ready to form an alliance even with Great Britain should Napoleon take possession of New Orleans. When convinced that Louisiana had been ceded to France, he instructed Robert R. Livingston, American minister in Paris, to open negotiations for

---

[1] Talleyrand to Napoleon, March 3, 1800. *Ibid.*, Vol. LI, fol. 357.

[2] Instructions to General Victor, who was to command the French forces in Louisiana. Henry Adams, *History of the United States*, II, 5-12.

[3] *Clark Papers*, p. 37.

the purchase of New Orleans and the Floridas. "The day that France takes possession of N. Orleans," he wrote, "fixes the sentence which is to restrain her forever within her low water mark. It seals the union of two nations who in conjunction can maintain exclusive possession of the ocean. From that moment we must marry ourselves to the British fleet and nation."[1]

[1] *Writings of Jefferson*, ed. Ford, VIII, 145.

Chapter XX

Last Years

I T IS not possible to fix definitely the date when Clark
returned from St. Louis. That he was at Louisville in
June, 1799, is established by a letter written by his
brother William.[1] Conditions at Mulberry Hill were greatly altered after the death of his mother in April of that
year. Three months later his father died. Jonathan and
George Rogers were among the executors of their father's
will, but to William, as chief heir, was given the home farm
with twenty-four slaves, an estate of 7,000 acres of Kentucky lands, and additional lands north of the Ohio.[2] The
bequest to George Rogers consisted only of a man and a
woman slave, for any property in his own name was subject to seizure by his creditors.

For three years he continued to live at Mulberry Hill,
but he was dependent on the generosity of his brother. Life
at best was lonely for him. He was land poor and in debt
because of advance payments made for supplies to sustain
his troops. An indebtedness to William for $2,100 was met
through the transfer of 74,000 acres of Kentucky land on
the Ohio (1803).[3] An additional 15,000 acres were disposed

[1] To Jonathan Clark, Jonathan Clark Papers, II, 50, Draper Collection. As
noted in the previous chapter, steps leading toward an understanding between
France and the United States were well under way by the close of 1798.

[2] English, *Conquest of the Northwest*, I, 46.

[3] These 73,962 acres were immediately below the mouth of the Tennessee
River. The two separate entries of June 7, 1784, and of June 8 of that year were

457

of the following year in the cancellation of another debt for 434 pounds. William finally sold his own farm and residence in order to meet the further pressing obligations of his brother.[1]

Clark was embittered at what he interpreted as ingratitude by Virginia, and he writes: "I have little hopes of ever geting anything from the State of Virginia as I find by your Letters that they are loath to come to tryall and I suppose never will."[2] Was he seeking some relief for burdens which seemed intolerable by the method with which he was already too familiar, described in the terse, pained expression of brother to brother. "I am sorry to inform you that Brother George has given up more to that vice which has been so injurious to him than ever."[3]

He continued, however, to give attention, as chairman of the Commission, to the allotment of lands to soldiers of the Illinois Regiment.

Glimpses of his life are seen also in a letter from his nephew, John O'Fallon, whom Clark adopted as his son. He writes of the coming, each year, of Indian chiefs and warriors in order to smoke the pipe of peace and friendship with their conqueror, "the first man living, the great and invincible long knife."[4] These visits were continued after

---

made because of treasury warrants granted by Virginia to Clark. The ownership, however, was in dispute, for a military warrant covering the same tract had been subsequently issued to a Colonel Porterfield, of the Virginia Continental line. Although Clark was finally awarded his claim, there remained the necessity of extinguishing the right held by the Chickasaw tribe. This was not accomplished until 1818, after his death. In the meantime the land had been sold for $30,000, but the purchaser, Charles S. Todd, failed to comply with the contract.

[1] Testimony of William Clark. Draper MSS, 5 K 255.

[2] To Jonathan Clark, January 8, 1800. Draper MSS, 2 L 53.

[3] To Jonathan Clark, June 1799, Jonathan Clark Papers, II, 50, Draper Collection.

[4] Draper MSS, 34 J 10.

he took up his residence at Clarksville (1803). This town, when founded, he had proclaimed as the commercial rival-to-be of Louisville. But it continued the typical frontier community of twenty houses with tavern and general store. Residents kept in touch with the world outside by the ferry to Louisville and the old Vincennes trace.

For six years Clark lived in this "deserted village," attending the meetings of the Commission on the Illinois Grant, taking part in the elections and other public affairs, and running a small stone grist-mill. This mill was located near his home, a log house of two rooms with gables facing up and down the river. The cabin stood on a point of land overlooking the falls—one of the most picturesque and wild spots to be found on the Ohio. Here he lived attended by his servants. Here he was visited by Josiah Espy, in 1805, who writes:

I had the pleasure of seeing this celebrated warrior at his lonely cottage seated on Clark's Point. This point is situated at the upper end of the Falls, particularly the lower rapid, commanding a full and delightful view of the falls, particularly the zigzag channel which is only navigated at high water. The general has not taken much pains to improve this commanding and beautiful spot, but it is capable of being made one of the handsomest seats in the world. General Clark has now become rather frail and helpless but there are the remains of great dignity and manliness in his countenance, person and deportment, and I was struck with perhaps a fancied likeness to the great and immortal Washington.[1]

A project, in which he was much interested, was for the construction of a canal extending from Clarksville to a point a mile and a quarter above the falls. In his application, which was granted by the trustees of the village, he provided that the control of a strip of land through which the canal was to pass should be vested in his brother Wil-

---

[1] Journal of Josiah Espy, 1805, *Ohio Valley Historical Series, Miscellaneous*, p. 14.

liam for the erection of mills, wharfs, storehouses, "or any kind of water-works that may be of public utility or for the erection of gates and locks for the passage of boats and vessels."[1] It was his estimate that the construction of the stone containing walls and a lock with a 20-foot lift would cost about $150,000. A company was incorporated and the strip of land was purchased by December, 1804, but after years of favorable consideration the plan was abandoned.[2]

Relations between the three brothers were, as already noted, most intimate.[3] It was to his youngest brother that the General appealed for the adjustment of his financial embarrassments. Their interest in military affairs was mutual, and they shared in the collection and study of the remains of extinct animals. Before his cabin there were the petrified specimens of the vertebrae and tusks of the mammoth, as he called it, and petrified fish and terrapins.[4]

Pride in his brother's ability may be seen in a letter which he wrote President Jefferson. Jefferson, jealous for the interests of the United States after the acquisition of Louisiana by France, sought to ascertain the best site for a fort at the mouth of the Ohio River. His Secretary of War submitted the inquiry to William Clark. He, in turn, passed the letter on to his brother, who, in making a direct reply to Jefferson, states the results of his observations. He then pays a tribute to his brother in language which could not have failed to arrest the attention of the President:

I suggest to you Sir, if worthy of your attention, any further information, and the best perhaps that can be obtained of that country, may be got from my brother William, who is now settled at Clarksville in the Indian Territory. I have long since laid aside all Idea of Public Affairs. By bad fortune, and ill health I have become incapable of persuing those enterpriseing active pursuits which I have been fond of from

[1] Draper MSS, 35 J 10. [2] See Lewis Collins, *Kentucky*, II, 375.
[3] Jonathan, the eldest, and William, the youngest, of the sons.
[4] Draper MSS, *Trip* 1868, IV, 25 S 136.

my youth—but I will with the greatest pleasure give my bro William every information in my power on those or any other points which may be of Service to your Administration. He is well qualified almost for any business—If it should be in your power to Confer on him any post of Honor and profit, in this Country in which we live, it will exceedingly gratify me—I seem to have a right to expect such a gratification when asked for, but what will greatly heighten it is that I am sure it gives you pleasure to have it in your power to do me a service.[1]

Evidently the application proved effective. Shortly after Captain William Clark, as the associate of Captain Meriwether Lewis and their small party of men, embarked at Clarksville (October 8, 1803)—an epochal event in the village—on their journey of exploration which was to extend "even to the Western Ocean." After the lapse of two years we find William writing of their success: "Great joy in camp, we are in view of the ocian, this great Pacific Octean which we have been so long anxious to see" (November 7, 1805).

At the same time General Clark was preparing a memorial which in equally forceful language describes the hardships undergone and states the significance of the capture of Vincennes. Without this event the triumphant note of William Clark could not have been uttered.

In his petition to Congress he asked that there should be confirmed to him a quantity of land equal in amount to the grant made in his favor by the Piankashaw tribe and their confederates in 1779. He had disclaimed title to this grant, two and a half leagues square, situated at the falls of the Ohio, but his right thereto was conceded by the unanimous vote of the Assembly of Virginia. While the question was still under consideration in the Council, the claims of the state were transferred to the federal government.

My reason [he declares] for not soliciting Congress before this, was the great number of Petitions before them, and the prospect I yet had

[1] *Ibid.*, 11 C 27.

of a future support, but those prospects are vanished. I engaged in the Revolution with all the Ardour that Youth could possess. My Zeal and Ambition rose with my success, determined to Save those Countries which had been the Seat of my toil, at the hazard of my life and fortune.

At the most gloomy period of the War, when a Ration could not be purchased on Public Credit I risked my own, gave my Bonds, Mortgaged my Lands for supplies, Paid strict attention to every department, flattered the friendly and confused the hostile tribes of Indians by my emissaries, baffled my internal enemies (the most dangerous of the whole to Public Interest) and carried my Point. Thus at the end of the War I had the pleasure of seeing my Country Secure, but with the loss of my Manual activity and a prospect of future indigence, demands of very great amount were not paid, others with depreciated Paper, Suits commenced against me for those sums in specie, My military and other lands earned by my Service as far as they would extend were appropriated for the payment of those debts, and demands yet remaining to a considerable amount more than remains of a shattered fortune will pay—this is truly my situation—I see no other resource remaining, but to make application to my Country for redress—hoping that they will so far ratify the Grant as to allow to your Memorialist an equal quantity of land now the property of the United States.[1]

In his invitation to his friend John Breckenridge, formerly senator from Kentucky, to assist in the plea before Congress, he makes it clear that he has really no regrets for the sacrifices he was called upon to make during the Revolution: "Although the quantity called for is considerable it will not more than compensate me for the losses I have actually sustained by my involving myself so imprudently in the publick expenses which I doubt without assistance I never shall get clear off, but a country was at stake, and if it was imprudence, I suppose I should do the same should I again have a similar Field to pass through."[2]

An adverse report by the Committee on Public Lands defeated the petition. The alternative request in the me-

[1] October 29, 1805. Draper MSS, 54 J 50.
[2] Draper MSS, 54 J 49.

morial, "or for such other relief as may seem proper," was likewise ineffective.

In the meager correspondence during the following three years, chiefly letters to Clark, glimpses may be gotten of his real nature. He possessed unusual power over men. In that period when Jefferson was exclaiming to Washington, "The energetic genius of Clark is not altogether unknown to you," Clark was receiving the loyal and enthusiastic support of men such as Major Joseph Bowman, outstanding military leader; of Colonel John Todd, Jr., trained lawyer and organizer of orderly civil government; of Pierre Gibault, the Kaskaskia priest; and of Gabriel Cerré, French merchant and trader, who, as Clark stated, was one of the "most eminent men in the Countrey of great influance among the people."[1] In years of retirement he secured the friendship of young men through the charm of his conversation, for he was an authority on the history, geography, and the development of the West. The founders and defenders were personally known to him. As we have seen, he was a lover of natural history. Jefferson refers to him as his chief authority on the Indian, and John J. Audubon, after a personal interview, acknowledges his indebtedness to him on bird life.[2]

"I recollect with signal pleasure and advantage my short visit to you," one young man writes: "I long to repeat it and draw a little more out of that treasure of information which is to be found nowhere else."[3]

Before returning to Clarksville, after his absence of three years, William Clark, then in St. Louis, hastened to send his brother an account of the journey to the Pacific.

[1] "Memoir," Clark Papers, 229.

[2] Writings of Jefferson, ed. Ford, VII, 223. Audubon, Birds of America, VI, 183. III, 6.

[3] October 17, 1806. Draper MSS, 55 J 73.

He gives an outline of the route taken, discusses the delay on their return due to snows in the Rocky Mountains, and describes the Indians and the products of the country passed through. He was especially interested in the large numbers of beaver seen on the way.

Early in 1808 Clark was the recipient of a letter from President Jefferson, who was interested in making a collection of the remains of extinct animals which were to be presented to the National Institute of France. With Jeffersonian precision he asks to have included the ribs, back-bones, leg-bones, thigh, horn, hips, shoulder blades, parts of upper and under jaw teeth of the mammoth and elephant. " . . . . I avail myself on this occasion," he concludes, "of recalling myself to your memory of assuring you that time has not lessened my friendship for you. We are both now grown old, you have been enjoying in retirement the recollection of the services you have rendered your country and I am about to retire without an equal consciousness that I have not occupied places in which others could have done more good; but in all places & times I shall wish you every happiness and salute you with great friendship and esteem."[1]

The breadth of his interests during these years may be seen also through the communications of two of his nephews. "All his leisure time was occupied in reading," one of them states. "His fine and extensive library which he took to Point of Rocks was by gifts and loans reduced to a mere skeleton by the year 1809." An entry in Clark's diary on the day he proposed to the Governor and Council of Virginia the conquest of the Northwest is here suggestive: "Got to Williamsburg bought 2 shirts and a Book £ 5."[2]

"He rarely, if ever, spoke of himself or of his achievements," this nephew continues. His "unselfishness was a

---

[1] December 19, 1807. English, *Conquest of the Northwest*, I, 57.

[2] "Diary," *Clark Papers*, 27.

marked characteristic and he was always willing to divide all he possessed with a friend or with those he imagined in need." These recollections of later years have their foundation in two typical schoolboy letters from the same nephew. "I am greatly Ob(liged) to you for the horse you have sent me. But I am now in as great labyrinth as before. It is uncertain when my saddle will be done. . . . . I wish you could contrive me up Uncle for I have no other resource but you. Kit says he wishes to go, but I am ashamed to ask such a thing, and nothing but necessity could Compell me to do so. Mamma is very uneasy about me, not knowing what to do, I wish Uncle you would form some plan and send me word as soon as you possibly can."[1]

Three months later he again sought relief, despite certain traditional boyish misgivings:

. . . . And you will look over my very bad writing as the pen I write with is a very bad one.[2] . . . . Nevertheless Uncle, you were never out of my mind. . . . . I have often tried to embrace an opportunity to write to you, but Uncle the weather and everything proving So much against my wishes, that I have postponed from time to time untill I am afraid you have quite given me out, and I am so situated it is very Seldome I hear of any thing remarkable and when it comes to my knowledge it has passed almost over all the state, and as to going to Lexington that is the last place I would wish to go, because I pass unnoticed by every body and as a person I suppose not worth their notice. . . . . I have never received a letter as I expected from Uncle William and I suppose you can very easily guess what has been my Situation ever since in respect to money. But Uncle William has written to Major Morrison To Furnish me with Book's and what else I may be in want of; but I am afraid it will prove as bad as ever because I have been to see the major twice, Since I heard of his receiving a letter from Uncle William respecting myself, but he was so much engaged in publick business that

[1] November 18, 1808. Draper MSS, 55 J 64. The letter was written by John O'Fallon, then in Lexington attending school. John O'Fallon became a well-known merchant in St. Louis.

[2] February 19, 1809. Draper MSS, 55 J 65.

he attended very little to me, and he said before he furnished me with those little things I said I was in need of, he must receive a note from Mr. Moore certifying my being in need of those things. I think Uncle that is rather too hard, he must certainly think me a very inconsiderate youth that knowing my income would spend more than it could afford; but I know Uncle William did it for the best. My Studies I am at present engaged in are Navigation Ferguson's lectures and the French, the latter of which I am studying with a Mr. Dupoe a man highly deserving the business he is engaged in. Mr. Moore's Family is very much distressed on account of the death of Mr. Moore the Father who departed this life on the 17th inst. he was very well known as a man of an unblemished character and the rearing of all his children to pursue the same road.

The memories revived in the mind of the uncle by the closing paragraph may be surmised. "I know of nothing worth relating except that there is a great stir in Lexington about one of the states wishing to revolt (perhaps Mas^{ts}) on account of the embargo's being prolonged."

The reply of another nephew to the request for some books was: "I have sent you the life of Fred^k. the 2nd, but I suppose you have Read them. We have no Other Books that will Suit you as you are not fond of [MSS unintelligible] I will try and get some for you—perhaps I will be down this afternoon."[1] Probably the last letter written in his own hand was addressed to still another of his nephews, requesting a loan of fifty dollars which was to be used in paying workmen who were engaged in finishing his house.[2]

The letter from one of his brothers-in-law gives evidence also of the high estimate in which he was held by his family. "When I saw you at the Springs the other day, you told me you were busily engaged in finishing your house. That is well enough, but I sh^d feel better satisfied if you would come & spend the Winter with me. Every thing that

---

[1] Draper MSS, 55 J 63.
[2] Temple Bodley, *Clark*, p. 365, note.

is in my power to make your situation comfortable shall be done & think you had better come."[1]

Six months after (1809), because of an accident, he was forced to quit Clark's Point. Stricken with paralysis of his right side, he fell unconscious in front of the fireplace in his cabin and his right leg was badly burned.[2] From this stroke he never fully recovered. An infection of his right foot and leg made amputation necessary. The pain and danger connected with such an operation, with no anaesthetic nor antiseptics, may readily be imagined. Upon his own request he was cheered by the strains of martial music during the two hours required by the surgeons in performing this task. This weird scene was described shortly after by his nephew, George Rogers Clark Sullivan:

Your Uncle George is with us in high spirits, and the wound healed up. I have stayed with him every night since he has been in town, that is about 5 weeks. I never new a man in my life to stand it so well as he did the day it was taken off. he sent for the drummer and fifer to come and play. Floyd then took the hint and had all the men placed around the house with two drums and two fifers and played for about two hours and his leg was taken off in the mean time. In the evening they returned and played for about an hour, and then ten at night four elegant violins two drums two fifes marched around the house for about an hour playing elegant marches.[3]

Thereafter he lived at Locust Grove, 8 miles from Louisville, the home of his sister Lucy, who was the wife of Major William Croghan. During the remaining nine years of his life he received every possible attention. A wheel chair enabled him to go about the house, and he was supplied with a carriage for trips to town. His interest in the allotment of lands to his Illinois troops was still unflagging.

[1] Draper MSS, 55 J 63. The letter was written by Owen Gwathney.

[2] That paralysis affected his right side is established by a letter of Major William Croghan, a brother-in-law. Draper MSS, 55 J 82.

[3] Draper MSS, 12 C 1. The letter was sent to his cousin, John O'Fallon.

Three times, within the year following the operation, the minutes of the Commissioners show that he was in attendance at all their sessions as chairman.[1]

Among the messages of respect and confidence of which he was then the recipient were two which served to revive the memories of those years when he participated in deeds of heroism with which his name must always be linked. It was Francis Vigo, the Italian trader, who, on January 29, 1779, when Clark was in doubt regarding his next move, brought him "every Inteligence that I could wish to have."[2] From Vincennes this faithful friend through the years writes:

When I saw that on a late occasion, on the fourth of July last, the citizens of Jefferson County and vicinity, from a spontaneous impulse of gratitude and esteem had paid an unfeigned tribute of respect to the veteran to whose skill and valor America and Kentucky owe so much, I then repelled the unwelcome idea of national ingratitude and my sentiments chimed in unison with those of the worthy citizens of Kentucky towards the saviour of this once distressed Country. . . . . Please Sir to accept this plain but genuine offering from a man whom you honoured once with your friendship, and who will never cease to put up prayers to heaven that the evening of your days may be serene and happy.[3]

Clark wrote in reply:

A letter from a man who has always occupied a distinguished place in my affection & esteem, must insure the warmest and most cordial reception. An affection, the result not so much as being associated in the placid stream of tranquility, & the benign sunshine of peace, as Companions amidst the din of war, & those struggles, when the indefatigable exertion of every muscle and nerve was demanded. But it may be enough to remark, that while the one is the effect of your uniformly discreet and irreproachable conduct on the intricate path of civil and domestic life, the other is wrought by a strong sense of that gratitude due from your adopted Country: having myself both witnessed & experienced the signal advantages flowing to our Common Country from

[1] *Clark Papers* (1781–83), pp. 457, 458.

[2] *Ibid.* (1771–81), p. 138.   [3] July 15, 1811. Draper MSS. 55 J 77.

your inestimable conduct, & what is more enhancing to such Services, having rendered them at a time when the cloud on which our fate hung, assumed the most menacing aspect.

When I contemplate the glowing affection with which your letter is fraught, and only a revival of such you in past time, ah! better times troubles as they were, were wont to evince for me, I am so filled with correspondent feelings, that I am at a loss for words to express them.

How happy would I be could the sentiments of entreaty to a trueful providence, in the conclusive part of your letter, for a serene & happy evening, be realized; but that providence, submitting as I do with manly patience to his decrees, has long since denied me that boon. He has cut asunder the life's tenderest string.[1]

The second note of cheer came through an act of the legislature of Virginia, passed almost to the day a third of a century after Hamilton, responding to the demand "immediate surrender," marched out of Fort Sackville in the presence of Clark's bedraggled troops drawn up on parade, and the American colors were run up. By this law he was granted a life pension of $400 a year. It was also voted to present him with a sword to be manufactured at the state armory.[2]

[1] Clark to Vigo, August 1, 1811. *Illinois Regiment Commission Report*, p. 102. There is no real basis for the statement: "A tradition is preserved in the family that he was fascinated with the beauty of the daughter of the Spanish governor of St. Louis, when he relieved that post from attack. Observing a want of courage in the governor, he broke off his addresses to the girl, saying to his friends: I will not be the father of a race of cowards." *Cyclopedia of American Biography* (New York: Appleton, 1887), I, 627. Mr. Bodley has preserved the questionable tradition in another form. Bodley, *Clark*, pp. 368, 369. Of Clark's five brothers, Jonathan and William were the only ones who married. John, the third son, was a captain in one of the Virginia continental regiments. Richard, the fourth son, was a captain under George Rogers, and Edmund, the fifth son, was commissioned a lieutenant, at the age of seventeen, while in school. This was at the close of the Revolution. Clark's four sisters, Ann, Lucy, Elizabeth, and Frances Eleanor, were all married. For Clark genealogical tables, see English, *Conquest of the Northwest*, II, 1142–53.

[2] The bill became a law February 20, 1812. Draper MSS, 55 J 78. Bowman's "Journal," *Clark Papers* (1771–81), p. 162.

Two years before, William Clark had once more urged that a suitable pension should be awarded his brother.[1] The act which finally passed was due to the effort of General Charles Fenton Mercer. In sending a copy to Clark, he wrote as follows:

I am persuaded, that had you [Major Croghan] been present, you would have approved of the course, which I pursued, which sustained the honor and dignity of General Clark, while it interested the tenderness, the generosity, and the magnanimity of the General Assembly of Virginia. . . . . I told them, the "Story of the sword," and urged, as a reason, why they should present to the gallant veteran, another, that he had with haughty sense of wounded pride and feeling, broken and cast away that which this state formerly gave him. . . . .[2] It is due, also, to their motives to state, that the sum of four hundred dollars, was the only sum, with which it was proposed to fill the blank in the engrossed bill, ... about one half of a Colonell's full pay. I knew it exceeded any annuity ever granted by this Commonwealth for past services.[3]

Governor James Barbour, in addition to his official message which accompanied the sword, took the occasion, as he wrote Clark, for "an expression of my own feelings. . . . .

[1] Draper MSS, 55 J 71.

[2] Varying statements have been made with reference to the swords presented to Clark. The evidence is clear that the Virginia Assembly voted to present "an elegant sword" to him, June 12, 1779. *Clark Papers* (1771–81), p. 362. Lyman C. Draper based his statement regarding the refusal of Clark to receive it on the testimony, which he himself secured, of Clark's nephews, Colonel George Croghan and Dr. John Croghan. Clark lived for a number of years in their home, and it seems probable they knew all of the facts connected with the incident. Dr. Draper wrote: "He had drawn on Oliver Pollock of New Orleans, as the agent of Virginia to pay for provisions he had purchased of Charles Gratiot, the father of General Gratiot, & that draft was protested, & the protest & the sword reached Clark about one and the same time. Clark was soured, took the fine sword, walked out on the bank of the river with none present but his servant, thrust the blade deep into the ground, & gave the hilt a kick with his foot, broke it off & sent it into the river, & sent word to the Governor of Virginia, that he would have no such hollow-hearted insignias while they refused his starving soldiers the common necessaries of life." Draper MSS, 10 J 204. A complete statement of the controversy over the swords may be found in English, *Conquest of the Northwest*, II, 871–84.

[3] Draper MSS, 55 J 79.

I have dwelt with rapture upon the distinguished part you acted in that great drama, being always convinced, that it only wanted the adventitious aid of numbers, to make it amongst the most splendid examples of skill and courage, which any age or country has produced."[1]

Judged by his reply to this tribute of the Governor, Clark's words, on the occasion when the sword was actually presented, were an expression of gratitude. "Flattering indeed, he says, it is to him to find that his exertions when doing his Duty Should meet the Approbation of so respectable a body of his fellow Citizens as Your Excellency & the General Assembly of Virginia. The Genl flatters himself that some Conveyance will Shortly offer by which the Sword (voted to him by the General Assembly) may be forwarded . . . . he says he is much obliged by your polite offer of transmitting to him the money the Assembly voted him & says he will probably trouble you."[2]

On February 1, 1813, he attended for the last time a meeting of the board on the Illinois grant.[3] Shortly after, a second stroke of paralysis left him with mind impaired,

---

[1] *Jour. Va. House of Delegates* (1812–13), p. 30.

[2] Draper MSS, 55 J 82. Communication by Major William Croghan. On March 17, 1812, Major Croghan also wrote General Mercer: "The Act of Assembly which you were so principally Instrumental in Geting passed which Gives Genl Clark a pention Came duly to hand, Immediately communicated it to the General, who will ever with Gratitude remember your very Friendly attention to him, he wished me to Inform you that had he it in his power he would Write to you and endeavor to Express his Gratitude & feelings." Draper MSS, 55 J 81.

There seems to be no foundation for the traditional story to the effect that when the Committee waited on Clark to present the sword he received them in gloomy silence and exclaimed after receiving their compliments: "When Virginia needed a sword, I gave her one. She sends me now a toy. I want bread! He thrust the sword into the ground and broke it with his crutch" (Appleton *Cyclopedia of American Biography*, I, 627). Dr. Draper stated, after his interview with Colonel George Croghan and Dr. John Croghan: "The second sword, presented to him by Virginia in 1812, is now possessed by Col. Geo. Croghan." Draper MSS, 10 J 204.

[3] *Clark Papers* (1781–83), p. 459.

with loss of speech, and incapable of moving about.[1] Five years later death came through a stroke of apoplexy (February 13, 1818).

Members of the circuit court then in session at Louisville voted to attend the funeral services at Locust Grove in a body and to wear crepe on the left arm for thirty days.[2] Officers of the Revolution in the neighborhood adopted the same resolution. On Sunday (February 15), "a very stormy, snowy day," services, military and religious, were conducted which were attended by "a large assemblage of persons."[3] One sentence only of the oration given by Judge John Rowan was reported: "The mighty oak of the forest has fallen, and now the scrub oaks may sprout all around."[4]

---

[1] Upon his request, a will bequeathing certain properties to relatives was drawn up by his brother William (November 15, 1815). It was signed by his mark, but the document was never regarded as valid by his relatives. Draper MSS, 35 J 112. For the later adjustments under the will, see English, *Conquest of the Northwest*, II, 1123–41. Twenty-five thousand dollars were received as a final settlement with Virginia. Of this amount, $22,000 were awarded Clark's heirs.

[2] Draper MSS, 12 J 42.

[3] *Western Courier*, Louisville, February 21, 1818.

[4] The nature of the address may be gathered from the obituary which was also prepared by Judge Rowan.

"The father of the Western Country is no more! Genl George Rogers Clark whose character is rendered illustrious by his distinguished public Services during the War of our Revolution departed this life at his residence in this county on the morning of the 13th inst. in the 66th year of his age. At an early period of life he stepped forth at the call of his country to execute one of the boldest and most arduous designs recorded in the history of nations. He was placed by the state of Virginia at the head of a corps consisting of not more than 400 men destined to operate against the British & Savages then occupying the Country West of the Alleghany Mountains. To ordinary men such a design would have appeared to be fraught with dangers and difficulties the most overwhelming and insurmountable: but to Gen¹ Clarke it presented a theatre for the exercise of that ardent heroism and sublime genius which lighted his path to victory, and covered his name with glory and renown. At the head of this little Spartan band he

Two thoughts come to the mind of the visitor who stands, in beautiful Cave Hill Cemetery, before the little memorial stone which marks the grave of George Rogers Clark.[1] One is of Vincennes (1786). Many of the events with which his name was connected during the last half of his life were fashioned by that incident. About them there may still arise much controversy. But the dominating thought is of Kaskaskia (July 4, 1778) and of Vincennes (February 25, 1779). These days recall events which must always stand out as epochal in the history of our nation.[2]

---

pierced the gloom of the Western forests, encountering hunger, cold and toil in their most aggravated shapes. With celerity unrivalled he traversed this immense region. On every side he spread terror & dismay. Kaskaskia, & Vincennes The two great rallying points of the enemy successively yielded to the valor of his arms. Such was the irresistible majesty of his presence, that disciplined valor was awed into submission, savage ferocity into humble subservience. So indelible were the impressions which he made that his conquests were no where succeeded by revolt." Draper MSS, 55 J 85.

[1] Clark's body was brought from Locust Grove to Cave Hill Cemetery (Louisville), 1869. It was my privilege to visit this cemetery in the company of Colonel Reuben T. Durrett, of Louisville, an acknowledged authority on Kentucky history and especially on the later years of the career of General Clark.

[2] This view has been recently presented in a striking way by Dr. J. Franklin Jameson: "But if," he said, "the Northwest had not been acquired by the heroic action of George Rogers Clark, all the territory to the westward, which the map shows to be more than half of the United States, would never have been acquired; but if the "cribs and cabins" of the United States, to use an old phrase, had been confined to the Alleghany Mountains, it could never have had that career of imperial greatness that we see before us now." (January 18, 1927).

Hearing before the Joint Committee on the Library, Congress of the United States, Sixty-ninth Congress, second session, on S. J. Res. 139 and H. J. Res. 307. "A Joint Resolution Providing for the Participation of the United States in the Celebration in 1929 of the One Hundred and Fiftieth Anniversary of the Conquest of the Northwest Territory by George Rogers Clark, Authorizing an Appropriation for the Construction of a Permanent Memorial in the City of Vincennes, State of Indiana, and for Other Purposes."

APPENDIX I

Clark's Memoir

The original of this document is the possession of the Wisconsin Historical Society.[1] It consists of 128 pages of manuscript and purports to give a detailed account of events with which Clark was connected in Virginia, Kentucky, and the Northwest from the close of the year 1773 to September, 1779. Attention was first called to the Memoir by Mann Butler in his *History of Kentucky*.[2] John B. Dillon, who owned a copy, made extensive use of it in his *Historical Notes of the Discovery and Settlement of the Territory of the United States Northwest of the River Ohio*. This volume, which was published in 1843, contains extracts from the document. The Memoir was published, slightly abridged, by Dillon in his *History of Indiana*. The entire document was printed for the first time (1896) by W. H. English in his *Conquest of the Northwest*.[3]

Early writers on the period, following Mann Butler, have accepted this narrative of events by Clark as trustworthy. Dillon accepted the facts as stated in the Memoir, and novelists such as Winston Churchill, in *The Crossing*, and Maurice Thompson, in *Alice of Old Vincennes*,

[1] In this discussion I have made free use of an article, "The Value of the Memoir of George Rogers Clark as an Historical Document," which I presented before the Mississippi Valley Historical Association and which appeared in the *Proceedings* of that Association (IX [1918], Part II, 249-70).

Two manuscript copies of the Memoir are in existence. One, which formerly belonged to John B. Dillon, is in the possession of the estate of W. H. English, Indianapolis. The other was owned by Colonel Reuben T. Durrett, of Louisville, but is now the property of the University of Chicago.

[2] Published in 1834. It is said that Mann Butler owned the original. William H. English, *Conquest of the Country Northwest of the River Ohio, 1778-83; and Life of General George Rogers Clark* (Indianapolis, 1896), I, 456.

[3] *Ibid.*, I, 457-555. It was printed as one of the *George Rogers Clark Papers, 1771-81*, ed. James, *Ill. Hist. Soc. Colls.* (Springfield, 1912), VIII, 208-302.

adopted the statements without criticism; in fact, the substance of these novels is made up largely from this source.[1] The value of the Memoir as a historical source was first questioned by Theodore Roosevelt in *The Winning of the West*. Evidently accepting the view of Dillon as to the time when it was written, Mr. Roosevelt says: "It was written at the desire of Presidents Jefferson and Madison, and therefore some thirty or forty years after the events of which it speaks. Valuable though it is as the narrative of the chief actor, it would be still more valuable had it been written earlier; it undoubtedly contains some rather serious errors." Mr. Roosevelt describes the Memoir as "written by an old man who had squandered his energies and sunk into deserved obscurity." Elsewhere he writes: "Unfortunately, most of the small western historians who have written about Clark have really damaged his reputation by the absurd inflation of their language. They were adepts in the forcible-feeble style of writing, a sample of which is their rendering him ludicrous by calling him 'the Hannibal of the West,' and the 'Washington of the West.' Moreover, they base his claims to greatness not on his really great deeds, but on the half-imaginary feats of childish cunning he related in his old age."[2]

While it would be futile to attempt to prove that the Memoir is wholly trustworthy, it is regarded as worth the effort to try to determine, first, when it was written; and, second, what portions may be approved.

In the correspondence carried on between Clark and John Brown, delegate in Congress from Kentucky, it is shown that at least one hundred pages, the greater part of the Memoir, were written in the years 1789 and 1790. The essential portions of these letters follow:

NEW YORK, July 5, 1789

DEAR GENL: . . . . I must beg that you will pardon the liberty which I am going to take. I have a request to make of you and as it is one of consequence, I must premise that I am not only seconded in makeing it but urged to it by some of the most important Characters in the Union—it is—that you will favor the World with a Narrative of your Campaigns in the Western Country. The

---

[1] Dillon wrote: "Extracted from the MSS Memoirs of General George Rogers Clark, composed by himself at the united desire of Presidents Jefferson and Madison," John B. Dillon, *A History of Indiana, from Its Earliest Exploration by Europeans to the Close of the Territorial Government in 1916* (Indianapolis, 1859), p. 115.

[2] Theodore Roosevelt, *The Winning of the West* (New York, 1889), II, 36, 55, 82, notes.

United States now find themselves in possession of a territory N.W. of the Ohio of vast extent & of immense value to which all turn their Eyes as being the only certain fund for the discharge of the National Debt and although it is confest by all that we owe it to your enterprise & successful exertions, yet the incredible Difficulties & Dangers you incountered, and the gallant exploits which led to & secured the acquisition are but partially & imperfectly known. All wish to know it & you alone are in possession of this Information & should you decline to communicate it the latest Posterity will regret the loss of what would constitute the most interesting Pages in the Annals of the Western World & would be an ornament to the History of the American Revolution. Mr. Madison whose literary and Political Character now attracts the attention of all America is so much engaged in the success of this application that he has desired me to inform you that to lessen the task, if you will furnish the material & it is agreeable to you he will carefully attend to the arrangement & style so as to usher it into the world in a Dress suitable to the importance of the Subject.

You cannot be too minute in the details of the Causes and effects, of Views and Measures, of occurrances and transactions during those successful campaigns. Circumstances & facts which may appear unimportant to you will not be thought so by others. Copies of the Letters which passed between you & the Executive of Virginia of Treaties with & of speeches to & from the Indians may be inserted with great propriety, and 'tis important to preserve them & they must necessarily throw great light upon the Subject. . . . .[1]

Sir Yr. Mo Hble Servt.

J. Brown

Genl G. R. Clark

Louisville, Jan. 20th, 1789 [1790][2]

Dear Sir: Your favor of the 5th July came safe to hand. . . . . The requisition you make, Sir, by your letter, is such, that a compliance will be in some degree, destroying a resolution that I have long concluded on, that of burying the rise and progress of the War in this quarter in oblivion; which is in my power as all light cast on it by another person, must be faint indeed. Great part of the most material papers are either lost, or made use of as waste paper, and finding my nature such that it was impossible for me to be void of some affection for the people I had suffered so much for, in the establishment of their interests, that I have frequently destroyed papers that were of such a nature that the reading of them would in some measure cool that spark that still remained, and tend to

---

[1] The original of this letter is in the Draper MSS, 53 J 80. The significance of the correspondence between Brown and Clark was first noted by Mrs. Minnie G. Cook, who printed portions of it in the *Virginia Magazine of History and Biography*, XV, 205.

[2] The two letters by Clark which follow were printed in the *Commonwealth* (Frankfort, Kentucky, July 25, 1838), Draper MSS, 27 CC29.

aggravate the crime of the people—that by having nothing about me that might frequently fall in my way and renew my ideas, and by attempting, if possible, to forget the various transactions that have happened, I might again reconcile myself to live in a country that I was always fond of, and with people whose prosperity I have, until lately, studied with delight. For the want of these helps alluded to, it would require time and recollection to collect materials necessary to compose a true narrative of this department. Some papers I can collect, and will immediately set about this business, and as soon as finished, enclose them to you, probably in four or five months. I shall take no other pains than that of stating facts, and occurrences, &c. If this is to make its appearance in the world, there is no person I could be more happy in their handling the subject than Mr. Madison. You wil be pleased to favor me in presenting my most sincere thanks to that gentleman for his expression in my favor.

Yours, with much esteem,

GEO. R. CLARK

The Hon. John Brown

JEFFERSON, July 15th, 1790

DEAR SIR: . . . . As to the Narrative; I have been at a great deal of trouble in attempting to recover several copies, that I was in hopes were in the hands of Captains Harrison and Brashears, at the Natchez, and others, but found myself disappointed, and have set about the business without those helps, have tasked myself to spend two days in the week, and have got through about one hundred pages. I wish, before I close this business, to receive every querie of importance on the subject that yourself and Mr. Madison could imagine. The more I enter into this business, the better I am pleased at the undertaking, and frequently, I suppose, experience the same feeling that actuated me at the time of those transactions. I believe, that through myself, every thing past, relative to this country may be known. If this should fortunately meet with a quick passage, I may probably get an answer from you in two months. Judging from the progress I make, to be nearly closing this business by that period.

Please present my respects to Mr. Madison.

Am, Sir, y'r Hble ser'vt

GEO. R. CLARK

JEFFERSON, July 29, 1790

DEAR SIR: In my last, of this inst., I informed you of the progress I have made in the narrative you wish for. I have advanced but slowly for the want of papers that have been destroyed by one means or other. Of course I require more study and recollection to go on with this business. The papers relative to the years '78 and '79 are those that I have been at the greatest loss for. Some, I have recovered. In the Winter of 1779, on the request of Col. G. Mason, of Fairfax, I wrote him a pamphlet that contained great part of our proceedings up to that time. I have wrote to him for it, in hopes that he might find it among his old papers, but have got no answer from him. As he is convenient to you, by post, I should thank you to try and recover it for me and send it by the first opportunity. If I get this, I shall be tolerably complete, and correct in what I have done.

I am, Sir, y'r h'ble servant.

Geo. R. Clark

The Hon. John Brown

New York, 27 April, 1790[1]

Dear General: . . . . Your favor of the 20th August signifying your willingness to favor the World with a Narrative of your Campaigns in the Western Country gave me as well as many of your friends in this quarter great pleasure. I hope you have not relinquished a work which would make so important an addition to the History of the Revolution, Mr. Madison will chearfully undertake to revise & arrange the collection of facts should you please to put it into his Hands but begs you to desend in the recital even to minutia. . . . .

I am with sentiments of esteem Your friend & Hble Ser[t]

J. Brown

Genl Clark

Philad[A], 8th Dec[r], 1790[2]

Dear General: I had not the pleasure to receive your letters of the 15th and 29 of July untill yesterday. They had been detained with all my other letters written from Kentucke since that date by my Brother near Staunton in expectation of my paying him a visit during the late recess of Congress. But a tour which I made through Vermont & the Eastern States prevented me of that pleasure & also of writing to you more frequently. It affords real satisfaction to me as also to Mr. Madison (to whom I have communicated the contents of your letters) to find you have made so great progress in compiling your Narrative of the Western Campaigns. I hope you will persevere to the completion of this interesting work which I am fully persuaded will make an important addition to the History of the American Revolution. Neither Mr. Madison nor myself can undertake to propose queries to you not being sufficiently acquainted with the subject, but we fully unite in the request that in collecting materials you will not use a sparing hand. Many things may appear very interesting to others which you might think unimportant & any redundancy which may be thus created can easily be retrenched upon a revisal. By next Post I shall write to Col[o] Mason for the Pamphlet you mention & should it come to hand I shall be carful to forward it to you by the first opportunity. . . . .

I am with great respect Yours &c

J. Brown

[1] The original is in the Draper MSS, 53 J 88.　[2] *Ibid.*, 53 J 89.

From the correspondence between Jefferson and Judge Harry Innes, of Kentucky, it appears probable that the Memoir was nearly completed during the year 1791. "Will it not be possible," wrote Jefferson, March 7, 1791, "for you to bring General Clark forward? . . . . We are made to hope he is engaged in writing the account of his expeditions north of Ohio. They will be valuable morsels of history, and will justify to the world those who have told them how great he was."[1] Judge Innes replied on May 30, 1791, as follows: "Since the reception of your letter I have seen Genl Clark and find he is writing the History of his Expeditions and will complete the work in the course of this summer."

In the further effort to reach some conclusion on the trustworthiness of the Memoir, comparison has been made, wherever possible, with other documents of the period. Among these sources, which have passed unchallenged, are Clark's Diary, Clark's letter to George Mason, known as the Mason Letter, Clark's Journal, and Joseph Bowman's Journal.[2] Proof is abundant that Clark, when he undertook to write the Memoir, strove to collect all his correspondence which bore on the various phases discussed. That, so far as possible, he made use of this correspondence is evident from his annotations, such as: "See my letter to him [governor of Virginia]," "Refer to Maj^r Bowman's Journal," and "This copy is lost." The Diary and Bowman's Journal were in his possession. Clark tried unsuccessfully to locate the Mason Letter,[3] and his Journal was

[1] Writings of Thomas Jefferson, ed. W. C. Ford (New York, 1895), V, 295.

[2] These documents are to be found in *Clark Papers* (1771–81), pp. 20–28, 114–54, 164–68, and 155–64.

[3] The original manuscript of this letter is now in the possession of Mr. R. C. Ballard Thruston, of Louisville, Kentucky. The location of the letter was unknown for a number of years. Clark's correspondence at the time he was writing the Memoir was published in the *Frankfort Commonwealth* toward the close of the year 1826 and called attention to it. Lyman C. Draper, with this clue, took up the search for the missing document and wrote to Colonel George Mason, who was living at Hollin Hall, Virginia, the family home. Colonel Mason replied, February 8, 1827: "The narrative, to which you refer, written by Col. George Rogers Clark & sent to my Grand-Father is in my possession. It is not only a highly interesting, but very valuable document; and I have long since destined it for the safe keeping of some Public Institution. I cannot therefore, consign it to the hands of any Individual, much less those of an entire Stranger, as you are to me Sir—for individual purposes. It will soon be presented to the Historical Society of Kentucky; and it will then be at their discretion to give

in the possession of the British.[1] The narrative of events in the Memoir, between December 25, 1776, when ten men went to the Ohio River to bring on the gunpowder which Clark had secured from the Virginia legislature for the defense of Kentucky, to March 30, 1778, when he was prepared to descend the Ohio on the Illinois expedition, shows a close adherence to the statements given in the Diary. On December 29, 1776, McClelland's Fort was attacked by the Indians; Harrodsburg, on March 7, 1777; and numerous other attacks on the white settlements followed. Benjamin Linn and Samuel Moore, who had been sent as special agents by Clark, returned on June 22 with an account of conditions in the French villages of the Illinois country. The arrival of Colonel John Bowman at Harrodsburg on September 2 with a company of men from Virginia gave renewed courage to the defenders of Kentucky. On October 1 Clark set out for Virginia in order to make an appeal to the Governor for aid in the defense of these settlements. Governor Patrick Henry favored granting this request, and on January 2 Clark received orders for carrying it into effect. Twelve hundred pounds of public money were granted for the use of the expedition, and on January 4 Clark set out for Fort Pitt, where he received supplies from General Hand, the commandant at that post.

In testing the narrative of the Memoir between March 30, 1778, the date when the Diary ends and January 29, 1779, when Bowman's

----

you, or any other Gentleman, access to it." In a postscript, dated February 10, he stated that the manuscript had that day been sent to that institution. When the Kentucky Historical Society dissolved, the Mason Letter came into possession of Hon. Henry Pirtle, then president of the society. It was published in 1869, with an introduction by Mr. Pirtle, as *Col. George Rogers Clark's Sketch of His Campaign in the Illinois in 1778–79*, Ohio Valley Historical Series, No. 3 (Cincinnati, 1869); and by English in his *Conquest of the Northwest*, I, 411–53.

[1] Clark's Journal gives the earliest known account of events connected with the capture of Vincennes after February 23, 1779. William Myers, the bearer of this official message to Governor Henry, was killed by the Indians near the falls of the Ohio. According to custom, the Indian agents, instead of sending the originals of important captured letters to their superior officers, forwarded copies of such portions as they chose to select. A copy of the Journal taken from the Canadian archives was published in the *American Historical Review*, I, 91–94. Three weeks after the death of Myers, Clark prepared another account of the capture of Vincennes, one copy of which was sent to Governor Henry and the other to Thomas Jefferson. *Writings of Thomas Jefferson*, ed. Washington (New York, 1853), I, 222.

Journal begins, comparison is made with the Mason Letter. As already stated, Clark did not possess this document.

On March 29 Clark received a message from Major William Bailey Smith containing the information that he had recruited four companies of men on the Holston River and was sending them to Kentucky. Two companies under Captain Joseph Bowman and Captain Leonard Helm were to join Clark at Redstone. On May 12, with 150 frontiersmen, together with a number of private adventurers and some twenty settlers with their families, Clark set out from Redstone.[1] After taking on stores at Pittsburgh, liberally granted by General Hand, and at Wheeling, they proceeded cautiously down the Ohio, not knowing when they might be surprised by Indian war parties. Reaching the mouth of the Kanawha, they learned that this post had been attacked by the Indians the day before.[2] Descending the river, they were joined by Captain James O'Hara with his company who were on their way to the Arkansas on "publick business."[3] The mouth of the Kentucky, where they landed, was at first selected by Clark as a suitable spot to fortify as a protection for immigrants coming down the river. But the falls of the Ohio, while fulfilling this requirement, would in addition furnish the site for a fort necessary to protect the Kentucky settlements and the Illinois country.[4] On May 27 they reached the falls, where Clark learned that instead of the four companies expected from the Holston, only part of a company under Captain Dillard had arrived in Ken-

[1] *Clark Papers*, pp. 27 (Diary), 117 (Mason Letter), 220 (Memoir). The Memoir says "late in may"; also that he was accompanied by three companies of men. Each of these companies contained fifty men. Major Smith's companies were to contain two hundred men.

[2] *Ibid.*, pp. 117 (Mason Letter), 220 (Memoir). The Memoir says 250 Indians, and the Mason letter, "a large Body of Indians." Joseph Bowman to George Brinker, July 30, 1778: "by a superior body of Indians—appearing to be about two hundred in number." *Ibid.*, p. 614.

[3] *Ibid.*, pp. 117 (Mason Letter), 221 (Memoir). The Mason Letter says: "on his way to the Ozark." General Hand to General Horatio Gates, April 24, 1778: "I am preparing to send Capt. O'Hara with a detachment to the Arkansas with the provisions for Capt. Willing." Reuben G. Thwaites and Louise P Kellogg, *Frontier Defense on the Upper Ohio, 1777-78*, Draper Series (Madison, 1912), III, 278.

[4] *Clark Papers*, pp. 117 (Mason Letter), 221 (Memoir). The Mason Letter says: "after spending a day or two, We set out," while the Memoir gives the reasons for choosing the falls of the Ohio as a suitable place to fortify.

tucky.[1] At first Clark took possession of an island in the rapids in order the more easily to prevent desertions. Then for the first time he disclosed to his followers the real object of the expedition. Because of dissatisfaction among the Holston men the boats were guarded to prevent their escape. A few men escaped, but some of them were captured by horsemen the next day.[2] On June 26 they set off from the falls, and on the fourth day reached the mouth of the Tennessee, where final preparations were made for the march to Kaskaskia.[3] The boats were concealed near Fort Massac, and the expedition proceeded in a northwesterly course. The events which followed were: The guide became bewildered and lost the route, but soon located it again;[4] the arrival within three miles of Kaskaskia on July 4;[5] boats were secured by which they crossed the river and then captured the town.[6] Clark delayed making his proclamation to the people for a few days, and meantime Captain Joseph Bowman, on July 8; captured Cahokia.[7] The other Illinois villages followed the example of Kaskaskia and Cahokia by taking the oath of allegiance to the United States. Friendly correspondence was begun with the Spanish officer at St. Louis, and Father Gibault brought about the transfer of authority at Vincennes. Clark deceived the French by his statement that the troops he had brought with him were only a detachment of the larger army stationed at the falls of the Ohio. For five weeks Clark was engaged in treating with the Indian tribes assembled at Cahokia.[8]

Word was received by Clark that an expedition was to move from Pittsburgh against Detroit.[9] Captain Helm was authorized to proceed to Ouiatanon with a party of men in order to counteract the influence

[1] The Mason Letter gives the name "Delland" and also "Dillard." *Ibid.*, p. 118.

[2] *Ibid.*, pp. 118 (Mason Letter), 222, 223 (Memoir).

[3] The Memoir does not give the day in June, but the Mason Letter says that it was June 26. *Ibid.*, pp. 118, 223.

[4] *Ibid.*, pp. 119 (Mason Letter), 226 (Memoir).

[5] Mason Letter: "we got within three miles of the Town Kaskaskias." Memoir: "within a few miles of the Town." *Ibid.*, pp. 119, 227.

[6] The Mason Letter says Clark divided his men into two divisions; the Memoir, three. *Ibid.*, pp. 120, 227.

[7] The Memoir gives "Maj^r Bowman," and the Mason Letter, "Capt Bowman." *Ibid.*, pp. 122, 232, 233.

[8] *Clark Papers*, pp. 122, 125–29 (Mason Letter), 234–38, 243–61 (Memoir).

[9] *Ibid.*, pp. 131 (Mason Letter), 259 (Memoir).

of a British agent at that post. The expedition was successful in that from twenty to thirty Chippewa warriors were captured, but the British emissary escaped.[1] With the setting in of winter, preparations were begun at Detroit for an expedition which was at first thought by Clark to be intended against the army from Pittsburgh, but which he later learned was to come against the Illinois towns.[2]

For the events between January 29, 1779, when Colonel Francis Vigo gave information on the capture of Vincennes, to March 20 of the same year, when Clark returned to Kaskaskia after his victory over Hamilton, the sources, in addition to the Memoir and the Mason Letter are Bowman's Journal, Clark's Journal, and Hamilton's Report.[3] In a marginal note by Clark in the Memoir he says: "Refer to Maj^r Bowman's Journal for the particulars of this march." While there can be no doubt that this Journal was carefully followed by Clark, there are a number of incidents not mentioned therein which are included in the Memoir and the Mason Letter.

The afternoon of February 23, when they reached the Warrior's Island, within two miles of Vincennes, is referred to as a "delightful day."[4] Here they captured a hunter from Vincennes. Clark used this

---

[1] Mason Letter: "but a few days before the Captains arrival Mr Celeron thought proper to make his Escape. . . . . About forty in number being made Prisoners." Memoir: "the Emisary (I forget his name)." *Ibid.*, pp. 130, 259.

[2] Mason Letter: "A Young Man at the Town of Cohos holding a Correspondance and sending Intilligence to Governour Hambletons Party was Detected & punished accordingly." Memoir: "one Denny an Inhabitant of Kohokia was taken up by Maj^r Bowman for writing through the Indians to his friend near DeTroit given dangerous Information his Letters was intercepted and him self tied to the tail of a Cart and by drum Received a lash at every Door in Town and Burnt in the Hand for other Misdemeneours." *Ibid.*, pp. 132, 261.

[3] Major Joseph Bowman was one of Clark's most trusted associates. His Journal gives a brief statement of the important events between January 29 and March 20, 1779. *Ibid.*, pp. 155–64. The original of this document has not been located. There is a copy in the Draper MSS, 47 J 131. Another copy is in the Library of Congress, Letters to Washington, 1779, fol. 91. The Journal has been published in the *Louisville Literary News*, November 24, 1840, in *Clark's Campaign in the Illinois*, and in English, *Conquest of the Northwest*, I, 568. The report prepared by Lieutenant-Governor Hamilton covers events from November, 1776, to June, 1781. The original is in the British Museum. See *Clark Papers*, pp. 174–207.

[4] Mason Letter: "Laying in this Grove some time to dry our Clothes by the Sun." *Ibid.*, p. 141.

prisoner, "who was not permited to see our numbers," to carry a letter to the inhabitants of the village.[1] Several of his men also "sent ther Compliments to ther Friends under borrowed Names well known at S[t] Vincents and the person supposed to have been at Kentucky."[2]

About sundown, Clark ordered the march to begin with colors flying and drums braced. By marching to and fro, a light elevation of land obstructing the view so that only the flags could be seen from the town, the impression was made that a force of one thousand men was approaching.[3]

[1] Mason Letter: "but would not suffer him to see our Troops except a few." Memoir: "the soldiers all had instructions that ther common conversation when speaking of our Numbers should be such that a stranger overhearing must suppose that their was near 1000 of us." *Ibid.*, pp. 141, 278.

[2] Mason Letter: "Sending the Compliments of several Officers that was known to be Expected to reinforce me, to several Gentlemen of the Town." *Ibid.*, p. 141.

[3] Mason Letter: "I march'd time enough to be seen from the Town before dark but taking advantage of the Land, disposed the lines in such a manner that nothing but the Pavilions could be seen, having as many of them as would be sufficient for a thousand Men, which was observed by the Inhabitants, who had Just Receiv'd my letter counted the different Colours and Judged our number accordingly But I was careful to give them no oppertunity to seeing our Troops before dark, which it would be before we could Arrive." Memoir: "Raising Volunteers in the Illinois every person that set about the business must have a set of Colurs given him which they brought with them to the am[t] of 10 or 12 pair these ware displayed to the best advantage and as the Low plain we march through was not a perfect level but have frequent Risings in it of Seven or Eight Feet higher than the common Level which was covered with Water and they Gen[ly] Run in an oblique direction to the Town we took the advantage of on[e] of them march through the Water under it which compleatly prevented our Men being Numbered but our Colours shewed considerably above the height as they ware fixed to long poles procured for the purpose and at a distance made no despicable appearance and as our young frenchmen had while we lay on the Warriours Island decoyed and taken several Fowlers with their Horses officers ware mounted on those and Rode about more compleatly to deceiv the Enemy in this manner we moved and directed our march in such a manner as to suffer it to be dark before had avancd more than half way to the Town." *Clark Papers*, pp. 141, 279.

Thwaites, in his *How George Rogers Clark Won the Northwest* (Chicago, 1903), p. 56, quotes: "But taking advantage of the Land, disposed the lines in such a manner that nothing but the Pavilions [doubtless shelter huts of boughs] could

So completely were the British surprised that Lieutenant-Governor Hamilton was not aware of the approach of the enemy and believed the rifle shots to have been fired by drunken Indians until one of his men was wounded by a shot fired through a porthole. A Piankashaw, son of the chief of that tribe, tendered Clark the services of one hundred warriors, but the offer was declined.[1] The firing was almost continuous throughout the night.[2] Captain Lamothe had been sent out by Hamilton on a scouting expedition. On returning, some of his men were made prisoners, and Clark, finding that he could not capture the whole party, withdrew his troops shortly before daybreak to allow their entrance into the fort.[3] About nine o'clock Clark sent a messenger to

---

be seen, having as many of them as would be sufficient for a thousand Men." In the second edition of his book (Chicago, 1904), however, he changed his explanation to "referring to the enemy's banners."

On this point Roosevelt prefers for some unknown reason to follow Clark's Journal in place of the Mason Letter, which had been previously accepted by him. Referring to Clark's Journal, he writes: "This is not only the official report, but also the earliest letter Clark wrote on the subject and therefore the most authoritative. The paragraph relating to the final march against Vincennes is as follows: 'At sun-down I put the divisions in motion to march in the greatest order & regularity & observe the orders of their officers. Above all to be silent— the 5 men we took in the canoes were our guides.' " Roosevelt continues, "This effectually disposes of the account, which was accepted by Clark himself in his old age, that he ostentatiously paraded his men and marched them to and fro with many flags flying, so as to impress the British with his numbers. Instead of indulging in any such childishness (which would merely have warned the British, and put them on their guard), he in reality made as silent an approach as possible, under cover of the darkness." Roosevelt, *The Winning of the West*, II, 78, n. 2. This does not dispose, however, of the deception, the details of which are given in both the Mason Letter and the Memoir.

For the tradition of a somewhat similar march, see Claude H. Van Tyne, "The American Revolution," *The American Nation: A History* (New York, 1905), IX, 283; Edmund Flagg, "The Far West; or, a Tour beyond the Mountains," in Reuben G. Thwaites, *Early Western Travels*, XXVII, 88.

[1] *Clark Papers*, pp. 142 (Mason Letter), 280, 281 (Memoir).

[2] Mason Letter: "Never was a heavier fireing kept up on both sides for eighteen Hours with so little damage done." Memoir: "and the firing continued without Intermission (except about 15 minutes a little before Day)." *Ibid.*, pp. 142, 281.

[3] Mason Letter: "Capt Lemote was sent out to intercept them; being out on our Arival could not get in the Fort." Hamilton's report: "we despaired of

Hamilton demanding the surrender of the fort, for he was especially solicitous about letters from Virginia which the British had taken with two prisoners the day before.[1] There followed the conference at the little French church and an agreement on the terms of surrender.[2] Clark's

Captain La Mothe's party regaining the fort, but to our great surprize and joy about half-an-hour before sunrise they appear'd and got into the Fort over the Stockades which were upright, and 11 feet out of the ground." Memoir: "after some deliberation on the subject we concluded to Risque the Reinforcement in preference to his going again among the Indians. . . . a little before Day the Troops was withdrawn from the Fort except a few parties." *Ibid.*, pp. 142, 186, 283, 284.

Roosevelt says, "Clark in his 'Memoir' asserts that he designedly let them through, and could have shot them down as they tried to clamber over the stockade if he had wished. Bowman corroborates Hamilton, saying: 'We sent a party to intercept them, but missed them. However, we took one of their men, ... the rest making their escape under the cover of the night into the fort.' Bowman's journal is for this siege much more trustworthy than Clark's 'Memoir.' In the latter, Clark makes not a few direct misstatements, and many details are colored so as to give them an altered aspect." Roosevelt, *The Winning of the West*, II, 8

[1] Mason Letter: "knowing of the Prisoners lately taken and by the discription I had of them I was sure of their being the Express from Williamsburg (but was mistaken) to save the papers and Letters." Bowman's Journal: "about 9 O Clock the Col. sent a flag to Govr Hamilton." Clark's Journal: "about 8 o'clock I sent a flag of truce with a letter." Memoir: "about nine Oclock in the morning of the 24th Learning that two prisoners they had brought in the Day before had a considerable number of Letters with them I supposed it an Express that we expected about this time which I new to be of the greatest moment to us as we had not received one Since our arrival in the countrey and not being fully acquainted with the character of our Enemy we were doubtfull that those papers might be destroyed to prevent which I sent a flag Demanding the Garison and desiring Govr Hamilton not to destroy them with some threats in case he did if his Garison should fall into my Hands his answer was that they ware not disposed to be awed into any thing unbecoming British Subjects." *Clark Papers*, pp. 143, 160, 165, 285.

[2] *Ibid.*, pp. 143, 144, 145 (Mason Letter), 162 (Bowman's Journal), 167 (Clark's Journal), 286, 287, 288, 289 (Memoir). Clark's Journal: "I told Capt Helm Sir you are a prisoner on your parole, I desire you to reconduct G. H. into the Fort and there remain till I retake you." Memoir: "Cap^{tn} Helms attempted to moderate our fixed determination I told him that he was a British prisoner and it was doubtfull whether or not he could with propriety Speak on the subject."

men clamored for the capture of Detroit, but he wished to add to his force before undertaking that project.[1] Looking toward gaining the friendship of the French at that post, he paroled the volunteers who had accompanied the British.[2] After dealing with the Indians in the vicinity of Vincennes, Clark returned to Kaskaskia, where he overcame an uprising of the Delawares.[3] Clark's disappointment was extreme when, in August, the expedition against Detroit was again postponed because of the failure to respond to his call for troops.[4]

A number of statements made in the Mason Letter, dealing chiefly with special days, are corrected in the Memoir. Clark set out for Williamsburg October 1, 1777, not in August.[5] Father Gibault and Dr.

[1] *Clark Papers*, pp. 146 (Mason Letter), 290–93 (Memoir). Memoir: "Kentuck we new could immediately furnish perhaps 200 Men." Mason Letter: "did not doubt of getting two or three hundred Men from Kentucky."

[2] Memoir: "A compleat company of Volunteers from DeTroit of Cap^{tn} Lamoths mostly composed of young men was drawn up and when expecting to be sent of into a strange cuntrey and probaly never again returning. . . . and that as we new that sending them to the States whare they would be confined in a Jail probably for the course of the war would make a great number of our Friends at DeTroit unhappy we had thought proper for their sakes to suffer them to return home . . . . in a few Days they set out (and as we had spies that went among them as Traders we learned that they made great havack to the British interest on their return." *Ibid.*, p. 291.

[3] *Ibid.*, pp. 149 (Mason Letter), 298 (Memoir).

[4] Mason Letter: "Receiving letters from Col^o Bowman at Kentucky informing me that I might expect him to Reinforce me with three hund^d men . . . . on my arrival at St Vincents the first of July, instead of two or three hundred Men that I was promised; I found only about thirty Volunteers, meeting with a Repulse from the Shawnees got discouraged Consequently not in the power of the Com^d to March them as Militia, being for some time, (as I hinted before) suspicious of a disappointment, I had conducted matters so as to make no Ill impression on the minds of the Savages in case I should not proceed as the whole had suspected that my design was against Detroit." Memoir: "I received an express from Kentucky wharin Col Bowman informed me that he could furnish 300 good men . . . . my self with a party of Horse reached the opost in four Days. . . . . Instead of 300 Men from Kentucky thare appeared about 30 Volunteers commanded by Cap^{tn} McGary. . . . . Col. Bowman had turned his attention against the Shawnees Town and got repulsed and his men discouraged." *Ibid.*, pp. 150, 299, 300.

[5] *Ibid.*, pp. 115 (Mason Letter), 218 (Memoir). Clark's Diary gives October 1, 1777. *Ibid.*, p. 24.

Laffont started for Vincennes July 14, 1778.[1] Clark's expedition left Kaskaskia for Vincennes February 5, 1779.[2]

The narrative of the Memoir may be tested in still another way, for it is to be noted that there are here numerous statements of fact not corroborated by any of the following four documents: Clark's Diary, the Mason Letter, Clark's Journal, or Bowman's Journal, but the truth of which is confirmed by other documents of the time. As we have seen, the date of the first entry in the diary is December 25, 1776. Clark's relation to the West during the preceding two years is described in the Memoir, constituting eight printed pages. So far as it has been possible to make a comparison, only a minor error in a date has been noted.[3] The attempt to settle Kentucky by James Harrod and his associates during the spring of 1774 and their return to the site of Harrodsburg after Dunmore's war;[4] the purchase of land by Colonel Richard Henderson from the Cherokee and the settlement of Boonesborough;[5] Clark's coming to Kentucky as a surveyor for the Ohio company early in 1775;[6] his determination to contest the claims of Colonel Henderson and the meeting at Harrodsburg in which Clark and Jones were elected delegates to the Virginia assembly;[7] the application to Governor Henry and the Virginia council for 500 pounds of powder for the defense of Kentucky and the return to Kentucky with the powder, which had been stored at Pittsburgh.[8]

[1] *Clark Papers*, p. 238 (Memoir). Clark gave his instructions to Dr. Laffont, July 14. Mason Letter: "In a few days the Priest, Doct[r] Lefont, the Principal, with a few others set out." *Ibid.*, pp. 53, 122.

[2] Mason Letter: "By the 4th day of Janu[y] I got every thing Compleat and on the 5th I marched." Bowman's Journal: "[February] 5th . . . . about three O Clock crossed the Kaskaskias River with our Baggage and Marched about a League from the Town." Memoir: "5th of February." *Ibid.*, pp. 139, 156, 269.

[3] The general meeting at Harrodsburg for selecting deputies to the Virginia assembly was June 8, 1776, instead of June 6. *Ibid.*, p. 209 (Memoir). For the petition for election, see *ibid.*, pp. 11–13.

[4] *Ibid.*, p. 208 (Memoir). For Harrod's settlement, 1774, see Harrison's Journal, April 7–9, 1774, in Reuben G. Thwaites and Louise P. Kellogg, *Documentary History of Dunmore's War, 1774* (Madison, 1905), p. 121.

[5] Henderson's Journal in *Filson Club Publications*, XVI, 169–80.

[6] Clark to Jonathan Clark, April 1, 1775, and July 6, 1775, in *Clark Papers*, p. 9. See also *ibid.*, p. 209 (Memoir).

[7] Clark to Jonathan Clark, February 26, 1776, and the petition from the people of Kentucky. *Ibid.*, pp. 11–16.

[8] *Ibid.*, pp. 210–15 (Memoir). See also the journal of the executive council, August 23, 1776, *ibid.*, p. 18.

Similarly, it is seen that on later events the Memoir is not only more complete than either of the four sources referred to, but it contains statements supplementary to them. Such are the following: Governor Henry and his conferences with Thomas Jefferson, George Mason, and George Wythe, and their promise to use influence to secure 300 acres of land for each soldier if the expedition were successful;[1] Henry's secret and public instructions to Clark;[2] order on Pittsburgh for boats and ammunition;[3] on the expedition to Kaskaskia, they "shot the falls during a total eclipse of the sun;"[4] the letter from Colonel

[1] Order of council, January 2, 1778: "The Governor informed the Council that he had had some conversation with several Gentlemen who were well acquainted with the Western Frontiers of Virginia." Letter of Wythe, Mason, and Jefferson to Clark, January 3, 1778: "We think it just & reasonable that each Volunteer entering as a common Soldier in this Expedition, should be allowed three hundred Acres of Land." Memoir: "he had several private Counsills composed of select gen[tn] . . . . the Expedition was resolved on and as an Incouragement to those that would Ingage in s[d] service and Instrument of writing was sign wharein those Gen[tn] promised to use their Influance to procure from the assembly 300 Acres of Land Each in case of suckness." *Clark Papers*, pp. 33, 37, 219.

[2] Memoir: "finding from the Governors conversation to me in Gen[l] upon the subject that he did not wish an implicit attention to his instructions." *Ibid.*, p. 219. For the "Secret Instructions" and "Public Instructions" to Clark, see *ibid.*, pp. 34, 36.

[3] Patrick Henry to General Edward Hand, January 2, 1778. *Ibid.*, p. 36.

[4] A letter from W. S. Burnham addressed to Simon Newcomb, who was at the time in charge of the National Observatory at Washington, brought the following reply:

WASHINGTON, July 22, 1886

DEAR SIR: I have much pleasure in acknowledging receipt of your letter of July 20th, inquiring whether an eclipse of the sun was visible at Louisville, Ky., about the first of June, 1778.

I find by reference to the ephemenides that on the morning of June 24th, 1778, there was a total eclipse of the sun visible in this country, the moon's shadow passing over the northern part of the Gulf of Mexico.

At Louisville the sun must have been four-fifths or even nine-tenths covered about nine o'clock in the morning. It may interest you to know that this was one of the recurrences of the great eclipse of 1868.

Yours very truly,

S. NEWCOMB

John Campbell, who was at Pittsburgh, announcing the treaty between France and America;[1] circumstances connected with the capture of Cahokia by Joseph Bowman and his occupancy of the old fort as a means of defense;[2] Clark's relation to Cerré;[3] Winston and Murray were using their influence at Kaskaskia for the Americans;[4] subterfuge used by Clark in his letter to the people of Vincennes;[5] the agreement with Blackbird, chief of the Chippewa;[6] the appearance of the Indian squaws in a canoe having in their possession a quarter of buffalo;[7] the

[1] Draper MSS, 47 J 22. In a letter written from Pittsburgh Clark was informed of the celebration at that place, May 26, on account of the report that France had acknowledged the independence of the United States, that a treaty of commerce had been made between the representatives of the two nations, and that hostilities between Great Britain and France were to begin. John Campbell to Clark, June 8, 1778, in the *American Historical Review*, VIII, 497. A dispatch announcing the success of the American representatives at Paris was received by Congress May 3, 1778. Francis Wharton, *The Revolutionary Diplomatic Correspondence of the United States* (Washington, 1889), II, 568.

[2] "I caused a Court of sivil Judicature to be Established at Kohas Elected by the people Maj^r Bowman to the supprise of the people held a pole for a Majestacy and was Elected and acted as Judge of the Court." *Clark Papers*, p. 235 (Memoir). The early records of this court are given in Alvord, *Cahokia Records*, Illinois Historical Collections (Springfield, 1907), II, 2–8.

[3] *Clark Papers*, p. 228 (Memoir). Two pages are given to Cerré. The same facts are brought out in a letter from Cerré to Clark, July 11, 1778. *Ibid.*, pp. 47–49. See Alvord, *Kaskaskia Records*, Illinois Historical Collection (Springfield, 1909), V, 49.

[4] *Ibid.*, p. 28; *Clark Papers*, p. 229 (Memoir).

[5] *Ibid.*, p. 238 (Memoir). "I have been charmed to learn from a letter written by Governor Abbott to M. Rocheblave that you are in general attached to the cause of America." Clark to the inhabitants of Vincennes, July 13, 1778. *Ibid.*, p. 52.

[6] Patrick Henry to the Virginia delegates in congress, November 16, 1778: "The Great Blackbird, a Chippewa Chief, has also sent a belt of peace to Col. Clark, influenced, he supposes, by the dread of Detroit's being reduced by the American arms." Memoir: "I told him that I was happy to find that this business was likely to end so much to both our satisfactions and so much to the advantage and Tranquility of Each of our people that I should amediately [write] the Govr of Virginia of what passed between us and that I knew that it would give him [and] all the Americans great pleasure." *Ibid.*, pp. 72, 255. See also the Mason Letter, in *ibid.*, p. 129.

[7] *Ibid.*, p. 276; *The Winning of the West*, II, 76. In the Clark MSS, Virginia State Archives, is an order, March 12, 1779, signed by Joseph Bowman, which

completion of Fort Sackville;[1] supplies of ammunition secured from the French;[2] conference of Clark and Hamilton during which Clark assured Hamilton that the garrison would fall and that if the defense were persisted in it would not be possible to save a single man.[3]

Detroit then became Clark's objective, for the garrison at that post did not exceed eighty men and the majority of the French were disaffected.[4] Until the middle of October, 1779, Clark was at Louisville, from which post he superintended military affairs in the west and prepared for the advance on Detroit.[5]

---

is as follows: "Issue to that squaw that Furnished our men with Provisions on our way to Attact Governor Hemilton one Bushl Corn and five pounds of Pork."

[1] Hamilton's Report: "The fort was on the 22nd of February in a tolerable state of defence the Work proposed being finish'd." Memoir: "we now found that the Garison had known nothing of us that having finished the Fort that eavening." *Clark Papers*, pp. 185, 280.

[2] Hamilton's Report: "On our arrival at St. Vincennes a strict search was made for Gunpowder, all that was to be found in the place was put into the Magazine, and a heavy fine was laid on those who should be found to conceal any, nevertheless Colonel Clarke was supplyed by the Inhabitants, his own to the last ounce being damaged on his March." Memoir: "Col¹ Legress Maj^r Bosseron and others had buried the Greatest part of their powder and Ball this was amediately produced and we found our selves well supplyed." *Ibid.*, pp. 192, 281.

[3] Hamilton's Report: "He told me it was in vain to think of persisting in the defence of the Fort, ... that if from a spirit of obstinacy I persisted when there was no probability of relief and should stand an Assault, not a single Soul should be spared." Memoir: "I told him . . . . That he by this time must be sensible that the Garison would Fall . . . . and the Result of an Inraged body of Woodmen breaking in must be obvious to him it would be out of the power of an American officer to save a single man." *Clark Papers*, pp. 190, 286.

[4] Clark to Patrick Henry, April 29, 1779: "On hearing of my success against Mr. Hamilton, and were so certain of my embracing the fair opportunity of possessing myself of that post, that the merchants and others provided many necessaries for us on our arrival; the garrison, consisting of only eighty men, not daring to stop their diversions." Memoir: "DeTroit opened full in our View not more than 80 men in the Fort great part of them Invalids and we found that a considerable Number of thar prinsipal Inhabitants was disaffected to the British cause." *Ibid.*, pp. 172, 290.

[5] Memoir: "Col. Rogers who had been sent to the mississippi for a very considerable Quantity of Goo[d]s geting a reinforcement at the Falls on his passage to Pittsburgh, a little above Licking Creek got totally defeated himself

It is to be noted that many of the documents used in testing the accuracy of statements in the Memoir have been made public for the first time within the past few years. But there are other events referred to which cannot thus be tested, for they are given in the Memoir alone. In the histories of Kentucky and elsewhere these statements have been accepted without criticism. Such are: the treatment meted out to the men who escaped from Corn island by the inhabitants of Harrodsburg;[1] methods of keeping the men in good spirits, such as the assistance of the little "antick drummer";[2] making light of the fears of the volunteers; and Clark's orders to go out and kill some deer. On the twenty-second of February, when the men were almost despairing, Clark blackened his face with gunpowder and sprang forward into the icy water. His men followed, taking up the song of those in front. The night of February 23 was so cold that ice from one-half to three-fourths of an inch thick formed on the still water. Clark, at sunrise, promised them that a few hours more would bring them in sight of Vincennes. He then plunged into the water, giving orders to Captain Bowman to take the rear with twenty-five men and shoot any refusing to march. In cross-

---

and almost the whole of his party consisting of about 70 men were killed or made prisoners among the Latter those of Note ware Col. John Campbell and Cap[tn] Abraham Chapline." Benjamin Logan to Clark, October 17, 1779: "from the alarming news we have received of the defeat of Col[o] Rodgers & Campble." Robert Todd to Clark, October 16, 1779: "I have by chance heard of the disaster of Col. Rogers and the supposed loss of two Boats which had roused & alarm'd them here not a little." *Ibid.*, pp. 302, 371.

[1] *Ibid.*, p. 223 (Memoir); *The Winning of the West*, II, 40.

[2] Memoir:"a little Antick Drummer afforded them great divertion by floating on his Drum &c." *Clark Papers*, p. 271. Writers have enlarged upon this account. "In one of the companies was a small boy who acted as drummer. In the same company was a sergeant, standing six feet two inches in his stockings, stout, athletic, and devoted to Clark. Finding that his eloquence had no effect upon the men, in persuading them to continue their line of march, Clark mounted the little drummer on the shoulders of the stalwart sergeant, and gave orders to him to plunge into the half frozen water. He did so, the little drummer beating the *charge* from his lofty perch, while Clark, sword in hand, followed them, giving the command as he threw aside the floating ice—'Forward!' Elated and amused by the scene, the men promptly obeyed, holding their rifles above their heads, and in spite of all obstacles, reached the high land beyond them safely." John Law, *Colonial History of Vincennes* (Vincennes, 1858), p. 32, note. See also Thwaites, *How George Rogers Clark Won the Northwest*, p. 52.

ing the Horseshoe Plain many were saved from drowning by the canoes; others clung to their stronger companions and to logs and bushes. Fires were built when the strongest reached an island, but some of the men were restored only as two of their companions took them by the arms and forced them to run up and down. Arriving in sight of the town, a horseman who was out shooting ducks was captured, and from him Clark learned that the fort had been completed, that a large number of Indians had just entered the town, and that the French were lukewarm to the British.[1]

Finally, it is to be noted that certain incidents have been introduced into the account of Clark's conquest, supposedly coming from the Memoir, but for which there is no evidence whatsoever in that document. The most familiar and most striking of these, furnishing excellent material for the historical pageantry of our time, are: the description of the dance at Kaskaskia when that post was captured;[2] the defense of Vincennes by Captain Helm and his single companion;[3] their marching out with the honors of war; the story of Helm's drinking toddy with Hamilton before the fireplace in Fort Sackville and Clark's ordering his riflemen to fire at the chimney so as to knock the mortar into the toddy.[4]

[1] *Clark Papers*, pp. 272–77 (Memoir); *The Winning of the West*, II, 72–77.

[2] *Ibid.*, p. 46, note.

[3] "There is an anecdote respecting Captain Leonard Helm, evincing an intrepidity which would ill be omitted: it has been communicated to the author through the friendly interest of Judge Underwood, and his venerable relative, Edmund Rogers, Esq., of Barren county, a brother of Captain John Rogers, and personally intimate with Clark and his officers for years. It is as follows: When Governor Hamilton entered Vincennes, there were but two Americans there, Captain Helm, the commandant, and one Henry. The latter had a cannon well charged, and placed in the open fort gate, while Helm stood by it with a lighted match in his hand. When Hamilton and his troops got within good hailing distance, the American officer in a loud voice, cried out, 'Halt.' This stopped the movements of Hamilton; who in reply demanded a surrender of the garrison. Helm exclaimed with an oath, 'No man shall enter until I know the terms,' Hamilton answered, 'You shall have the honors of war'; and then the fort was surrendered with its garrison of one officer and one private." Mann Butler, *A History of the Commonwealth of Kentucky* (Cincinnati, 1836), p. 79, note.

[4] "The story of Helm drinking toddy by the fireplace when Clark retook the fort, and of the latter ordering riflemen to fire at the chimney, so as to knock the

It is evident from these tests that the Memoir can no longer be thought of as the reminiscences of an old man who strove for the dramatic in his presentation of facts. Although the language is stilted occasionally, especially in the speeches before Indian councils, it is not conspicuously so when compared with the Mason Letter and Clark's Journal describing similar events. These two documents, together with Clark's Diary and Bowman's Journal, will always constitute the main sources for the history of the West during the period between December 25, 1776, and the close of August, 1779. But from the evidence presented it may confidently be asserted that the Memoir must be accepted as a trustworthy supplement to each of them, at times, and to all of them on a number of essential points.

---

mortar into the toddy, may safely be set down as pure—and very weak—fiction. When Clark wrote memoirs, in his old age, he took delight in writing down among his exploits all sorts of childish stratagems; the marvel is that any sane historian should not have seen that these were on their face as untrue as they were ridiculous." *The Winning of the West*, II, 63, note.

APPENDIX II

Clark on the Mound Builders[1]

OHIO RIVER

SIR: I have some whare in your Museum read a long account of the march of de Soto through these Cuntreys he is brought to Lexington taken to the Mouth Muskinggum Cross to the Mississury &c &c Fortifying the Cuntrey he passed through and all those emence works are ascribed to him. I think the world ought to be undeceived in this point so great a stranger to the western Cuntrey as M. Webster appears to be ought to have informed himself better before he ventured to have pamed [palmed] his conjectures on the World. I dont suppose their is a person living that knows the Geography and Natural History of the back Cuntrey better if so well as I do myself it hath been my study for many years I have made the calculation and venture to inform you that if their was paved Roads from each of those fortifications to the other through out the western Cuntrey that De Soto could not have Visited the whole of those works with his army in four years allowing him the common season for marching. Those works are numerous in every part of the western cuntrey but more so in the Pittsburg Cuntrey than else whare there you will find them on tops of High Mountains they are larger as you descend towards the Mississippi, there is not a place on the Ohio that we have attempted to fortify from Pitt down but we find antient works, Soto might have been on the Ohio but no vestiges remain to prove it. as to his being the author of those Fortifications it is quite out of the question they are more numerous than he had men, and many of them would have required fifty Thousand men to have ocupied Some of them have been fortified Towns others Incampments, intrenched but the greatest parts have been common

[1] Letter addressed to Matthew Carey, editor of the *American Museum*. Draper MSS, 53 J 81.

Garisoned Forts Many of them with Towers of earth of considerable
height to defend the walls with arrows and other Missive weapons,
that they had commerce is evident because the mouths of every River
hath been fortified whare the Land was subject to floods, it hath been
raised out of the way of water, that they ware a numerous people is
also evident not only from their numerous Works but also their habitations raised in low Lands I had frequently observed scattered in what
we call the low Cuntrey on the Ohio Little mounds that I took to be
graves such as Mr. Jefferson describes which is frequent all over this
cuntrey but could not what could induce the people to bring their dead
Several miles from the High into the Lands for burial in the Spring
1780 I lay a considerable time near the mouth of the Ohio I was extremely anctious to find some high Ground near the point I had every
Acre of the Cuntrey for several miles explored but found the[m] Subject to inundation and was about to Move when a man came runing
into camp almost out of breath & with Joy informed me that he had
found a spot of high Land not far from that they had not befor noticed.
pleased with the information I went to the place and to my astonishment found the foundation of a Town raised in that low cuntrey the
few stone that lay scattered we could easily discover that they came
from a Quary up the Misspi this plat was in the shape of an L with
the angle pointing up the Mississippy and might have contained about
forty Huts I viewed this with great pleasure although of no other use
to me at the time it explained to me the cause of little mounds that I
had observed in the Low cuntrey and informed me that the whole of
this cuntrey had been so populas that good Lands was scarce and that
they raised habitations throughout these low cuntries and for the con-
veniency of Commerce or some other cause they had raised the foundation of a Town at the point Suffitiently large to answer their purpose
I say at the point because I make no doubt but that it was very near
it when built although at a very considerable distance at present as
the Rivers have left it I neglected at the time noticeing which River
it was probably on as I make no doubt it was on the bank of one or
the other I rather [think] the Mississippy as the Lands on that River
is Higher than those of Ohio in those parts That they had great armies
in the fleld is Evident the fortifed Lines in different parts would have
required enormous armies to man them one in the choctaw Cuntrey is
Several miles in length the one Mr Carver mentions and many others
in different directions but at considerable distances from each other
That important passes were attended to by them is evededent because

many them are Fortified. Thousands of Men have passed the Cumber
Land gap and perhaps but few of them have tain [taken] notice of the
Curiosity there the gap is very narrow and what is genely view'd as a
little Hill that nearly fills up the gap is an antient fortress for the defence of the place a fine spring breaking out within a few yards of it
that they made use of wells is evident becaus they yet appear in many
places as little Basons by the earth washing in: The one in the antient
fortress at Louisville was the year fill up by Cap^tn Patton who made
use of parts of the old wall for that purpose: Covered ways to water
is Common Caseways across Marshes is frequent the High Road across
little Grave Creek and I suppose does at present pass over an antient
Causeway made of sand and Gravell across a Marsh

The Indian tradition give an acc^t of those works they say they
ware the works of their forefathers and that they were formerly as
numerous as the Trees in the woods that they affronted the Great
Spirit and he made them kill one another the works on the Mississippi
near the Caw River is one of the largest we know of[1] the Kaskaskias
Chief, Babtist, gave me a history of it he said that was the palace of
his forefather when they covered the whole and had large Towns that
all those works we saw their was the Fortifications round the Town
which must have been very considerable that the Smaller works we so
[saw] far within the larger was the real palace that the little Mountain
we their saw flung up with a bason on the top was a Tower that contained part of the guards belonging to the prince as from the Top of
that height they could defend the Kings House with their arrows &c
I had some whare seen an antient account of the Town of Kohokia
formerly containing 10,000 M their is not one of that nation at present
known by that name being frequently at that place recollecting this
Story I one day set out with a party Gent^n to see whether we could
discover signs of such population we easily and evidently traced the

---

[1] Cahokia Mound, or "Monk's Mound," the most imposing monument of
the Mound Builders within the United States, is located 6 miles from East St.
Louis. Its shape is that of a truncated pyramid with a base extending 1,080
feet from north to south and 710 feet from east to west and covering a greater area than the greatest of the Egyptian pyramids. From the top, 100 feet
above the original suface, may be seen within a radius of two miles some sixty
other mounds, which vary in height from 10 to 50 feet. On some of them farm-
houses have been constructed, large trees are growing on others, while the faint
outlines of still others may still be seen after the years during which they have
been cultivated. This mound is now a part of the Illinois State Park System.

Town for upwards of five miles in the beautifull plain below the present Town of Kohokia their could be no deseption hear because the remains of antient works are thick the whole Mounds &c nature never formed a more beautifull than this several leagues in length and about four Miles in breadth from the River to the High land and but few Trees or scrubs to be seen this Town appear to have occupied that part of the nearest the River but not on it as their is a strip of lower Land. Fronting nearly the sentor of this Town on the Heights is pinicle called Shugar from its figure it is frequently Visited by Strangers as a mear curiosity. My visit was perhaps from different motives I was not disappointed I at once saw that it was a hill shaped by a rill breach or Brook breaking through the Heights it had formed a very narrow Ridge this had been cut across the point shaped in the form of a Shugar loaf perhaps to place an Idol or a Temple on as it could not be more conspicuous it is of very considerable height and you are obliged to wind round it to assend on horse back. I think the world is to blame to express such great ancziety to know who it was that built those numerous and formidable works and what hath become of those people they will find them in the Kaskaskias peorias Kohokias (now extinct) Piankishaws Kicabaws Cherokees and such old nations that say they grew out of the ground where they now live and that they ware formerly as numerous as the Trees in the woods but affronting the great spirit he made war among the nations and they destroyed each other this is their Tradition and I see no reason why it should not be received as good History at least as good as great part of ours. at what time this great revolution should have happened which certainly hath taken place in this Quarter I never could get any satisfactory Acc[t] only that it had been the case as it is beyond their Calculation of time but I am convinced that it is anteriour to five Hundred years and I dont think it difficult to make a tolerable Satisfactory conjecture of the time at least within a few Ages it may appear strange how it should be possible to discover this but so it is[1]

[1] This letter was first published by Henry R. Schoolcraft in *Archives of Aborginal Knowledge* (Philadelphia, 1860), IV, 133–36. The letter was sent to Schoolcraft by Lyman C. Draper. In commenting on the letter, Schoolcraft writes: "General Clark has discussed this question well. The extensive personal knowledge of this gentleman of these western antiquities; of the manners and customs of the aborigines; of Indian defensive works, and of military science generally, in which latter he so much distinguished himself, give great weight to his opinions. He deems these encampments, ditches, and lines of

defence, to be due entirely to the ancestors of the present race of Indians. In favor of this conclusion he adduces the additional testimony of Indian tradition" (p. 145).

In the discussion on American antiquities by Dr. W. H. Holmes, no reference is made to this letter nor to the statement of Mr. Schoolcraft. His conclusion, however, is as follows: "During the second half of the century researches extending over a large part of the United States were rapidly initiated, and a vast body of substantial information was brought together and published by individuals, societies, and institutions, and by the government. During this period a gradual change took place in the view of students regarding the Mound Builders, and at the close of the century there was practical unanimity in the view that the builders of the great earth works were the ancestors of the Indian tribes found in possession of the general region, and that the culture represented is not of a grade especially higher than that of the tribes first encountered by the whites in the lower Mississippi Valley and in some of the Gulf states to the east." (W. H. Holmes, "Handbook of Aboriginal American Antiquities." *United States Bureau of American Ethnology Bulletin 60* [Washington, 1919], pp. 15, 16.)

Appendix III

Improvement in River Navigation

Clark to John Brown:[1]

BEARGRASS, January 30th, 1790

. . . . I doubt Sir, you will smile at the contents of this letter, as it may appear to border a little on the marvellous, when I inform you of an invention that will give a new turn to the face of things throughout the Western country.

Frequently navigating those rivers in the course of the War, with various kinds of vessels, I was led to believe that great improvement might be made, which I was determined to study, when I should have leisure to apply myself. But at that period, Mr. Rumsey and others amused us with vessels so constructed as to answer every desirable purpose. This I believed they would have done, having a similar idea myself. They failing, I again resumed the study, and soon found that it was necessary to make myself master of the mechanical powers, which I did, and to my astonishment, found that by a combination of those powers properly applied, that a boat of any size, with a small given force (either by men or horses on board) would be forced against a stream that no number of oars applied in the common way, could move her. I was highly pleased with the discovery for sometime, but viewing the simplicity of the machine, I got discouraged, supposing it impossible but that every mechanical genius that turned his attention that way must know it, and that it had been tried and found not to answer the purpose. Not being able to discover any defect, and further to satisfy myself, I had the machine actually made on a small scale and proved every conjecture beyond a doubt. It moves any number of oars you choose to apply, with more regularity and despatch than men can possibly do. By multiplying the powers, the velocity of a vessel so fixed, will be as great as possible for it to pass through the water. I am not good at description, otherwise I should attempt to give you

[1] Draper MSS, 27 CC 29, 30.

a draught of this machine, and not wishing others, that are capable, to see it, I hope you will excuse me. What I wish you would do for me, is, to get a resolution of Congress in my favor, granting me the sole use of those vessels for fourteen years, throughout the Continent. I have already contracted for a boat of the size I wish, and within a month from the time I receive such a resolution, I will set her to work. Then all doubts respecting the expeditious navigation of those rivers will immediately vanish. The experiment is already made, and you need be in no doubt about it. I have raised every objection against it that my ingenuity could possible suggest, without being able to find a fault. With the small one I have, I can make every experiment I could wish to make. The request, if granted, may perhaps make me some amends for my public losses. Pray honor me with an answer to this letter as soon as possible. . . . .

I am, with great respect, Sir, your humble servant,

GEO. R. CLARK

The Hon. John Brown
John Brown to Clark:[1]

NEW YORK 27th April 1790

DEAR GENERAL: Your favor of the 30th Jan' came to hand this Morning. The Act of Congress which you will find inclosed contains all the information I can give you relative to obtaining a Patent Right for the Discovery you have made—Several applications for Patent Rights for supposed improvements in Navigating of Boats have been made but as yet no patents have issued. M' Jefferson has accepted the appointment of Secretary of State & is now in the discharge of the duties of that Office. . . . .

I am with sentiments of esteem,

Your friend & Hble Sert,

J. BROWN

Clark to John Brown:

JEFFERSON, July, 15th, 1790

DEAR SIR: I received your favor on the new construction of boats. The little machine remains as it did when I wrote you on the subject, without my being able to make any improvements or find a defect. The papers you were so kind as to enclose, gave much satisfaction to the neighbors. I hope you will continue those favors. . . . .

Please present my respects to Mr. Madison.

Am, Sir, y'r h'ble ser'vt

GEO. R. CLARK

The Hon. John Brown

[1] Draper MSS, 53 J 88.

Appendix IV
Speech of Chief Logan

Logan, whose Indian name was Tah-goh-jute, was a noted Mingo chief. His father was French, but as a boy was captured by the Indians and became an influential chief of the Cayuga. Logan's mother was of this tribe. For a number of years he lived in western Pennsylvania, and then, 1772, moved to a Mingo village located on Tetlow Creek. Among the pioneers he was noted for his sobriety, honesty, and friendship for the whites. In later life he drank to excess and is said to have become ferocious toward everyone. He met his death, 1780, at the hand of one of his relatives.

In the original statement regarding Logan made by Jefferson, *Notes on Virginia* (1781), he wrote:

The principles of their society forbidding all compulsion, they are to be led to duty and to enterprise by personal influence and persuasion. Hence eloquence in council, bravery and address in war, become the foundations of all consequence with them. To these acquirements all their faculties are directed. Of their bravery and address in war we have multiplied proofs, because we have been the subjects on which they were exercised. Of their eminence in oratory we have fewer examples, because it is displayed chiefly in their own councils. Some, however, we have of very superior lustre. I may challenge the whole orations of Demosthenes and Cicero, and of any more eminent orator, if Europe has furnished more eminent, to produce a single passage, superior to the speech of Logan, a Mingo Chief, to Lord Dunmore, when Governor of this State. And, as a testimony of their talents in these lines, I beg leave to introduce it. In the Spring of the year 1774, a robbery and murder were committed on an inhabitant of the frontiers of Virginia, by two Indians of the Shawnee tribe. The neighboring whites, according to their custom, undertook to punish this outrage in a summary way. Col. Cresap, a man infamous for the many murders he had committed on those much-injured people, collected a party, and proceeded down the Kanhaway in quest of vengeance. Unfortunately a canoe of women and children, with one man only, was seen coming from the opposite shore, unarmed, and unsuspecting a hostile attack from the whites. Cresap and his party concealed themselves on the bank of the river, and the moment the canoe reached the shore, singled out their objects, and at one fire killed every person in it. This happened to be the family of Logan, who had long been distinguished as a friend of the whites. This unworthy return provoked his vengeance.[1]

Luther Martin, son-in-law of Cresap, in a letter published in 1797, pronounced the speech not genuine and the statement made about Captain Cresap without foundation. A controversy followed, and this led Jefferson to make a careful investigation of the facts. This was the origin of the letter from Clark. It is difficult to understand why he did not incorporate the letter, along with others, in the new edition of his *Notes on Virginia*.[2]

In response to the criticism of Martin, Jefferson wrote: "I knew nothing of the Cresaps, and could not possibly have a motive to do them an injury with design. I repeated what thousands had done before, on as good authority as we have for most of the facts we learn through life, and such as, to this moment, I have seen no reason to doubt. That anybody questioned it, was never suspected by me, till I saw the letter of Mr. Martin in the Baltimore paper. I endeavored then to recollect who among my contemporaries, of the same circle of society, and consequently of the same recollections might still be alive."[3]

"I do not mean to notice Mr. Martin, or to go in the newspapers on the subject," he asserts in a statement to one of his friends (January 1, 1798), "but I am still anxious to inquire into the foundation of that story, and if I find anything wrong in it it shall be corrected, and what is right supported either in some new edition of that work or in an appendix to it."[4]

A similar inquiry was addressed to Dr. Samuel Brown, a well-known physician in Lexington and professor in Transylvania University.

[1] Thomas Jefferson, *Notes on the State of Virginia*, ed. J. W. Randolph (Richmond, 1853). The first edition appeared in 1781. A new edition was printed in 1800. Mr. Randolph used the first edition.

[2] These letters are to be found in Appendix IV, *Notes on Virginia* (ed. 1853). The letter from Clark was written June 17, 1798. One of the letters used is of April 4, 1799.

[3] *Notes on Virginia* (ed. 1853), p. 242.

[4] *Writings of Thomas Jefferson*, ed. Ford, VII, 185.

Jefferson to Dr. Brown:

PHILADELPHIA, Mar. 25, 98

"O! that mine enemy would write a book!" has been a well known prayer against an enemy. I had written a book, & it has furnished matter for abuse for want of something better. Mr. Martin's polite attack on the subject of Cresap and Logan, as stated in the Notes on Virginia, had begun before you left us; it has continued and still continues. . . . . I suppose it probable that General Clarke may know something of the facts relative to Logan or Cresap. I shall be much obliged to you for any information you can procure on this subject. . . . . I am in hopes in connecting with it some account of Kentucky that your information & his together will be able to correct & supply what I had collected relative to it in a very early day. Indeed it was to Genl Clarke that I was indebted for what degree of accuracy there was in most of my statements. I wish you to attend particularly to the overflowage of the Mississippi, on which I have been accused of error. Present me affectionately to the General & assure him of my constant remembrance & esteem."[1]

Dr. Brown to Clark:

I remember to have had some conversation with you respecting the affair when at your house; and, although the variety and important nature of the events which your conversations suggested, have in some degree effaced from my memory that distinct recollection of this particular event, which I ought to have before I should attempt to communicate your account of it to Mr. Jefferson, yet still I am pretty certain that as you related the story, any mistakes that have crept into the Notes on Virginia are not attributable to Mr. Jefferson but to Logan himself, or to those by whom his speech was originally published. I think you informed me that you were with Cresap at the time Logan's family was murdered, that Cresap was not the author of the massacre, that Logan actually delivered the speech as reported in the Notes of Virginia.[2]

CLARK'S LETTER ON THE SPEECH OF LOGAN[3]

June 17th, 1798

SIR: your letter was handed to me by Mr. Thruston, the matter therein contained was new to me; I find myself hurt that Mr. Jefferson should

[1] *Ibid.*, p. 223.   [2] Draper MSS, 48 J 2.

[3] Jefferson Papers, May 9, 1798—January 24, 1799, Library of Congress, p. 104.

those people and their associates. The War was raged with all its savage Fury until the following fall when a Treaty of Peace was held at Dunmores Camp within five miles of Chilicothe—the Indian Capitol on the Siothe—Logan did not appear—I was acquainted with him and wished to be informed of the Reason of his absence by one of the Interpreters, The answer that he gave to my Enquiry was "that he was like a Mad Dog, that his Bristles had been up and had not yet fallen, but that the Good Talks now going forward might allay them." Logans speech to Dunmore now came forward as related to Mr. Jefferson and was generally believed and indeed not doubted to have been genuine and dictated by Logan. The Army knew it was wrong so far as it respected Cresap and afforded me opportunity to rally that Gentleman on the Subject—I discovered that Cresap was displeased and told him that he must be a very great Man, that the Indians shouldered him with everything that happened—he smiled and said that he had a great mind to tomahawk Greathouse about the Matter—What is here related was Fact, I was intimate with Cresap, and better acquainted with Logan at that time than with any other Indian in the Western Country, and had a knowledge of the Conduct of both Parties. Logan is Author of [the] Speech as related by Mr. Jefferson, and Cresaps conduct was such as I have herein related.

I have gone through a Relation of every Circumstance that has any Connection and Information you desire, and hope it will be satisfactory to yourself and Mr. Jefferson.

I am

Your mos ob.t Serv.t

G. R. CLARK

Doct.r Sam.l Brown

LETTER OF DR. SAMUEL BROWN TO JEFFERSON[1]

LEXINGTON Sept. 4th 1798

DEAR SIR: The letter you did me the honor of writing me, in March last, I intended to have answered long since; and to enable me to do so, the more to your satisfaction I took the earliest opportunities of informing General Clarke and several other gentlemen, who had been companions of his youthful campaigns, of the illiberal attack made on you by the Attorney General of Maryland. I have deferred replying to your friendly letter hereto, from an expectation of collecting from

[1] Jefferson Papers, May 9, 1798—January 24, 1799, Library of Congress, p. 104.

have been attacked with so much Virulence on a Subject which I know he was not the Author of, but except a few Mistakes of Names of Persons or Places the story is substantially true, I was of the first and last of the active officers who bore the Weight of that War, and on Perusing some Old Papers of that Date I find some Memoirs, but independent of them I have a perfect recollection of every Transaction relative to Logan's story—the Conduct of Cresap I am perfectly acquainted with, he was not the Author of that Murder, but a Family of the Name of Greathouse—But some transactions that happened under the Conduct of Capt.n Cresap a few Days previous to the Murder of Logan's Family gave him sufficient grounds to suppose it was Cresap who had done him the Injury; but to enable you fully to understand the subject of your Enquiry, I shall relate the Incidents that gave rise to Logan's suspicions, and will enable Mr. Jefferson to do Justice to himself and the Cresap Family, by being made fully acquainted with Facts.

Kentucky was explored in 1773; a Resolution was formed to make Settlement in the Spring following and the Mouth of the little Kenhawa was appointed the Place of Rendevous—in order to descend the River from thence in a Body; Early in the Spring the Indians had done some Mischief, Reports fom their towns were alarming which caused many to decline meeting and only eighty or ninety men assembled at the Place of Rendevous where we lay for some Days; a small Party of Hunters which lay about ten miles below us were fired on by the Indians whom the Hunters bear off and returned to our Camp, this and many other Circumstances led us to believe that the Indians were determined to make War; the whole of our Party was exasperated, and resolved not to be disappointed in their Project of forming a Settlement in Kentucky, as we had every necessary Store that could be thought of.

An Indian Town called Horse-Head Bottom on the Siotho and nearest its Mouth lay most in our way, we resolved to cross the country and surprise it; who was to command was the question; there were but few among us who had experience in Indian Warfare, and they were such as we did not chose to be commanded by. We knew of Capt Cresap being upon the River about 15 Miles above with some Hands settling a new Plantation and intending to follow us to Kentucky as soon as he had fixed his People, we also knew that he had had Experience in a former War. It was proposed and unanimously agreed on to send for him to command the Party. Messengers were dispatched and in half an Hour returned with Cresap; he had heard of our Revolution by some of his Hunters who had fallen in from those of our Camp, and had set out to come to us; we now thought our little Army (as we called it) complete and the Destruction of the Indian Town inevitable, a Council was called and to our astonishment our intended General was the Person who dissuaded us from the Enterprize, alledging that appearances were suspicious, but that there was no certainty of a War, that if we made the Attempt proposed he had no doubt of Success, but that a War at any Rate would be the Result, that we should be blamed for it and perhaps justly; but that if we were determined to execute the Plan he would lay aside all Considerations, send for his People and share our Fortunes; he was then asked what Measure he would recommend to us, his answer was that we should return to Wheeling a convenient Post to obtain Intelligence of what was going forward, that a few weeks would determine the Matter, and as it was early in the Spring, if we should find that the Indians were not hostilely disposed we should have full Time to prosecute our intended Settlements in Kentucky. The Measure was adopted, and in two hours the whole Party was on its way. As we ascended the River we met Killbuck an Indian Chief [Delaware] with a small Party; We had a long Conference but obtained very little satisfaction from him. It was observed that Cresap did not attend this Conference but kept on the opposite side of the River; he said that he was afraid to trust himself with the Indians; that Killbuck had frequently attempted to waylay and Kill his father, and he was doubtful that he should [be] tempted to put Killbuck to Death. On our arrival at Wheeling the whole country being pretty much settled thereabouts, the Inhabitants appeared to be much alarmed, and fled to our Camp from every Direction—we offered to cover their neighborhood with Scouts, until we could obtain further Information, if they would return to their Plantations but nothing we could say would prevail, by this time we got to be a formidable party as all the Hunters and Men without Families &c. in that quarter joined us. Our Arrival at Wheeling was soon known at Pittsburgh, the whole of that Country at that time being under Jurisdiction Virginia Doctor Connelly had been appointed by Dunmore Cap. Commandant of the District then called West Augusta; He Connelly hearing of us, sent a message addressed to the Party, informing us that a War was to be apprehended, and requesting that we would keep our Position for a few days that Messengers had been sent to the Indian Towns whose Return he daily expected, and the Doubt respecting a war with the Indians would then be cleared up. The Answer we returned was

that we had no Inclination to decamp for some time, and during our stay we should be careful that the Enemy should not harrass the Neighborhood, But before this Answer could reach Pittsburgh he had sent a second express addressed to Capt Cresap as the most influential man amongst us informing him that the Messengers had returned from the Indian Towns and that a War was inevitable and begged him to use his influence with the Party to get them to cover the Country until the Inhabitants could fortify themselves The Time of the Reception of this letter was the Epoch of open Hostilities with the Indians—The War Post was planted a Council called and the Letter read and the Ceremonies used by the Indians on so important Occasion and War was formally declared—The same Evening two Scalps were brought into Camp—The following Day some Canoes of the Indians were discovered descending the River, taking advantage of an Island to cover themselves from our view They were chased by our Men 15 miles down the River they were forced ashore and a Battle ensued a few were wounded on both Sides and we got one scalp only, on examining their canoe we found a considerable quantity of ammunition and other warlike Stores—On our Return to camp a Resolution was formed to march next day and attack Logan's Camp on the Ohio about 30 miles above Wheeling—we actually march about five Miles and halted to take some refreshments, here the Impropriety of Executing the proposed Enterprize was agreed the Conversation was brought forward by Cresap himself; it was generally agreed that those Indians had no hostile Intentions, as it was a hunting Camp composed of Men Women and Children with all their stuff with them This we knew as I myself and others then present had been at their Camp about four weeks before that Time on our way down from Pittsburgh. In short every Person present especially Cresap (upon reflection) was opposed to the projected Measure We returned and on the same evening decamped and took the Road to Redstone—it was two Days after this that Logan's Family was killed, and from the manner in which it was done it was viewed as a horrid murder by the whole Country. From Logans hearing that Cresap was at the head of this party at Wheeling it was no wonder that he considered Cresap as the Author of his Family's Destruction.

Since the receipt of your Letter I have procured the Notes on Virginia, they are now before me; the action was more barbarous than therein related by Mr. Jefferson; those Indians used to visit and receive visits from the neighboring whites on the opposite Shore, were on a Visit at Greathouses at the Time they were masacr

different sources, a variety of statements, and facts relative to the murder of Logans family. But as most of the gentlemen to whom I wrote on the subject, reside in remote parts of the country, at a distance from Post Roads, I am induced to attribute their silence to the want of safe modes of conveying their letters to Lexington. I am, however, happy, in having it in my power to transmit to you, an interesting letter from your good friend General Clarke, which, indeed, appears to me, to render further investigation quite unnecessary. The only point for which you contend (viz) that Logan is really the author of the speech ascribed to him, in your Notes on Virginia is now established beyond the possibility of a contradiction. The incidents in General Clarkes narrative follow each other in a manner so simple and so natural as to afford to every liberal and candid enquirer, the highest internal evidence of their reality.

To those who have the happiness of being acquainted with that truly great man, his statement will bring the fullest conviction. His memory is singularly accurate, his veracity unquestionable. To such respectable authority I can suppose no one capable of objecting, except Mr. Luther Martin. I have shown General Clarkes letter to Major Morrison, the Supervisor of the Ohio District, who resided near Pittsburg when the transaction respecting Logan occurred. He assures me that he knows most of them as stated in the letter to be true for they are within his own recollection.

Col. Peterson who likewise lived in that Country about that time mentioned to me a circumstance which appears worthy of notice. There were, then, in that, as in almost every other frontier, two parties—by the one Capt. Cresap was considered as a wanton violator of Treaties as a man of a crual and inhuman disposition, by the other he was esteemed as an intrepid warrior & as a just avenger of savage barbarities. You probably became first acquainted with his character at Williamsburg the seat of Government; General Clarke joined him in the War-Path, This circumstance will, perhaps, in some measure, account for the very different sentiments, which two Gentlemen so capable of appreciating Cresaps character, may have entertained respecting it.

Should you judge it advisable at the present time, I could easily obtain from General Clarke the substance of his narrative and have it published here as an answer to spontaneous enquiries of my own. It can be done without you appearing at all in the business. This however I shall not attempt to do without your permission; yet I wish that Genl Clarkes statement could be made public in some shape or other, as it would doubly mortify Mr. Martin to have his assertions refuted without receiving a reply from you whom he has so seduously labored to draw forth into the field of controversy. I can assure you that your friends in this quarter are highly gratified at the silent contempt with which you have treated that redoutable Hero of Federalism, and it is with heartfelt pleasure that I further assure you, that nothing which old Tories aristocrats, and governmental Sycophants can say against you, will in any degree, diminish the confidence, which the good citizens of this State repose in your abilities & patriotism. Never was a State more unanimous in execrating the measures supported by your Enemies who, I trust, will soon prove themselves to be what I have long thot them, the enemies of Liberty and their Country.

I have Sir The honor

To be yo ms obt

SAM BROWN

Letters of Clark pertaining to His Relations with the French Government, 1798, 1799

TRADUCTION D'UNE LETTRE DE SAMUEL FULTON DU 6 THERMIDOR[1]

Je viens de recevoir une lettre du G^l G. R Clark dont je m'empresse de vous communiquer copie pour vous faire connaître la situation facheuse de ce brave officier et en même tems pour vous prier de faire quelques démarches en sa faveur, afin qu'il ne devienne pas la victime de ses cruels ennemis.

Ci joint vous trouvéres une copie fidele de cette lettre dont j'ai remis l'original du directoire.

Philadelphie le 3 Juin 1798.

LETTRE DU G^I CLARK AU COLONEL FULTON A PARIS

Je m'empresse de vous apprendre la situation facheuse dans laquelle notre pais est sur le point d'etre plongé par une faction anglaise qui s'est emparée des rênes du Gouvernement. La guerre avec la republique francaise parâit inevitable on prend toutes les mesures hostiles imaginables comme vous pourrés vous enconvaincre par la lecture des journaux ci joints.

La guerre des etats unis avec la Rep. parait inevitable

Les oreilles frappées des vociferations horribles vomies par tous les malveillans contre la genereuse mation a laquelle tout vrai americain est redevable de sa liberté je n'ai plus pu ni empêcher de venir à la capitale, afin de connaitre la source de ces etonnantes plaintes et griefs, mais je vois clai remt [sic] que *l'or seul de l'Angleterre* en est le cause. A mon arrivee ici, je fus aussitot menacé d'incarceration, Mais apres une plus mûre deliberation j'ai ete invité a donner ma demission au consul general de France ou a me retirer des Etats Unis.

J'ai refusé de faire le premier, comme vous pouve bien l'imaginer mais je crois que je serai oblige de souscrire a la seconde proposition.

[1] *Affaires Étrangeres, États Unis*, Vol. XLVIII, fol. 130.

Mais n'ayant rien appris de vous depuis près d'un an, ni recu des instructions du Directoire, j'allai trouver le Consul francais pour concerter avec lui s'll conviendroit que je passasse en France, mais je trouvai en lui un homme ou trop timide ou peu enclin a donner un avis. Nayant pu rien obtenir de satisfesant de sa part, je me rendit sur le champ chez le Ministre d'Espagne et luy fis part de ma situation

Il m'offrit aussitot toute la protection qu'un ami et allie de la France pouvait accorder a un de ses officiers, et il m'a meme prie

Le ministre d'espagne invite le Gal Clark a se rendre sur le Mississippi

d'aller a St. Louis sur le Mississipi et d'y cooperer avec le commandant de ce pays a dejouer toutes les tentatives hostiles que l'ennemi commun pourrait faire contre les etablissement espagnols sur le Mississipi, jus qu'a ce que je puisse obtenir les instructions du Directoire executif.

J'accepterai cette proposition jusqu'a a nouvel ordre en attendant je vous prie de communiquer cette lettre au directoire et le prier de m'envoyer des instructions pour regler ma conduite; Je suis bien persudé que ce n'est pas son intention qu'une personne qui a donne tant de gages de son attachement à la cause, soit entieremt oublie ou negligé dans un moment aussi important que celui-ci.

Vous n'aurés pas de la peine a croire que d'apres les depenses, que j'ai faites ces cinq dernieres annees pour soutenir la cause de la France, dans ce pais, je ne dois pas être fort á mon aise á present; Je vous prie

et les arrerajes de sa paye

donc de solliciter une partiè de ce qui peut m'être du de ma paye.

Consideres qu'il s'est ecoulé cinq ans depuis ma premiere nomination et que je n'ai pas encore recu un sol excepté ce que vous m'aves avancé. Je partirai sous peu de jours pour Kentukey afin d'y mettre notre propriete a l'abret de toute entreprise, car nous sommes menaces de confiscation, vous parce que vous servés en qualite de militaire en France, et moi parce que je suis chargé d'une mission dans les Etats Unis, quoique il y ait longtems que nous nous sommes expatriés.

De Kentuky je me rendrai incessamt [*sic*] a St. Louis ou je resterai jusqu'a ce que je puisse recevoir de vos nouvelles.

Si vous vous proposiés de venir vous même, je vous conseillerai de débarquer a quelque port du sud où vous n'etes pas connu, et de voyager le plus incognito que vous pourrés, jusqu'a ce que vous arrivies sur les bords du Mississipi.

Je n'ai plus rien a vous dire pour le present sinon d'assurer le directoire de mon attachemt [*sic*] inalterable a la cause de la France et sa constution [*sic*] republitaine et que j'attends avec une vive impatience d'ulterieures instructions—enfin que je me repose intieremt [*sic*] sur sa protection, car tout ce que je possede a present dans le monde est bien precaire.

EXTRAIT D'UNE LETTRE DU GENERAL CLARK[1]
MINISTERE DES RELATIONS EXTERIEURES
ÉTATS UNIS. ST. LOUIS, RIVE OCCIDENTALE DU MISSISSIPI,
23 fructidor au 6

Apres mon retour du Kentukey, le president Des etats unis Donna ordre de me faire arreter. Mais le Detachement quil envoya pour me prendre fut attaqué et desarmé par un certain nombre de volontaires que mes anciens camarades eurent le tems de rassembler. Je me retirai ensuite a St. louis Rive occidentale du mississipi.

La j'ai en soin d'observer les moyens de defense du pays et Le nombre des habitans et des troupes qui sont dans le haute Louisaine. Ce pays est hors d'etat de resister a une invasion ni les militaires ni les habitans ne sont attaches a l'espagne; il s'y trouve a peine deus mille hommes de troupes; en Cas De rupture avec les etats unis, la Louisiane deviendrait pour eux une facile proie, et il serait difficile de la leur arracher environ quinze cent familles sont Deja venues des etats unis s'etablir a St. louis, et si l'angleterre et les etats unis conquierent la Louisiane, Cinquante mille familles viendront s'y fixer des la premiere annee.

Que la france s'en empare l'emigration sera encore plus forte, ce pays procurera a la Republique un grand ascendant dans les etats unis, parce qu'il lui vaudra l'alliance des habitans Des plaines qui sont a l'ouest Des montagnes d'Alligany, habitans qui finiront par se Detacher du gouvernement federal.

Si le Directoire Executif Desire posseder la Louisiane, il n'y a pas de tems à perdre. Dans neuf mois au plus, il serait trop tard; ce pays serait conquis par l'amerique ou l'Angleterre.

en Soumettant ces remarques au Directoire, veuillez lui representer que depuis cinq ans que je suis au service de france en qualite de general je n'ai rien recu, et que je suis oblige de faire de continuels sacrifices.

[Sign] GEORGE R. CLARK

SAMUEL FULTON, AMERICAIN, AU CITOYEN REWBELL, MEMBRE DU DIRECTOIRE EXECUTIF. RECU LE IER NIVOSE AU 7[2]

CITOYEN DIRECTEUR: Je viens de recevoir une lettre d'1 Cen Georges Rogers Clark employé avec le Grade de General au Service de la Re-

[1] *Affaires Étrangeres, États Unis,* Vol. L, fol. 221.

[2] *Ibid.,* fols. 376, 377.

publique, aux Etats Unis, dont est ci-jointe le Traduction. Je m'adresse a votre humanite, vous priant d'avoir egard a ce brave homme qui S'est sacrifié pour son attachement a la france, oblige d'abandonner son bien et sa Patrie, et de se refugier dans la Partie [sic] espagnole.

il y a trois ans que je suis a Paris pour solliciter ce qui lui est dû de ses appointements comme General, ainsi que 4805 Piastres Gourdes quil a deboursées pour les preparatifs de l'expedition contre la Louisiane en 1794; mais sans le moindre espoir de reussir; le Departement de la Marine ayant toujours oppose des difficultes *in surmontables*. Tantot des pieces ne sont pas en règle selon la Comptabilité en france; sans considerer l'impossibilite d'accomplir cette Condition sur les bords du Mississipi. Tantot c'est le manque de fonds, et ensuite que la maniere de payer n'est pas fixee par le Directoire, dans son arrete du 28. Prairial an 5ᵉ qui portoit ordre de le payer avec tous les officiers employes dans l'expedition.

Veuillez donc, Citoyen Directeur, prendre en Consideration la malheureuse position d'un digne Republicain, et ordonner les moyens les plus efficaces pour l'execution de votre arrete dont Copie est egalement cijointe, afin que je puisse voler a son secours.

> Salut et Respect
> Samᵉˡ Fulton

Egalite Liberte

EXTRAIT DES REGISTRES DES DELIBERATIONS DU DIRECTOIRE EXECUTIF PARIS LE 28. PRAIRIAL AU 5ᵉ DE LA REPUBᵉ UNE ET INDIVISIBLE

Le Directoire Executif apres avoir entendu le rapport du Ministres des Relations experieures, arrête

Art. 1ᵉʳ

Les officiers employés dans l'expedition projettie en 1794 contre la Louisane et les florides, par le Cᵉⁿ Genet alors Ministre de la Republique francaise, pres les Etats Unis de L'Amerique, et d'apres L'autorisation formelle du Conseil executif provisoire seront payes de leurs Traitement sur les fonds mis a la disposition du Ministre de la Marine et des Colonies en egard a leurs Grades respectifs et a partir de L'epoque de leur Commission ou de leur brevet, Jusqu'a celle de la proclamation par laquelle le cᵉⁿ fauchet successeur du CᵉⁿGenet suspendit cette expedition.

Art. 2ᵉ

Chacun des dits officiers pour recevoir son traitement sera tenu de presenter au Ministre de la Marine et des Colonies une Commission signie du Cᵉⁿ Genet ou bien un Brevet delivré par les Chefs de L'expedition ci-dessus auquel Brevet devra etre jointe une declaration de la Legation francaise a Philadelphie constatant que ce Brevet a ete donné anterieurement a la Notification de la Proclamation de l'ex ministre fauchet. Dans L'un et L'autre cas les dits officiers prouveront par un Certificat de cette Legation que Le Traitement qu'ils reclament n'a point ete acquitté.

Art. 3ᵉ

Il ne sera accorde aucune indemnité aux dits officiers.

Art. 4

Les ministres de la Marine et des Relations exterieurs, chacun en ce qui le concerne, sont chargés de l'execution du present arrêté qui ne sera point imprime.

Pour Expedition Conforme Le President du Directoire Executif signé Carnot.

Par le Directoire Executif, Le secretaire General signé Lagarde.

Pour copie conforme signé Truguet.

Bibliography[1]

I. UNPUBLISHED SOURCES

Manuscripts in Archivo General de las Indias, Seville, Spain (transcripts in Ayer Collection, Newberry Library). Archives des Affaires Étrangères, Paris.

Memoir on the retrocession of Louisiana (1789), *États Unis*, Vol. III (William Smith Mason Library, Evanston).

Draper Manuscripts (in the Wisconsin Historical Library).

Haldimand Manuscripts (in the British Museum).

Innes Papers, Letters Relating to Kentucky Discontent, 1789–91 (Library of Congress).

Rufus King Papers, Navigation of the Mississippi and Indian Relations, New York Historical Society.

Letter of Clark to S. Brown, Jefferson Papers (Library of Congress).

Letter of Clark to George Mason (in the possession of J. S. Pirtle, Louisville).

Letters of Henry Knox, Secretary of War (Library of Congress).

Letters of James Madison (New York Public Library).

Letters of James Monroe (New York Public Library).

Letters of Timothy Pickering, Department of State; also Massachusetts Historical Society Collection.

Letters to Washington (Library of Congress).

George Morgan, Letter Books. 3 vols. (Carnegie Institute, Pittsburgh).

Pollock Papers, in Papers of the Continental Congress (Library of Congress).

Public Record Office (London), F.O.R., America.

Virginia State Archives: Clark Letters, Letter Book of Benjamin Harrison, Letter Book of Thomas Jefferson.

Washington Manuscripts (Library of Congress).

[1] Used in the preparation of this volume.

II. PUBLISHED SOURCES

ADAMS, JOHN QUINCY. *Writings*, ed. W. C. Ford. 7 vols. (New York, 1913–17).

ALMON, J. *The Remembrancer or Impartial Repository of Public Events.* 17 vols. (London, 1775–84).

ALVORD, CLARENCE W. (ed.). *Cahokia Records, 1778–90* (Springfield, 1907), *Collections of the Illinois State Historical Library*, Vol. II, *Virginia Series*. Vol. I.

———. *Kaskaskia Records, 1778–90* (Springfield, 1909), *Collections of the Illinois State Historical Library*, Vol. V, *Virginia Series*, Vol. II.

———, AND CLARENCE EDWIN CARTER (eds.). *The Critical Period, 1763–65* (Springfield, 1915), *Collections of the Illinois State Historical Library*, Vol. X.

———, AND C. E. CARTER (eds.). *The New Régime, 1765–67* (Springfield, 1916), *Collections of the Illinois State Historical Library*, Vol. XI.

American Archives (4th and 5th series), ed. Peter Force, 9 vols. (Washington, 1837–53).

American State Papers, Public Lands. 8 vols. (Washington, 1833–61).

———, *Foreign Relations*, 6 vols. (Washington, 1833).

———, *Indian Affairs*, 2 vols. (Washington, 1832).

———, *Miscellaneous*, 2 vols. (Washington, 1834).

BALLAGH, JAMES C. (ed.). *Letters of Richard Henry Lee.* 2 vols. (New York, 1911, 1914).

BECKWITH, H. W. *Collections of the Illinois State Historical Library*, Vol. I (Springfield, 1903).

BILLON, FREDERIC L. *Annals of St. Louis in Its Early Days under French and Spanish Domination* (St. Louis, 1886).

———. *Annals of St. Louis from 1804 to 1821, Being a Continuation of the Author's Previous Work* (St. Louis, 1888).

BRACKENRIDGE, HENRY M. *Journal of a Voyage up the River Missouri; Performed in Eighteen Hundred and Eleven* (2d ed., Baltimore, 1816). Reprinted in R. G. Thwaites, *Early Western Travels*, Vol. VI.

BRADBURY, JOHN. *Travels in the Interior of America, in the Years 1809, 1810, 1811; Including a Description of Upper Louisiana Together with the States of Ohio, Kentucky, Indiana and Tennessee, with the Illinois and Western Territories, etc.* (2d ed. London, 1814). Reprinted in Thwaites, *Early Western Travels*, Vol. V.

BUTTERFIELD, CONSUL W. (ed.). *Washington-Irvine Correspondence* (Madison, 1882)

Calendar of Virginia State Papers and Other Manuscripts. 11 vols. (Richmond, 1875–93).

Canadian Archives Reports, 1872–1921 (Ottawa, 1873–1922).

Chicago Historical Society's Collections, Vols. I–V (Chicago, 1882–1908).

CIST, C. *The Cincinnati Miscellany.* 2 vols. (Cincinnati, 1845).

COLLOT, G. H. V. *Voyage dans L'Amerique Septrionale.* 2 vols. (Paris, 1826).

Correspondence of Clark and Genet, ed. F. J. Turner, *American Historical Association Report,* 1896 (Washington, 1897).

CRAIG, NEVILLE B. (ed.). *The Olden Time.* 2 vols. (Pittsburgh, 1846–48).

DENNY, MAJOR E. *A Military Journal, Record of Upland and Denny's Journal* (Philadelphia, 1860).

Documents Relative to the Colonial History of the State of New York. 11 vols. (Albany, 1856).

FRANKLIN, BENJAMIN. *Writings,* ed. A. H. Smyth. 10 vols. (New York, 1905–7).

HENING, WILLIAM WALLER. *Statutes at Large, Being a Collection of the Laws of Virginia, 1619–1792.* 13 vols. (Richmond, 1819–23).

HENRY, WILLIAM WIRT. *Patrick Henry; Life, Speeches and Correspondence.* 3 vols. (New York, 1891).

HOUCK, LOUIS. *The Spanish Régime in Missouri: A Collection of Papers and Documents Relating to Upper Louisiana, Principally within the Present Limits of Missouri, during the Dominion of Spain, from the Archives of the Indies,* Seville, etc. 2 vols. (Chicago, 1909).

"Intercepted Letters and Journal of George Rogers Clark, 1778, 1779," *American Historical Review,* Vol. I (New York, 1896).

JAMES, JAMES ALTON (ed.). *George Rogers Clark Papers, 1771–81* (Springfield, 1912), *Collections of the Illinois State Historical Library,* Vol. VIII, *Virginia Series,* Vol. III.

———. *George Rogers Clark Papers, 1781–84* (Springfield, 1926), *Collections of the Illinois State Historical Library,* Vol. XIX, *Virginia Series,* Vol. IV.

JAY, JOHN. *Correspondence and Public Papers,* ed. H. P. Johnson. 4 vols. (New York, 1890–93).

JEFFERSON, THOMAS. *Writings,* ed. P. L. Ford. 10 vols. (New York, 1892–99).

———. *Writings,* ed. H. A. Washington. 9 vols, (Philadelphia, 1853).

Journals of the Continental Congress, 1774–89 (Library of Congress). 23 vols. (Washington, 1904–15).

KELLOGG, LOUISE PHELPS (ed.). *Frontier Advance on the Upper Ohio, 1778–79* (Madison, 1916), *Wisconsin Historical Collections*, Vol. XXIII.

———. *Frontier Retreat on the Upper Ohio, 1779–81* (Madison, 1917), *Wisconsin Historical Collections*, Vol. XXXIV.

LITTELL, WILLIAM. *Political Transactions*, ed. Temple Bodley (Louisville, 1926), *Filson Club Publications*, Vol. XXI.

MASON, E. G. *John Todd's Papers*, in *Chicago Historical Society Collections*, Vol. IV (Chicago, 1890).

———. *John Todd's Record Book*, in *Chicago Historical Society Collections*, Vol. IV (Chicago, 1890).

———. *Rocheblave Papers*, in *Chicago Historical Society Collections*, Vol. IV (Chicago, 1890).

Michigan Pioneer and Historical Collections. 39 vols. (Lansing, 1877—).

The Colonial and State Records of North Carolina, ed. Walter Clark. 30 vols. (Raleigh, 1885–1914).

Pennsylvania Archives. 12 vols. (Philadelphia, 1852–56).

Pennsylvania Colonial Records. 16 vols. (Philadelphia, 1851–53).

PIRTLE, HENRY (ed.). *Colonel George Rogers Clark's Sketch of his Campaign in the Illinois in 1778–79* (Cincinnati, 1869), Ohio Valley Historical Series, No. 3.

PITTMAN, PHILIP. *The Present State of the European Settlements on the Mississippi* (London, 1770). (2d ed., edited by Frank H. Hodder, Cleveland, 1906.)

POPE, J. *Tour in the Southern and Western Territories in 1790* (Richmond, 1792).

RICHARDSON, J. D. *Messages and Papers of the Presidents*. 10 vols. (Washington, 1896–99).

ROBERTSON, JAMES A. (ed.). "Spanish Correspondence concerning the American Revolution," *Hispanic American Historical Review*, I, 299.

———. *Louisiana under Spain, France, and the United States, 1785–1807* (Cleveland, 1911).

ST. CLAIR, A. *A Narrative of the Manner in which the Campaign against the Indians, 1791, Was Conducted* (Philadelphia, 1812).

Secret Journals of the Acts and Proceedings of Congress. 4 vols. (Boston, 1821).

SHEPHERD, W. R. "Wilkinson and the Spanish Conspiracy," *American Historical Review*, IX, 490, 748.

SMITH, W. H. *St. Clair Papers.* 2 vols. (Cincinnati, 1882).

STEINER, BERNARD C. (ed.). *The Life and Correspondence of James McHenry* (Cleveland, 1907).

STODDARD, AMOS. *Sketches, Historical and Descriptive, of Louisiana* (Philadelphia, 1812).

THWAITES, REUBEN G. (ed.). *Early Western Travels, 1748-1846.* 32 vols. (Cleveland, 1904).

——, AND KELLOGG, LOUISE P. (eds.). *Documentary History of Dunmore's War, 1774* (Madison, 1905).

——. *The Revolution on the Upper Ohio, 1775-77* (Madison, 1908).

TURNER, FREDERICK J. "George Rogers Clark and the Kaskaskia Campaign, 1777-78," *American Historical Review*, Vol. VIII (New York, 1903).

——. "The Correspondence of Clark and Genet," *Report of American Historical Association* (Washington, 1896).

——. "Correspondence of French Ministers to the United States, 1791-97," *Report of American Historical Association, 1903,* Vol. II (Washington, 1904).

——. "Mangourit Correspondence," *Report of American Historical Association,* 1897 (Washington, 1897).

VOLNEY, C. F. *View of the Climate and Soil of the United States of America.* Trans. (London, 1804).

WASHINGTON, GEORGE. *Writings,* ed. W. C. Ford. 14 vols. (New York, 1889-93).

——. *Writings,* ed. Jared Sparks. 12 vols. (Boston, 1834-37).

——. *Diaries,* ed. J. C. Fitzpatrick. 4 vols. (Boston, 1925).

WHARTON, FRANCIS (ed.). *The Revolutionary Diplomatic Correspondence of the United States.* 6 vols. (Washington, 1889).

Wisconsin Historical Collections, Vols. I-XX (Madison, 1855—).

WILKINSON, JAMES. *Memoirs of My Own Times.* 3 vols. (Philadelphia, 1816).

WITHERS, ALEXANDER S. *Chronicles of Border Warfare,* ed. R. G. Thwaites (Philadelphia, 1816).

GENERAL MATERIAL

ADAMS, HENRY. *History of the United States.* 9 vols. (New York, 1889-91).

ALDEN, G. H. *New Governments West of the Alleghanies before 1780* (Madison, 1897), *University of Wisconsin Bulletin,* Vol. II, No. 1.

ALDEN, G. H. "The State of Franklin," *American Historical Review*, Vol. VIII (New York, 1903).

ALVORD, CLARENCE W. *The Illinois Country, 1673–1818* (Springfield, 1920), *Centennial History of Illinois*, Vol. I.

———. "Conquest of St. Joseph, Michigan, by the Spaniards in 1781," *Missouri Historical Review*, Vol. II (Columbia, Missouri, 1907).

———. *The Mississippi Valley in British Politics: A Study of the Trade, Land Speculation, and Experiments in Imperialism Culminating in the American Revolution*, 2 vols. (Cleveland, 1917).

———. "Virginia and the West: An Interpretation," *Mississippi Valley Historical Review*, Vol. III (Cedar Rapids, 1916).

———. "Eighteenth-Century French Records in the Archives of Illinois," *Annual Report of American Historical Association, 1905* (Washington, 1906).

BECK, L. C. *A Gazetteer of the States of Illinois and Missouri* (Albany, 1823).

BEMIS, SAMUEL FLAGG. *Pinckney's Treaty* (Johns Hopkins University Press, 1926).

BENTON, E. J. *The Wabash Trade* (Baltimore, 1903), *Johns Hopkins University Studies XXI*.

BEVERIDGE, ALBERT J. *The Life of John Marshall.* 4 vols. (Boston, 1916).

BOGGESS, A. C. *The Settlement of Illinois, 1778–1830* (Chicago, 1908), *Chicago Historical Society Collections*, Vol. V.

BOND, B. W. *The Monroe Mission to France, 1794–96* (Baltimore, 1907). *Johns Hopkins University Studies in Historical and Political Science Series XXV*, Nos. 2–3.

BOYD, C. E. "The County of Illinois," *American Historical Review*, Vol. IV.

BRACKENRIDGE, H. M. *View of Louisiana* (Pittsburgh, 1814).

BREESE, S. *The Early History of Illinois* (Chicago, 1884).

BROWN, H. *History of Illinois* (New York, 1844).

BUTLER, MANN. *A History of the Commonwealth of Kentucky* (Louisville, 1834).

Butterfield, C. W. *History of the Girtys* (Cincinnati, 1890).

CARSON, W. W. "Transportation and Traffic on the Ohio," *Mississippi Valley Historical Review*, Vol. VII (Cedar Rapids, 1920).

CARTER, C. E. *Great Britain and the Illinois Country, 1763–74* (Washington, 1910).

CHANNING, EDWARD. *A History of the United States* (New York, 1905).

COFFIN, VICTOR. *The Province of Quebec and the Early American Revolution* (Madison, 1896), *University of Wisconsin Bulletin*, Vol. I.

CORWIN, E. S. *French Policy and the American Alliance* (Princeton University Press, 1916).

COULTER, E. M. "The Efforts of the Democratic Societies of the West to Open the Navigation of the Mississippi," *Mississippi Valley Historical Review*, Vol. XI (Cedar Rapids, 1924).

COX, I. J. "The Indian as a Diplomatic Factor," *Ohio Archaeological and Historical Quarterly*, Vol. XVIII.

CRAIG, O. J. "Ouiatanon," *Indiana Historical Society Publications*, Vol. II (Indianapolis, 1895).

DAVIDSON, A., AND STUVÉ, B. *A Complete History of Illinois* (Springfield, 1874).

DILLON, J. B. A. *History of Indiana* (Indianapolis, 1859).

DOUGLAS, W. B. "Jean Gabriel Cerré: A Sketch," *Illinois State Historical Society Transactions, 1905* (Springfield, 1906).

DRAKE, DANIEL. *Pioneer Life in Kentucky*, ed. C. D. Drake (Cincinnati, 1870).

DUNN, J. P. "Father Gibault," *Illinois State Historical Society Transactions, 1905* (Springfield, 1906).

———. *Indiana* (Boston, 1905).

DURRETT, REUBEN T. "Centenary of Louisville," *Filson Club Publications*, Vol. VIII (Louisville, 1893).

ENGLISH, WILLIAM HAYDEN. *Conquest of the Country Northwest of the River Ohio, 1778–83*, and *Life of George Rogers Clark*. 2 vols. (Indianapolis, 1897).

Filson Club Publications, Nos. 1–31 (Louisville, 1884–1926).

GAYARRÉ, C. E. A. *History of Louisiana*. 4 vols. (New Orleans, 1903).

GIBBS, GEORGE. *Memoirs of the Administration of Washington and Adams*. 2 vols. (New York, 1846).

GREEN, T. M. *The Spanish Conspiracy* (Cincinnati, 1891).

HALL, JAMES. *The Romance of Western History* (Cincinnati, 1857).

HODGE, F. W. *Handbook of American Indians North of Mexico*, ed. F. W. Hodge. 2 vols. (Washington, 1910), Smithsonian Institution, Bureau of American Ethnology, *Bulletin 30*.

HASKINS, CHARLES H. "Yazoo Land Companies," *American Historical Association Papers*, Vol. V (New York, 1891).

HENDERSON, A. *Conquest of the Old Southwest* (New York, 1920).

———. "Spanish Conspiracy in Tennessee," *Tennessee Historical Magazine*, Vol. III.

———. "Isaac Shelby and the Genet Mission," *Mississippi Valley Historical Review*, Vol. VI (Cedar Rapids, 1920).

HOLMES, W. H. *Handbook of Aboriginal American Antiquities* (Washington, 1919), Smithsonian Institution, Bureau of American Ethnology, *Bulletin 60*.

HOUCK, LOUIS. *History of Missouri*. 3 vols. (Chicago, 1908).

HULBERT, ARCHER B. *Historic Highways*. 16 vols. (Cleveland, 1902).

JAY, WILLIAM. *Life of John Jay, with Selections from His Correspondence*. 2 vols. (New York, 1833).

JAMES, JAMES ALTON. "Indian Diplomacy and the Opening of the Revolution in the West," *Wisconsin State Historical Society Proceedings* (Madison, 1910).

———. "Significance of the Attack on St. Louis, 1780," *Mississippi Valley Historical Society Proceedings, 1908–9* (Cedar Rapids, Iowa, 1910).

———. "French Diplomacy and American Politics," *Report of American Historical Association, 1911* (Washington, 1912).

———. "Significant Events during the Last Year of the Revolution in the West," *Mississippi Valley Historical Association Proceedings, 1912–13* (Cedar Rapids, 1913).

———. "Some Phases of the History of the Northwest, 1783–86," *Mississippi Valley Historical Association Proceedings, 1913–14*, Vol. VII (Cedar Rapids, 1914).

———. "Louisiana and American Diplomacy, 1795–1800," *Mississippi Valley Historical Review*, Vol. I (Cedar Rapids, 1914).

———. "Spanish Influence in the West during the American Revolution," *Mississippi Valley Historical Review*, Vol. IV, 1917.

———. "The Value of the Memoir of George Rogers Clark as an Historical Document," *Mississippi Valley Historical Association Proceedings*, Vol. IX (Cedar Rapids, 1918).

———. "To What Extent Was George Rogers Clark in Military Control of the Northwest at the Close of the American Revolution?" *Report of American Historical Association, 1917* (Washington, 1920).

———. "French Opinion as a Factor in Preventing War between France and the United States, 1795–1800," *American Historical Review*, Vol. XX (New York, 1925).

JAMES, JAMES ALTON. "The Significance of the Sesquicentennial Celebration of the American Revolution West of the Alleghany Mountains," *Illinois State Historical Society Journal*, Vol. XIX (Springfield, 1927).

JEFFERSON, THOMAS. *Notes on Virginia*, ed. J. W. Randolph (Richmond, 1853).

KINGSFORD, WILLIAM. *History of Canada*. 10 vols. (Toronto, 1887–98).

MARSHALL, HUMPHREY. *The History of Kentucky*. 2 vols. (Frankfort, 1824).

MASON, E. G. "British Illinois, Philippe de Rocheblave," *Chicago Historical Society's Collections*, Vol. IV (Chicago, 1890).

———. *Chapters from Illinois History* (Chicago, 1901).

McLAUGHLIN, A. C. "Western Posts and British Debts," *Report of American Historical Association* (Washington, 1895).

Mississippi Valley Historical Association Proceedings. 10 vols. (Cedar Rapids, 1907).

Mississippi Valley Historical Review. 11 vols. (Cedar Rapids, 1914–25).

Missouri Historical Review. 20 vols. (Columbia, Missouri, 1906–26).

MONETTE, J. W. *History of the Discovery and Settlement of the Valley of the Mississippi*. 2 vols. (New York, 1846).

MOREHEAD, J. T. *The First Settlement of Kentucky* (Frankfort, 1840).

OGG, F. A. *The Opening of the Mississsippi* (New York, 1904).

Ohio Archaeological and Historical Quarterly. 31 vols. (Columbus, Ohio, 1887–1926).

PARKMAN, FRANCIS. *The Old Régime in Canada*. 2 vols. (Boston, 1905).

PECK, JOHN MASON. *Annals of the West* (St. Louis, 1850).

———. *A Gazetteer of Illinois* (Philadelphia, 1831).

PAXSON, FREDERIC L. *History of the American Frontier, 1763–1893* (Boston, 1924).

PHILLIPS, PAUL C. *The West in the Diplomacy of the American Revolution* (Urbana, 1913), *University of Illinois Studies in the Social Sciences*, Vol. II, Nos. 2 and 3.

PRIESTLEY, H. I. *José de Galvez* (Berkeley, California, 1916).

QUAIFE, MILO MILTON. *Chicago and the Old Northwest, 1673–1835: A Study in the Evolution of the Northwestern Frontier Together with a History of Fort Dearborn* (Chicago, 1913).

RAMSEY, J. G. M. *Annals of Tennessee* (Philadelphia, 1853).

RANCK, G. W. *Boonesborough* (Louisville, 1901), *Filson Club Publications*, Vol. XVI.

RANDALL, JAMES G. "George Rogers Clark's Service of Supply," *Mississippi Valley Historical Review*, Vol. VIII, 1921–22 (Cedar Rapids, 1922).

REYNOLDS, JOHN M. *My Own Times, Embracing also the History of My Life* (Belleville, 1855).

———. *The Pioneer History of Illinois* (Belleville, 1852).

RILEY, FRANKLIN L. "Spanish Policy in Mississippi," *Report of American Historical Association, 1897*.

RIVES, W. C. *Life of James Madison.* 3 vols. (Boston, 1859–68).

RIVES, W. L. "Spain and the United States in 1795," *American Historical Review*, Vol. IV (New York, 1899).

ROOSEVELT, THEODORE. *The Winning of the West.* 4 vols. (New York, 1889–96).

ROWLAND, KATE MASON. *The Life of George Mason* 2 vols. (New York, 1892).

SCHOOLCRAFT, HENRY R. *Archives of Aboriginal Knowledge.* 6 vols. (Philadelphia, 1860).

SHALER, N. S. *Kentucky a Pioneer Commonwealth* (Boston, 1885).

SHORTT, ADAM, AND ARTHUR G. DOUGHTY (eds.). *Canada and Its Provinces: A History of the Canadian People and Their Institutions by One Hundred Associates.* Vols. I–V (Toronto, 1914).

SIEBERT, WILBUR H. "Loyalists in West Florida and the Natchez District," *Mississippi Valley Historical Review*, Vol. II (Cedar Rapids, 1916).

STEVENSON, MARY L. C. "Colonel Thomas Cresap," *Ohio Archaeological and Historical Society Publications*, Vol. X (Columbus, 1887).

SHEPHERD, W. R. "Wilkinson and the Spanish Conspiracy," *American Historical Review*, Vol. IX.

STIPP, G. W. *The Western Miscellany* (Xenia, Ohio, 1827). Sometimes quoted as Bradford, *Notes on Kentucky*.

THWAITES, REUBEN G. *How George Rogers Clark Won the Northwest* (Chicago, 1903).

———. *Daniel Boone* (New York, 1903).

TURNER, FREDERICK J. "Western State-Making in the Revolutionary Era," *American Historical Review*, Vol. I (New York, 1896).

———. "The Old West," *Wisconsin Historical Society Proceedings, 1908* (Madison, 1908).

———. *The Character and Influence of the Indian Trade in Wisconsin* (Baltimore, 1891), *Johns Hopkins University Studies in Historical and Political Science*, Series IX.

Turner, Frederick J. "Genet's Projected Attack on Louisiana," *American Historical Review*, Vol. III, 650.

———. "The Policy of France toward the Mississippi Valley," *American Historical Review*, Vol. X.

———. "Diplomatic Contest for the Mississippi Valley," *Atlantic Monthly*, XCIII, 676, 807.

———. *The Frontier in American History* (New York, 1921).

VanTyne, Claude H. *The American Revolution, 1776–83* (New York, 1905), American Nation Series, Vol. IX.

Whitaker, A. P. "The Spanish Intrigue in the Old Southwest," *Mississippi Valley Historical Review*, Vol. XIII.

———. "The Muscle Shoals Speculation," *Mississippi Valley Historical Review*, Vol. XIII.

———. *The Spanish American Frontier, 1783–95* (Boston, 1927).

Winsor, Justin. *Narrative and Critical History of America.* 8 vols. (Boston, 1884–89).

———. *The Mississippi Basin, 1697–1763* (Boston, 1895).

———. *Westward Movement* (Boston, 1897).

Wisconsin Historical Society Proceedings. 20 vols. (Madison, 1875—).

INDEX

Abbott, Edward, lieutenant governor at Vincennes, 53

Adams, John: attitude toward France, 439–46

Adet, P. A., French minister plenipotentiary and the West, 432

Alcudia, Duke de la. *See* Godoy, Manuel de

Alien law, 444

Aranda, Count de: Spanish ambassador at Paris, 98; Jay accomplishes nothing in negotiations with, 362

Arkansas, fortified Spanish post, 107

Basel, Treaty of, 431

Bibliography, 516–26

Bird, Henry: leads expedition against Kentucky, 198; attacks Ruddles Station, 209; retreats, 209

Blue Licks, battle of, 272–74

Boone, Daniel: removal to Yadkin River, 1; explorer, 11; warns settlers at Harrodsburg, 16; founds Boonesborough, 22; associated with Clark, 56; colonel and leader at Blue Licks, 272

Boonesborough: capital of Transylvania, 22; attack on (1777), 56

Bosseron, François, 198

Bowman, John: defender of Kentucky (1777), 57, 58; ordered by Clark to assist in expedition against Detroit, 153; fails, 171

Bowman, Joseph: captain under Clark, 115, 116, 117; with Clark at capture of Vincennes, 142; major, 145; journal of, 479, 483

Brant, Joseph: surprises Colonel Lochry, 243; influence on Iroquois at close of Revolution, 312; criticizes policy of English regarding treatment of Indians, 338, 339

Brodhead, Daniel: in command Fort Pitt (1778), 68; leads expedition for capture of Detroit, 173–75; accused of land-jobbing and speculation, 236; refuses to assist Clark, 237; leads expedition against the Delawares, 238

Brown, John: representative from Kentucky in the Continental Congress, associate of Wilkinson, 381; not insurrectionist, 448

Brown, Samuel, 503, 504

Bryan's Station: location of, 268; attack on, 268–71

Butler, Richard, Indian commissioner, 307, 308

Cahokia: capture of, 121; Indians assembled at, 128

Carmichael, William, 222

Carondelet, Baron de: governor of Louisiana, 422; fears invasion of force under Clark, 423, 434

Cerré, Gabriel: leader at Kaskaskia, 123; goes to St. Louis, 176

Chartres, Fort, 70, 71, 72; abandoned, 86

Cherokee Indians, attack on Carolinas and Georgia, 48

Chilicothe, stronghold of Shawnee: attacked by Clark, 278; messengers sent to, by Clark, 282

Christian, William, colonel: leads Virginians for attack upon Cherokee, 49; shot by Indians, 345

Clark, George Rogers: accounts of, investigation by commissioners, 260; accounts of, Virginia refuses to accept, 417; and alien law, 444–49; and amputation of leg, 467; ancestors of, 1, 2; and appeals: for ammunition to protect Kentucky, 25, 26, for co-operation of French

for expedition against British (1777), 112–14, for retaliatory expedition against Indians (1782), 277, for personal financial help, 291, 292, for retaliatory expedition against the Wabash, for help from Virginia, 436, for help from Congress, 462; place of birth of, 2; burial of, 472, 473 n.; and canal at falls, 459, 460; and Cave Hill Cemetery, burial in (1769), 473 n.; and Clarksville, resided at, 459; commissioned: in Dunmore's War, 14, captain, 17, delegate to Virginia Assembly from Fincastle County, 25, major, 56, lieutenant-colonel, 114, brigadier-general, 231; to hold treaty with Indians in Northwest, 334, French officer, 420, 426, 437; criticism of, 275, 288, 352, 354, 376, 378, 380, 392; criticism of, Clark's attitude toward, 401; and defense of Kentucky, 25, 55, 56, 184, 211, 212, 261, 276; and Detroit, see Detroit; diary of, 479, 480; and drinking: Clark accused of drunkenness, 352, "grown temperate," 412, becomes more intemperate, 458; and education, 3, 4, 5, interest in study of extinct animals, 304, on board of trustees of Transylvania Seminary, 326, student of history and geography, 463, knowledge of animals, 464, reader, 466; and forts: at mouth of Ohio (Fort Jefferson), 196, 197, Ft. Nelson, 275; and France: relation of Clark to Genet, 411, 412, officer in army of, 420, 426, attempts to collect debts from, 428, 429; and French inhabitants: in Illinois country, 74, social life, 75, influence of Church, 76, fur trade, 76, farmers, 76, houses, 78, 79, 80, slaves, 79, trade, 81, 82, 83, 84, Clark wins favor, 120, 121, 127, 148, 170, government for, 160–62; and Illinois Regiment, bounty lands for, 298, 299, 459; impoverished, 277, 288, 289, 393, 418, 457; and Indians: Clark's policy toward, 128, 129, 130, 152, 153; recommends policy toward (1783), 290, 291, advises governor,

300, Clark as Indian commissioner, 306, general policy toward, 347, 393, 415, regard for, 458; as inventor, 413, 500, 501; and Jefferson (see Thomas Jefferson), 2; journal of, 479, 483; and Kaskaskia, see Kaskaskia; land of, exchanges of flour for troops, 277; land, Clark holds quantities of, 324, 457; and Locust Grove, 472; and Logan's speech, 18, 19, 502–8; and Mason letter, 479–94; memoir of: writing of, 412, value of as historical document, 479–94; and mounds, Indian, 412, 413, 495–99; and Mulberry Hill, 411, 457; obituary of, 472 n.; paralysis of, 467, 471, 472; pension of, voted by Virginia, 469; and Piankashaw grant, 461, 462; rebuked by Governor Harrison, 275, 330; and Shawnee expedition, 211–13, 277, 278; sisters of (Ann, Lucy, Elizabeth, Frances, Eleanor), 469 n.; and Spanish territory: desires to found colony in, 392, plans to lead expedition into, 405, plan to invade in the interests of France, 422, 423, still Clark's goal, 436, 449; as surveyor, 5, 10, 20, lays out town, 21, at close of Revolution, 299; and swords, 469, 470 n., 471 n.; and Vincennes expedition, see Vincennes; and Wabash expedition, 354, 355

Clark, Ann, mother of George Rogers, 1, 2, 3; residence of at Mulberry Hill, 411; death of, 457

Clark, John, brother of George Rogers, 469 n.

Clark, John, father of George Rogers, 1, 2, 3; residence of at Mulberry Hill, 411; death of, 457

Clark, Jonathan, oldest brother of George Rogers: education of, 3; looks after interests of George Rogers, 416, 417

Clark, Richard, brother of George Rogers, 469 n.

Clark, William, youngest brother George Rogers: protects interests of brother, 436; appointment of as explorer of West due to influence of George Rogers, 460, 461

Clarksville: to become important center, 329; expedition from to Vincennes, 354

Collot, Victor, 432, 433

Connolly, John, Indian commissioner, 12; character, 13; capture, 36

Continental currency, in Illinois country, 166, 167

Convention of 1800, 455

Cornplanter, chief of Seneca, 307; presented to Congress, 339

Cornstalk, Shawnee chieftain in Dunmore's War, 17, 18

Crawford, William, colonel: friend of Washington, 264; leads expedition against Shawnee, 265–68

Creek Indians: attack on Carolinas, 48; message sent by Clark, 282

Cresap, Michael: relation to Chief Logan, 14, 15, 502–4; captain in Dunmore's War, 17

Croghan, William, 299, 300

Crusat, Francisco, Spanish governor at St. Louis, plans to capture St. Joseph, 220; and basis for Spanish claim of territory, 221

Cumberland settlements, 186

Davie, William R., 454

Delaware Indians: war against by Clark, 154, 155; treaty with, 335

De Leyba, Fernando, lieutenant governor St. Louis, 123; urges Clark's assistance in defense of St. Louis, 207

Democratic societies of West, 424, 425

De Peyster, Arent S.: in charge at Detroit, 172; fears attack by Clark, 276; deceives Indians about cession of Northwest, 311

Detroit: key to fur trade, 29; garrison (1776), 30; expedition against, planned (1778), 65; effect on, capture of Vincennes, 148, 149, 150; Clark determines to capture, 169–72; Clark's disappointment, 171, 172; British on defense at, 173; Clark

plans attack on (1781), 229–50; Clark still urges expedition against, 252; fears expedition, 261, 262; Clark urges capture of, 348

Dodge, John: inaugurates iron rule at Kaskaskia, 341; refuses assistance to Clark, 358

Dunmore, Earl of, governor of Virginia, 6

Dunmore's War, 14–20

DuPont, Victor, 451, 452

Ellsworth, Oliver, 454

Falls of Ohio: Clark's expedition reaches falls, 116, 117; base for Clark during Revolution, 116; Clark returned to, after capture Vincennes, 175; John Todd opposed to fort at, 250; Clark ordered to garrison, 257; difficulties encountered 257, 258

Fauchet, Joseph, French minister plenipotentiary, 431

Florida Blanca, Count of, 99; refuses to make treaty with United States (1780), 223; refuses to yield position (1781), 228; refuses to discuss navigation of Mississippi, 364

Floyd, John, county lieutenant, Jefferson County: on conditions in Kentucky, 246; in charge of division against Shawnee, 211, 213, 277, 278

Fort Chartres: location of, 70; means of defense, 70

Fort Finney, 335

Fort Harmar, 333, 334

Fort Jefferson, near mouth of Ohio, 196, 197; attacked by Chickasaw and Choctaw, 215; partially deserted, 216; evacuated, 244, 245

Fort McIntosh, treaty with Indians, 309

Fort Massac, 117

Fort Nelson: at falls of Ohio, 259; expedition planned against, 259; Clark depends upon, 260; importance, 275, 281, 286

Fort Patrick Henry. See Vincennes

Fort Pitt. *See* Pittsburgh

Fort Sackville, 122

Franklin, Benjamin: plan for colonies beyond Alleghany Mountains, 7, 8; wins favor of d'Aranda, 98; congratulates Jay on outcome of Spanish mission (1780), 224; member secret committee Congress, 293

Franklin, state of: founded, 387; inhabitants represented as desirous of putting themselves under the rule of Spain, 388; failure of plan, 388

Fredericksburg (Virginia), 4, 5

French: attitude toward America, at Detroit (1778), 66; desire of about revolution in United States, 438

French Revolution, 410

Frontier: Kentucky (1776), 55, 56; frontiersmen of, characterized, 64; Kentucky (1779), 179, 180, 181, 193, 194; at close of Revolution, 325; attitude of men of toward closing Mississippi River by Spain, 371; attitude of Spaniards toward men of, 373; attitude toward East, 392; attitude toward France, 430; attitude toward Spain, 420; attitude toward alliance with Great Britain, 447

Fulton, Samuel: agent of Clark, 429, 432; again before French government, 436

Galvez, Bernando de, governor of Louisiana (1778): friend of United States, 94, 97; refuses to surrender Pollock to British, 95; wins neutrality of Indians, 96; aid from, 101, 106; welcomes Willing, 104; orders to attack British posts, 200; plans to capture British posts, 201; captures Mobile and Pensacola, 201, 202

Galvez, Josef de, president of the Council of the Indies: friendly toward the United States, 94; objects to attitude of America on free navigation of the Mississippi, 364

Gardoqui, Diego de: aids the United States, 101; negotiates with John Jay (1780), 224; first Spanish envoy to United States, 365; plan for dis-

membement of West, 385, 386; leaves United States, 400

Genet, Edmond: comes to United States, 410; instructions of, 411; letter from Clark, 411; in Charleston, 419; in Philadelphia, 420; relation to Jefferson, 421; recalled, 425, 426

George, Robert, 154

Gerry, Elbridge, 439

Gibault, Pierre, 120, 121, 122

Gibson, George, captain, 92

Gibson, John, colonel: ordered to join Clark against Detroit, 234; Colonel Brodhead refuses his permission, 241

Girty, Simon, Indian interpreter, 37; becomes Tory, 64, 68; attacks Americans, 183; leader of Indians at Blue Licks, 271–74; influence on Wabash Indians at close of Revolution, 313

Godoy, Manuel de (Duke of Alcudia), Spanish minister, 431, 432

Great Britain: employment of Indians, 35–51, 52, 53; declares war against Spain, 200; plans to capture New Orleans, Natchez, St. Louis, 201; continues in control of Northwest, 309; plans for alliance with United States, 442; attitude toward in West, 446

Greathouse, 505

Green, Thomas: proposes to found county at the mouth of the Yazoo River, 372; relation to Clark, 372; statement of Kentucky committee regarding, 377

Grimaldi, Marquis of, Spanish prime minister, 99, 100

Haldimand, Frederick: commander at Niagara, 147; attitude toward terms of Treaty of Paris, 319, 327

Hamilton, Henry, lieutenant-governor at Detroit, 39, 40, 41; Indian policy of, 43, 45, 46, 51, 52, 53; captures Vincennes, 131–35; taken prisoner by Clark, 144, 146

Hand, Edward, brigadier general in command at Fort Pitt (1777), 58, 59, 60, 61, 62

Harmar, Josiah, colonel: in charge of artillery at Fort McIntosh, 308; forbids survey of land not within particular state, 331; defeat of by Indians, 415

Harrison, Benjamin, governor: rebukes Clark, 275; congratulates Clark, 284, 290; rebukes Clark for taking possession of land north of Ohio River, 330

Harrod, William, 117

Harrodsburg: first permanent settlement in Kentucky, 21, 22; attacked (1777), 56

Helm, Leonard: captain under Clark, 115, 117; sent to Vincennes, 122; captured by Hamilton, 134; took Ouiatenon, 145, 146; in charge at Vincennes, 153

Henderson, Richard, judge: organizes Transylvania Company, 21, 22; plan defeated by Clark, 24; grants of land, 27; and Cumberland settlements, 190–92

Henry, Patrick: appeals to, by Clark for defense of Kentucky, 25, 26; appeals to governor of Cuba, 102, 103; grants authority to Clark for expedition, 114, 115; sets up county government for Illinois, 157, 158; urges Kentucky to assume self-defense, 351; member of Virginia Company, 402

Hutchins, Thomas, geographer of United States: conducts first systematic survey of lands in Northwest, 332; associate of George Morgan for founding colony in Spanish territory, 395

Illinois Regiment, bounty lands, 298, 299

Illinois settlements, 69, 70, 71; government of, by British, 88; British plan to capture (1780), 198, 199; condition of (1781), 247, 248

Immigration to Louisiana: Spain encourages, 98, 391; attitude of Jefferson toward, 391, 392

Indians, at opening of Revolution, 30, 31, 32, 33, 37

Innes, Harry: early associate of Wilkinson, 381; as federal judge, 401

Iron Banks, 197

Iroquois Indians: cession of 1768, 7; cession of 1785, 309

Irvine, William: plans expedition against Shawnee, 267, 268; to co-operate with Clark, 276; fails, 280

Jay, John, president of Congress, appointed minister plenipotentiary to carry on negotiations for treaty with Spain (1779), 221–28; appointed to deal with Gardoqui on navigation of Mississippi, 365; advises Congress to consent to closing Mississippi, 367; attitude of sections toward navigation of the Mississippi, 368; attitude of the West toward, 381

Jefferson, Thomas: one of committee to pass on Clark's plan, 114; gives Clark free hand for capture of Detroit, 193; assists Clark in plans (1781), 230; interest in extinct animals, 304; friendship for Clark, 305; proposes Clark lead exploring expedition to the West, 305; secures appointment of Clark as Indian commissioner, 306; and rectangular survey, 332; attitude toward American migration to Louisiana, 391, 392; understands Western problems, 406; urges Clark be brought forward, 416; and Genet, 421; relation to Létombe, 439; war with France, would remain neutral, 440; attitude toward alliance with Great Britain, 446, 456; continued interest in Clark, 460; high regard for Clark, 464

Kaskaskia: spies sent to by Clark (1777), 69; population of, 69; Clark directed to capture, 115; march to, 118; capture of, 119; Clark returns to, after capture of Vincennes, 153, 154; effects of Clark's victories, 177, 178; people of, chafe under American rule, 196; Clark urged court to punish offenders, 341; Clark recommends people of, to resume French customs, 349

Kentucky: defense of, by Clark, 184; winter (1779) in, 185, 186; immigration (1780), 199, 211, 212; condition of, in 1781, 244, 245, 246; attacked (1782), 269; petitions to be made independent state, 303; immigration to, 322, 323; numbers of inhabitants killed by Indians, 325; raided (1786), 345; Patrick Henry urged people of, to defend themselves, 351; population of, 361; steps leading to independence of, 398; admitted into Union, 407; democratic societies in, 424, 425; attitude of people of, toward alliance with Great Britain, 447, 448

King's Mountain, battle of, 218-20

La Balme, Augustin Mottin de: inspector general of cavalry, 213; plan for capture of Detroit, 214; death, 215

Land speculation: Virginians in Illinois country, 85; Illinois Land Company, 87; Wabash Land Company, 87; Kentucky, 182, 183; at close of Revolution, 324, 330

Langlade, Charles, 198, 208

Las Casas, Luis de la, governor of Havana, 428

Lee, Arthur, Indian commissioner, 308

Lee, Charles, general, 91, 92, 98

Le Gras, J. M. P., 342

Lernoult, Richard B., 149

Létombe, 439

Linctot, Geoffrey, 170

Liston, Robert, English minister, 435

Logan, Benjamin: associated with Clark (1777), 56; second in command retaliatory expedition, 212; urges Clark be made leader of retaliatory expedition against Wabash Indians, 352; ordered to return to Kentucky by Clark to secure additional force to march against Wabash Indians, 355; leads expedition against Shawnee, 356

Logan, Chief: relation to whites, 14; speech of, 18, 19, 502-10

Louisiana: British trade in, 90, 91; impossible for Spain to hold, 409, 410; French designs on, 420, 426, 428, 431, 432

Louisville: government set up, 178, 179, 180; conditions in (1785), 328

McCarty, Richard, 163, 164

McGary, Hugh, major: conduct at Blue Licks, 272, 273; ordered for court martial, 357

McGillivray, Alexander, 400

McIntoch, Lachlan, 63, 67, 68

McKee, Alexander: invades Kentucky, 268; influence on Detroit Indians at close of Revolution, 313

Madison, James: in same school with Clark, 3; opposes contention of Spaniards on free navigation of Mississippi, 365; attitude toward Jay's proposal, 369

Marshall, John, 441

Mason, George: as friend of Clark, 5; one of committee to pass on Clark's plan, 114

Michaux, André, 420, 422

Michillimackinac, 149, 150, 173

Miro, Esteban, Spanish governor of New Orleans: and Wilkinson, 383, 384, 385; and Robertson, 389

Mississippi navigation: negotiations with Spain on (1780), 224, 225; Congress refuses to yield free navigation, 225; recedes from position (1781), 226; Florida Blanca refuses to negotiate, 227, 228

Monroe, James: contemplates going to West, 280; criticism of Clark, 352; attitude toward Jay's proposal, 369

Montgomery, John: captain under Clark, 117, 170, 175; ordered to retire from Illinois, 198

Morgan, George: plan for Indians in Revolution, 33; Indian commissioner, 44, 50; plan for attack on Detroit, 54; plans for colony in Spanish territory, 394, 395

Morris, Robert: member secret committee of Congress, 293; testimony on services of Oliver Pollock, 296

Mounds, Indian, Clark's theory on origin of, 495–99

Mulberry Hill: Clark with his father at, 411; continues to reside with brother at, 457

Murray, William Vans, 454

Muscle Shoals, 189; colony projected, 402

Nashville, 188, 191

Navarro, Martin de, intendant of Louisiana, 382

New Madrid, 395

New Orleans: British plan to capture, 90; United States would demand, 409

Northwest: in Treaty of Paris, 283; effects of Clark's victories on cession of, 283, 284, 285; Iroquois cede rights to, 308, 309; objections to treaty by British, 320; Congress provides for sale of lands in, 332; survey, 332

O'Fallon, James, 404

Otto, Louis-Guillaume, 450, 451

Ouiatanon, trading-post, 73; captured, 145, 146

Paine, Thomas, 418, 419

Paris, Treaty of (1783), 283

Pinckney, Charles Cotesworth: minister to France, 439; member of commission, 441

Pinckney, Thomas, 430

Pittsburgh: at opening of Revolution, 30, 31; and conference of Indians (1776), 38, 39; flour shipped from, 255, 256; condition of, in 1781, 256

Pollock, Oliver: buys powder from Spaniards at New Orleans, 93; appointed commercial agent for United States, 105; fits out ships by aid of Galvez, 107; aids Clark, 124, 125, 126; funds exhausted, 155; goods secured from Spanish, 183; financier of Revolution in West, 292–95; in custody at Havana, 296; payment by Congress, 297; informs United States on policy of Spain toward navigation of the Mississippi, 366

Reed, Joseph, president of Pennsylvania, 236

Richmond (Virginia), 4, 5

Robertson, James: and Watauga Association, 8; and Cumberland settlements, 186–92; represents condition of settlements, 389; turned to Spanish for assistance, 389–90; as brigadier general, 390

Rocheblave, Philippe de Rastel, 109, 110, 111, 119

Ruddle's Station, attacked by British, 209

St. Clair, Arthur, Indian commissioner, 12, 13; plan for capture of Detroit, 41, 42; defeat by Indians, 415

St. Louis, 72; Spanish trade center, 89; British plan to capture, 201; expedition against, 202, 203, 204, 205; Clark prevents capture of, 206, 207

San Ildefonso, treaty of, 455

San Lorenzo, treaty of, 430; delay in fulfilling conditions of, 435

Saunders, John: Clark's guide to Kaskaskia, 118; partner with Clark in hunting, 327

Sebastian, Benjamin, 381, 402

Sectionalism: spirit of, in Kentucky, 374; attitude of Virginia toward, 375, 381

Selby, Isaac, 217, 218

Sevier, John: and Watauga Association, 8; at battle of King's Mountain, 219; governor of state of Franklin, 387; defeated, 387

Shawnee Indians: and colonists, 12; Clark goes against, 277, 278; effect Clark's expedition on, 286; not at treaty of Fort McIntosh, 308; treaty with, 336, 337

Sinclair, Patrick, 202

South Carolina Yazoo Company, 403

Spain: suggests terms of treaty between United States and (1779), 221; refuses alliance with United States, 222–24; loan to United States (1780), 223; Congress refuses to yield right of free navigation to Mississippi, 225; no American vessels to be admitted to Spanish ports, 360; attitude of West toward policy of, 370, 371; Spaniards at New Orleans seize American boats, 359–60

Spanish Intrigue, 385, 390, 391; collapse of, 397, 398

Talleyrand, Charles Maurice de, master of French foreign policy, 439; bribe asked from the United States, 440; and Gerry, 449, 450; suggests treaty with United States, 453

Tennessee Company, 402

Todd, John Jr.: associate of Clark in defense of Kentucky, 56; county lieutenant of Illinois, 158, 159, 160, 161, 162; problems of, 164–67; elected delegate from county of Kentucky to Virginia assembly, 168; severs relations with Illinois, 167; killed at battle of Blue Licks, 274

Todd, Levi, colonel: goes to defense of Bryan's Station, 270; urged that Clark lead retaliatory expedition against Wabash Indians, 352

Unzaga, governor of Louisiana, 91

Vigo, Francis: friend of United States, 136; creditor for Clark, 156; friendship in old age, 468

Vincennes: location of, 73; population of, 73; Hamilton captures, 131–35; captured by Clark, 137–44; anarchy at, 341, 342; Clark sends troops to rescue of, 344; Americans at, petition Congress for relief, 349; condition of Americans, desperate, 351; expedition to, 354; mutiny of troops on way to Wabash villages, 355; Garrison at, established by Clark, 357

Virginia: treasury empty, 254; claims in Northwest and cession, 301; grants rights to settlers in Kentucky at close of Revolution, 324

Virginia Company, 402

Wabash Indians, expedition against, 354, 355

Washington, George: favors attack on Detroit (1781), 231; on lack of virtue among certain inhabitants, 235, 236; on refusal of British to surrender posts, 318, 319; travels of, 361; attitude toward West, 400, 401; proclamation against plan of O'Fallon, 406; proclamation against Genet's project, 427

Watauga settlement, 8; attack by Indians, 48; ceded to Confederation by North Carolina, 386; petition for protection against Indians, 386; decides to secede from North Carolina, 387

West. See Frontier

White, James: superintendent of Indian affairs and delegate in Congress of Confederation, 386; plan for dismemberment of West, 376; visits Cumberland settlements, 388

Wilkinson, James: comes to Kentucky, 374; chairman of committee to interview Clark regarding the Vincennes episode, 376; in New Orleans, 381–83; memorial to Spanish governor, 383, 384, 385; opposed to plan of George Morgan, 395; and trade with New Orleans, 396; as corrupt politician, 399; reasserts his friendship for Spain, 402; fails to respond to call of Spanish governor at New Orleans, 434

Willing, James, 104–7

Wolcott, Oliver, Indian commissioner, 307

Wythe, George, 114

Yazoo Company, 403

Yazoo River, 377

Yrujo, Marquis de Casa, Spanish minister, 435

Zane, Andrew, 60